Adobe® DREAMWEAVER® CS5

INTRODUCTORY

Gary B. Shelly

Dolores J. Wells

COURSE TECHNOLOGY
CENGAGE Learning™

SHELLY CASHMAN SERIES®

Australia • Canada • Denmark • Japan • Mexico • New Zealand • Philippines • Puerto Rico • Singapore • South Africa • Spain • United Kingdom • United States

COURSE TECHNOLOGY
CENGAGE Learning™

Adobe® Dreamweaver® CS5
Introductory
Gary B. Shelly, Dolores J. Wells

Vice President, Publisher: Nicole Pinard

Executive Editor: Kathleen McMahon

Product Manager: Jon Farnham

Associate Product Manager: Aimee Poirier

Editorial Assistant: Lauren Brody

Director of Marketing: Cheryl Costantini

Marketing Manager: Tristen Kendall

Marketing Coordinator: Stacey Leasca

Print Buyer: Julio Esperas

Director of Production: Patty Stephan

Content Project Manager: Matthew Hutchinson

Development Editor: Lisa Ruffolo

Copyeditor: Harry Johnson

Proofreader: Foxxe Editorial

Indexer: Rich Carlson

QA Manuscript Reviewers: Jeffrey Schwartz, Serge Palladino, Danielle Shaw, Susan Whalen

Art Director: Marissa Falco

Cover Designer: Lisa Kuhn, Curio Press, LLC

Cover Photo: Tom Kates Photography

Text Design: Joel Sadagursky

Compositor: Bill Smith Group

For product information and technology assistance, contact us at
Cengage Learning Customer & Sales Support, 1-800-354-9706
For permission to use material from this text or product, submit all requests online at **cengage.com/permissions**
Further permissions questions can be emailed to
permissionrequest@cengage.com

Microsoft and the Office logo are either registered trademarks or trademarks of Microsoft Corporation in the United States and/or other countries. Course Technology, a part of Cengage Learning, is an independent entity from the Microsoft Corporation, and not affiliated with Microsoft in any manner.

Library of Congress Control Number: 2010930203

ISBN-13: 978-0-538-47374-3
ISBN-10: 0-538-47374-6

Course Technology
20 Channel Center Street
Boston, MA 02210
USA

Cengage Learning is a leading provider of customized learning solutions with office locations around the globe, including Singapore, the United Kingdom, Australia, Mexico, Brazil, and Japan. Locate your local office at: **international.cengage.com/region**

Cengage Learning products are represented in Canada by Nelson Education, Ltd.

For your course and learning solutions, visit **www.cengage.com**

To learn more about Course Technology, visit **www.cengage.com/coursetechnology**

Purchase any of our products at your local college bookstore or at our preferred online store at **www.CengageBrain.com**

Printed in the United States of America
1 2 3 4 5 6 7 14 13 12 11

Adobe® DREAMWEAVER® CS5 INTRODUCTORY

Contents

Preface   vii

Adobe Dreamweaver CS5

INTRODUCTION
Web Site Development and Adobe Dreamweaver CS5

Objectives	**DW 1**
The Internet	**DW 2**
The World Wide Web and Web Browsers	**DW 2**
Accessing the Web	DW 2
Web Browsers	DW 3
Types of Web Sites	**DW 5**
Planning a Web Site	**DW 7**
Planning Basics — Purpose	DW 7
Planning Basics — Content	DW 8
Web Site Navigation	**DW 9**
Design Basics — Navigation Map	DW 9
Developing a Web Site	**DW 11**
Development Basics — Typography, Images, Page Layout, and Color	DW 12
Reviewing and Testing a Web Site	**DW 14**
Publishing a Web Site	**DW 14**
Publishing Basics — Domain Name, Server Space, and Uploading	DW 14
Maintaining a Web Site	**DW 17**
Methods and Tools Used to Create Web Sites	**DW 17**
Web Site Languages	**DW 17**
Web Page Authoring Programs	**DW 20**
Adobe Dreamweaver CS5	**DW 20**
Chapter Summary	**DW 22**
Learn It Online	**DW 23**
Apply Your Knowledge	**DW 23**
Extend Your Knowledge	**DW 25**
Make It Right	**DW 25**
In the Lab	**DW 26**
Cases and Places	**DW 30**

CHAPTER ONE
Creating a Dreamweaver Web Page and Local Site

Objectives	**DW 33**
What Is Adobe Dreamweaver CS5?	**DW 34**
Project — Montana Parks Web Site Home Page	**DW 34**

Overview	DW 35
Starting Dreamweaver	**DW 36**
To Start Dreamweaver	DW 36
The Dreamweaver Environment and Workspace	**DW 38**
Document Tab	DW 39
Document Window	DW 39
Panels and Panel Groups	DW 39
Status Bar	DW 40
Vertical/Horizontal Bars	DW 41
Application Bar	DW 41
Toolbars	DW 42
Opening and Closing Panels	DW 43
To Display the Standard Toolbar, Change the Icon Colors, and Close and Open Panels	DW 43
Defining a Local Site	**DW 45**
Creating the Local Root Folder and Subfolders	DW 46
Using Site Setup to Create a Local Site	DW 46
To Use Site Setup to Create a Local Web Site	DW 47
To Copy Data Files to the Local Web Site	DW 52
Removing or Editing a Web Site	DW 54
Preparing Your Workspace and Saving a Web Page	**DW 55**
Rulers	DW 55
The Index Page	DW 55
To Hide the Rulers, Change the .html Default, and Save a Document as a Web Page	DW 55
Web Page Backgrounds	**DW 59**
To Add a Background Image to the Index Page	DW 60
Adding Text to a Web Page	**DW 62**
To Hide the Panel Groups	DW 62
Adding Text	DW 63
To Add a Heading and Introductory Paragraph Text	DW 63
Deleting Web Pages	DW 65
Formatting Features	**DW 65**
Property Inspector Features	DW 65
Collapsing/Hiding the Property Inspector	DW 66
Applying Text-Related Features	DW 68
Text Headings	DW 68
To Format Text with the Heading 1 Style	DW 68
Centering Text	DW 70
To Center the Web Page Heading	DW 70
Types of Lists	DW 71
To Create an Unordered List	DW 72
Bold Formatting	DW 73
To Bold Text	DW 73
Understanding Line Breaks	DW 74
To Add a Line Break	DW 74

To Add Your Name and Date .... DW 75
Web Page Titles .... **DW 76**
   To Change the Web Page Title .... DW 77
Other Web Page Enhancements .... **DW 77**
   Special Characters .... DW 77
Check Spelling .... **DW 78**
   To Check Spelling .... DW 79
Previewing a Web Page in a Browser .. **DW 80**
   Selecting a Browser .... DW 80
   To Select Primary and Secondary Target Browsers DW 81
   To Preview the Web Page .... DW 83
Printing a Web Page .... **DW 83**
   To Print a Web Page .... DW 84
Dreamweaver Help System .... **DW 84**
Disabling the Welcome Screen and
   Quitting Dreamweaver .... **DW 85**
   To Disable the Welcome Screen, Close the
      Web Site, and Quit Dreamweaver .... DW 85
Starting Dreamweaver and Opening a Web Page **DW 85**
Chapter Summary .... **DW 86**
Learn It Online .... **DW 87**
Apply Your Knowledge .... **DW 87**
Extend Your Knowledge .... **DW 89**
Make It Right .... **DW 90**
In the Lab .... **DW 91**
Cases and Places .... **DW 97**

CHAPTER TWO
Adding Web Pages, Links, and Images
Objectives .... **DW 99**
Introduction .... **DW 100**
Project — Two New Pages, Links, and Images **DW 100**
   Overview .... DW 101
   Copying Data Files to the Local Web Site DW 102
   Starting Dreamweaver and Opening a Web Site DW 103
   To Start Dreamweaver and Open the
      Montana Parks Web Site .... DW 104
Managing a Web Site .... **DW 105**
The Files Panel .... **DW 105**
   The Home Page .... DW 105
Adding Pages to a Web Site .... **DW 106**
   To Open a New Document Window ...... DW 106
   Creating the Montana National Parks and
      Preserves Web Page .... DW 109
   To Create the Montana National Parks and
      Preserves Web Page .... DW 109
   Creating the Lewis and Clark National Historical
      Trail Web Page .... DW 111
   Entering Text for the Lewis and Clark National
      Historical Trail Web Page .... DW 112
Images .... **DW 113**
   Image File Formats .... DW 113
   Background Colors and Background Images DW 115
   Assets Panel .... DW 117
   Accessibility .... DW 117
   Invisible Elements .... DW 118
   To Set Invisible Element Preferences and Turn
      on Visual Aids .... DW 119
   Opening a Web Page .... DW 122
   To Open a Web Page from a Local Web Site DW 123
   Inserting an Image into a Web Page .... DW 123
   To Insert an Image into the Index Page DW 124
   Property Inspector Image Tools .... DW 126

   Aligning the Image and Adjusting the Image Size DW 127
   To Align an Image .... DW 128
   Adjusting Space Around Images .... DW 129
   To Adjust the Image Size and the Horizontal Space DW 130
   Image Editing Tools .... DW 141
   To Crop and Modify the Brightness/Contrast of
      an Image .... DW 142
Understanding Different Types of Links **DW 145**
   Relative Links .... DW 146
   To Add Text for Relative Links .... DW 147
   To Create a Relative Link Using Point to File DW 148
   To Create a Relative Link Using the Context Menu DW 150
   To Create a Relative Link to the Home Page DW 153
   Creating an Absolute Link .... DW 155
   To Create Absolute Links .... DW 155
   E-Mail Links .... DW 156
   To Add an E-Mail Link .... DW 156
   Changing the Color of Links .... DW 159
   Editing and Deleting Links .... DW 159
Dreamweaver Views .... **DW 159**
   Using Code View and Design View ..... DW 159
   To Use Design View and Code View Simultaneously DW 160
   Modifying Source Code .... DW 161
   Live View .... DW 161
   To Use Live View .... DW 161
Quitting Dreamweaver .... **DW 162**
Chapter Summary .... **DW 162**
Learn It Online .... **DW 163**
Apply Your Knowledge .... **DW 164**
Extend Your Knowledge .... **DW 165**
Make It Right .... **DW 166**
In the Lab .... **DW 168**
Cases and Places .... **DW 174**

CHAPTER THREE
Tables and Page Layout
Objectives .... **DW 177**
Introduction .... **DW 178**
Project — Formatted Tables with Images **DW 178**
   Overview .... DW 181
Starting Dreamweaver and Opening a Web Site **DW 182**
   Copying Data Files to the Local Web Site DW 183
Adding Pages to a Web Site .... **DW 184**
   Creating the Nez Perce National Historic Trail
      Web Page .... DW 185
Understanding Tables and Page Layout **DW 188**
   Inserting a Table into the Nez Perce National
      Historic Trail Page .... DW 189
   Using the Insert Bar .... DW 189
   To Display the Insert Bar and Select the Layout Tab DW 190
   Layout Tab .... DW 190
   Table Defaults and Accessibility ...... DW 191
Table Layout .... **DW 193**
   To Insert a Table .... DW 193
   Property Inspector Table Features ..... DW 195
   Cell, Row, and Column Properties ..... DW 196
   Table Formatting Conflicts .... DW 197
   Understanding HTML Structure in a Table DW 198
   Selecting the Table and Selecting Cells DW 198
   Centering a Table .... DW 201
   To Select and Center a Table .... DW 201
   Changing the Default Cell Alignment for Text DW 202
   To Change Vertical Alignment from Middle to Top DW 203

Specifying Column Width | DW 204
To Specify Column Width | DW 205
Adding an ID | DW 205
To Add a Table ID to the Nez Perce National
   Historic Trail Table | DW 206
Adding Text to the Nez Perce National Historic
   Trail Web Page | DW 206
To Add Text to the Nez Perce National Historic
   Trail Web Page | DW 208
Adding a Second Table to the Nez Perce
   National Historic Trail Web Page | DW 209
To Add a Second Table to the Nez Perce
   National Historic Trail Web Page | DW 210
Adjusting the Table Width | DW 212
To Adjust the Table Width, Center the Text,
   and Add the Table ID | DW 212
Editing and Modifying Table Structure | DW 215
Merging Cells and Adding Images | DW 216
To Merge Two Cells in a Table | DW 217
To Disable the Image Tag Accessibility Attributes
   Dialog Box | DW 218
To Add Images to a Table | DW 219
Creating the Glacier National Park Web Page | DW 225
Spanning Rows and Columns | DW 228
To Merge Cells in Row 1 | DW 230
Adding Text to the Table | DW 230
To Add and Format Text for the Glacier National
   Park Web page | DW 231
Adding Images and Image Borders | DW 234
To Add Images, Image Borders, and a Table Border | DW 235
Head Content | **DW 241**
Head Content Elements | DW 241
To Add Keywords and a Description to the Index
   Page | DW 242
Publishing a Web Site | **DW 246**
Quitting Dreamweaver | **DW 246** Chapter Summary
| **DW 247**
Learn It Online | **DW 248**
Apply Your Knowledge | **DW 249**
Extend Your Knowledge | **DW 251**
Make It Right | **DW 252**
In the Lab | **DW 254**
Cases and Places | **DW 263**

Appendices

Appendix A
Adobe Dreamweaver CS5 Help
Getting Help with Dreamweaver CS5 | **APP 1**
The Dreamweaver Help Menu | APP 1
Exploring the Dreamweaver CS5 Help System | **APP 3**
Using the Contents Panel | APP 4
To Find Help Using the Contents Panel | APP 5
Using the Search Feature | APP 6
To Use the Search Feature | APP 6
Context-Sensitive Help | **APP 8**
To Display Context-Sensitive Help on Text
   Using the Question Mark | APP 8
To Use the Options Menu to Display Context-
   Sensitive Help for the Files Panel | APP 9
Using the Reference Panel | **APP 10**

To Use the Reference Panel | APP 10
Apply Your Knowledge | **APP 12**

Appendix B
Dreamweaver and Accessibility
Web Accessibility | **APP 13**
Using Screen Readers with Dreamweaver | **APP 13**
Activating the Accessibility Dialog Boxes | APP 14
To Activate the Image Tag Accessibility Attributes
   Dialog Box | APP 14
Inserting Accessible Images | APP 16
To Insert Accessible Images | APP 16
Navigating Dreamweaver with the Keyboard | **APP 18**
Using the Keyboard to Navigate Panels | APP 18
To Use the Keyboard to Hide and Display the
   Property Inspector | APP 19
Operating System Accessibility Features | **APP 20**
To Turn On High Contrast | APP 20

Appendix C
Publishing to a Web Server
Publishing to a Remote Site | **APP 22**
Defining a Remote Site | APP 23
To Define a Remote Site | APP 23
Connecting to a Remote Site | APP 27
To Connect to a Remote Site | APP 27
Uploading Files to a Remote Server | APP 28
To Upload Files to a Remote Server | APP 29
Remote Site Maintenance and Site Synchronization | APP 30
Apply Your Knowledge | **APP 31**

Appendix D
Customizing Adobe Dreamweaver CS5
Changing Screen Resolution | **APP 33**
To Change the Screen Resolution | APP 34

Index | **TK**

Quick Reference Summary | **QR 1**

Preface

The Shelly Cashman Series® offers the finest textbooks in computer education. We are proud of the fact that our previous Dreamweaver books have been so well received. With each new edition of our Dreamweaver books, we make significant improvements based on the software and comments made by instructors and students. For this Adobe Dreamweaver CS5 text, the Shelly Cashman Series development team carefully reviewed our pedagogy and analyzed its effectiveness in teaching today's Dreamweaver student. Students today read less, but need to retain more. They need not only to be able to perform skills, but to retain those skills and know how to apply them to different settings. Today's students need to be continually engaged and challenged to retain what they're learning.

With this Adobe Dreamweaver CS5 text, we continue our commitment to focusing on the user and how they learn best.

The Shelly Cashman Approach

A Proven Pedagogy with an Emphasis on Project Planning

Each chapter presents a practical problem to be solved, within a project planning framework. The project orientation is strengthened by the use of Plan Ahead boxes, which encourage critical thinking about how to proceed at various points in the project. Step-by-step instructions with supporting screens guide students through the steps. Instructional steps are supported by the Q&A, Experimental Step, and BTW features.

A Visually Engaging Book that Maintains Student Interest

The step-by-step tasks, with supporting figures, provide a rich visual experience for the student. Call-outs on the screens that present both explanatory and navigational information provide students with information they need when they need to know it.

Supporting Reference Materials (Appendices and Quick Reference)

The appendices provide additional information about the Application at hand and include such topics as the Help Feature and customizing the application. With the Quick Reference, students can quickly look up information about a single task, such as creating a site, and find page references of where in the book the task is illustrated.

Objectives of This Textbook

Adobe Dreamweaver CS5: Introductory is intended for a first course that offers an introduction to Dreamweaver CS5 and creation of Web sites. No experience with a computer is assumed, and no mathematics beyond the high school freshman level is required. The objectives of this book are:

- To teach the fundamentals of Dreamweaver CS5
- To expose students to proper Web site design and management techniques
- To acquaint students with the proper procedures to create Web sites suitable for coursework, professional purposes, and personal use
- To develop an exercise-oriented approach that allows learning by doing
- To introduce students to new input technologies
- To encourage independent study and provide help for those who are working independently

Integration of the World Wide Web

The World Wide Web is integrated into the Dreamweaver CS5 learning experience by (1) BTW annotations; (2) BTW, Q&A, and Quick Reference Summary Web pages; and (3) the Learn It Online section for each chapter.

End-of-Chapter Student Activities

Extensive end-of-chapter activities provide a variety of reinforcement opportunities for students where they can apply and expand their skills.

Instructor Resources

The Instructor Resources include both teaching and testing aids and can be accessed via CD-ROM or at **www.cengage.com/login**.

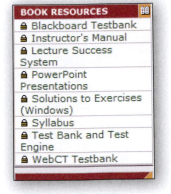

BOOK RESOURCES
- 🔒 Blackboard Testbank
- 🔒 Instructor's Manual
- 🔒 Lecture Success System
- 🔒 PowerPoint Presentations
- 🔒 Solutions to Exercises (Windows)
- 🔒 Syllabus
- 🔒 Test Bank and Test Engine
- 🔒 WebCT Testbank

INSTRUCTOR'S MANUAL Includes lecture notes summarizing the chapter sections, figures and boxed elements found in every chapter, teacher tips, classroom activities, lab activities, and quick quizzes in Microsoft Word files.

SYLLABUS Easily customizable sample syllabi that cover policies, assignments, exams, and other course information.

FIGURE FILES Illustrations for every figure in the textbook in electronic form.

POWERPOINT PRESENTATIONS A multimedia lecture presentation system that provides slides for each chapter. Presentations are based on chapter objectives.

SOLUTIONS TO EXERCISES Includes solutions for all end-of-chapter and chapter reinforcement exercises.

TEST BANK & TEST ENGINE Test Banks include 112 questions for every chapter, featuring objective-based and critical thinking question types, and including page number references and figure references, when appropriate. Also included is the test engine, ExamView, the ultimate tool for your objective-based testing needs.

DATA FILES FOR STUDENTS Includes all the files that are required by students to complete the exercises.

ADDITIONAL ACTIVITIES FOR STUDENTS Consists of Chapter Reinforcement Exercises, which are true/false, multiple-choice, and short answer questions that help students gain confidence in the material learned.

Content for Online Learning

Course Technology has partnered with the leading distance learning solution providers and class-management platforms today. To access this material, instructors will visit our password-protected instructor resources available at www.cengage.com/coursetechnology. Instructor resources include the test banks in Blackboard- and Web CT-compatible formats. For additional information or for an instructor user name and password, please contact your sales representative.

CourseNotes

Course Technology's CourseNotes are six-panel quick reference cards that reinforce the most important and widely used features of a software application in a visual and user-friendly format. CourseNotes serve as a great reference tool during and after the student completes the course. CourseNotes are available for software applications such as Adobe Dreamweaver CS5, Photoshop CS5, Microsoft Office 2010, and Windows 7. Topic-based CourseNotes are available for Best Practices in Social Networking, Hot Topics in Technology, and Web 2.0. Visit www. cengage.com/ct/ coursenotes to learn more!

course|notes™
quick reference guide

A Guided Tour

Add excitement and interactivity to your classroom with "*A Guided Tour*" product line. Play one of the brief mini-movies to spice up your lecture and spark classroom discussion. Or, assign a movie for homework and ask students to complete the correlated assignment that accompanies each topic. "*A Guided Tour*" product line takes the prep work out of providing your students with information about new technologies and applications and helps keep students engaged with content relevant to their lives; all in under an hour!

About Our Covers

The Shelly Cashman Series is continually updating our approach and content to reflect the way today's students learn and experience new technology. This focus on student success is reflected on our covers, which feature real students from Bryant University using the Shelly Cashman Series in their courses, and reflect the varied ages and backgrounds of the students learning with our books. When you use the Shelly Cashman Series, you can be assured that you are learning computer skills using the most effective courseware available.

Textbook Walk-Through

The Shelly Cashman Series Pedagogy: Project-Based — Step-by-Step — Variety of Assessments

Plan Ahead boxes prepare students to create successful projects by encouraging them to think strategically about what they are trying to accomplish before they begin working.

Step-by-step instructions now provide a context beyond the point-and-click. Each step provides information on why students are performing each task, or what will occur as a result.

Adding Text to a Web Page

In Dreamweaver, you can create a Web page in several ways: (1) add text to a new document; (2) open an existing HTML document, even if it was not created in Dreamweaver; (3) copy and paste text; and (4) import a Word or Excel document or tabular data.

In this chapter, you create the index page for the Montana Parks Web page by typing the text in the Document window. Entering text into a Dreamweaver document is similar to typing text in a word-processing document. You can position the insertion point at the upper-left corner of the Document window or within another object, such as a table cell. Pressing the ENTER key creates a new paragraph and inserts a blank line. Web browsers automatically insert a blank line of space between paragraphs. To start a new single line without a blank line between lines of text requires a **line break**. You can insert a line break by holding down the SHIFT key and then pressing the ENTER key.

Plan Ahead

Select the words and fonts for the text.
Most informational Web pages start with a heading, include paragraphs of text, provide one or more lists, and end with a closing line. Before you add text to a Web page, consider the following guidelines for organizing and formatting text:

- **Headings:** Start by identifying the headings you will use. Determine which headings are for main topics (Heading 1) and which are for subtopics (Heading 2 or 3).
- **Paragraphs:** For descriptions or other information, include short paragraphs of text. To emphasize important terms, format them as bold or italic.
- **Lists:** Use lists to organize key points, a sequence of steps, or other information you want to highlight. If amount or sequence matter, number each item in a list. Otherwise, use a bullet (a dot or other symbol that appears at the beginning of the paragraph).
- **Closing:** The closing is usually one sentence that provides information of interest to most Web page viewers or that indicates where people can find more information about your topic.

To Hide the Panel Groups

The following step shows how to provide more workspace by hiding the panel groups.

1
- Click Window on the Application bar and then click Hide Panels to close the Files panel and the Property inspector (Figure 1–40).

Figure 1–40

Other Ways
1. Press F4

To Add a Background Image to the Index Page

When you copied the data file earlier in this chapter, you copied an image to the Montana Parks Web site pages. The following steps illustrate how to use that background image to the index page.

1
- Click Modify on the Application bar and then click Page Properties to display the Page Properties dialog box.
- Click the Appearance (HTML) category to display options for adding a background image to the page (Figure 1–36).

Figure 1–36

2
- Click the Background image Browse button to display the Select Image Source dialog box (Figure 1–37).

Q&A
Why should I use a background image on my Web pages? Background images add texture and visual interest to your Web pages.

Figure 1–37

Explanatory callouts summarize what is happening on screen.

Navigational callouts in red show students where to click.

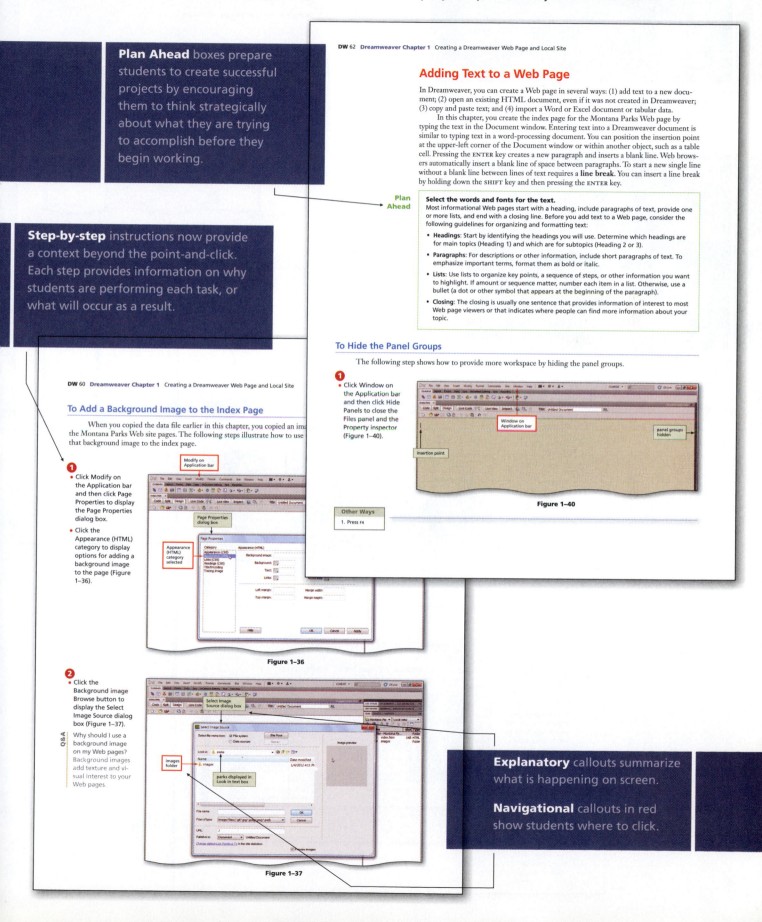

Textbook Walk-Through

Q&A boxes offer questions students may have when working through the steps and provide additional information about what they are doing right where they need it.

Experiment Steps within our step-by-step instructions, encourage students to explore, experiment, and take advantage of the features of the Dreamweaver CS5 user interface. These steps are not necessary to complete the projects, but are designed to increase the confidence with the software and build problem-solving skills.

3 • Type **Montana Parks** in the Site name text box to name the site (Figure 1–15).

Q&A
Is the site name necessary?
This name is required, but it is for reference only. It is not part of the path and is not visible to viewers of your site.

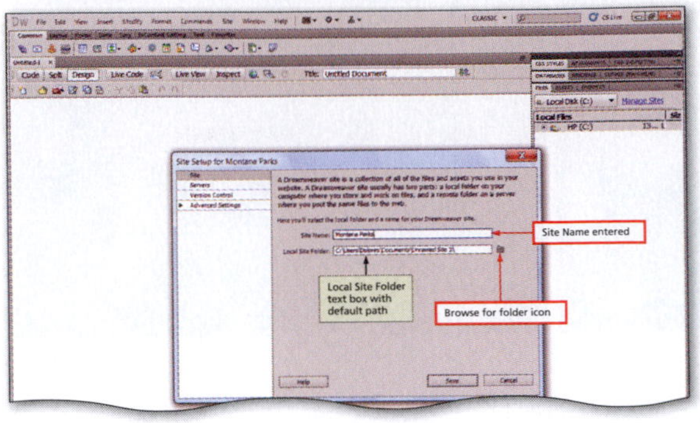

Figure 1–15

4 • Click the Browse for folder icon to display the Choose Root Folder dialog box.
  • Navigate to where you will store your Web site files (Figure 1–16).

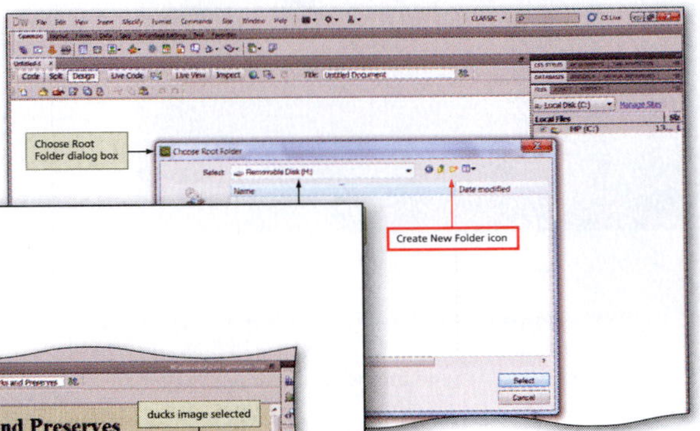

–16

ir instructor to
te. Other options

e letter from
hat the device

4 • Click the Brightness and Contrast tool in the Property inspector to display the Brightness/Contrast dialog box (Figure 2–53).

Q&A
What should I do if a Dreamweaver dialog box is displayed warning that adjusting the brightness and contrast permanently alters the image?
Click the 'Don't show me this message again' check box, and then click the OK button.

Figure 2–53

5 🄿 **Experiment**
  • Drag the Brightness slider and the Contrast slider so you can see how changing the value of each affects the ducks image.
  • Drag the Brightness slider to the left and adjust the setting to –10 to change the brightness level.
  • Drag the Contrast slider to the right and adjust the setting to 20 to change the contrast level (Figure 2–54).

Q&A
What are the ranges for the Brightness and Contrast settings?
The values for the Brightness and Contrast settings range from –100 to 100.

Figure 2–54

Chapter Summary A concluding paragraph, followed by a listing of the tasks completed within a chapter together with the pages on which the step-by-step, screen-by-screen explanations appear.

BTW

Quick Reference
For a table that lists how to complete tasks covered in this book using the keyboard, see the Quick Reference at the end of this book.

Quitting Dreamweaver

After you add pages to your Web site, including images and links, and then view your pages in a browser, Chapter 2 is complete.

To Close the Web Site and Quit Dreamweaver

The following steps show how to close the Web site, quit Dreamweaver, and return control to Windows.

1 Click the Close button on the right corner of the Dreamweaver title bar to close the Dreamweaver window, the Document window, and the Montana Parks Web site.

2 Click the Yes button if a prompt is displayed indicating that you need to save changes.

Chapter Summary

Chapter 2 introduced you to images and links, and discussed how to view source code and use Live view. You began the chapter by copying data files to the local site. You added two new pages, one for Lewis and Clark National Historical Trail and one for Montana National Parks and Preserves, to the Web site you started in Chapter 1. Next, you added images to the index page. Following that, you added a background image and page images to the two new pages. Then, you added relative links to all three pages. You added an e-mail link to the index page and absolute links to the Montana National Parks and Preserves and Lewis and Clark National Historical Trail pages. Finally, you learned how to view source code. The items listed below include all the new Dreamweaver skills you have

Preserves

istorical

urn on

e (DW 123)
V 124)

al Space

st of an

11. Add Text for Relative Links (DW 147)
12. Create a Relative Link Using Point to File (DW 148)
13. Create a Relative Link Using the Context Menu (DW 150)
14. Create a Relative Link to the Home Page (DW 153)
15. Create Absolute Links (DW 155)
16. Add an E-Mail Link (DW 156)
17. Use Design View and Code View Simultaneously (DW 160)
18. Use Live View (DW 161)

Dreamweaver Chapter 1

STUDENT ASSIGN

Learn It Online

Test your knowledge of chapter content and key terms.

Instructions: To complete the Learn It Online exercises, start your browser, click the Address bar, and then enter the Web address **scsite.com/dwCS5/learn**. When the Dreamweaver CS5 Learn It On-line page is displayed, click the link for the exercise you want to complete and then read the instructions.

Chapter Reinforcement TF, MC, and SA
A series of true/false, multiple choice, and short answer questions that test your knowledge of the chapter content.

Flash Cards
An interactive learning environment where you identify chapter key terms associated with displayed definitions.

Practice Test
A series of multiple choice questions that test your knowledge of chapter content and key terms.

Who Wants To Be a Computer Genius?
An interactive game that challenges your knowledge of chapter content in the style of a television quiz show.

Wheel of Terms
An interactive game that challenges your knowledge of chapter key terms in the style of the television show *Wheel of Fortune*.

Crossword Puzzle Challenge
A crossword puzzle that challenges your knowledge of key terms presented in the chapter.

Apply Your Knowledge

Reinforce the skills and apply the concepts you learned in this chapter.

Adding Text and Formatting a Web Page
Instructions: In this activity, you modify a Web page by adding a background image, changing the heading style, adding bullets, and centering text (Figure 1–69 on the next page). To use Dreamweaver effectively, it is necessary to create a new site for the Apply Your Knowledge exercises in this book. Make sure you have downloaded the data files for Chapter01\apply, which are available in the Data Files for Students folder. See the inside back cover of this book for instructions on downloading the Data Files for Students, or contact your instructor for information about accessing the required files.

Learn it Online Every chapter features a Learn It Online section that is comprised of six exercises. These exercises include True/False, Multiple Choice, Short Answer, Flash Cards, Practice Test, and Learning Games.

Apply Your Knowledge This exercise usually requires students to open and manipulate a file from the Data Files that parallels the activities learned in the chapter. To obtain a copy of the Data Files for Students, follow the instructions on the inside back cover of this text.

Textbook Walk-Through

Extend Your Knowledge

Extend the skills you learned in this chapter and experiment with new skills. You may need to use Help to complete the assignment.

Adding Text and Formatting a Web Page

Instructions: In this activity, you modify a Web page by adding a background image, inserting line breaks, and centering text (Figure 1–70). To use Dreamweaver effectively, it is necessary to create a new site for the Extend Your Knowledge exercises in this book. Make sure you have downloaded the data files for Chapter01\extend, which are available in the Data Files for Students folder. See the inside back cover of this book for instructions on downloading the Data Files for Students, or contact your instructor for information about accessing the required files.

Figure 1–70

Perform the following tasks:

1. Start Dreamweaver. Use the Site Setup dialog box to define a local site. Enter **Extend Exercises** as the name of the new site.

2. Using the Browse for folder icon next to the Local Site Folder text box, in the *your name* folder. Enter **extend** as the name of the subfolder. select it as the local site folder.

3. In the Advanced Settings category of the Site Setup for Extend Exercises, Browse for folder icon next to the Default Images folder text box. In the folder named images. Open the images folder, and then select it as the

4. Make sure the path in the Default Images folder text box ends with *your name*. Click the Site category and make sure the path in the Local site folder *name*\extend. Click the Save button in the Site Setup for Extend Exercises settings for the new site.

5. Using Windows Explorer or the Windows Computer tool, copy the ex Chapter01\extend folder into the *your name*\extend folder for the Exten the extend_bkg.jpg from the Chapter01\extend\images data files folder images folder for the Extend Exercises Web site.

6. Open the extend.htm page. If necessary, expand the Property inspector. Verify that the HTML button on the left side of the Property inspector is selected.

7. Click the Page Properties button in the Property inspector and apply the extend_bkg background image to the Web page.

8. Type your name and the current date where indicated.

9. Apply the Heading 2 style to the first three lines.

10. On the Format menu, use the Underline command on the Style submenu to underline the third line.

11. Select the next four lines containing the names of flowers and bullet the text. Press SHIFT+ENTER at the end of the first bulleted item, and then press SHIFT+ENTER again to insert a blank, unbulleted line. Do the same to insert a blank line between each of the remaining bulleted items.

12. Center all of the text. Bold the bulleted list, your name, and the date.

13. Enter **Mary's Flower Shoppe** as the title of the document.

14. Save your document and then view it in your browser, comparing your Web page to Figure 1–70. Submit your work in the format specified by your instructor.

Make It Right

In this activity, you analyze a Web page, correct all errors, and/or improve the design.

Adding Text and Formatting a Web Page

Instructions: In this activity, you modify an existing Web page by formatting and adjusting text and adding data (Figure 1–71). To use Dreamweaver effectively, it is necessary to create a new site for the Make It Right exercises in this book. Make sure you have downloaded the data files for Chapter01\right, which are available in the Data Files for Students folder. See the inside back cover of this book for instructions on downloading the Data Files for Students, or contact your instructor for information about accessing the required files.

Figure 1–71

Extend Your Knowledge projects at the end of each chapter allow students to extend and expand on the skills learned within the chapter. Students use critical thinking to experiment with new skills to complete each project.

Make It Right projects call on students to analyze a file, discover errors in it, and fix them using the skills they learned in the chapter.

In the Lab

Create a document using the guidelines, concepts, and skills presented in this chapter. Labs are listed in order of increasing difficulty.

Lab 1: Modifying the Computer Repair Services Web Site

Problem: Now that Bryan has a basic Web page for his Computer Repair Services Web site, he wants to make the page more appealing to visitors. He asks you to help him add images of computers to his Web page.

Image files for the Bryan's Computer Repair Services Web site are included with the data files. See the inside back cover of this book for instructions for downloading the data files or see your instructor for information on accessing the files in this book.

You need to add two new pages to the Bryan's Computer Repair Services Web site: a services page and a references page. In this exercise, you will add relative and absolute links to each page. You also will add a background image to the new pages. Next, you will insert images on all three pages and use the settings in Table 2–4 to align the images and enter the alternate text. You then will add an e-mail link to the home page and relative links from the two new pages to the home page. The pages for the Web site are shown in Figures 2–77a, 2–77b, and 2–77c. (Software and hardware settings determine how a Web page is displayed in a browser. Your Web pages may be displayed differently in your browser from the pages shown in the figures.)

(a)

(b)

(c)

Figure 2–77

In the Lab Three all new in-depth assignments per chapter require students to utilize the chapter concepts and techniques to solve problems on a computer.

---

12. Create an absolute link from the Fair Credit Billing Act text in the answer to question 3. In this link, use the following as the URL: http://www.ftc.gov/bcp/edu/pubs/consumer/credit/cre16.shtm. Save the questions page (Figure 2–79c).

13. View the Web site in your browser and verify that your external and relative links work. *Hint:* Remember to check the link for the image on the theft.htm page. Submit the documents in the format specified by your instructor.

Cases and Places

Apply your creative thinking and problem solving skills to design and implement a solution.

• Easier •• More Difficult

• 1: Modify the Favorite Sports Web Site

In Chapter 1, you created a Web site named Favorite Sports with a Web page listing your favorite sports and teams. Now, you want to add another page to the site. Create and format the new page, which should include general information about a selected sport. Create a relative link from the home page to the new page and from the new page to the home page. Add a background image to the new page and insert an image on one of the pages. Include an appropriate title for the page. Save the page in the sports subfolder. For a selection of images and backgrounds, visit the Dreamweaver CS5 Media Web page (scsite.com/dwcs5/media).

• 2: Modify the Hobbies Web Site

Several of your friends were impressed with the Web page and Web site you created about your favorite hobby in Chapter 1. They have given you some topics they think you should include on the site. You decide to create an additional page that will consist of details about your hobby and the topics your friends suggested. Format the page. Add an absolute link to a related Web site and a relative link from the home page to the new page and from the new page to the home page. Add a background image to the new page. Create an e-mail link on the index page. Title the page with the name of the selected hobby. Save the page in the hobby subfolder. For a selection of images and backgrounds, visit the Dreamweaver CS5 Media Web page (scsite.com/dwcs5/media).

•• 3: Modify the Politics Web Site

In Chapter 1, you created a Web site and a Web page to publicize your campaign for public office. Develop two additional pages to add to the site. Apply a background image to the new pages. Apply appropriate formatting to the two new pages. Scan a picture of yourself or take a picture with a digital camera and include the picture on the index page. Add a second image illustrating one of your campaign promises. Include at least two images on one of the new pages and one image on the other new page. Add alternate text for all images, and then add appropriate H Space and V Space property features to position the images. Create e-mail links on all three pages and create relative links from the home page to both pages and from each of the pages to the home page. Create an absolute link to a related site on one of the pages. Give each page a meaningful title and then save the pages in the government subfolder. For a selection of images and backgrounds, visit the Dreamweaver CS5 Media Web page (scsite.com/dwcs5/media).

Cases & Places exercises call on students to create open-ended projects that reflect academic, personal, and business settings.

Web Site Development and Adobe Dreamweaver CS5

Objectives

You will have mastered the material in this chapter when you can:

- Describe the Internet, the Web, and their associated terms

- Specify the difference between a Web page and a Web site

- Define Web browsers and identify their main features

- Identify the 13 types of Web sites

- Discuss how to plan, design, develop, test, publish, and maintain a Web site

- Identify the methods and tools for creating a Web page and Web site

- Recognize the basic elements within HTML/XHTML

- Discuss the advantages of using Web page authoring programs such as Dreamweaver

Web Site Development and Adobe Dreamweaver CS5

The Internet

The **Internet**, sometimes simply called the **Net**, is a global network connecting millions of computers. Within this network, a user who has permission at any one computer can access and obtain information from any other computer within the network. A **network** is a group of computers and associated devices that are connected by communications facilities. A network can span a global area and involve permanent connections, such as cables, or temporary connections made through telephone or other communications links. Local, regional, national, and international networks constitute a global network. Each of these networks provides communications, services, and access to information.

No one person or organization is responsible for the birth of the Internet. Its origin, however, can be traced to the early 1960s when the Advanced Research Projects Agency (ARPA), working under the U.S. Department of Defense, began a networking project. The purpose of the project was to create a network that would allow scientists at different locations to share military and scientific information. Today, the Internet is a public, cooperative, and self-sustaining facility that hundreds of millions of people worldwide access.

The World Wide Web and Web Browsers

The World Wide Web (WWW), also called the Web, is one of the more popular services on the Internet. The Web consists of a system of global network servers, also known as Web servers, that support specially formatted documents and provide a means for sharing these resources with many people at the same time. A network server is known as the host computer, and your computer, from which you access the information, is called the client. Hypertext Transfer Protocol (HTTP) enables the transfer of data from the host computer to the client.

Accessing the Web

Users access Web resources, such as text, graphics, sound, video, and multimedia, through a Web page. A unique address, or Uniform Resource Locator (URL), identifies every Web page. The URL provides the global address of the location of the Web page. URLs are discussed later in this Introduction. Viewing data contained on a Web page requires a Web browser, a software program that requests a Web page, interprets the code contained within the page, and then displays the contents of the Web page on your computer display device.

Web Browsers

Web browsers contain special buttons and other features to help you navigate through Web sites. The more popular Web browser programs are **Microsoft Internet Explorer, Mozilla Firefox, Google Chrome, Safari,** and **Opera**. This book uses Internet Explorer as the primary browser. When you start Internet Explorer, it opens a Web page that has been set as the start, or home, page (Figure I–1). Using the browser's Tools menu, the user can designate any page on the Web as the home page or start with a blank page. Important features of Internet Explorer are summarized in Table I–1.

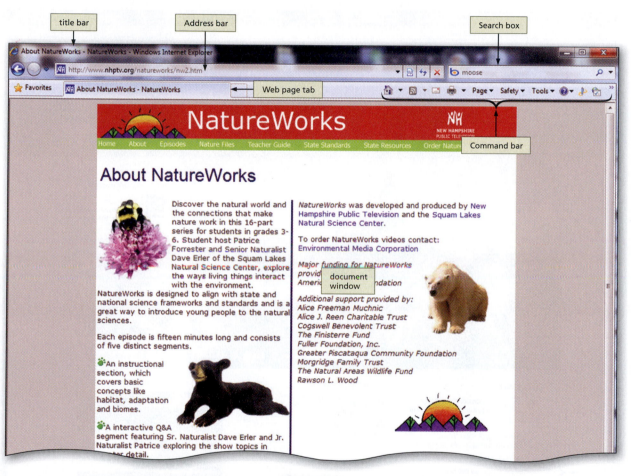

Figure I–1

Table I–1 Internet Explorer Features	
Feature	**Definition**
Title bar	Displays the name of the Web page you are viewing
Search box	Allows Web searches using your favorite search provider
Command bar	Contains buttons, boxes, and menus that allow you to perform tasks quickly
Address bar	Displays the Web site address, or URL, of the Web page you are viewing
Document window	Contains the Web page content
Web page tab	Provides the option to use tabs to switch from one site to another in a single browser window

Nearly all Web pages have unique characteristics, but most share the same basic elements. On most Web pages, you will find headings or titles, text, pictures or images, background enhancements, and hyperlinks. A **hyperlink**, or **link**, can connect to another place in the same Web page or site — or to an entirely different Web page on a server in another city or country. Normally, you click the hyperlink to follow the connected pathway. Figure I–2 contains a variety of link types. Clicking a link causes the Web page associated with the link to be displayed in a browser window. Linked pages can appear in the same browser window, in a new tab, or in a separate browser window, depending on the HTML or XHTML code associated with the link. HTML and XHTML are discussed later in this Introduction.

Figure I–2

Most Web pages are part of a **Web site**, which is a group of related Web pages that are linked together. Most Web sites contain a home page, which generally is the first Web page visitors see when they enter the site. A **home page** (also called an **index page**) typically provides information about the Web site's purpose and content. Most Web sites also contain additional content and pages. An individual, a company, or an organization owns and manages each Web site.

Accessing the Web requires a connection through a regional or national Internet service provider (ISP), an online service provider (OSP), or a wireless service provider (WSP). Figure I–3 illustrates ways to access the Internet using these service providers.

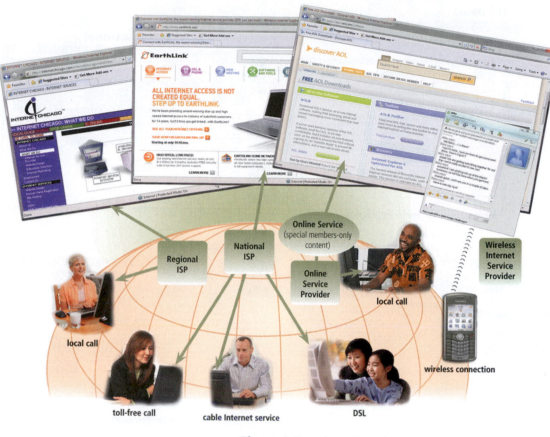

Figure I–3

An **Internet service provider** (**ISP**) provides temporary connections to individuals or businesses through its permanent Internet connection. Similar to an ISP, an **online service provider** (**OSP**) provides additional member-only services such as financial data and travel information. America Online and CompuServe are examples of OSPs. A **wireless service provider** (**WSP**) provides Internet access to users with Web-enabled devices or wireless modems. Generally, all of these providers charge a fee for their services.

Types of Web Sites

Web sites are classified as 13 basic types: portal, news, informational, business/marketing, blog, wiki, social networks, educational, entertainment, advocacy, Web application, content aggregator, and personal, all shown in Figure I-4 on the next page. A **portal** Web site (Figure I–4a) provides a variety of Internet services from a single, convenient location. Most portals offer free services such as search engines; local, national, and worldwide news; sports; weather; reference tools; maps; stock quotes; newsgroups; chat rooms; and calendars. A **news** Web site (Figure I–4b) contains news articles relating to current events. An **informational** Web site (Figure I–4c) contains factual information, such as research and statistics. Governmental agencies and nonprofit organizations are the primary providers of informational Web pages. A **business/marketing** Web site (Figure I–4d) contains content that promotes or sells products or services. A **blog** (Figure I–4e), short for Weblog, uses a regularly updated journal format to reflect the interests, opinions, and personality of the author and sometimes of site visitors. A **wiki** (Figure I–4f) is a collaborative Web site that allows users to create, add to, modify, or delete the Web site content via their Web browser. Most wikis are open to modification by the general public. An **online social network** (Figure I–4g) is an online community that encourages members to share their interests, stories, photos, music, and videos with other members.

(a) portal

(b) news

(c) informational

(d) business/marketing

(e) blog

(f) wiki

(g) online social network

(h) educational

(i) entertainment

(j) advocacy

(k) Web application

(l) content aggregator

(m) personal

Figure I–4

An **educational** Web site (Figure I–4h) provides exciting, challenging avenues for formal and informal teaching and learning. An **entertainment** Web site (Figure I–4i) offers an interactive and engaging environment and contains music, video, sports, games, and other similar features. Within an **advocacy** Web site (Figure I–4j), you will find content that describes a cause, opinion, question, or idea. A **Web application** (Figure I-4k) uses a browser that allows users to access and interact with software that is connected to the Internet. A **content aggregator** (Figure I–4l) is a business that gathers and organizes Web content and then distributes the content to subscribers free or for a fee. **RSS** 2.0 (**Really Simple Syndication**) is used to distribute content to subscribers. A **personal** Web site (Figure I–4m) is published by an individual or family and generally is not associated with any organization. As you progress through this book, you will have an opportunity to learn more about different types of Web pages.

Planning a Web Site

Thousands of individuals create and publish Web pages every day, some using word processing software or markup languages, such as HTML and XHTML, to create their pages. Others use professional design and management editors such as Dreamweaver. Although publishing a Web page or a Web site is easy, advanced planning is paramount in ensuring a successful Web site. Publishing a Web site, which makes it available on the Internet, is discussed later in this Introduction.

Planning Basics — Purpose

Those who rush into the publishing process without proper planning tend to design Web sites that are unorganized and difficult to navigate. Visitors to this type of Web site often lose interest quickly and do not return. As you begin planning your Web site, consider the following guidelines to ensure that you set and attain realistic goals.

Purpose and Goal   Determine the purpose and goal of your Web site. Create a focus by developing a purpose statement, which communicates the intention of the Web site. Consider the 13 basic types of Web sites mentioned previously. Will your Web site consist of just one basic type or a combination of two or more types?

Target Audience   Identify your audience. The people who visit your Web site will determine the success of your site. Although you welcome all visitors, you need to know as much as possible about the primary group of people you wish to reach — your target audience. To learn more about the visitors to your Web site, determine whether you want to attract people with similar interests, and consider the gender, education, age range, income, profession/job field, and computer proficiency of your target audience.

Web Technologies   Evaluate whether your potential visitors have access to high-speed broadband media or to baseband media, and use this information to determine what elements to include in your Web site. **Broadband** can transmit many moving images or a vast quantity of data at a high speed. Media and hardware such as **T1 lines, DSL** (**digital subscriber lines**), **ISDN** (**Integrated Services Digital Network**), **fiber optics**, and **cable modems** work with broadband. **Baseband** transmits one signal at a time over a telephone line and includes media and hardware such as 56K modems. Baseband works well with a Web site composed mostly of text and small images. Web sites that contain many images or multimedia, such as video and animations, generally require broadband connections. Increasingly, people are using **mobile Web technologies** to access the Internet using a smartphone or other handheld device connected to a wireless network.

Web Site Comparison Visit other Web sites that are similar to your proposed site. What do you like about these sites? What do you dislike? Look for inspirational ideas. How can you make your Web site better?

Planning Basics — Content

To ensure a successful Web experience for your visitors, consider the following guidelines to provide appropriate content and other valuable Web page elements.

Value-added Content Consider the different types of content you can include within your Web site. Use the following questions as guidelines:

- What topics or concepts do you want to cover?
- How much information will you present about each topic and how will you present it?
- What will attract your target audience to your Web site?
- What methods will you use to keep your audience returning to your site?
- What changes will you have to make to keep your site updated?

Text Text accounts for the bulk of content on most Web pages, so be brief and incorporate lists whenever possible. Statistical studies indicate that most people tend to scan the page, picking out individual words and sentences. Use common words and simple language, and check your spelling and grammar. Create your textual content to accomplish your goals effectively by highlighting key words, using bulleted lists, maintaining one idea per paragraph, and including meaningful subheadings.

Images After text, images constitute the next most commonly included content. Ask yourself these questions with respect to your use of images:

- Will you have a common logo or theme on all of your Web pages?
- Are these images readily available?
- What images will you have to locate?
- What images will you have to create?
- How many images per page will you have?

Color Palette The color palette you select for your Web site can enhance or detract from your message or goal. Instead of thinking in terms of your favorite colors, consider how color can support your goal. Ask yourself the following questions:

- Do your selected colors work well with your goal?
- Did you use a color palette generator to select a well-balanced set of colors?
- Did you limit the number of colors to a selected few?

BTW

Web Site Development
To develop a Web site, start with and organize your content. Then create your navigation map.

Multimedia Multimedia adds interactivity and action to your Web pages. Animation, audio, and video are types of **multimedia**. If you plan to add multimedia, determine whether the visitor will require plug-ins. A **plug-in** extends the capability of a Web browser. Some of the more commonly used plug-ins are Shockwave Player, Adobe Flash, and Windows Media Player. Most plug-ins are free and can be downloaded from the Web.

Web Site Navigation

Predicting how a visitor will access a Web site or at what point the visitor will enter the Web site structure is not possible. The importance of a navigation structure, however, cannot be overemphasized. Visitors can arrive at any page within a Web site by a variety of ways: a hyperlink, a search engine, a directory, typing a Web address directly, and so on. On every page of your Web site, you must provide clear answers to the three basic questions your visitors will ask: Where am I? Where do I go from here? How do I get to the home page? A well-organized Web site provides the answers to these questions. Once the visitor arrives at a Web site, **navigation**, the pathway through your site, must be obvious and intuitive. Individual Web pages cannot be isolated from the rest of the site if you want it to be successful. At all times and on all pages in your site, you must give the visitor a sense of place, of context within the site. Most Web designers use a navigation map to help the user visualize the navigation pathway.

Design Basics — Navigation Map

A site map is essential, even for a modestly sized site. A site map, or **navigation map**, outlines the structure of the entire Web site, showing all pages within the site and the connections from one page to the others. The navigation map acts as a road map through the Web site, but does not provide details of the content of the individual pages. Web site navigation should be consistent from page to page, so your visitors do not have to guess where they are within the site each time they encounter a new page. All pages in the site should contain a link to the home page. Consider the types of structures in Figure I-5 for site navigation:

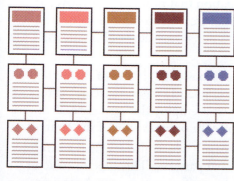

(a) Linear Structure

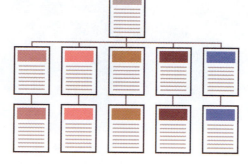

(b) Hierarchical Structure

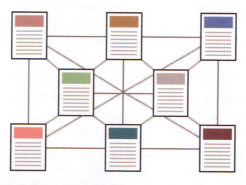

(c) Web Structure

(d) Grid Structure

Figure I–5

Structure The goal and the type of Web site often determine the structure selected for a specific Web site. Create a navigation map to serve as a blueprint for your navigational structure. Consider the following navigational structures and determine which one best meets your needs.

Figure I–6

- In a **linear structure** (Figure I–5a on the previous page) the user navigates sequentially, moving from one page to the next. Information that flows as a narrative, as a timeline, or in logical order is ideal for sequential treatment. Simple sequential organization, however, usually works only for smaller sites. Many online tutorials use a linear structure.

- A **hierarchical structure** (Figure I–5b on the previous page) is one of the better ways to organize complex bodies of information efficiently. Because many visitors are familiar with hierarchical charts, many Web sites employ this structure. Be aware that effective hierarchical structures require thorough organization of the content.

- A **Web structure** (Figure I–5c on the previous page), which also is called a **random structure**, places few restrictions on organizational patterns. This type of structure is associated with the free flow of ideas and can be confusing to a user. A random structure is better suited for experienced users looking for further education or enrichment and is not recommended if your goal is to provide a basic understanding of a particular topic. If a Web site is relatively small, however, a random structure could work well.

- Use a **grid structure** if your Web site consists of a number of topics of equal importance (Figure I–5d on page DW 9). Procedural manuals, events, and item lists work well in a grid structure.

- Large Web sites frequently use a **hybrid structure**, a combination of the previous listed structures, to organize information. See Figure I–6.

Tools   Determine the tool necessary to create the navigation map (Figure I–7). For small Web sites, you might want to consider using the organizational chart included in the Microsoft PowerPoint application.

For larger, more diverse Web sites, you can chart and organize your content using Visio Professional, Flow Charting PDQ, FlowCharter Professional, and SmartDraw.

Navigation Elements   The more common types of navigation elements include text, buttons, images, image maps, a site index, a menu, a search feature, and navigation bars. Depending on the complexity of your Web site, you may want to include some or all of these elements.

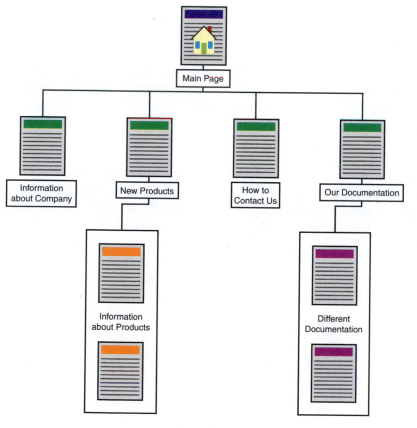

Figure I–7

Developing a Web Site

Once you have established a structure for your Web site, you can begin developing the site. Make text and images the main focus because they are the more common elements. Then consider page layout and color.

Development Basics — Typography, Images, Page Layout, and Color

Typography, images, page layout, and color are the key design elements that will make up your finished Web site. Correct use of these elements plays an important part in the development process. Consider the following guidelines:

Typography As in all media, good **typography**, the appearance and arrangement of the characters that make up your text, is vital to the success of your Web page. A font consists of all the characters available in a particular style and weight for a specific design. Text always should be easy to read, whether in a book, magazine, Web page, or billboard. Keep readability in mind as you select fonts, especially when you consider that some of your visitors might only be viewing them on screen, and others might print them.

When selecting a font, determine its purpose on your Web page. Is it to be used for a title? For on-screen reading? Is it likely to be printed? Will the font fit in with the theme of the Web site? Is it a Web-safe font, such as Times New Roman, Courier, or Arial? **Web-safe fonts** are the more popular fonts and the ones that most visitors are likely to have installed on their computers. Also, while visitors to your Web page may never consciously notice the design of the text characters, or the **typeface**, it often subconsciously affects their reaction to the page.

Images Images can enhance almost any Web page if used appropriately. Without the visual impact of shape, color, and contrast, Web pages can be visually uninteresting and will not motivate the visitor to investigate their contents. Consider the balance between the number of images and page performance as you develop your site. When adding images, consider your potential audience and the technology they have available. Remember that a background image or a graphical menu increases visitor download time. You may lose visitors who do not have broadband access if your Web page contains an excessive number of graphical items.

BTW

Keep the Page Simple
Some Web pages take a long time to download or view if they contain multiple elements and appear very "busy." Simple pages download faster and make an immediate impression on the reader.

Page Layout The importance of proper page layout cannot be overemphasized. A suitable design draws visitors to your Web site. Although no single design system is appropriate for all Web pages, establish a consistent, logical layout that allows you to add text and images easily. The Web page layouts shown in Figure I–8 illustrate two different layouts. The layout on the left (Figure I–8a) shows a page with centered headings and other centered elements, which break up the page and can be difficult to read. The page layout on the right (Figure I–8b) presents strong visual contrast by organizing headings and some types of graphics on the left, while displaying other types of graphics on the right.

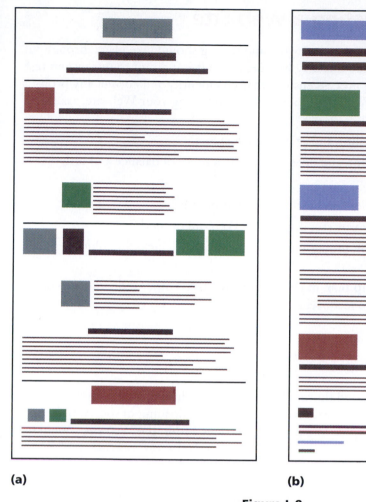

(a)   **(b)**

Figure I–8

Maintaining consistency and updating changes throughout a site are two of the biggest challenges facing Web designers. A **template,** a special type of document, can help with these challenges. Dreamweaver provides several page layout templates that can be modified easily. In laying out your Web pages, consider the following guidelines to ensure that visitors have the best viewing experience:

- Include only one topic per page.
- Control the vertical and horizontal size of the page.
- Start text on the left to match the way most people read text.
- Use concise statements and bulleted points to get your point across; studies indicate most people scan the text.

Color   When creating a Web page, use color to add interest and vitality to your site. Include color in tables, as backgrounds, and with fonts. Use the right combination of colors to decorate the layout and tie the Web site pages together.

Reviewing and Testing a Web Site

Some Web site developers argue that reviewing and testing should take place throughout the developmental process. While this may be true, it also is important to review and test the final product. This ongoing process ensures that you identify and correct any problems before publishing to the Web. When reviewing and testing your Web site, ask the following questions:

- Is the Web site free of spelling and grammatical errors?
- Is the page layout consistent, and does it generate a sense of balance and order?
- Are any links broken?
- Do multimedia interactivity and forms function correctly?
- Do the more widely used browsers display the Web site properly?
- Does the Web site function properly in different browsers, including older browser versions?
- Have you initiated a **group test**, in which you have asked other individuals to test your Web site and provide feedback?

Publishing a Web Site

After your Web site has been tested thoroughly, it can be published. **Publishing** a Web site, making it available to your visitors, involves the actual uploading of the Web site to a server. After you complete the uploading process, all pages within the Web site should be tested again.

Publishing Basics — Domain Name, Server Space, and Uploading

With your Web site thoroughly tested and any problems corrected, you must make the site available to your audience by obtaining a domain name, acquiring server space, and uploading the site. Consider the following to ensure site availability:

Obtain a Domain Name　To allow visitors to access your Web site, you must obtain a domain name. Visitors access Web sites by an IP address or a domain name. An **IP address (Internet Protocol address)** is a number that uniquely identifies each computer or device connected to the Internet. A **domain name** is the text version of an IP address. The **Domain Name System (DNS)**, an Internet service, translates domain names into their corresponding IP addresses. The **Uniform Resource Locator (URL)**, also called a Web address, tells the browser on which server the Web page is located. A URL consists of a communications protocol, such as **Hypertext Transfer Protocol (HTTP)**, the domain name, and sometimes the path to a specific Web page (Figure I–9).

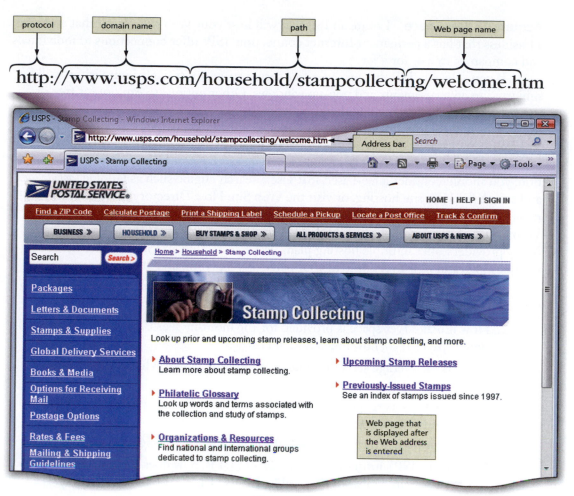

Figure I–9

Domain names are unique and must be registered. The **Accredited Registrar Directory** provides a listing of **Internet Corporation for Assigned Names and Numbers (ICANN)** accredited domain name registrars. Your most difficult task likely will be to find a name that is not registered. You can locate a name by using a specialized search engine at one of the many accredited domain name registrars listed on the ICANN Web site (*icann.org/registrars/accredited-list.html*). In addition to registering your business name as a domain name, you may want to register the names of your products, services, or other related names. Expect to pay approximately $10 to $35 per year for a domain name.

Consider the following guidelines when selecting a domain name:

- Select a name that is easy to pronounce, spell, and remember.
- Select a name that relates to the Web site content and suggests the nature of your product or service.
- If the Web site is a business, use the business name whenever possible.
- Select a name that is free and clear of trademark issues.
- Purchase variations and the .org, .net, and .mobi versions of your domain name.
- Some ISPs will obtain a domain name for you if you use their service to host your Web site.

Acquire Server Space   Locate an ISP that will host your Web site. Recall that an ISP is a business that has a permanent Internet connection. ISPs offer connections to individuals and companies free or for a fee.

If you select an ISP that provides free server space, most likely your visitors will be subjected to advertisements and pop-up windows. Other options to explore for free or inexpensive server space include the provider from which you obtain your Internet connection; online communities, such as Bravenet (*bravenet.com*), Tripod (*www.tripod.lycos.com*), and webs.com (*www.webs.com*); and your educational institution's Web server. If the purpose of your Web site is to sell a product or service or to promote a professional organization, you should consider a fee-based ISP. Use a search engine such as Google (*google.com*) and search for Web site hosting, or visit the Web Site Host Directory (*www.websitehostdirectory.com*), where you will find lists of Web hosting plans, as well as reviews and ratings of Web hosting providers. Selecting a reliable provider requires investigation on your part. Many providers offer multiple hosting plans. When selecting an ISP, consider the following questions and how they apply to your particular situation and Web site:

1. What is the monthly fee? Is a discount available for a year-long subscription? Are setup fees charged?

2. How much server space is provided for the monthly fee? Can you purchase additional space? If so, how much does it cost?

3. What is the average server uptime on a monthly basis? What is the average server downtime?

4. What are the server specifications? Can the server handle many users? Does it have battery backup power?

5. Are **server logs**, which keep track of the number of accesses, available?

6. What is the ISP's form of connectivity — that is, how does it connect to the Internet: dial up, DSL, wireless, cable, ISDN, T1, T3, or some other way?

7. Is a money-back guarantee offered?

8. What technical support does the ISP provide, and when is it available? Does it have an online knowledge base?

9. Does the server on which the Web site will reside have CGI scripting capabilities and Active Server Page (ASP) support?

10. Does the server on which the Web site will reside support e-commerce, multimedia, and **Secure Sockets Layer (SSL)** for encrypting confidential data such as credit card numbers? Are additional fees required for these capabilities?

11. Does the ISP support Dreamweaver and other Web site development software programs?

12. Are mailboxes included in the package? If so, how many?

Publish the Web Site   You must publish, or upload, the files from your computer to a server where your Web site then will be accessible to anyone on the Internet. Publishing, or uploading, is the process of transmitting all the files that make up your Web site from your computer to the selected server or host computer. The files that make up your Web site can include Web pages, PDF documents, images, audio, video, animation, and others.

A variety of tools and methods exist to manage the upload task. Some of the more popular of these are FTP (file transfer programs), Windows Web Publishing Wizard, Web Folders, and Web authoring programs such as Dreamweaver. These tools allow you to link to a remote server, enter a password, and then upload your files. Dreamweaver contains a built-in function similar to independent FTP programs. The Dreamweaver FTP function to upload your Web site is covered in Appendix C.

Maintaining a Web Site

Most Web sites require maintenance and updating. Some types of ongoing Web maintenance include the following:

- Changing content, either by adding new text and images or by deleting obsolete material
- Checking for broken links and adding new links
- Documenting the last change date (even when no revisions have been made)

Use the information from the server logs provided by your ISP to determine what needs to be updated or changed. Statistics contained within these logs generally include the number of visitors trying to access your site at one time, what resources they request, how long they stay at the site, at what point they enter the site, what pages they view, and what errors they encounter. Learning to use and apply the information contained within the server log will help you to make your Web site successful.

After you make updates or changes to the site, notify your viewers with a What's New announcement.

Methods and Tools Used to Create Web Sites

Web developers have several options for creating Web pages: a text editor, an HTML or XHTML editor, software applications, or a WYSIWYG text editor (discussed in detail on page DW 20). Microsoft Notepad and WordPad are each examples of a **text editor**. These simple, easy-to-use programs allow you to enter, edit, save, and print text. An **HTML** or **XHTML editor** is a more sophisticated version of a text editor. In addition to basic text-editing functions, these programs include advanced features such as syntax highlighting, color coding, and spell checking. Software applications such as Microsoft Word, Microsoft Excel, and Adobe Publisher provide a Save as Web Page or Save as HTML command. This feature converts the application document into a file Web browsers can display. Examples of a WYSIWYG text editor are programs such as Microsoft Expression Web and Adobe Dreamweaver. These programs provide an integrated text editor with a graphical user interface that allows you to view the code and the document as you create it.

A Web developer can use any of these options to create Web pages. Regardless of the option selected, however, it still is important to understand the specifics of HTML and XHTML.

Web Site Languages

Web pages are written in plain text and saved in the **American Standard Code for Information Interchange**, or **ASCII** (pronounced ASK-ee), format — the most widely used coding system to represent data. Using the ASCII format makes Web pages universally readable by different Web browsers regardless of the computer platform on which they reside.

The language of the Web is not static; it evolves just like most other languages. HTML (Hypertext Markup Language) has been the primary language of the Web and most likely will continue to be so for at least the near future. HTML is useful for creating headings, paragraphs, lists, and so on, but is limited to these general types of formatting. XHTML is a rewritten version of HTML using XML (Extensible Markup Language).

Unlike HTML, **Extensible Hypertext Markup Language (XHTML)** is an authoring language that defines the structure and layout of a document so that it displays as a Web page and is compatible with Web browsers such as Microsoft Internet Explorer,

BTW

W3C
The World Wide Web Consortium (W3C) develops and updates Web protocols. For example, they specified the most recent changes to XHTML, and are directing an effort to make it easier for people to browse the Web on mobile devices.

BTW

Test Web Pages
To test a Web page, you can use the Adobe Browser Lab at *https://browserlab.adobe.com* to see how your pages are displayed in a variety of browsers and versions of browsers.

Mozilla Firefox, Safari, or Google Chrome. Browser rules for interpreting HTML are flexible. XHTML, however, requires Web designers to adhere strictly to its markup language rules.

Two components constitute a Web page: source code and document content. The **source code**, which contains elements, acts as the program instructions. The **elements** within the source code control the appearance of the document content. Browsers display the **document content**, or the text and images. The browser interprets the elements contained within the code, and the code instructs the browser how to display the Web page. For instance, if you define a line of text on your Web page as a heading, the browser knows to display this line formatted as a heading.

All XHTML element formats and HTML tags start with a left angle bracket (< or less than symbol), are followed by the name of the element, and end with a right angle bracket (> or greater than symbol). Most elements have a start and an end element and are called **two-sided elements**. End elements are the same as start elements except they are preceded by a forward slash (/). Some XHTML elements, such as the one used to indicate a line break <br />, do not have an end element. Instead, the right angle bracket is preceded by a space and forward slash. These are known as **one-sided elements**, or **self-closing elements**. In some browsers, the end element can be omitted from certain elements, such as the end element for a new paragraph, </p>. Unlike HTML, however, XHTML standards require you to include both the start and end elements for all two-sided elements.

Some elements can contain an **attribute**, or **property**, which is additional information placed within the angle brackets. Attributes are not repeated or contained in the end element. Some attributes are used individually, while other attributes can include a value modifier. A **value modifier** specifies conditions within the element, and should always be enclosed in double quotation marks. For example, you can use a value modifier to specify the font type or size or the placement of text on the page. To create and display a centered heading, for instance, you would use the following code:

```
<h1 style="text-align:center">This is the largest header
element and the text will be centered</h1>
```

In this example, h1 is the XHTML element, text-align is the attribute, and center is the value modifier. Notice that the attribute does not appear as part of the end element, </h1>.

You can use the Dreamweaver Code window and Microsoft Notepad or WordPad (text editors) to create XHTML documents. Place each element in a pair around the text or section that you want to define (**mark up**) with that element. Use lowercase characters when typing XHTML elements.

XHTML elements also format the hyperlinks that connect information on the World Wide Web. While XHTML elements number in the hundreds, some are used more than others. All documents, however, require four basic elements. Figure I–10 illustrates the basic elements required for all XHTML documents. Table I–2 summarizes the more commonly used XHTML elements.

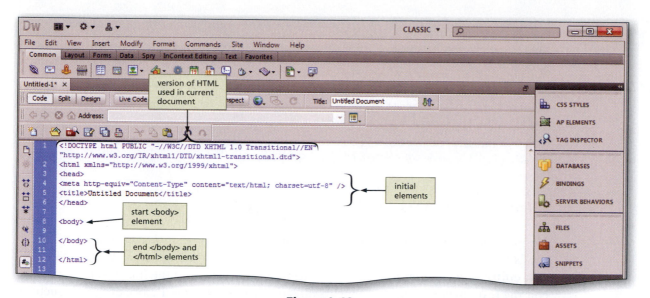

Figure I–10

Table I–2 Commonly Used XHTML Elements

Element (tags)	Structure
<html>...</html>	Encloses the entire XHTML document
<head>...</head>	Encloses the head of the XHTML document
<body>...</body>	Encloses the body of the XHTML document

Element (tags)	Title and Headings
<title>...</title>	Indicates the title of the document
<h1>...</h1>	Heading level 1
<h2>...</h2>	Heading level 2
<h3>...</h3>	Heading level 3
<h4>...</h4>	Heading level 4
<h5>...</h5>	Heading level 5
<h6>...</h6>	Heading level 6

Element (tags)	Paragraphs, Breaks, and Separators
<p>...</p>	Paragraph
 	Line break
<hr />	Horizontal rule
<ol>...</ol>	Ordered, numbered list
<ul>...</ul>	Unordered, bulleted list
<li>...</li>	List item, used with <ol>, <ul>, <menu>, and <dir>
<dl>...</dl>	Definition of glossary list
<dt>...</dt>	Definition term; part of a definition list
<dd>...</dd>	Definition corresponding to a definition term

Element (tags)	Character Formatting
...	Bold text
<u>...</u>	Underlined text
<i>...</i>	Italic text

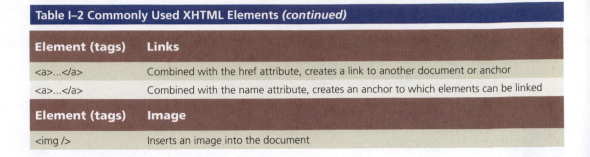

Element (tags)	Links
<a>...</a>	Combined with the href attribute, creates a link to another document or anchor
<a>...</a>	Combined with the name attribute, creates an anchor to which elements can be linked
Element (tags)	**Image**
<img />	Inserts an image into the document

Web Page Authoring Programs

Many of today's Web page authoring programs, including Dreamweaver, are What You See Is What You Get (WYSIWYG) text editors. As mentioned earlier, a **WYSIWYG text editor** allows a user to view a document as it will appear in the final product and to edit the text, images, or other elements directly within that view. Before programs such as Dreamweaver existed, Web page designers were required to type, or hand-code, Web pages. Educators and Web designers still debate the issue surrounding the necessity of knowing HTML and XHTML. Technically, you do not need to know either HTML or XHTML to create Web pages in Dreamweaver; however, an understanding of HTML and XHTML will help you if you need to alter Dreamweaver-generated code. If you know HTML and XHTML, then you can make changes to the code and Dreamweaver will accept the changes.

Adobe Dreamweaver CS5

The standard in visual authoring, Adobe Dreamweaver CS5 is part of the Adobe Creative Suite, which includes Adobe Flash, Fireworks, Photoshop, Illustrator, InDesign, Acrobat, and other programs depending on the particular suite. Dreamweaver provides features that access these separate products. Some of the new Dreamweaver CS5 features include the following:

- Integrated content management system (CMS) support
- New rendering mode that displays the design like a standard-based browser
- CSS inspection
- Integration with Adobe BrowserLab, PHP custom class code hinting, and Business Catalyst
- Enhanced CSS starter page

Dreamweaver makes it easy to get started and provides you with helpful tools to enhance your Web design and development experience. Working in a single environment, you create, build, and manage Web sites and Internet applications. In Dreamweaver, you can customize the workspace environment to fit your particular needs.

Dreamweaver contains coding tools and features that include references for HTML, XHTML, XML, CSS, and JavaScript as well as code editors that allow you to edit the code directly. Using **Adobe Roundtrip technology**, Dreamweaver can import Microsoft Office or other software Web pages and delete the unused code. Downloadable extensions from the Adobe Web site make it easy to add functionality to any Web site. Examples of these extensions include shopping carts and online payment features.

Instead of writing individual files for every page, you can use a database to store content and then retrieve the content dynamically in response to a user's request. Implementing and using this feature, you can update the information once, in one place, instead of manually editing many pages. Another key feature is **Cascading Style Sheets styles** (**CSS styles**). CSS styles are collections of formatting definitions that affect the appearance of Web page elements. You can use CSS styles to format text, images, headings, tables, and so forth. Implementing and applying this feature, you can update the formatting one time across many Web pages.

Dreamweaver provides the tools that help you author accessible content. These accessible pages comply with government guidelines and Section 508 of the Federal Rehabilitation Act. Accessibility is discussed in more detail as you progress through the book.

Dreamweaver allows you to publish Web sites with relative ease to a local area network, which connects computers in a limited geographical area, or to the Web, so that anyone with Internet access can see them. The concepts and techniques presented in this book provide the tools you need to plan, develop, and publish professional Web sites, such as those shown in Figure I–11 and Figure I–12.

Figure I–11

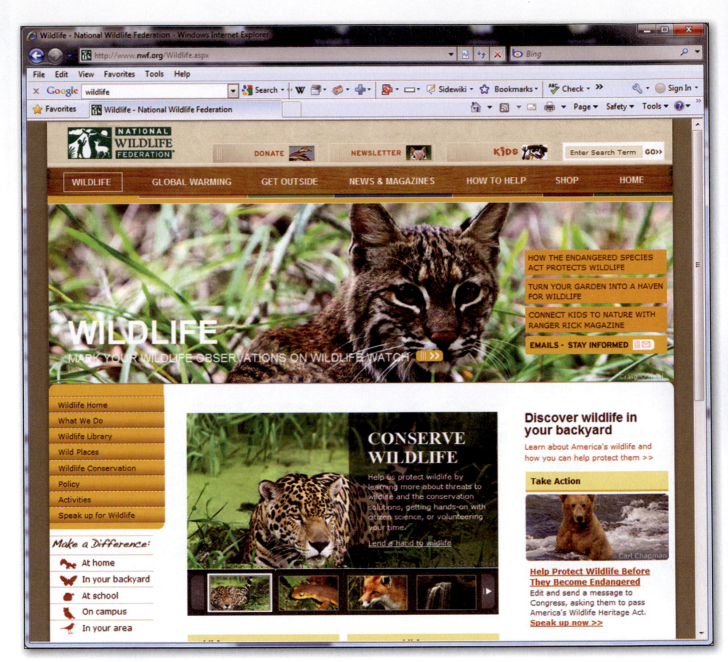

Figure I–12

Chapter Summary

The Introduction to Web Site Development and Adobe Dreamweaver CS5 provided an overview of the Internet and the World Wide Web and the key terms associated with those technologies. An overview of the basic types of Web pages also was presented. The Introduction furnished information on developing a Web site, including planning basics. The process of designing a Web site and each phase within this process were discussed. Information about testing, publishing, and maintaining a Web site also was presented, including an overview of obtaining a domain name, acquiring server space, and uploading a Web site. Methods and tools used to create Web pages were introduced. A short overview of HTML and XHTML and some of the more commonly used HTML tags and XHTML elements were presented. Finally, the advantages of using Dreamweaver in Web development were discussed. These advantages include a WYSIWYG text editor; a visual, customizable development environment; accessibility compliance; downloadable extensions; database access capabilities; and Cascading Style Sheets.

Learn It Online

Test your knowledge of chapter content and key terms.

Instructions: To complete the Learn It Online exercises, start your browser, click the Address bar, and then enter the Web address `scsite.com/dwcs5/learn`. When the Dreamweaver CS5 Learn It Online page is displayed, click the link for the exercise you want to complete and then read the instructions.

Chapter Reinforcement TF, MC, and SA
A series of true/false, multiple choice, and short answer questions that test your knowledge of the chapter content.

Flash Cards
An interactive learning environment where you identify chapter key terms associated with displayed definitions.

Practice Test
A series of multiple choice questions that test your knowledge of chapter content and key terms.

Who Wants To Be a Computer Genius?
An interactive game that challenges your knowledge of chapter content in the style of a television quiz show.

Wheel of Terms
An interactive game that challenges your knowledge of chapter key terms in the style of the television show *Wheel of Fortune*.

Crossword Puzzle Challenge
A crossword puzzle that challenges your knowledge of key terms presented in the chapter.

Apply Your Knowledge

Reinforce the skills and apply the concepts you learned in this chapter.

Creating a Web Site

Instructions: As discussed in this Introduction, creating a Web site involves planning, designing, developing, reviewing and testing, publishing, and maintaining the site. Use the information contained in Table I-3 to develop a plan for creating a Web site.

Table I–3 Creating a Web Site	
Planning	
Web site name	What is your Web site name?
Web site type	What is the Web site type: portal, news, informational, business/marketing, educational, entertainment, advocacy, blog, wiki, social network, content aggregator, Web application, or personal?
Web site purpose	What is the purpose of your Web site?
Target audience	How can you identify your target audience?
Web technologies to be used	Will you design for broadband, baseband, or mobile? Explain your selection.
Content	What topics will you cover? How much information will you present on each topic? How will you attract your audience? What will you do to entice your audience to return to your Web site? How will you keep the Web site updated?
Text, images, and multimedia	Will your site contain text only? What type of images will you include? Where will you obtain your images? Will you have a common logo? Will plug-ins be required?
Designing	
Navigation map	What type of structure will you use? What tools will you use to design your navigation map?
Navigational elements	What navigational elements will you include?

Apply Your Knowledge *continued*

Table I–3 Creating a Web Site *(continued)*	
Developing	
Typography	What font will you use? How many different fonts will you use on your site?
Images	How will you use images to enhance your site? Will you use a background image?
Page layout	What type of layout will you use? How many topics per page? How will text be presented: bulleted or paragraph style? Will the audience need to scroll the page?
Color	What color combinations will you use for your site? To what elements will you apply the color(s) — fonts, background, tables, other elements?
Reviewing and Testing	
Review	What elements will you review? Will you use a group review?
Testing	What elements will you test? Will you use group testing?
Publishing	
Domain name	What is your domain name? Have you registered your domain name? What ISP will host your Web site? What criteria did you use to select the ISP?
Maintaining	
Ongoing maintenance	How often will you update your Web site? What elements will you update? Will you add additional features? Does your ISP provide server logs? Will you use the server logs for maintenance purposes?

Perform the following tasks:

1. Download and then use your word processing program to open the Apply I-1 Web Site Creation file. With the Apply I-1 Web Site Creation file open in your word processing program, select a name for your Web site.

2. Use a specialized search engine at one of the many accredited domain name registrars to verify that your selected Web site name is available.

3. Answer each question in the Planning table. Use complete sentences to answer the questions. Type your answers in column 3.

4. Save the document with the file name Apply I-1_your initials. Submit the document in the format specified by your instructor.

Extend Your Knowledge

Extend the skills you learned in this chapter and experiment with new skills. You may need to use Help to complete the assignment.

Identifying Web Site Types

Instructions: As you learned in this Introduction, Web sites can be classified into 13 basic types. Use a browser such as Internet Explorer to identify Web site types.

Perform the following tasks:

Part 1: Web Site Types
1. Review the different types of Web sites described on pages DW 5-6.
2. Select three of the Web site types.

Part 2: Search for Web Sites
1. Start your word processing program.
2. Start your browser and search for each of your three selected Web site types. Locate at least two examples of each type.
3. Copy and paste the Web site address for each example, and then compose a short paragraph explaining how each Web site meets the selected criteria.

Make It Right

Analyze a Web site structure and suggest how to improve the organization or design.

Improving Navigation Structures

Instructions: Start your Web browser. Select and analyze a Web site and determine the navigation structure used within the Web site.

Figure I–5 (a) through (d) on page DW 9 contains examples of four types of navigation structures. This figure is reproduced as Figure I–13 on page DW 26. Select a Web site and review the structure of the Web site. Start your word processing program. Describe the structure used in your selected Web site. Include any suggestions you may have on how this structure could be improved. If you are using Microsoft Office Word 2007 or Word 2010, click the Insert tab on the Ribbon. In the Illustrations group, use the Shapes or SmartArt options to create an image of the structure. Save your document and submit it in the format specified by your instructor.

Make It Right *continued*

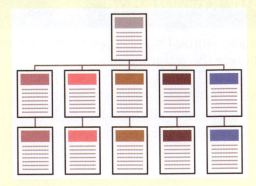

(a) Linear Structure

(b) Hierarchical Structure

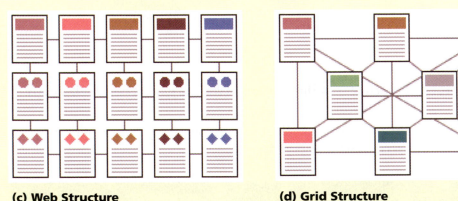

(c) Web Structure

(d) Grid Structure

Figure I–13

In the Lab

Design and/or create a document using the guidelines, concepts, and skills presented in this chapter. Labs are listed in order of increasing difficulty.

Lab 1: Using Internet Explorer

Problem: Microsoft Internet Explorer (IE) has many features that can make your work on the Internet more efficient. Using the Accelerators feature, for example, you can quickly display driving directions, translate and define words, or e-mail content to others without navigating to other Web sites. IE also includes other enhancements. Visit the Internet Explorer 8: Features Web page (Figure I–14 on page DW 27) and select three articles concerning topics with which you are not familiar. Read the articles and then create a word processing document detailing what you learned.

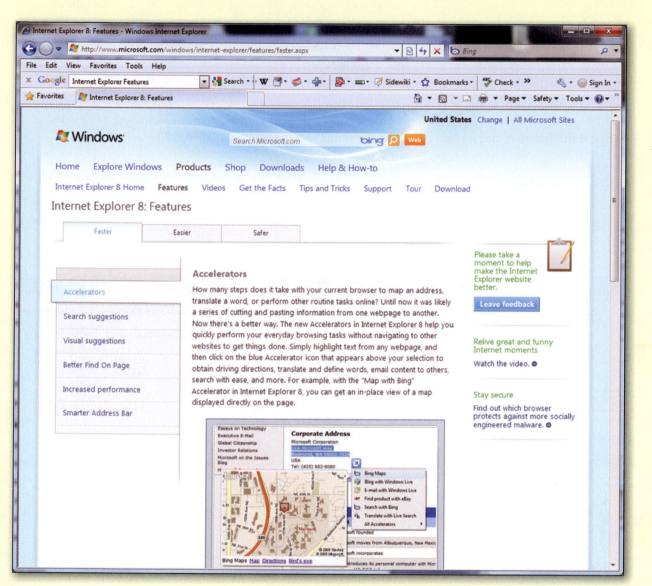

Figure I–14

Perform the following tasks:

1. Start your browser. Open the Internet Explorer 8: Features Web page (*www.microsoft.com/windows/ internet-explorer/features/faster.aspx*).

2. Scroll down the page, click a tab such as the Easier tab, and then scroll to display all the information on that tab.

3. Select three features with which you are not familiar.

4. Click the link for each article and read the article.

5. Start your word processing program.

6. List three important points that you learned from this Web site.

7. Write a summary of what you learned from each article. Include within your summary your opinion of the article and if you will apply what you learned or use it with your Web browser.

8. Save the document on a USB flash drive using the file name Lab I-1 IE Features.

9. Submit the document in the format specified by your instructor.

In the Lab

Lab 2: Identifying Types of Web Sites

Problem: A Web designer should be familiar with different types of Web pages and the sort of information displayed on these types of Web pages. This chapter describes 13 types of Web sites. Search the Internet and locate at least one example of each type of Web site.

Perform the following tasks:

1. Start your browser. Open the Google (google.com) search engine Web page (Figure I–15) and search for an example of each of the following types of Web sites: portal, news, informational, business/marketing, blog, wiki, social networks, educational, entertainment, advocacy, Web application, content aggregator, and personal.

Figure I–15

2. Start your word processing program.

3. Copy and paste the link for each of these Web page types into your word processing document.

4. Identify the type of Web page for each link.

5. Explain why you selected this Web page and how it fits the definition of the specific type.

6. Save the document with the file name Lab I-2 Web Page Types.

7. Submit the document in the format specified by your instructor.

In the Lab

Lab 3: Hosting a Web Site

Problem: Selecting the correct host or ISP for your Web site can be a confusing process. Many Web sites offer this service, but determining the best one for your particular needs can be somewhat complicated. Assume your Web site will sell a product. Compare several ISPs and select the one that will best meet your needs.

Perform the following tasks:

1. Review the information and questions on page DW 16 discussing the guidelines for acquiring active server space to host your Web site.

Figure I–16

2. Start your browser. Open Web page shown in Figure I–16 (*www.the10besthosts.com*).

3. Click one of the host server links and review the information relating to the services offered by your selected ISP.

4. Start your word processing program.

5. Read and answer the questions on page DW 16. Use the information provided in the list of services offered by your selected ISP.

6. Use your word processing program to write a short summary explaining why you would or would not select this ISP to host your Web site.

7. Save the document with the file name Lab I-3 Web Site Hosting. Submit the document in the format specified by your instructor.

Cases and Places

Apply your creative thinking and problem solving skills to design and implement a solution.

• EASIER •• MORE DIFFICULT

• 1: Research Web Site Planning

You are working as an assistant to the manager of Upscale Renovations, a firm that specializes in lawn and garden renovations. The marketing director is considering whether to create a Web site for Upscale Renovations, and asks you to conduct some research. Use a search engine such as Google (google.com) and research information about planning a Web site. Use your word processing program and write a two-page summary of what you learned. Save the document as Case I-1 Web Site Research. Check the spelling and grammar of the finished paper. Submit the document in the format specified by your instructor.

• 2: Explore Typography

Typography within a Web page is one of its more important elements. Start your browser and search for examples of Web sites that include what you consider appropriate typography and Web sites with inappropriate typography. Use your word processing program to define typography and to write a short summary of why you consider the Web sites to be appropriate and inappropriate. Copy and paste the Web site addresses into your document. Check the spelling and grammar of the finished paper. Save the document as Case I-2 Typography. Submit the document in the format specified by your instructor.

•• 3: Research Web Site Plug-ins

You are working as an intern in an animal shelter, helping the director design a Web site. He wants to show a video of the animals at the shelter on the site, and has heard that viewers might need a plug-in to view videos. He asks you to research the topic. Start your browser and search the Web for plug-ins. Prepare a list of and a short description of the plug-ins you found. Use your word processing program to create a summary statement describing how and why you could use each plug-in in a Web site. Include the link where you can download each of the plug-ins. Check the spelling and grammar of the finished paper. Save the document as Case I-3 Web Site Plug-ins. Submit the document in the format specified by your instructor.

•• 4: Create a Web Site Navigation Map

Make It Personal

In preparation for an upcoming wedding, the bride is asking members of the bridal party to create a personal Web site. Working with two or three members of your class, use a software program of your choice to create a navigation map for your proposed Web site. Show the link(s) from the home page to the other two pages. Use your word processing program and write a sentence or two describing the type of structure your group created and why you selected that structure. Check the spelling and grammar of the finished paper. Save the document as Case I-4 Navigation Map. Submit the document in the format specified by your instructor.

•• 5: Create Web Site Structures

Working Together

Each team member is to search the Internet for Web sites illustrating each of the Web site structures on page DW 9. Each team member then will use word processing software to write a minimum of 100 words describing the Web sites and explaining why he or she thinks the structure used is appropriate or inappropriate for that particular Web site. Check the spelling and grammar of the finished paper. Save the document as Case I-5 Web Site Structures. Submit the document in the format specified by your instructor.

1 Creating a Dreamweaver Web Page and Local Site

Objectives

You will have mastered the material in this chapter when you can:

- Describe Dreamweaver and identify its key features
- Start and quit Dreamweaver
- Describe the Dreamweaver window
- Define a local site
- Create and save a Web page
- Add a background image
- Open and close panels

- Display the Property inspector
- Format and modify text elements
- Define and insert a line break
- Change a Web page title and check spelling
- Preview and print a Web page
- Open a new Web page

1 | Creating a Dreamweaver Web Page and Local Site

What Is Adobe Dreamweaver CS5?

Adobe Dreamweaver CS5 is a powerful Web page authoring and Web site management software program with an HTML editor that is used to design, code, and create professional-looking Web pages, Web sites, and Web applications. The visual-editing features of Dreamweaver allow you to create pages without writing a line of code. Dreamweaver provides many tools and features, including the following:

- **Automatic Web page creation:** Dreamweaver provides tools you can use to develop Web pages without having to spend hours writing HTML code. Dreamweaver automatically generates the HTML code necessary to publish your Web pages.

- **Web site management:** Dreamweaver enables you to view a site, including all local and remote files associated with the selected site. You can perform standard maintenance tasks such as viewing, opening, and moving files and transferring files between local and remote sites.

- **Standard Adobe Web authoring tools:** Dreamweaver includes a user interface that is consistent across all Adobe authoring tools. This consistency enables easy integration with other Adobe Web-related programs such as Adobe Flash, Director, Shockwave, and ColdFusion.

Other key features include the integrated user interface, the integrated file explorer, panel management, database integration, and standards and accessibility support. Dreamweaver CS5 is customizable and runs on many operating systems including Windows 7, Windows Vista, Windows XP, Mac OS X, and others.

Project Planning Guidelines

The process of developing a Web site that communicates specific information requires careful analysis and planning. As a starting point, determine the type of and purpose of the Web site. Once the type and purpose are determined, decide on the content to be included. Design basics and Web site navigation then should be considered. Finally, creating a navigation map or flowchart will help determine the design that will be most helpful in delivering the Web site content. With the structure in place, the Web site is ready to be developed. Details of these guidelines are provided in the Introduction. In addition, each project in this book provides practical applications of these planning considerations.

Project — Montana Parks Web Site Home Page

To create documents similar to those you will encounter on the Web and in academic, business, and personal environments, you can use Dreamweaver to produce Web pages such as the Montana Parks and Recreation Areas Web page shown in Figure 1–1. This Web page is the index, or home, page for the Montana Parks Web site and provides interesting facts about three of Montana's parks and recreational areas. The page begins with a centered main heading, followed by two short informational paragraphs, and then an introductory sentence for a bulleted list. The list contains three bulleted items. A concluding sentence, the author's name, and current date end the page. A background image is applied to the page.

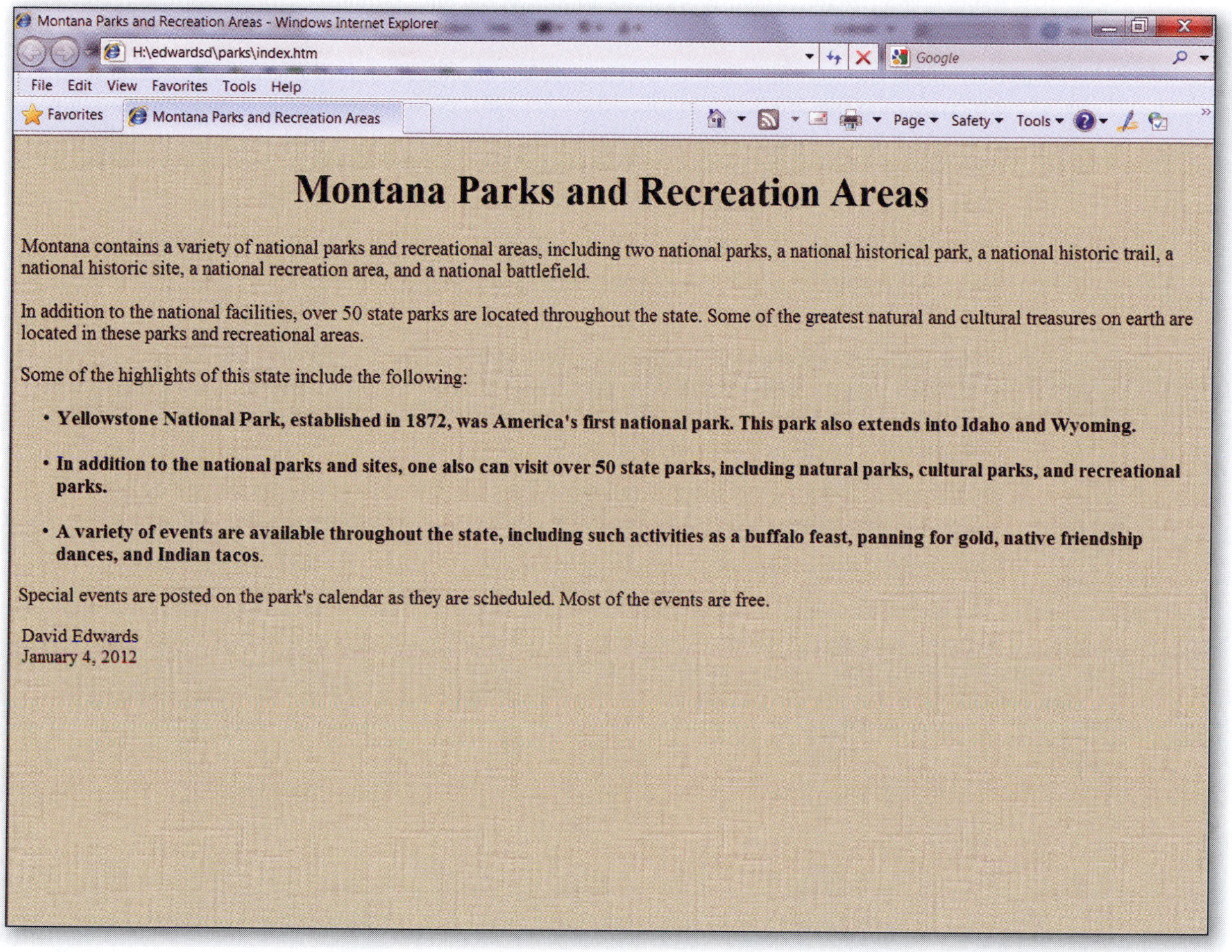

Figure 1–1

Overview

As you read this chapter, you will learn how to create the Web page shown in Figure 1–1 by performing these general tasks:

- Enter text in the document.
- Save the document.
- Add a background image.
- Format the text in the document.
- Insert a line break.
- Check spelling.
- Preview the Web page in a browser.
- Save and print the Web page.

General Project Guidelines

When creating a Dreamweaver Web site, the actions you perform and decisions you make will affect the appearance and characteristics of the entire Web site. As you create the home page, such as the page shown in Figure 1–1 on the previous page, you should follow these general guidelines:

1. **Review the Dreamweaver workspace window.** Become familiar with the various layouts and available panels.

2. **Determine the location for the local site.** Select the location and the storage media on which to save the site. Keep in mind that you will continue to modify pages and add new pages to the site as you progress through this book. Storage media can be a hard disk, USB flash drive, or read/write CD. If you are using a flash drive and intend to complete all exercises, the media storage capacity should be a minimum of 25 MB.

3. **Define the local site.** Create the local site using Dreamweaver's Site Setup dialog box.

4. **Add a background for the Web page.** Adding a background color or background image adds interest and vitality to a Web site.

5. **Select the words and fonts for the text.** Text accounts for the bulk of the content on most Web pages, but Web site visitors often avoid reading long blocks of text. It is best to be brief. Include headings to organize the text into sections. Use lists whenever possible. Use common words and simple language.

6. **Identify how to format various elements of the text.** Determine which text will be headings and subheadings, paragraphs, and bulleted and numbered lists on the Web page.

7. **Review final tasks.** Prepare to display a Web page to others by adding professional finishing touches such as a Web page title and by checking the spelling of the text.

   When necessary, more specific details concerning the above guidelines are presented at appropriate points in the chapter. The chapter also will identify the actions performed and decisions made regarding these guidelines during the creation of the Web site home page shown in Figure 1–1.

Starting Dreamweaver

If you are using a computer to step through the project in this chapter and you want your screen to match the figures in this book, you should change your screen's resolution to 1024 x 768. The browser used to display the Web page figures is Internet Explorer 8. The browser text size is set to Medium.

To Start Dreamweaver

Getting started in Dreamweaver is as easy as opening an existing HTML document or creating a new document. The following steps show how to start Dreamweaver based on a typical installation. You may need to ask your instructor how to start Dreamweaver for your computer.

1

- Click the Start button on the Windows 7 taskbar to display the Start menu (Figure 1–2).

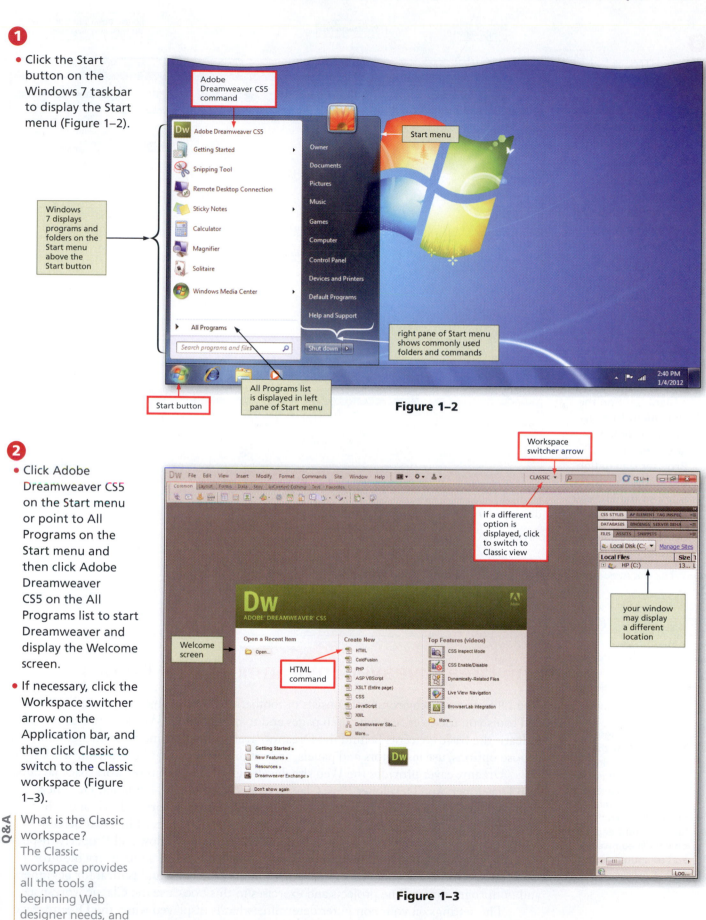

Adobe Dreamweaver CS5 command

Start menu

Windows 7 displays programs and folders on the Start menu above the Start button

right pane of Start menu shows commonly used folders and commands

Start button

All Programs list is displayed in left pane of Start menu

Figure 1–2

2

- Click Adobe Dreamweaver CS5 on the Start menu or point to All Programs on the Start menu and then click Adobe Dreamweaver CS5 on the All Programs list to start Dreamweaver and display the Welcome screen.

- If necessary, click the Workspace switcher arrow on the Application bar, and then click Classic to switch to the Classic workspace (Figure 1–3).

Workspace switcher arrow

if a different option is displayed, click to switch to Classic view

your window may display a different location

Welcome screen

HTML command

Q&A

What is the Classic workspace?
The Classic workspace provides all the tools a beginning Web designer needs, and omits features for advanced designers and programmers.

Figure 1–3

3

- Click HTML in the Create New column to close the Welcome screen and display the Dreamweaver workspace.

- If necessary, click the Maximize button to maximize the Dreamweaver window.

- If necessary, click the Design button on the Document toolbar to switch to Design view.

- If the Browser Navigation toolbar is displayed, right-click a blank spot on the Document toolbar, point to Toolbars, and then click Browser Navigation to remove the check mark so the Browser Navigation toolbar is not displayed in the Dreamweaver window.

- If the Insert bar is not displayed, click Window on the Application bar and then click Insert (Figure 1–4).

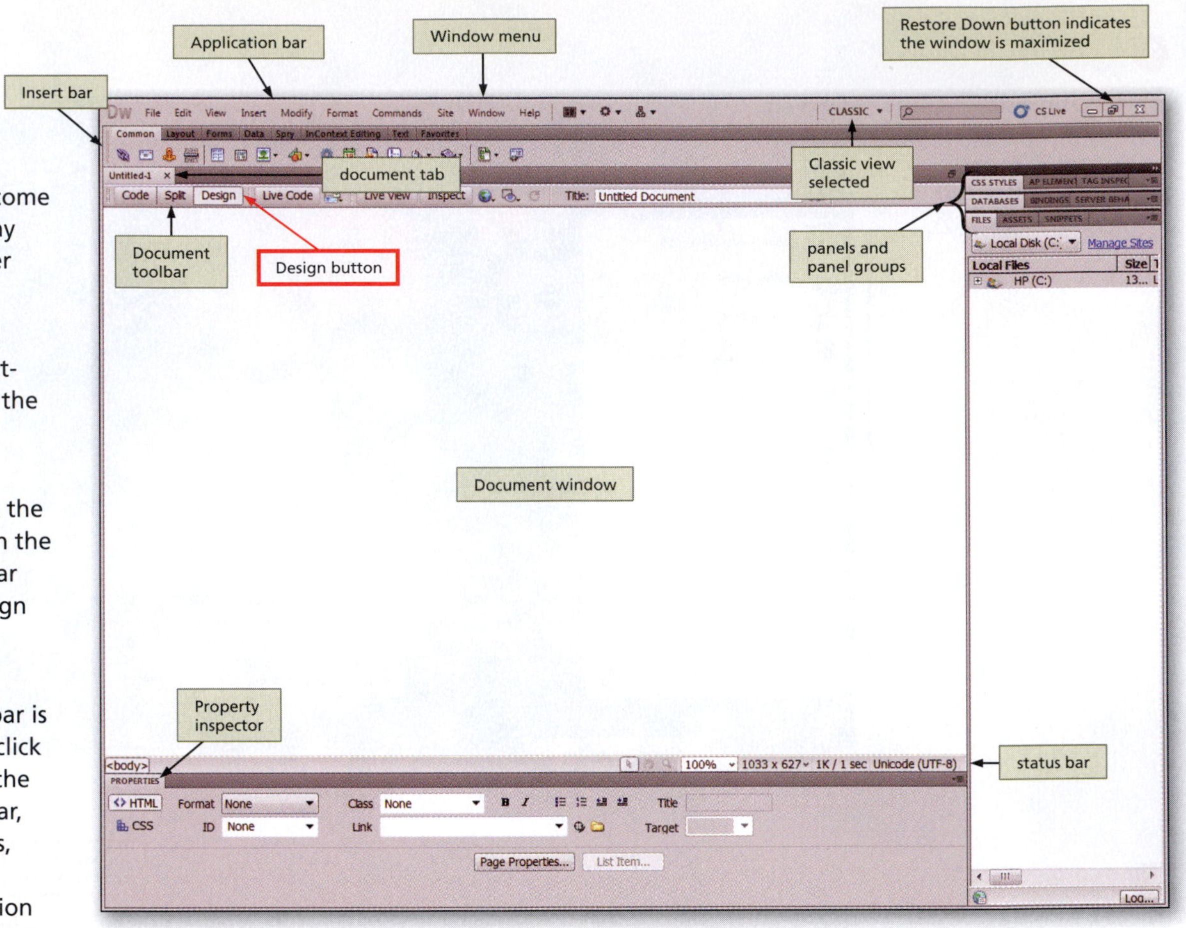

Figure 1–4

Q&A

What if a message is displayed regarding default file types?

If a message is displayed, click the Close button.

Other Ways

1. Double-click Dreamweaver icon on desktop

BTW

The Dreamweaver Window
The screen in Figure 1–4 shows how the Dreamweaver window looks the first time you start Dreamweaver after installation on most computers. Your screen might look different depending on your Dreamweaver and computer settings.

The Dreamweaver Environment and Workspace

The Dreamweaver environment consists of toolbars, windows, objects, panels, inspectors, and tools you use to create your Web pages and to manage your Web site. It is important to learn the basic concepts behind the Dreamweaver workspace and to understand how to choose options, use inspectors and panels, and set preferences that best fit your work style.

Dreamweaver provides the Web site developer with eight preset workspace layouts: App Developer, App Developer Plus, Classic, Coder, Coder Plus, Designer, Designer Compact, and Dual Screen. Programmers who work primarily with HTML and other languages generally select the Coder or App Developer workspace. The Dual Screen option requires two monitors. In this layout, the Document window and Property inspector are displayed on one monitor and the panels are displayed on a secondary monitor. The Classic workspace contains a visually integrated workspace and is ideal for beginners and nonprogrammers. The projects and exercises in this book use the Classic workspace.

The settings on your computer determine what is displayed when the Dreamweaver CS5 program starts. By default, the Welcome screen is displayed each time you start

Dreamweaver. The Welcome screen's visual representation is a good tool for beginners, but more proficient Dreamweaver users generally disable this feature. You will disable the Welcome screen at the end of this chapter. If you are opening Dreamweaver from a computer at your school or other location, most likely the program is set up and ready to use.

The screen in Figure 1–4 shows a typical Dreamweaver workspace, with some of the more commonly used components displayed. The **Dreamweaver workspace** is an integrated environment in which the Document window and panels are incorporated into one larger application window. The panel groups are docked, or attached, on the right. The Insert bar (also called the Insert panel) is located at the top of the Document window, and the Property inspector is located at the bottom of the Document window. You can move, resize, close, or collapse the panels to accommodate your individual preferences.

The next section discusses the following components of the Dreamweaver workspace: title bar, Document window, panels and panel groups, status bar, Application bar, and toolbars.

As you learn to use each of these tools, you will discover some redundancy. For example, to apply a font tag, you can access the command through the CSS Property inspector, the Format menu, or the Text category on the Insert bar. The different options accommodate various user preferences. The chapters in this book present the more commonly used methods. The Other Ways boxes describe additional methods to accomplish a task when they are available. As you become proficient working in the Dreamweaver environment, you will develop techniques for using the tools that best suit your personal preferences.

Document Tab

The **document tab** displays the Web page name, which is Untitled-1 for the first Web page you create in a Dreamweaver session, as shown in Figure 1–4. (The "X" is the Close button for the document tab.) After you save and name the Web page, the document tab reflects the changes by displaying the document name. When you make changes to the document, Dreamweaver includes an asterisk following the file name. The asterisk is removed after the document is saved, and the file path leading to the document's location is displayed to the right of the document tab.

Document Window

The **Document window** displays the current document, or Web page, including text, tables, graphics, and other items. In Figure 1–4, the Document window is blank. You work in the Document window in one of the following views: **Design view**, the design environment where you assemble your Web page elements and design your page (Figure 1–4 displays Design view); **Code view**, which is a hand-coding environment for writing and editing code; **Split view**, which allows you to see both Code view and Design view for the same document in a single window; **Live View**, which shows the page such as it would appear in a browser; **Live Code**, which displays any HTML code produced by JavaScript or server-side programming; or **Inspect Mode**, which evaluates the code. When you open a new document in Dreamweaver, the default view is Design view. These views are discussed in detail in Chapter 2.

Panels and Panel Groups

Panel groups are sets of related panels docked together below one heading. Panels provide control over a wide range of Dreamweaver commands and functions. Each panel group can be expanded or collapsed, and can be undocked or docked with other panel

BTW

Change the Insert Bar to a Menu
Right-click any category name on the Insert bar and then click Show as Menu to change the horizontal tabs on the Insert bar to a vertical menu.

groups. Panel groups also can be docked to the integrated Document window. This makes it easy to access the panels you need without cluttering your workspace. Panels within a panel group are displayed as tabs. Each panel is explained in detail as it is used in the chapters throughout the book. Some panels, such as the Insert bar and Property inspector, are stand-alone panels.

The **Insert bar** allows quick access to frequently used commands. It contains buttons for creating and inserting various types of objects — such as images, tables, links, dates, and so on — into a document. As you insert each object, a dialog box allows you to set and manipulate various attributes. The buttons on the Insert bar are organized into several categories, such as Common and Layout, which you can access through tabs. Some categories also have buttons with pop-up menus. When you select an option from a pop-up menu, it becomes the default action for the button. When you start Dreamweaver, the category in which you last were working is displayed.

The **Property inspector** displays settings for the selected object's properties or attributes. This panel is context sensitive, meaning it changes based on the selected object, which can include text, tables, images, and other objects. When Dreamweaver starts, the Property inspector is positioned at the bottom of the Document window and displays text properties if a Document window is open. Otherwise, the Property inspector is blank.

Status Bar

The **status bar** located below the Document window (Figure 1–5) provides additional information about the document you are creating.

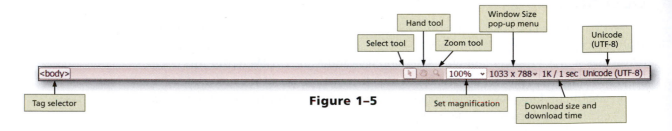

Figure 1–5

The status bar presents the following options:
- **Tag selector**: Click any tag in the hierarchy to select that tag and all its contents.
- **Select tool**: Use the Select tool to return to default editing after using the Zoom or Hand tool.
- **Hand tool**: To pan a page after zooming, use the Hand tool to drag the page.
- **Zoom tool**: Available in Design view or Split view, the Zoom tool can be used to check the pixel accuracy of graphics or to better view the page.
- **Set magnification**: Use the Set magnification pop-up menu to change the view from 6% to 6400%; default is 100%.
- **Window size**: Displays the Window size value, which includes the window's current dimensions (in pixels) and the Window size pop-up menu.
- **Download size and download time**: Displays the size and estimated download time of the current page. Dreamweaver CS5 calculates the size based on the entire contents of the page, including all linked objects such as images and plug-ins.
- **Unicode (UTF-8)**: An industry standard that allows computers to consistently represent and manipulate text expressed in most of the world's writing systems.

Vertical/Horizontal Bars

A vertical bar separates the panel groups from the Document window, and a horizontal bar separates the Property inspector from the Document window. Double-clicking the Property inspector bar hides or displays the Property inspector. The panel groups contain a Collapse to Icons/Expand Panels button (Figure 1–6). If your screen resolution is set to 800 × 600, a portion of the Property inspector may not be displayed when the panel groups are expanded.

Application Bar

The **Application bar** displays the Dreamweaver menu names (Figure 1–6). Each menu contains a list of commands you can use to perform tasks such as opening, saving, modifying, previewing, and inserting data into your Web page. When you point to a menu name on the Application bar, the area of the Application bar containing the name is selected.

To display a menu, such as the Edit menu (Figure 1–6), click the menu name on the Application bar. If you point to a menu command that has an arrow at its right edge, a submenu displays another list of commands. Many menus display some commands that appear gray, or dimmed, instead of black, which indicates they are not available for the current selection.

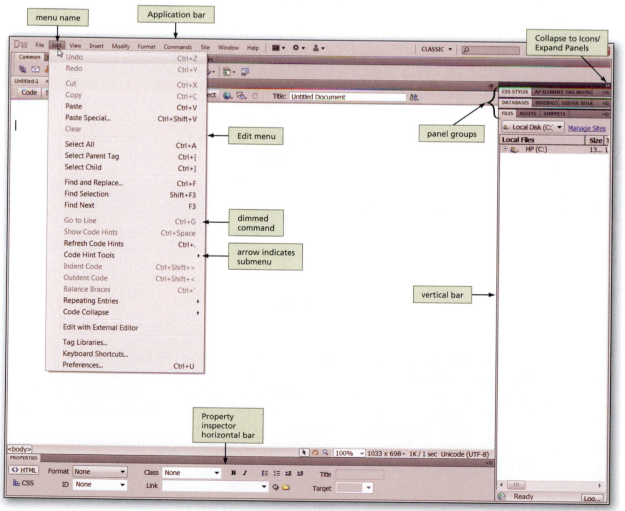

Figure 1–6

Toolbars

In the Classic workspace, or view, Dreamweaver can display four toolbars: Document, Standard, Style Rendering, and Browser Navigation. You can choose to display or hide the toolbars by clicking View on the Application bar and then pointing to Toolbars. If a toolbar name has a check mark next to it, it is displayed in the window. To hide the toolbar, click the name of the toolbar with the check mark, and it no longer is displayed. The Insert bar is considered a panel and was discussed previously in this chapter.

The **Document toolbar** (Figure 1–7) is the default toolbar displayed in the Document window. It contains buttons that provide different views of the Document window (e.g., Code, Split, and Design), the Document title, and some common operations, such as Preview/Debug in Browser, Refresh Design View, View Options, Visual Aids, and Check Browser Compatibility.

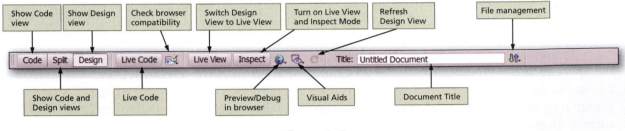

Figure 1–7

The **Standard toolbar** (Figure 1–8) contains buttons for common operations from the File and Edit menus: New, Open, Browse in Bridge, Save, Save All, Print Code, Cut, Copy, Paste, Undo, and Redo. The Standard toolbar is not displayed by default in the Dreamweaver Document window when you first start Dreamweaver. You can display the Standard toolbar through the Toolbars command on the View menu, or by right-clicking a blank area on the Document toolbar and then clicking Standard on the context menu. As with other toolbars and panels, you can dock or undock and move the Standard toolbar, so it might be displayed in a different location on your screen.

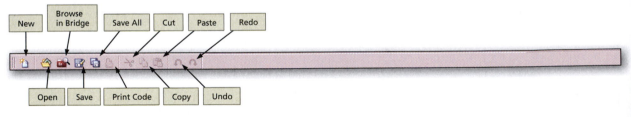

Figure 1–8

The **Style Rendering toolbar** (not shown by default) provides options for designing for different media types, such as screen, print, handheld, projection, TTY (teletype), television, CSS Styles, and Style Sheets. The CSS (Cascading Style Sheets) Styles button works independently of the other seven buttons and provides the option to disable or enable the display of CSS styles.

The **Browser Navigation toolbar** (also not shown by default) provides feedback regarding browser capability.

Opening and Closing Panels

The Dreamweaver workspace accommodates different work styles and levels of expertise. Through the workspace, you can open and close the panel groups and display or hide other Dreamweaver features as needed. To open a panel group, select and then click the name of a panel on the Window menu. Closing unused panels provides an uncluttered workspace in the Document window. To close an individual panel group, click Close Tab Group on the context menu accessed through the panel group's title bar (Figure 1–9) or click the Window menu and then click the panel name. To expand/collapse a panel, click the Expand Panels/Collapse to Icons button above the panel groups.

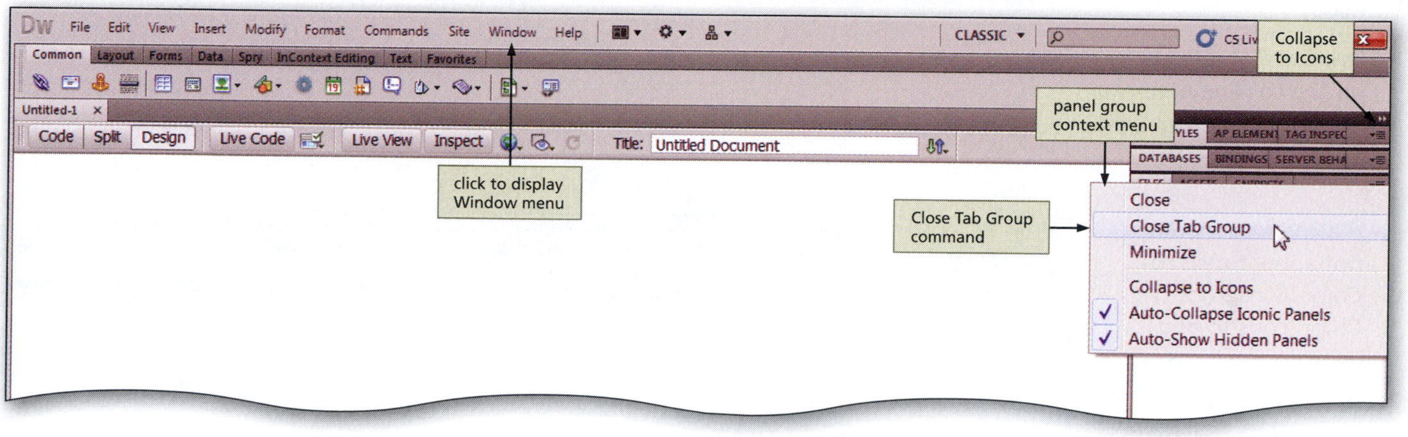

Figure 1–9

To Display the Standard Toolbar, Change the Icon Colors, and Close and Open Panels

The following steps illustrate how to display the Standard toolbar, change the icon colors, and close and open the panels.

1
- Click View on the Application bar to display the View menu.

- If necessary, click the down-pointing arrow at the bottom of the View menu to scroll the menu.

- Point to Toolbars, and then point to Standard on the Toolbars submenu to highlight Standard on the Toolbars submenu (Figure 1–10).

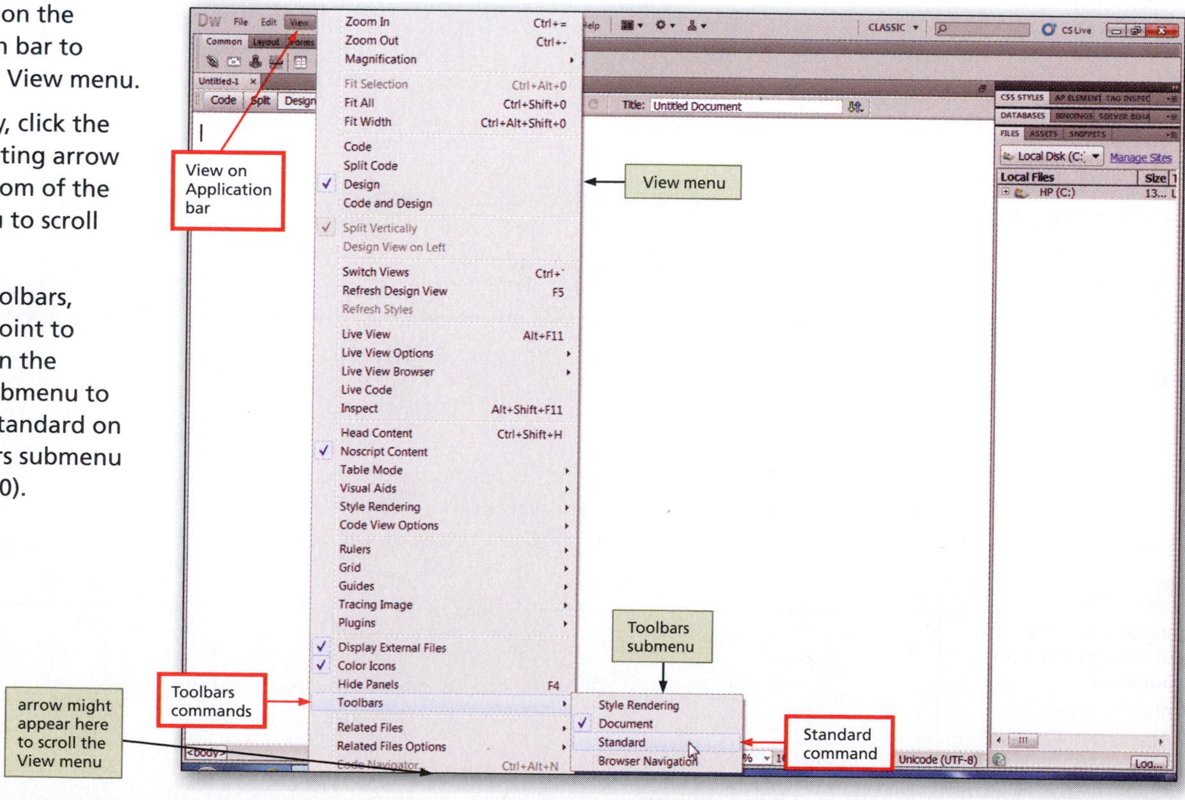

Figure 1–10

- Click Standard to display the Standard toolbar.

- If your Dreamweaver window does not display icons in color, right-click a blank spot on the Insert bar to display the context menu.

- Point to Color Icons on the context menu to highlight the command (Figure 1–11).

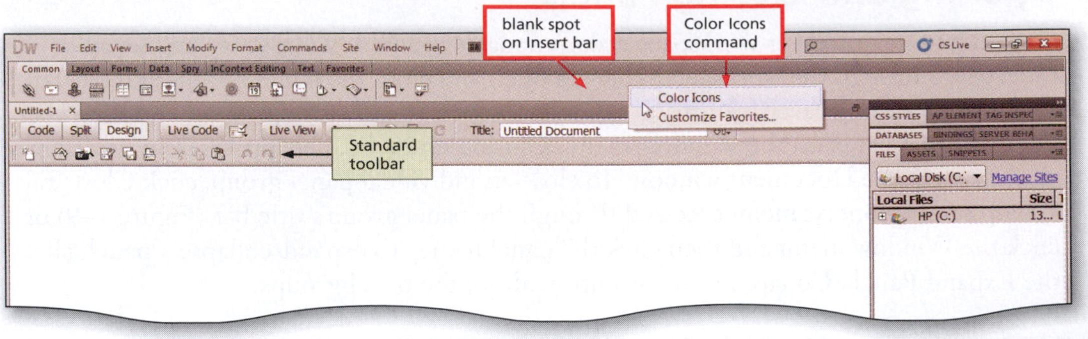

Figure 1–11

3

- If a check mark does not appear next to Color Icons, click Color Icons to add color to the icons.

- Press the F4 key to close all open panels and inspectors and to maximize the workspace available in the Document window.

- Press the F4 key again to redisplay the panels (Figure 1–12).

Q&A What is the fastest way to open and close panels?

The fastest way to open and close panels in Dreamweaver is to use the F4 key, which opens or closes all panels and inspectors at one time.

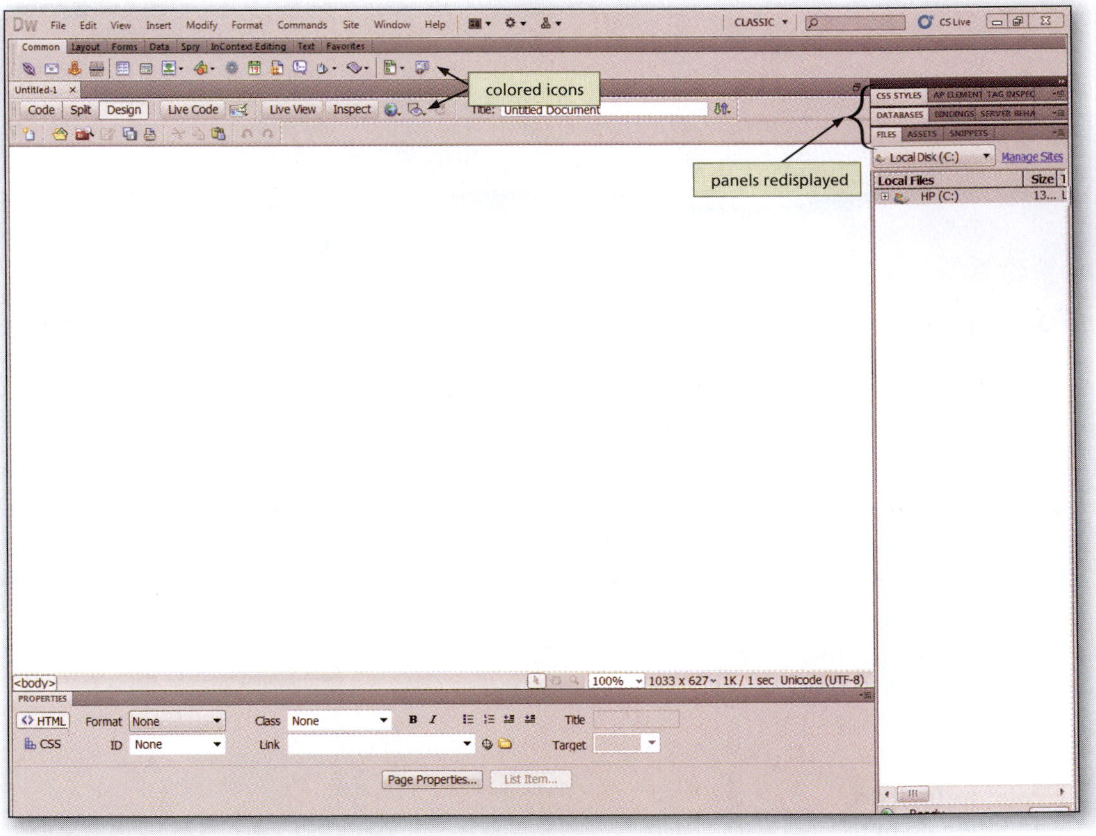

Figure 1–12

Q&A Can the location of the Standard toolbar change?

Yes. Previous settings determine the location of the Standard toolbar. It might be displayed below the Document toolbar or in another location in the Dreamweaver window.

Other Ways

1. Right-click blank area on toolbar, click Standard

2. Click View on Application bar, click Color Icons

Defining a Local Site

Web design and Web site management are two important skills that a builder of Web sites must understand and apply. Dreamweaver CS5 is a site creation and management tool. To use Dreamweaver efficiently, you first must define the local site. After defining the local site, you then publish to a remote site. Publishing to a remote site is discussed in Chapter 3 and Appendix C.

The general definition of a **site**, or Web site, is a set of linked documents with shared attributes, such as related topics, a similar design, or a shared purpose. In Dreamweaver, however, the term site can refer to any of the following:

- **Web site**: A set of pages on a server that are viewed through a Web browser by a visitor to the site.

- **Remote site**: Files on the server that make up a Web site, from the author's point of view rather than a visitor's point of view.

- **Local site**: Files on your computer that correspond to the files on the remote site. You edit the files on your computer, and then upload them to the remote site.

- **Dreamweaver site definition**: Set of defining characteristics for a local site, plus information on how the local site corresponds to a remote site.

All Dreamweaver Web sites begin with a local root folder. As you become familiar with Dreamweaver and complete the chapters in this book, you will find references to a **local site folder, local root folder, root folder**, and **root**. These terms are interchangeable. This folder is no different from any other folder on your computer's hard drive or other storage media, except for the way in which Dreamweaver views it. When Dreamweaver looks for Web pages, links, images, and other files, it looks in the designated root folder by default. Any media within the Web site that are outside of the root folder are not displayed when the Web site is previewed in a Web browser. Within the root folder, you can create additional folders and subfolders to organize images and other objects. A **subfolder** (also called a **nested folder**) is a folder inside another folder.

Dreamweaver provides two options to define a site and create the hierarchy: You can create the root folder and any subfolders, or create the pages and then create the folders when saving the files. In this book, you create the root folder and subfolders and then create the Web pages.

Determine the location for the local site.

Before you create a Web site, you need to determine where you will save the site and its files.

- If you plan to work on your Web site in various locations or on more than one computer, you should create your site on removable media, such as a USB flash drive. The Web sites in this book use a USB flash drive because these drives are portable and can store a lot of data.

- If you always work on the same computer, you probably can create your site on the computer's hard drive. However, if you are working in a computer lab, your instructor or the lab supervisor might instruct you to save your site in a particular location on the hard drive or on removable media such as a USB flash drive.

Plan Ahead

Creating the Local Root Folder and Subfolders

Several options are available to create and manage your local root folder and subfolders: Dreamweaver's Files panel, Dreamweaver's Site Setup feature, or Windows file management. In this book, you use Dreamweaver's Site Setup feature to create the local root folder and subfolders, the Files panel to manage and edit your files and folders, and Windows file management to download and copy the data files.

To organize and create a Web site and understand how you access Web documents, you need to understand paths and folders. The term path sometimes is confusing for new users of the Web. It is, however, a simple concept: A **path** is the succession of folders that must be navigated to get from one folder to another. Folders sometimes are referred to as **directories**. These two terms often are used interchangeably.

A typical path structure has a **master folder**, usually called the root and designated by the symbol "\". This root folder contains within it all of the other subfolders or nested folders. Further, each subfolder may contain additional subfolders or nested folders. These folders contain the Web site files. Most sites include a subfolder for images.

For this book, you first create a local root folder using your last name and first initial. Examples in this book use David Edwards as the Web site author. Thus, David's local root folder is edwardsd and is located on drive H (a removable disk). Next, for this chapter, you create a subfolder for the Montana Parks site and name it parks. Finally, you create another subfolder within parks and name it images. All Montana parks-related files and subfolders are stored within the parks folder. When you navigate through this folder hierarchy, you are navigating along the path. The path to the Montana Parks Web site is H:\edwardsd\parks\. The path to the images folder is H:\edwardsd\parks\images\. In all references to H:\edwardsd, substitute your last name and first initial and your drive location.

Using Site Setup to Create a Local Site

You create a local site using Dreamweaver's Site Setup dialog box. You work with two categories of settings:

- **Site category**: Enter the name of your site and the path to the local site folder. For example, you will use Montana Parks as the site name and H:\edwardsd\parks as the path to the local site. You can select the location of the local site folder instead of entering its path.

- **Advanced Settings category**: Enter Local Info settings, which include the path to the default images folder. For example, you will use H:\edwardsd\parks\images as the path to the folder containing the Web site images. You can select the location of the images folder instead of entering its path.

  Local Info settings also include options for specifying the types of links you will create in your site (relative to the document or to the site), and entering the URL of your Web site if you are using site-relative links. You also can check links for case-sensitivity (useful if you are publishing your site on a UNIX server) and enable caching to store frequently used site data.

  Note that the paths you enter to the local site folder and the images folder are included as part of the Web site. If you use removable media to store your files and move to another computer, you must recreate the local site setup on that computer.

  After you have completed the site definition, the hierarchy structure is displayed in the Dreamweaver **Local Files** list in the Files panel. This hierarchy structure is similar to the Windows file organization. The Local Files list provides a view of the devices and folders on your computer and shows how these devices and folders are organized.

To Use Site Setup to Create a Local Web Site

You define a local site by telling Dreamweaver where you plan to store local files. Use the Site Setup dialog box and the following steps to create a local Web site. A USB drive is used for all exercises in this book. If you are saving your sites at another location or on removable media, substitute that location for Removable Disk (H:).

1
- Click Site on the Application bar to display the Site menu, and then point to New Site to highlight that command (Figure 1–13).

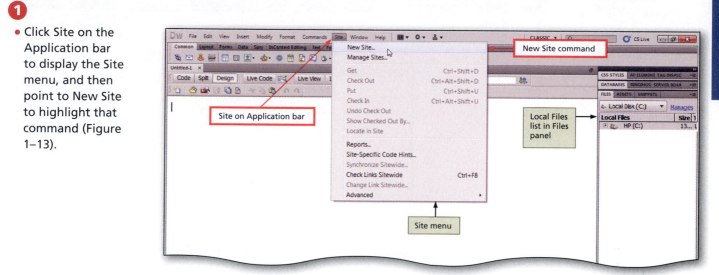

Figure 1–13

2
- Click New Site to display the Site Setup dialog box (Figure 1–14).

Q&A Should the name that appears in the Site Name text box be Unnamed Site 2?

Not necessarily. Your site number may be different.

Q&A What is the difference between the Local folder and the Remote folder?

The Local folder contains information about a Web site that you create on your computer, which is the way you develop a site. The Remote folder contains information about settings on a remote computer, such as a Web server, which is where you publish a site.

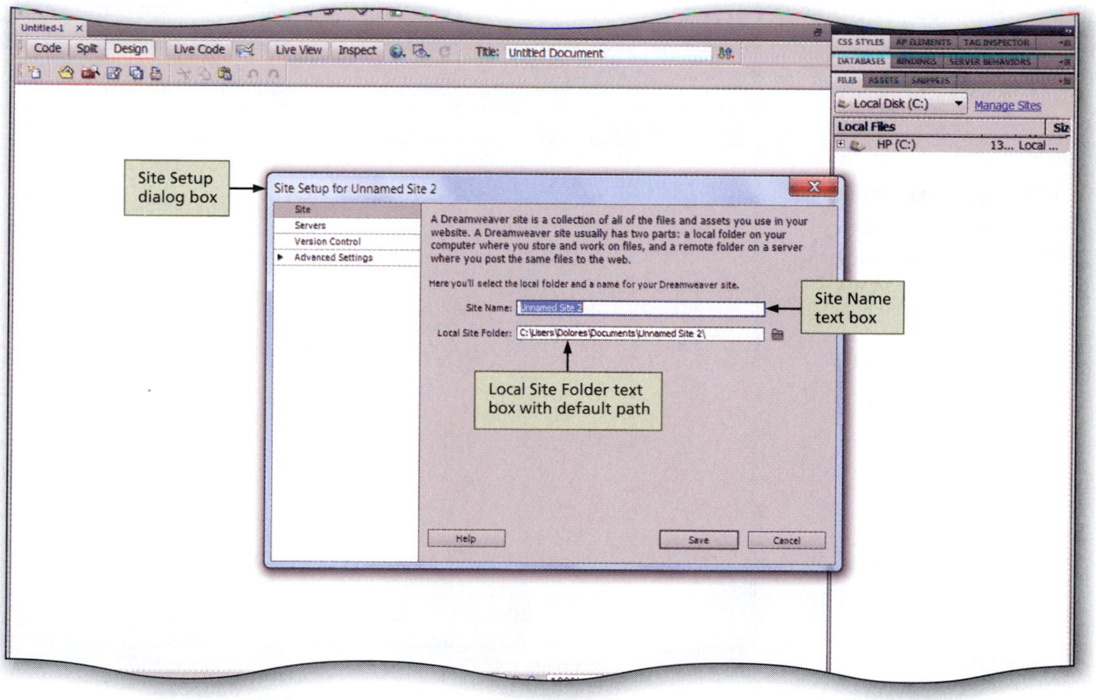

Figure 1–14

3

• Type **Montana Parks** in the Site name text box to name the site (Figure 1–15).

Q&A

Is the site name necessary?

This name is required, but it is for reference only. It is not part of the path and is not visible to viewers of your site.

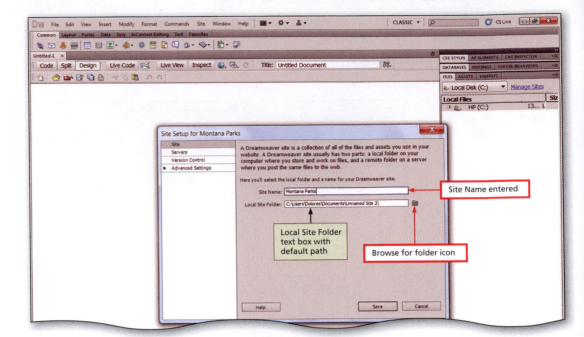

Figure 1–15

4

• Click the Browse for folder icon to display the Choose Root Folder dialog box.

• Navigate to where you will store your Web site files (Figure 1–16).

Q&A

On what drive should I store the Web site files?

Because most Web sites require many files, you should create the projects using a hard drive or removable drive with plenty of space — not the floppy drive (A:), if you have one. Steps in this chapter assume you are creating the local site on a USB drive. Check with your instructor to verify the location and path you will use to create and save your local Web site. Other options may include a CD-RW disc or a network drive.

Figure 1–16

Q&A

What if my USB flash drive has a different name or letter?

It is very likely that your USB flash drive will have a different name and drive letter from the one shown in Figure 1–16 and be connected to a different port. Verify that the device displayed in the Select text box is correct.

5

• Click the Create New Folder icon to create a folder for your local site (Figure 1–17).

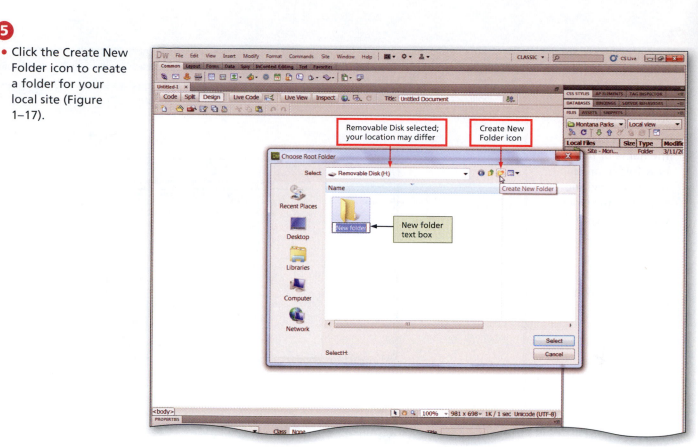

Removable Disk selected; your location may differ

Create New Folder icon

New folder text box

Figure 1–17

6

• For the root folder name, type your last name and first initial (with no spaces between your last name and initial) in the New folder text box. For example, type edwardsd. Press the ENTER key to rename the new folder, and then click the Open button to open the root folder (Figure 1–18).

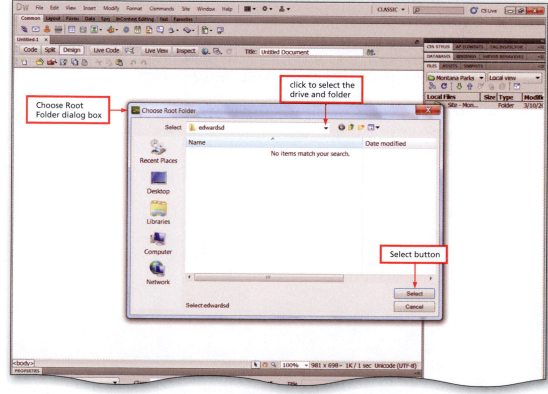

click to select the drive and folder

Choose Root Folder dialog box

Select button

Figure 1–18

7

- Click the Create New Folder icon to create a folder for the Montana Parks Web site.

- Type **parks** as the name of the new folder, press the ENTER key, and then click the Open button to create the parks subfolder and open it.

- Click the Select button to display the Site Setup dialog box (Figure 1–19).

Q&A Why should I create a folder on the drive for my Web site?

Organizing your Web site folders now will save you time and prevent problems later.

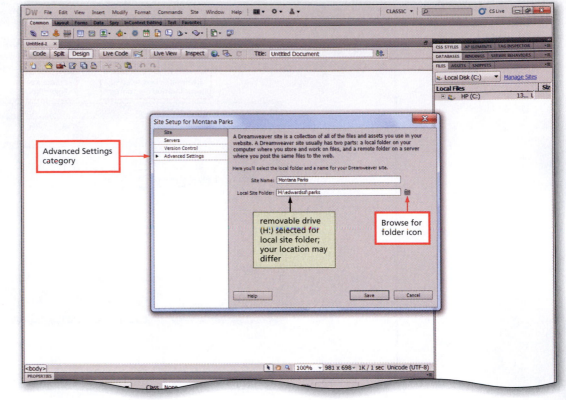

Figure 1–19

Create a main folder such as edwardsd for the sites in this book. (Substitute your last name and first initial for "edwardsd.") Create a subfolder in that main folder for the Montana Parks Web site. Finally, create a subfolder in the Montana Parks Web site folder for images.

Q&A Which files will I store in the parks folder?

The parks folder will contain all the files for the Montana Parks Web site. In other words, the parks folder is the local root folder for the Montana Parks Web site.

Q&A Am I finished defining the new Web site?

Not yet. Nearly every Web site displays graphics, photos, and other images, and you need to create a subfolder for these images.

8
- Click Advanced Settings in the category list to display the option for selecting the default images folder.

- Click the Browse for folder icon to specify the folder for the images.

- Navigate to the *your name*\parks folder.

- Click the Create New Folder icon to create a subfolder for images.

- Type **images** and then press the ENTER key to enter the name of the images subfolder.

- Click the Select button to select the images folder as the

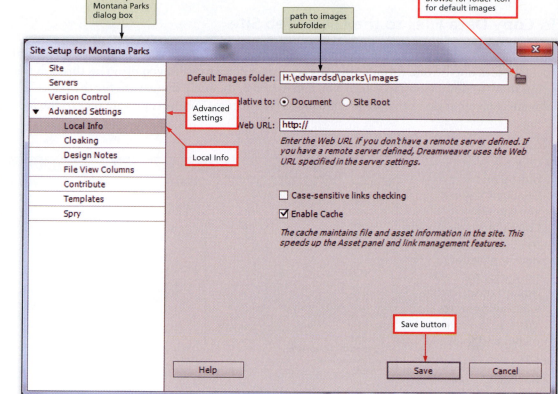

Site Setup for Montana Parks dialog box

path to images subfolder

Browse for folder icon for default images

Advanced Settings

Local Info

Save button

Figure 1–20

default folder for images and to display the Site Setup for Montana Parks dialog box (Figure 1–20).

9
- Click the Save button to save the site settings and display the Dreamweaver workspace. The Montana Parks Web site hierarchy is displayed in the Files panel (Figure 1–21).

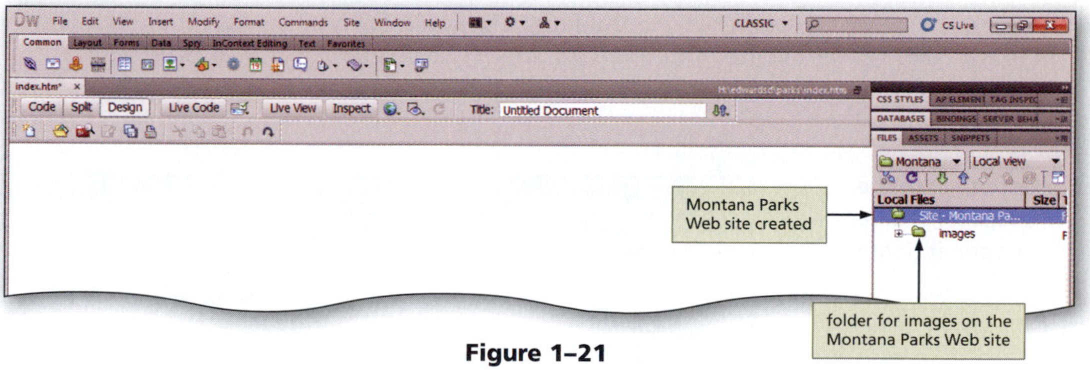

Montana Parks Web site created

folder for images on the Montana Parks Web site

Figure 1–21

Q&A What do the icons in the Files panel mean?

A small device icon or folder icon is displayed next to each object listed in the Files panel. The device icon represents a device such as the Desktop or a disk drive, and the folder icon represents a folder. Many of these icons have a plus or minus sign next to them, which indicates whether the device or folder contains additional folders. The plus and minus signs are controls that you can click to expand or collapse the view of the file hierarchy. In the Files panel, the site folders and files appear in a different color than non-site folders and files so that you easily can distinguish between the two.

Q&A What else does the Local Files list in the Files panel display?

The Local Files list displays a site, including local, remote, and testing server files associated with a selected site. In this chapter, you view only the local site.

Other Ways

1. Click Site button in Files panel, click Manage Sites, click New

To Copy Data Files to the Local Web Site

Your data files contain background images and text files for the Chapter 1 project and exercises. You can copy the data files one by one through the Dreamweaver Files panel as you progress through this chapter. Alternatively, using the Windows Computer tool, you can establish the basic framework for the parks Web site by copying all the files and images at one time. The following steps illustrate how to copy data files to the local Web site.

1
- Click the Start button on the Windows taskbar and then click Computer to display the Computer window. If necessary, right-click the background of the folder window, point to View on the context menu, and then click List.

- Navigate to the location of the data files for this book to display the files in the Computer window (Figure 1–22).

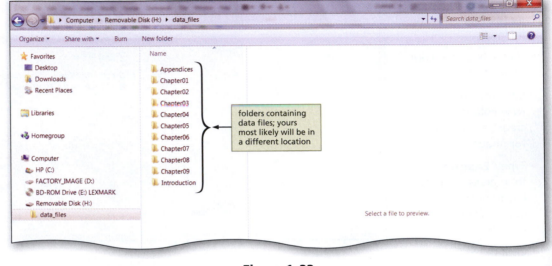

Figure 1–22

Q&A What if my data files are located on a different drive or folder?

In Figure 1–22, the location is Removable Disk (H:), a USB drive. Most likely your data files are stored in a different location. Your data files also could be stored in a folder with a name other than "data_files."

2
- Double-click the Chapter01 folder to open it (Figure 1–23).

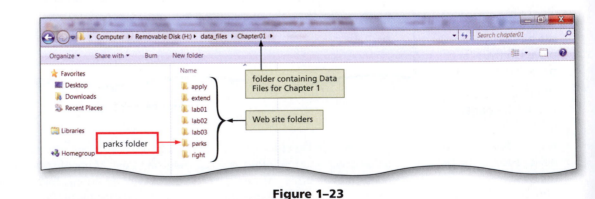

Figure 1–23

3
- Double-click the parks folder to open it (Figure 1–24).

Figure 1–24

4

- Right-click the parks_bkg image file to display a context menu.

- Point to the Copy command on the context menu to highlight the command (Figure 1–25).

Q&A

My context menu contains different commands. Is that a problem?

No. A file's context menu often changes depending on the programs on your computer. The Copy command, however, always appears on this menu.

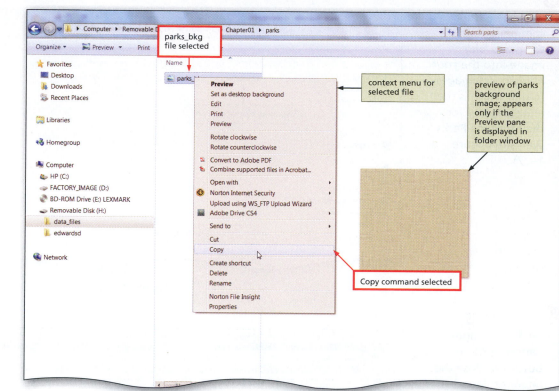

Figure 1–25

5

- Click Copy and then click the Back button the number of times necessary to navigate to the Computer window.

- Navigate to the drive containing the *your name* folder.

- Double-click the *your name* folder, double-click the parks folder, and then double-click the images folder to open the images folder for your Web site.

- Right-click anywhere in the open window to display the context menu.

- Point to the Paste command to highlight it (Figure 1–26).

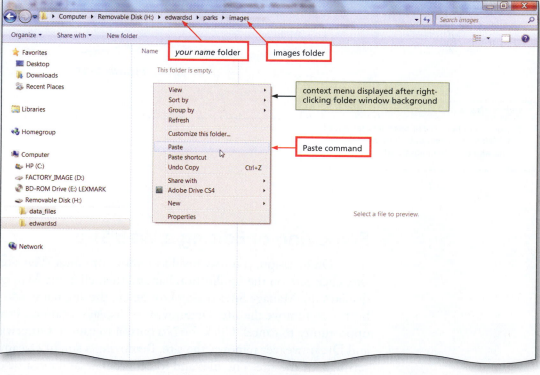

Figure 1–26

6

- Click the Paste command to paste the parks_bkg image into the *your name*\parks\images folder, which is the images folder for the Montana Parks Web site (Figure 1–27).

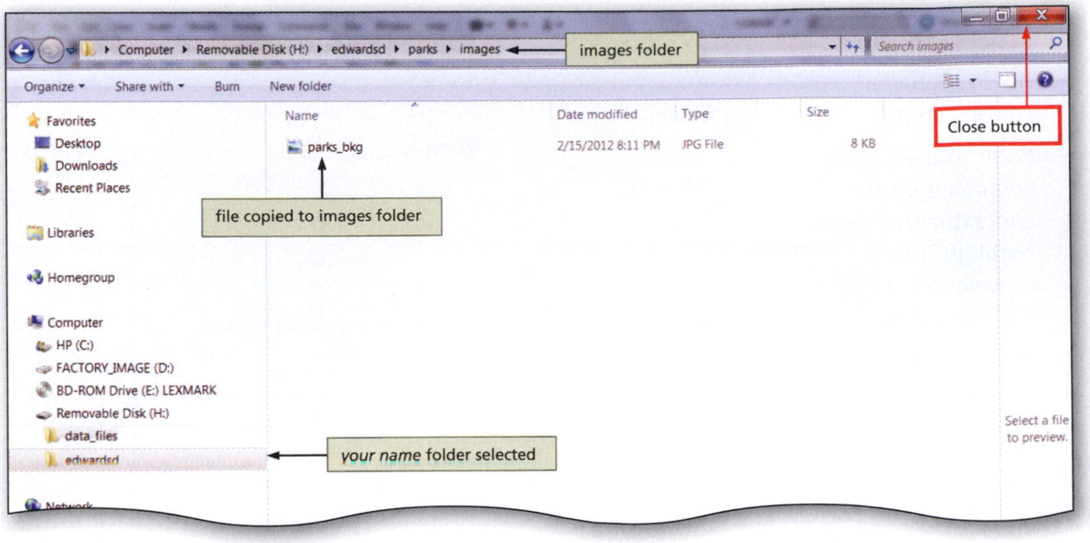

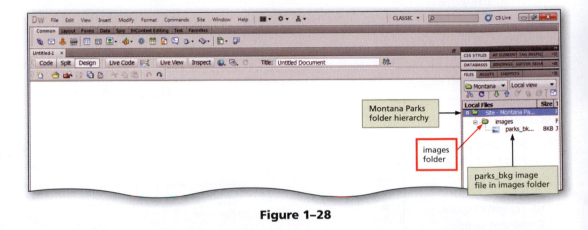

Figure 1–27

7

- Click the images window's Close button to close the images folder window.

- Double-click the images folder in the Dreamweaver Files panel to open the images folder (Figure 1–28).

Figure 1–28

Other Ways

1. Open data files folder, open images folder for Web site, select data files, hold down CTRL and drag to images folder

Removing or Editing a Web Site

On occasion, you may need to remove or edit a Web site. To remove or edit a Web site, click Site on the Application bar and then click the Manage Sites command. This displays the Manage Sites dialog box. Select the site name and then click the Remove button to remove the site. Dreamweaver displays a caution box providing you with an opportunity to cancel. Click the No button to cancel. Otherwise, click the Yes button, and Dreamweaver removes the site. Removing a site in Dreamweaver removes the settings for the site. The files and folders remain and must be deleted separately.

To edit a site, click the site name and then click the Edit button. Dreamweaver displays the Site Setup dialog box; from there, you can change any of the options you selected when you first created the site.

Preparing Your Workspace and Saving a Web Page

With the Montana Parks site defined and the data file copied to the site, the next step is to save the untitled Dreamweaver document. When you defined the site, you designated the local root folder (*your name*\parks). You can copy and paste files into this folder using Windows, or you can use Dreamweaver's file management tools to copy and paste. You also can save a Dreamweaver document into this folder. Dreamweaver treats any item placed in the folder as part of the site.

When a document is saved as a Web page, the Web page also remains in the computer's memory and is displayed in the Document window. It is a good practice to save when you first open the document and then save regularly while you are working in Dreamweaver. By doing so, you protect yourself from losing all the work you have done since the last time you saved.

Rulers

Rulers help you measure, organize, and plan your layout. They are turned off by default in the Classic workspace. When rulers are turned on, they appear on the left and top borders of the page, marked in pixels, inches, or centimeters. They especially are helpful when working with tables or layers. Rulers, however, sometimes can be distracting when first learning how to use Dreamweaver, so you will make sure they are turned off shortly.

The Index Page

The **home page** is the starting point for the rest of your Web site. For most Web sites, the home page is named index. This name has special significance because most Web servers recognize index.htm (or index.html) as the default home page.

Dreamweaver comes with a number of default commands. These defaults are stored in different categories in Dreamweaver's Preferences dialog box. Dreamweaver's default extension for new documents is .html. Although there is some debate about which extension to use — .htm or .html — most Web sites use .htm. You change the default through the Preferences dialog box. Therefore, when you save your document, Dreamweaver automatically adds the extension .htm to the file name. Documents with the .htm extension are displayed in Web browsers.

BTW

Best Practices for Naming Web Pages
To make sure your Web pages work well with most servers and browsers, name Web site files and folders using all lowercase characters, do not use spaces (use an underscore instead, as in file_name), do not use special characters such as @ or slashes, and keep the names short (up to eight characters).

To Hide the Rulers, Change the .html Default, and Save a Document as a Web Page

The home page for your Montana Parks Web site is named index.htm. The following steps show how to prepare your workspace by turning off the rulers, if necessary, and changing the .html default extension to .htm. You then save the untitled document as index.htm in the parks local root folder. If the Rulers are not displayed in your Document window, omit Steps 1 and 2.

1

• If Rulers are turned on, click View on the Application bar, point to Rulers, and then point to Show on the Rulers submenu to highlight the command (Figure 1–29).

Q&A

What should I do if rulers are not displayed in my Document window?

Skip Steps 1 and 2 and start with Step 3 to change the default file name extension.

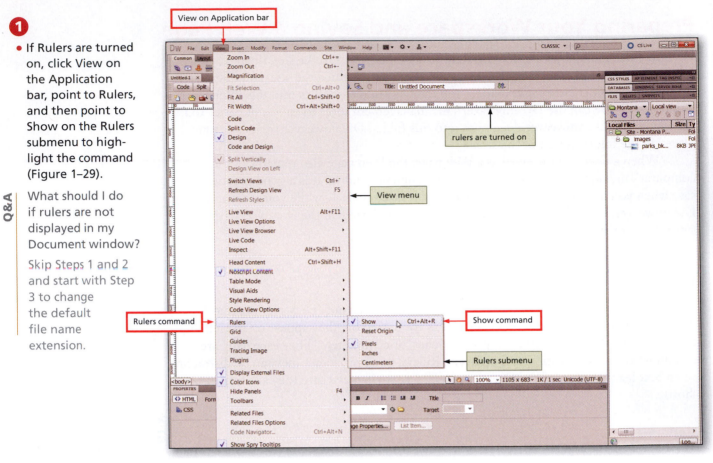

Figure 1–29

2

• Click Show to turn off the rulers (Figure 1–30).

Q&A

How can I display the rulers again later?

Perform Steps 1 and 2 again: click View on the Application bar, point to Rulers, and then click Show.

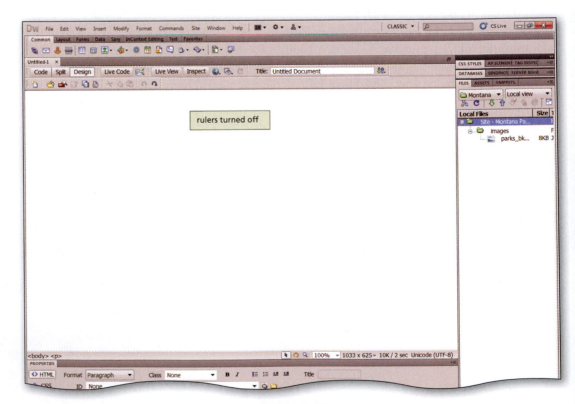

Figure 1–30

3

- Click Edit on the Application bar, and then click Preferences to display the Preferences dialog box (Figure 1–31).

Q&A

What if the Preferences dialog box displays a category of options different from the one shown in Figure 1–31?

The Preferences dialog box displays the last category of options used on your computer. You'll select the category for changing the default extension in the next step.

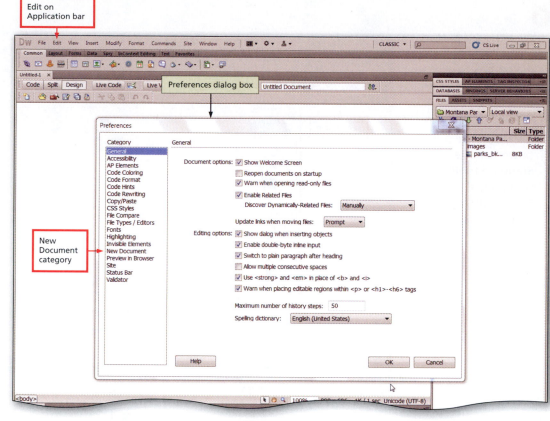

Figure 1–31

4

- Click the New Document category, if necessary, delete .html as the Default extension, and then type **.htm** to change the Default extension (Figure 1–32).

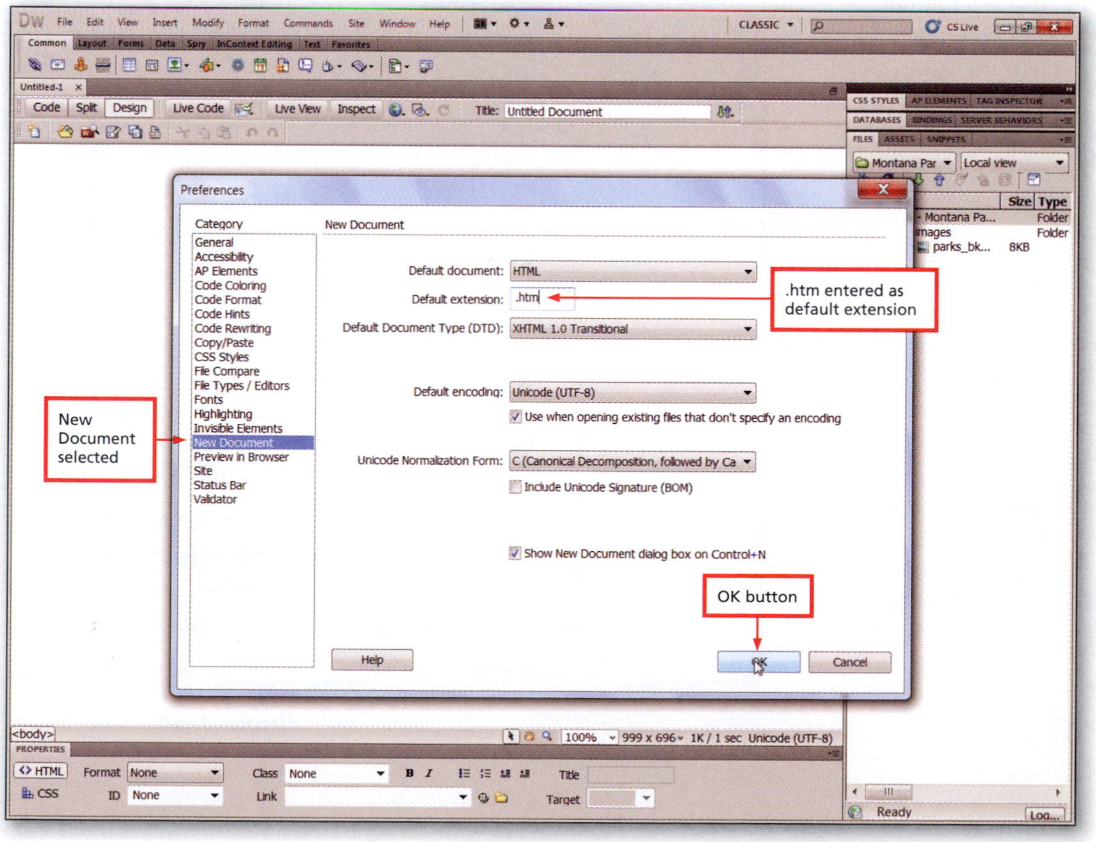

Figure 1–32

5

- Click the OK button in the Preferences dialog box to accept the setting and display the Document window.

- Click the Save button on the Standard toolbar to display the Save As dialog box (Figure 1–33).

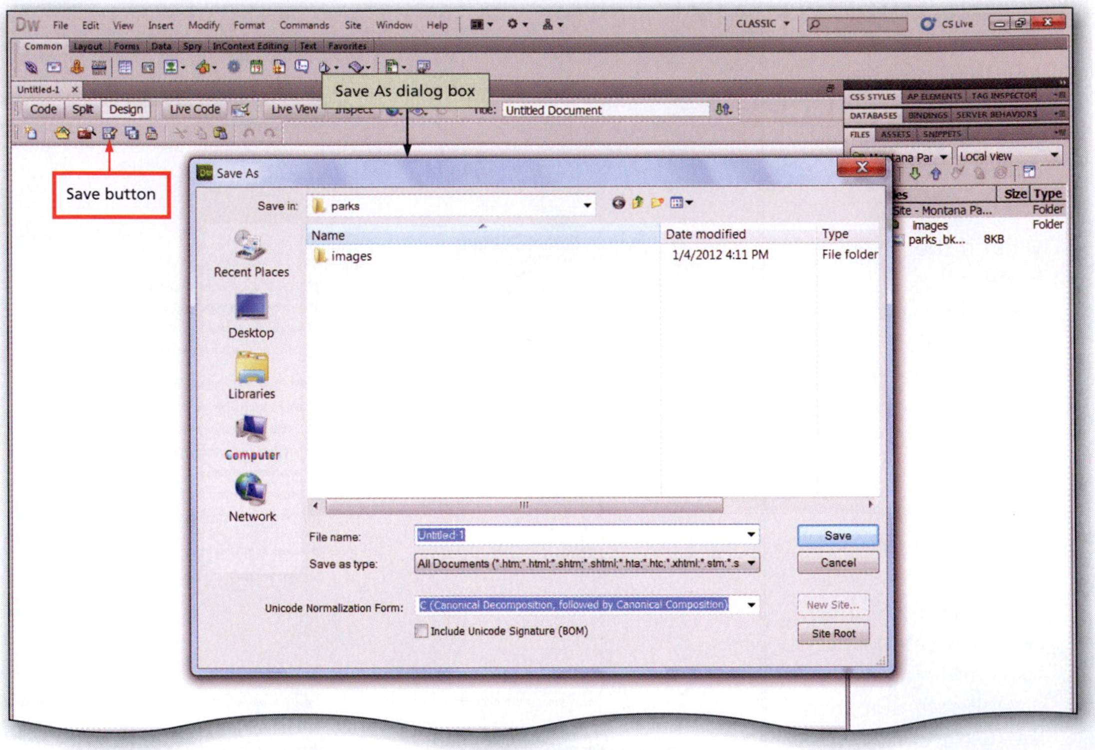

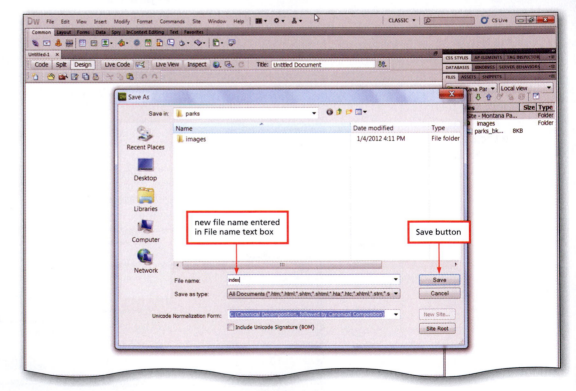

Figure 1–33

6

- Type **index** as the file name of the new document (Figure 1–34).

Q&A

Why is the file name specified in all lowercase characters?

Some Web servers are case sensitive, which means that they consider a file named "index" different from one named "Index." It's common practice among Web designers to use only lowercase characters for the names of all Web site files, including documents and images.

Figure 1–34

7

- Click the Save button to save the index. htm file in the Files panel under Local Files.

- Click the collapse icon next to the images folder to display only the images folder and the index.htm file in the Local Files list (Figure 1–35).

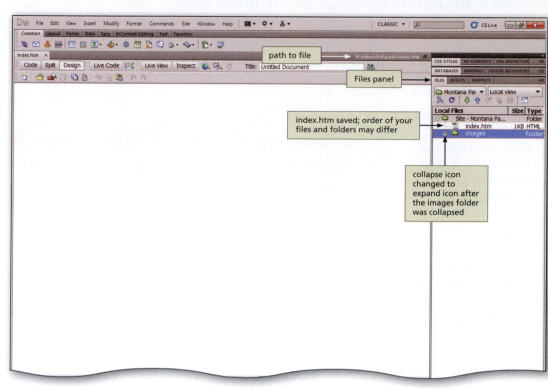

Figure 1–35

Other Ways

1. Press CTRL+ALT+R to turn rulers on and off

Web Page Backgrounds

Each new Web page you create is displayed with a default white or gray background and other default properties. You can modify these default properties using the **Page Properties** dialog box. The Page Properties dialog box lets you specify appearance, links, and many other aspects of page design. You can assign new page properties for each new page you create, and modify properties for existing pages. The page properties you select apply only to the active document.

Add a background for the Web page.

As you design and plan a Web page, consider the following guidelines for applying color and images to the background:

- You can change the default background and enhance your Web page by adding a background image or background color. If you use both a background image and a background color, the color appears while the image downloads, and then the image covers the color.

- Use a background image to add texture and interesting color to a Web page. You can find copyright-free background images on the Web or you can design them yourself.

- Be cautious when selecting or designing background images. Web page images displayed on top of a busy background image may not mix well, and text may be difficult to read. Images and image formats are discussed in more detail in Chapter 2.

Plan Ahead

To Add a Background Image to the Index Page

When you copied the data file earlier in this chapter, you copied an image file that will be the background for the Montana Parks Web site pages. The following steps illustrate how to use the Page Properties dialog box to add that background image to the index page.

1

- Click Modify on the Application bar and then click Page Properties to display the Page Properties dialog box.

- Click the Appearance (HTML) category to display options for adding a background image to the page (Figure 1–36).

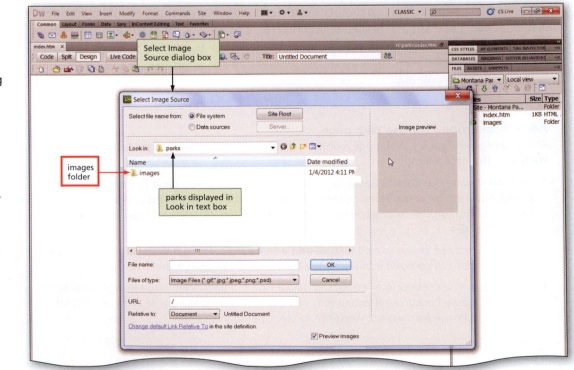

Figure 1–36

2

- Click the Background image Browse button to display the Select Image Source dialog box (Figure 1–37).

Q&A

Why should I use a background image on my Web pages? Background images add texture and visual interest to your Web pages.

Figure 1–37

3

• Double-click the images folder to display the images file list.

• If necessary, click the View Menu button and then click Details to display the file list in Details view.

• Click the parks_bkg file to select the file (Figure 1–38).

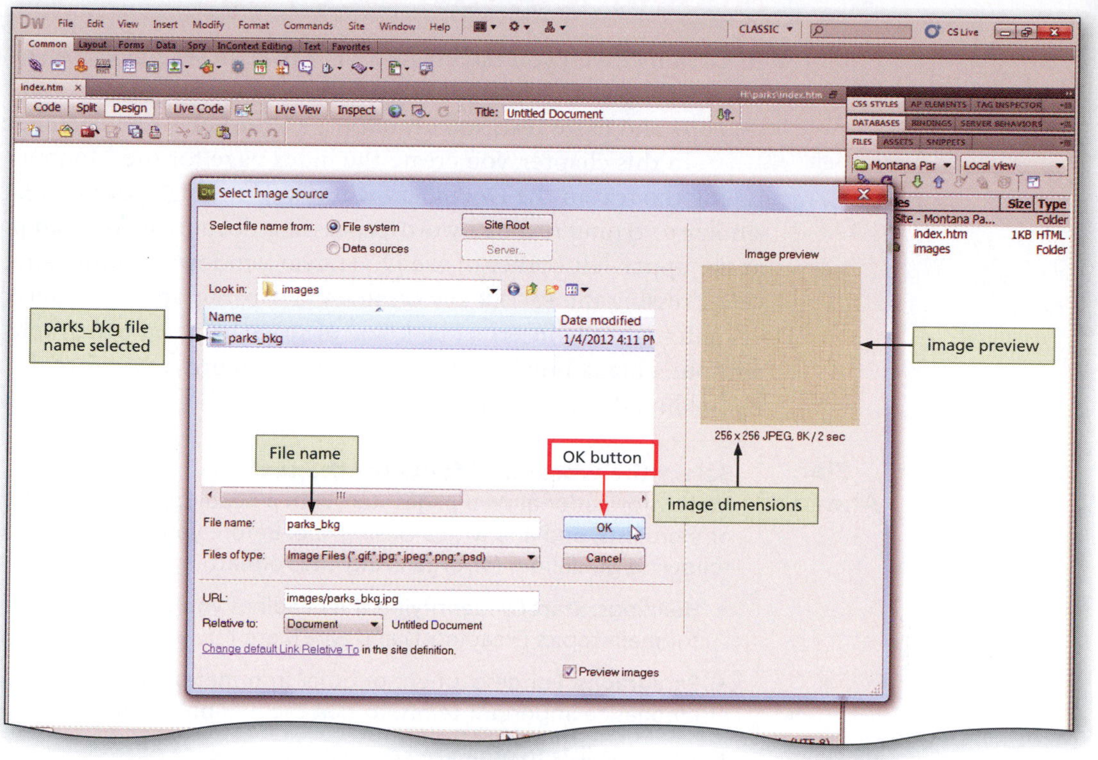

Figure 1–38

4

• Click the OK button to accept the background image and close the Select Image Source dialog box.

• Click the OK button to apply the image to the page.

• Click the Save button on the Standard toolbar to save the document (Figure 1–39).

Q&A How do I know the document is saved?

When the document is saved, the Save button on the Standard toolbar is dimmed.

Figure 1–39

Other Ways

1. Right-click Document window, click Page Properties on context menu

2. Click Page Properties button in Property inspector

3. Press CTRL+J

Adding Text to a Web Page

In Dreamweaver, you can create a Web page in several ways: (1) add text to a new document; (2) open an existing HTML document, even if it was not created in Dreamweaver; (3) copy and paste text; and (4) import a Word or Excel document or tabular data.

In this chapter, you create the index page for the Montana Parks Web page by typing the text in the Document window. Entering text into a Dreamweaver document is similar to typing text in a word-processing document. You can position the insertion point at the upper-left corner of the Document window or within another object, such as a table cell. Pressing the ENTER key creates a new paragraph and inserts a blank line. Web browsers automatically insert a blank line of space between paragraphs. To start a new single line without a blank line between lines of text requires a **line break**. You can insert a line break by holding down the SHIFT key and then pressing the ENTER key.

Plan Ahead

Select the words and fonts for the text.
Most informational Web pages start with a heading, include paragraphs of text, provide one or more lists, and end with a closing line. Before you add text to a Web page, consider the following guidelines for organizing and formatting text:

- **Headings**: Start by identifying the headings you will use. Determine which headings are for main topics (Heading 1) and which are for subtopics (Heading 2 or 3).

- **Paragraphs**: For descriptions or other information, include short paragraphs of text. To emphasize important terms, format them as bold or italic.

- **Lists**: Use lists to organize key points, a sequence of steps, or other information you want to highlight. If amount or sequence matter, number each item in a list. Otherwise, use a bullet (a dot or other symbol that appears at the beginning of the paragraph).

- **Closing**: The closing is usually one sentence that provides information of interest to most Web page viewers or that indicates where people can find more information about your topic.

To Hide the Panel Groups

The following step shows how to provide more workspace by hiding the panel groups.

1
- Click Window on the Application bar and then click Hide Panels to close the Files panel and the Property inspector (Figure 1–40).

Figure 1–40

Adding Text

Table 1–1 includes the text for the Montana Parks and Recreation Areas Web page. After typing each section of the document, you press the ENTER key to insert a blank line.

Table 1–1 Montana Parks and Recreation Areas Web Page Text	
Section	**Heading, Part 1, and Part 2 Text**
Heading	Montana Parks and Recreation Areas
Part 1 – first paragraph	Montana contains a variety of national parks and recreational areas, including two national parks, a national historical park, a national historic trail, a national historic site, a national recreation area, and a national battlefield.
Part 2 – second paragraph	In addition to the national facilities, over 50 state parks are located throughout the state. Some of the greatest natural and cultural treasures on earth are located in these parks and recreational areas.
Part 3 – bulleted list	Some of the highlights of this state include the following: Yellowstone National Park, established in 1872, was America's first national park. This park also extends into Idaho and Wyoming. In addition to the national parks and sites, you also can visit over 50 state parks, including natural parks, cultural parks, and recreational parks. A variety of events are available throughout the state, including such activities as a buffalo feast, panning for gold, native friendship dances, and Indian tacos.
Part 4 – closing paragraph	Special events are posted on the park's calendar as they are scheduled. Most of the events are free.

To Add a Heading and Introductory Paragraph Text

The following steps show how to add text to the Document window and insert blank lines between sections of text.

1
- Click in the Document window, type the heading **Montana Parks and Recreation Areas** as shown in Table 1–1, and then press the ENTER key to enter the heading for the Web page.

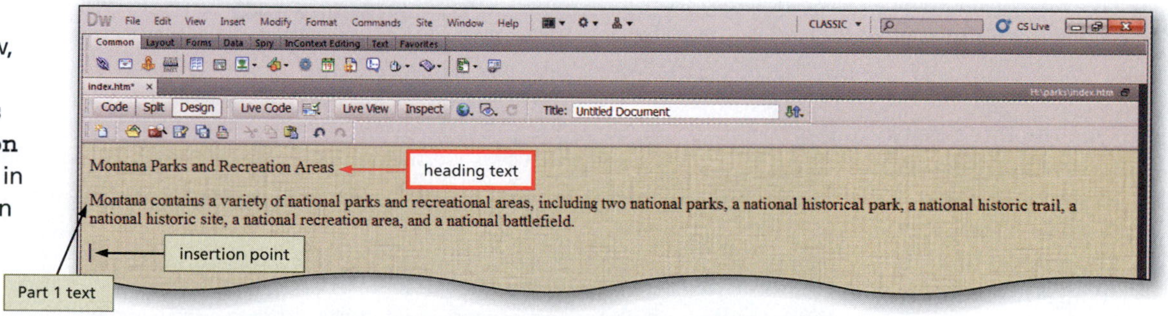

Figure 1–41

- Type the text of Part 1 as shown in Table 1–1, and then press the ENTER key (Figure 1–41).

Q&A

What should I do if I make a typing error?

Press the BACKSPACE key to delete text you typed, or select the text and then press the DELETE key. Correct your typing mistakes the way you would in a word-processing program.

2

- Type the text of Part 2 as shown in Table 1–1 on the previous page, and then press the ENTER key to insert a blank line (Figure 1–42).

Q&A

Why does my text wrap at different locations from those shown in Figure 1–42?

Where your text wraps depends on whether your Dreamweaver window is maximized, the screen resolution (which is 1024 x 768 in the figures in this book), and whether your computer has a standard or wide-screen monitor.

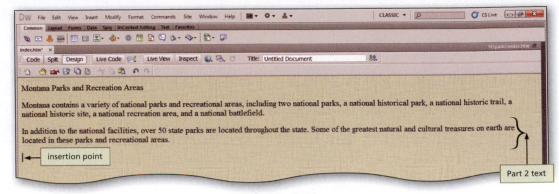

Figure 1–42

3

- Type the first line of the Part 3 text shown in Table 1–1, and then press the ENTER key to insert a blank line (Figure 1–43).

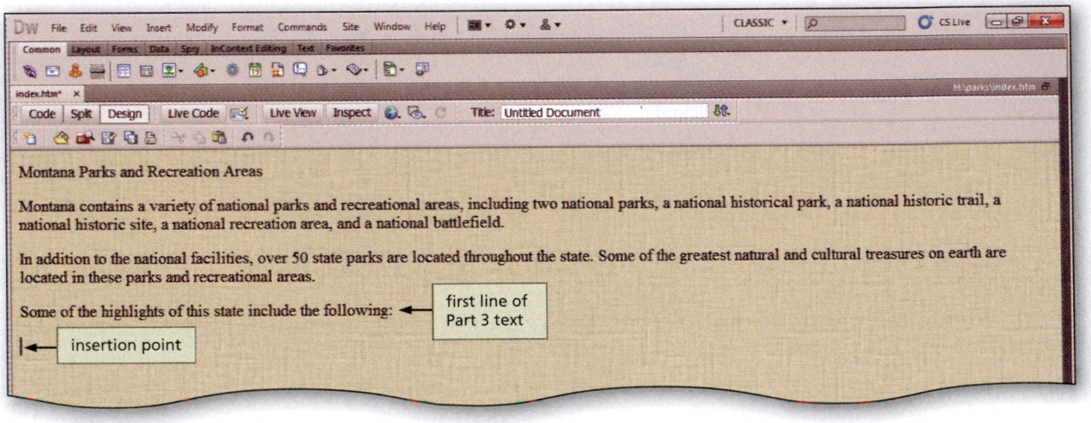

Figure 1–43

4

- Type the three items for the bulleted list as shown in Table 1–1. Press the ENTER key after each entry to insert space between the lines (Figure 1–44).

Q&A

When do I add bullets to the list?

You will add bullets when you format the text in the next section of this chapter.

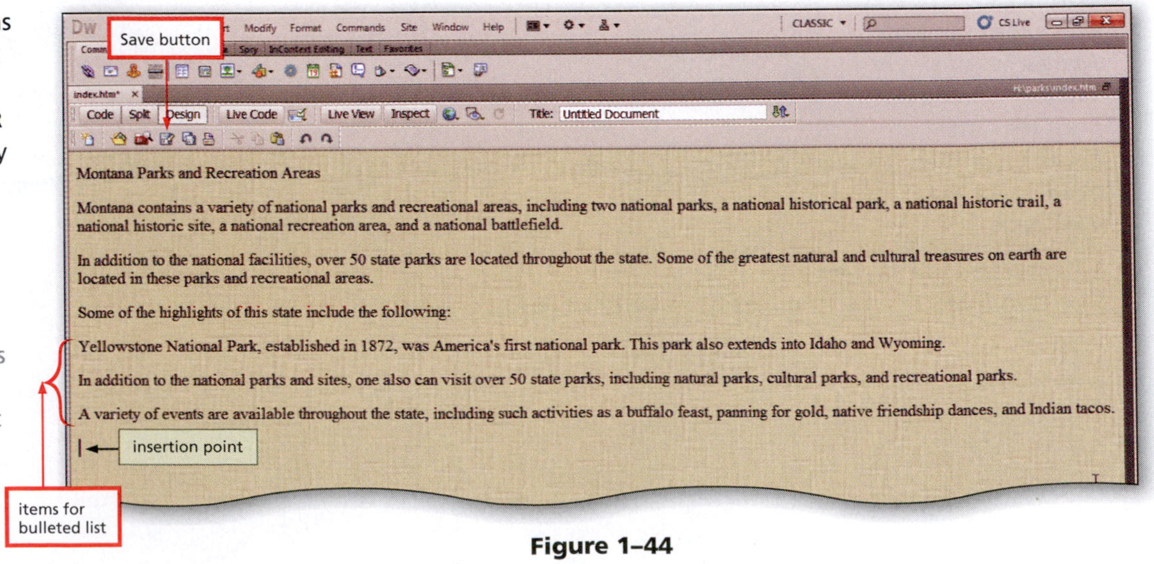

Figure 1–44

5
- Type the closing paragraph shown in Table 1–1, and then press the ENTER key to insert a blank line.

- Click the Save button on the Standard toolbar to save your work (Figure 1–45).

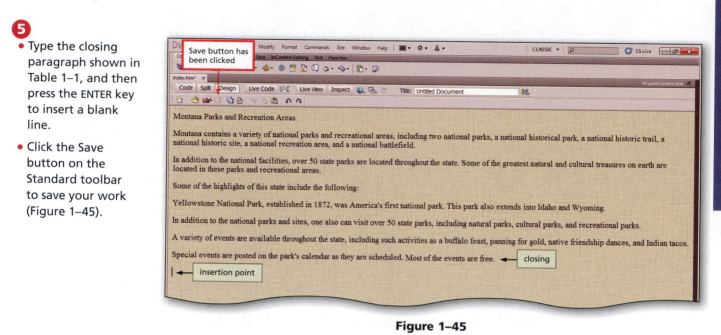

Figure 1–45

Deleting Web Pages

If you need to start over for any reason, you can delete a Web page file. Close the page, display the panel groups if necessary, right-click the name of the page you want to delete, point to Edit on the context menu, and then click Delete. You also can select a file and press the DELETE key. Dreamweaver will display a warning dialog box. If files are linked to other files, information will be displayed indicating how to update the links. To delete the file, click Yes in the dialog warning box or click No to cancel.

Formatting Features

The next step is to format the text on your Web page. **Formatting** means to change heading styles, insert special characters, and insert or modify other elements that enhance the appearance of the Web page. Dreamweaver provides three options for formatting text: the Format menu on the Application bar, the Insert bar Text category, and the Property inspector. To format the text for the Montana Parks index page, you use the text-related features of the Property inspector.

The Property inspector is one of the panels you use most often when creating and formatting Web pages. It displays the properties, or characteristics, of the selected object. The object can be a table, text, image, or some other item. The Property inspector is context sensitive, so its options change relative to the selected object.

Property Inspector Features

Divided into two sections, the HTML Property inspector lets you see the current properties of the selected object and alter or edit them. When the panel groups are closed, you can click the expander arrow in the lower-right corner of the Property inspector to collapse the Property inspector to show only the more commonly used properties for the selected element or to expand the Property inspector to show more options.

Collapsing/Hiding the Property Inspector

Displaying panels such as the Property inspector requires considerable window space. If you are finished working with a panel, it generally is better to collapse it or close it. **Collapsing** it leaves the title bar in the window. Double-clicking the horizontal bar collapses and expands the Property inspector. Pressing CTRL+F3 also collapses/expands the Property inspector. **Closing** the Property inspector removes it from the Document window. To close the Property inspector, display its context menu by right-clicking the Properties title bar and then selecting the Close Tab Group command. (You also can click the Options button on the Property inspector and then select Close Tab Group.) To open the Property inspector, click the Window menu and then click Properties.

By default, the Property inspector displays the properties for text in a blank document. Most changes you make to properties are applied immediately in the Document window. For some properties, however, you must apply changes by clicking outside a text box in the Properties inspector, pressing the ENTER key, or pressing the TAB key to switch to another property. The left side of the Property inspector contains two buttons: HTML and CSS. Most CSS options are discussed in detail in Chapter 5 of the Complete edition of this book. The following section describes the HTML-related features of the Property inspector (Figure 1–46).

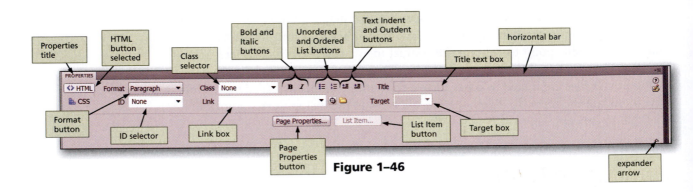

Figure 1–46

Format   The **Format button** allows you to apply a Paragraph, Heading, or Preformatted style to the text. Clicking the Format button displays a pop-up menu from which you can select a style.

The **Paragraph style** is the normal default style for text on a Web page. **Paragraph formatting** is the process of changing the appearance of text. **Heading styles** are used to create divisions and separate one segment of text from another. These formats are displayed based on how different browsers interpret the tags, offering little consistency and control over layout and appearance. When you apply a heading tag to text, Dreamweaver automatically adds the next line of text as a standard paragraph. You can use the **Preformatted style** when you do not want a Web browser to change the line of text in any way.

Class   Class displays the style that currently is applied to the selected text. If no styles have been applied to the selection, the Class text box shows None. If multiple styles have been applied to the selection, the text box is blank.

Bold and Italic   The **Bold button** and the **Italic button** allow you to format text using these two common font styles. Dreamweaver also supports a variety of other font styles, which are available through the Format menu Style command. To view these styles, click Format on the Application bar and then point to Style. The Style submenu contains a list of additional styles, such as Underline, Strikethrough, and Teletype.

Unordered List   Web developers often use a list to structure a page. An unordered list turns the selected paragraph or heading into an item in a bulleted list. If no text is selected before the **Unordered List button** is clicked, a new bulleted list is started. This command is also available through the HTML Property inspector and through the Application bar Format menu List command.

Ordered List   An ordered list is similar to an unordered list. This type of list, however, turns the selected paragraph or heading into an item in a numbered list. If no text is selected before the **Ordered List button** is clicked, a new numbered list is started. This command also is available through the HTML Property inspector and through the Application bar Format menu List command.

Definition List   A definition list is composed of items followed by an indented description, such as a glossary list. This command is available through the Application bar Format menu List command.

Indent and Outdent   To set off a block quote, you can use the Indent feature. The **Text Indent button** will indent a line or a paragraph from both margins. In XHTML and HTML, this is the blockquote tag. The **Text Outdent button** removes the indentation from the selected text by removing the blockquote tag. In a list, indenting creates a nested list, and removing the indentation removes the nesting from the list. A **nested list** is one list inside another list and is not the same as the block quote created by the Indent feature.

Title   Specifies the ScreenTip text for a hypertext link.

ID   Identifies the content of an element with a unique name; used to select an ID from any linked or external CSS style sheet. CSS style sheets are covered in Chapter 5.

Link   The **Link (Hyperlink) box** allows you to make selected text or other objects a hyperlink to a specified URL or Web page. To use the Property inspector to select the URL or Web page, you can (a) click the Point to File or Browse for File icon to the right of the Link box to browse to a page in your Web site and select the file name, (b) type the URL, or (c) drag a file from the Files panel into the Link box. Links are covered in detail in Chapter 2. The Insert menu on the Application bar also contains a Hyperlink option.

Page Properties   Clicking the Page Properties button on the Property inspector or the Properties command on the Modify menu opens the Page Properties dialog box.

List Item   If the selected text is part of a list, click the List Item button to set list properties for the text, such as the type of bullet or the starting number.

Target   In the **Target text box**, you specify the frame or window in which the linked page should load. If you are using frames, the names of all the frames in the current document are displayed in the list. If the specified frame does not exist when the current document is opened in a browser, the linked page loads in a new window with the name you specified. Once this window exists, other files can be targeted to it.

Understanding Fonts
The default font used for new Web pages is 12-pt Times New Roman. You can change the font of selected text using the Font submenu on the Format menu. Select Default to remove previously applied fonts. For HTML text, selecting Default displays the text in the browser's default font.

Applying Text-Related Features

The text for your Web page is displayed in the Document window. The next step in creating your Web page is to format this text. You use commands from the Property inspector and the Format menu on the Application bar to format the text.

Within Dreamweaver, you can format text before you type, or you can apply new formats after you type. If you have used word-processing software, you will find many of the Dreamweaver formatting commands similar to the commands within a word-processing program. At this point, your Web page contains only text, so the Property inspector displays attributes related to text.

To set block formatting, such as formatting a heading or an unordered list, position the insertion point in the line or paragraph and then format the text.

Text Headings

Just as in a word-processing document, designers use the heading structure in a Web page to set apart document or section titles. The six levels of HTML headings are Heading 1 through Heading 6. **Heading 1 <h1>** produces the largest text and **Heading 6 <h6>** the smallest. By default, browsers will display the six heading levels in the same font, with the point size decreasing as the importance of the heading decreases.

To Format Text with the Heading 1 Style

The following steps show how to format a heading.

1
- Click Window on the Application bar, and then click Properties to display the Property inspector.

- If necessary, scroll up and then position the insertion point anywhere in the heading text, Montana Parks and Recreation Areas to prepare for applying the Heading 1 format to that text (Figure 1–47).

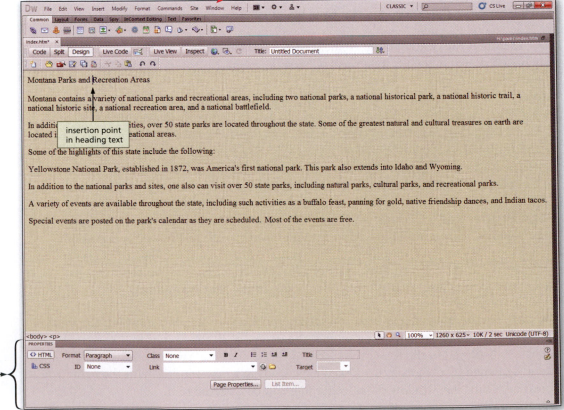

Figure 1–47

2

- Click the Format button in the Property inspector, and then point to Heading 1 to highlight the command (Figure 1–48).

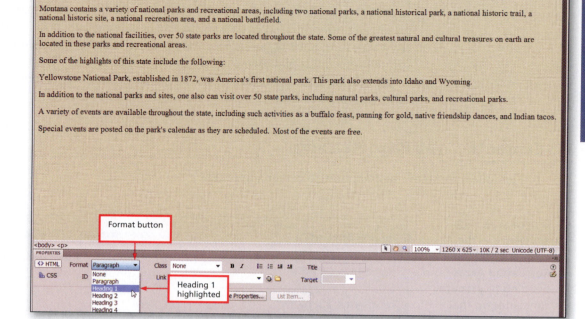

Figure 1–48

3

- Click Heading 1 to apply the Heading 1 style to the Montana Parks and Recreation Areas text (Figure 1–49).

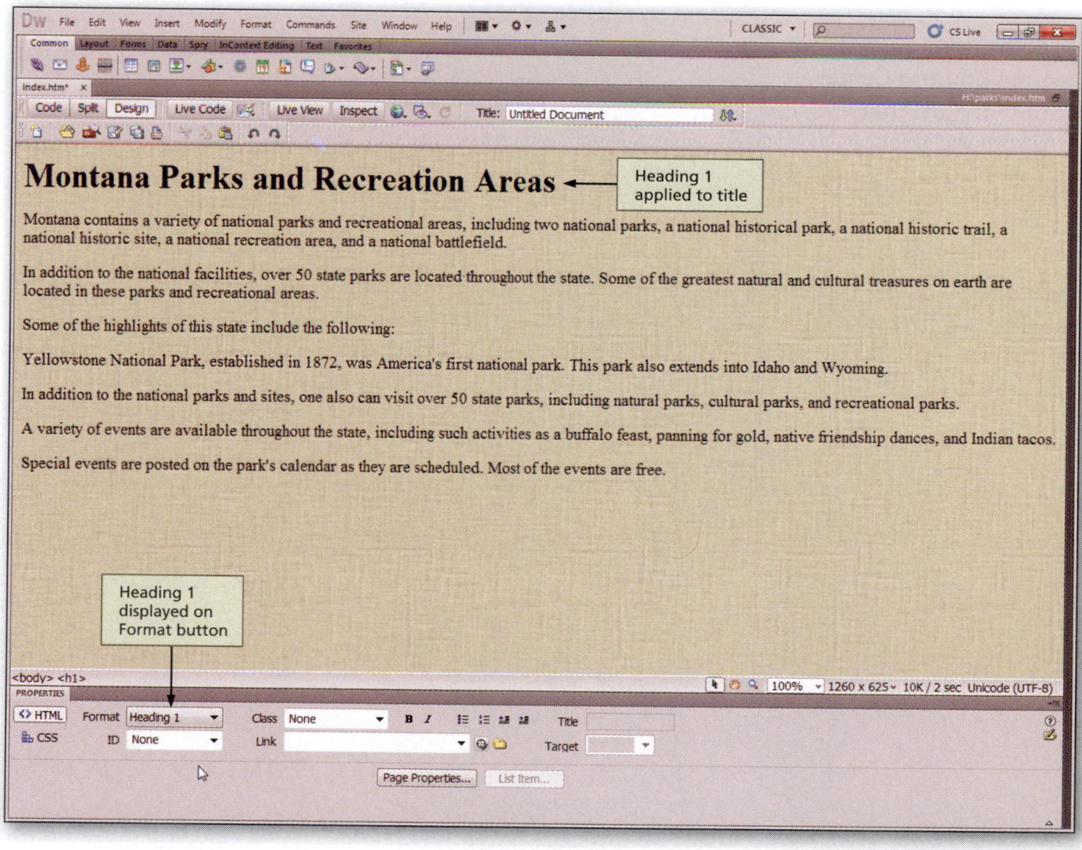

Figure 1–49

Other Ways

1. On Format menu, point to Paragraph Format, click Heading 1

2. Right-click selected text, point to Paragraph Format, click Heading 1

Centering Text

Using the Center command on the Align submenu on the Format menu allows you to center text. This command is very similar to the Center command or button in a word-processing program. To center a single line or a paragraph, position the mouse pointer anywhere in the line or paragraph, and then click the Format menu on the Application bar, point to Align, and then click Center to center the text. You do not need to select a single line or single paragraph to center it. To center more than one paragraph at a time, however, you must select all paragraphs.

To Center the Web Page Heading

The following steps illustrate how to center a heading.

1
- If necessary, click anywhere in the Montana Parks and Recreation Areas heading to prepare for centering that text.

- Click Format on the Application bar, point to Align, and then point to Center to highlight that command (Figure 1–50).

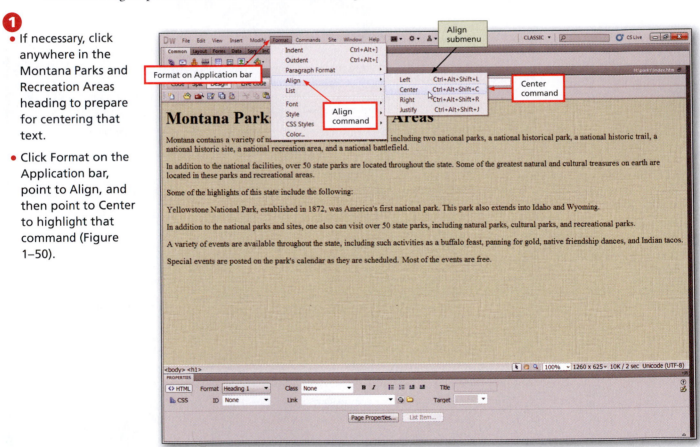

Figure 1–50

2

• Click Center on the Align submenu to center the heading (Figure 1–51).

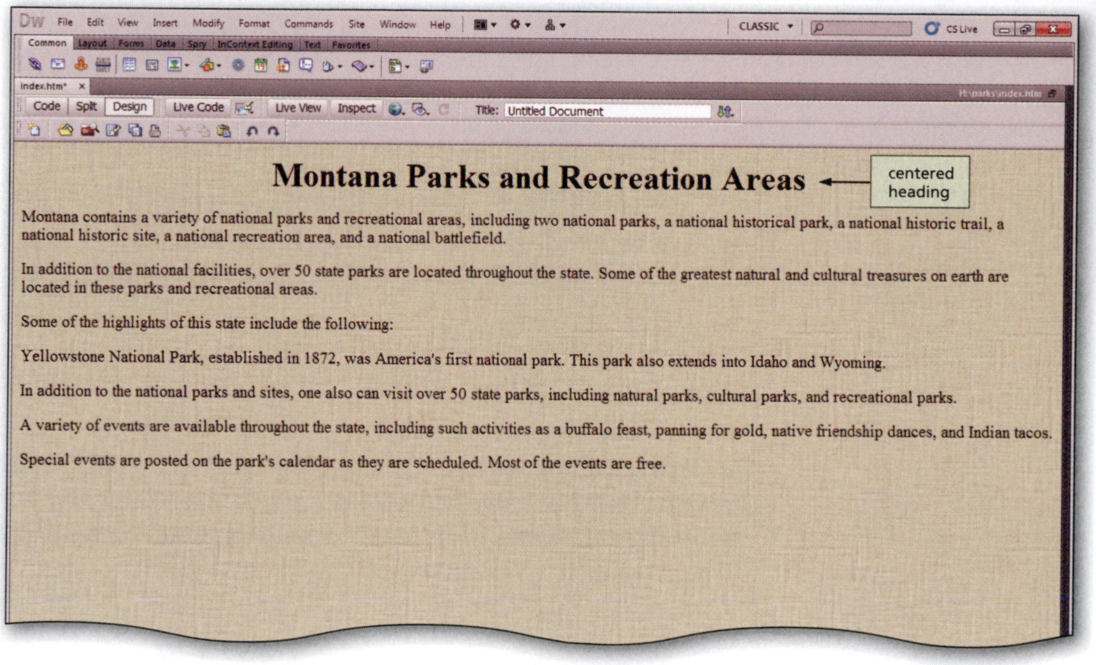

Figure 1–51

Types of Lists

One way to group and organize information is by using lists. Web pages can have three types of lists: ordered (numbered), unordered (bulleted), and definition. Ordered **lists** contain text preceded by numbered steps. Unordered lists contain text preceded by bullets (dots or other symbols) or image bullets. You use an unordered list if the items need not be listed in any particular order. **Definition lists** do not use leading characters such as bullet points or numbers. Glossaries and descriptions often use this type of list.

The Unordered List and Ordered List buttons are available in the Property inspector. You can access the Definition List command through the Application bar List command submenu. Through the List Properties dialog box, you can set the number style, reset the count, or set the bullet style options for individual list items or for the entire list. To access the List Properties dialog box, click anywhere in the list, and then click the List Item button in the Property inspector.

You can create a new list or you can create a list using existing text. When you select existing text and add bullets, the blank lines between the list items are deleted. Later in this chapter, you add line breaks to reinsert a blank line between each list item.

Other Ways

1. Right-click selected text, point to Align, click Center
2. Press CTRL+ALT+SHIFT+C

BTW

Lists
You can remove the bullets or numbers from a formatted list just as easily as you added them. Select the formatted list, and then click the button in the Property inspector that you originally used to apply the formatting.

To Create an Unordered List

The following steps show how to create an unordered (bulleted) list using existing text.

1
- Click to the left of the line that begins with "Yellowstone National Park".

- Drag to select the Yellowstone National Park paragraph and the next two paragraphs (Figure 1–52).

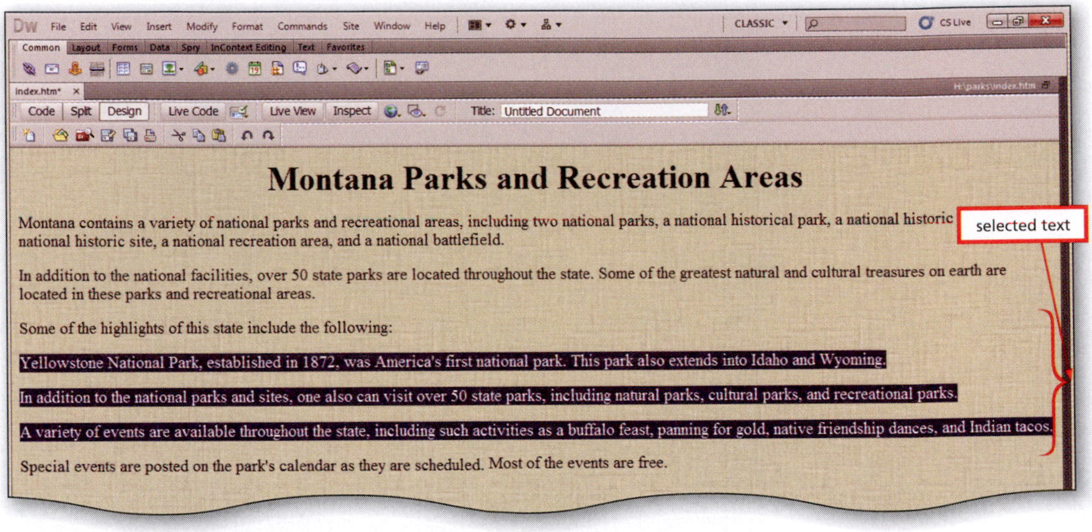

Figure 1–52

2
- In the Property inspector, click the Unordered List button to indent the text and add a bullet to each line (Figure 1–53).

  How do I start a list with a different number or letter?

  In the Document window, click the list item you want to change, click the Format menu, point to List, and then click Properties. In the List Properties dialog box, select the options you want to define.

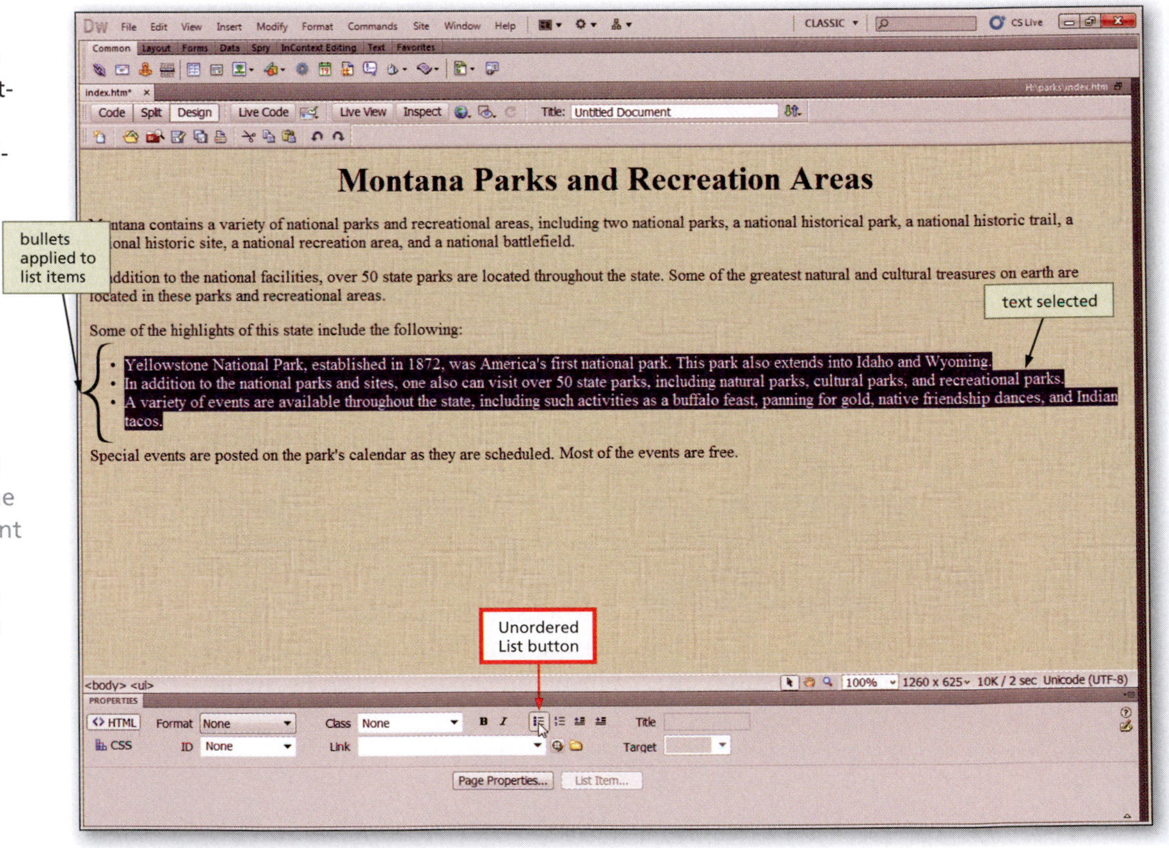

Q&A

Figure 1–53

Other Ways

1. On Format menu point to List, click Unordered List

2. Select text, right-click, point to List, click Unordered List

Bold Formatting

Other text formatting options are applying bold or italic styles to text. **Bold** characters are displayed somewhat thicker and darker than those that are not bold. *Italic* characters slant to the right. The Property inspector contains buttons for both bold and italic font styles. To bold text within Dreamweaver is a simple procedure. If you have used word-processing software, you are familiar with this process. You italicize text in a similar way.

To Bold Text

The following steps illustrate how to emphasize the bulleted items by applying bold formatting.

1
- If necessary, drag to select all of the lines of the bulleted points to prepare for formatting the lines.

2
- Click the Bold button in the Property inspector to bold the selected text.

- Click anywhere in the Document window to deselect the text (Figure 1–54).

Q&A

What other types of formatting can I apply to text?

To select fonts, apply underlining, colors, and other attributes to text, you can use the commands and submenus on the Format menu. Chapter 5 also explains how to use CSS to format text.

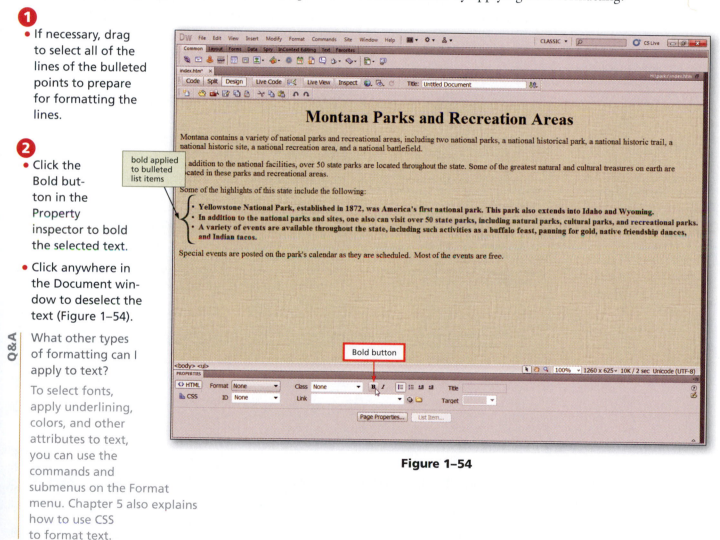

Figure 1–54

Understanding Line Breaks

When you added bullets to the items list earlier in this chapter, the blank line between each item was removed. Removing the blank line between items is a result of how Dreamweaver interprets the HTML code. A blank line between the bulleted items, however, will provide better spacing and readability when viewing the Web page in a browser. You can add blank lines in several ways. You might assume that pressing the ENTER key at the end of each line would be the quickest way to accomplish this. Pressing the ENTER key, however, adds another bullet. The easiest way to accomplish the task of adding blank lines is to insert line breaks. Recall that the line break starts a new single line without inserting a blank line between lines of text. Inserting two line breaks, however, adds a single blank line.

Dreamweaver provides a Line Break command through the Insert HTML Special Characters submenu. It is easier, however, to use the SHIFT+ENTER keyboard shortcut.

To Add a Line Break

The following steps show how to add a blank line between each of the bulleted items.

1 Click at the end of the first bulleted item to prepare for adding a line break.

2 Press the SHIFT+ENTER keys two times to insert a blank line (Figure 1–55).

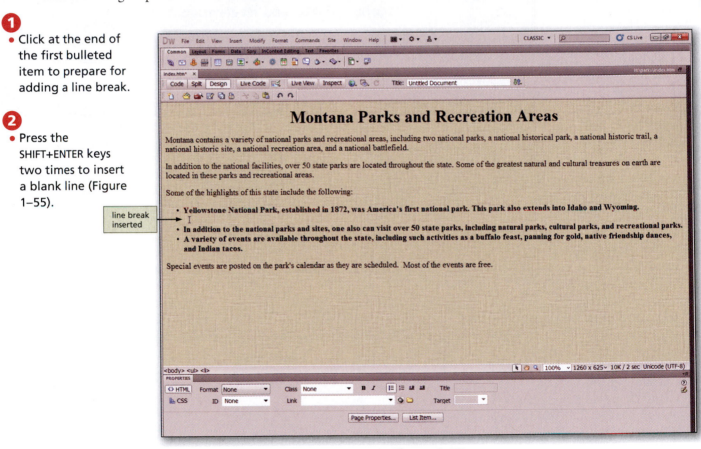

Figure 1–55

3

• Press the SHIFT+ENTER keys two times at the end of the second bulleted item to insert a blank line between the second and third bulleted list items (Figure 1–56).

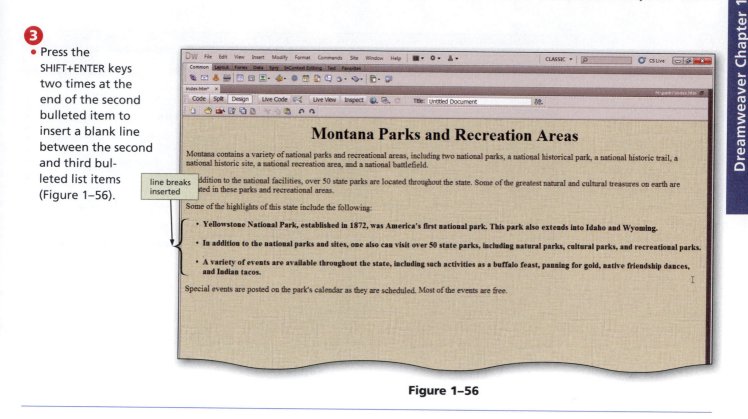

Figure 1–56

To Add Your Name and Date

When creating a Web document, it is a good idea to add your name and date to the document. Insert a single line break between your name and the date. The following steps show how to add this information to the page.

1

• If necessary, scroll down to display the closing paragraph.

• Click at the end of the closing paragraph to prepare for adding your name to the document.

• If necessary, press the ENTER key to move the insertion point to the next paragraph (Figure 1–57).

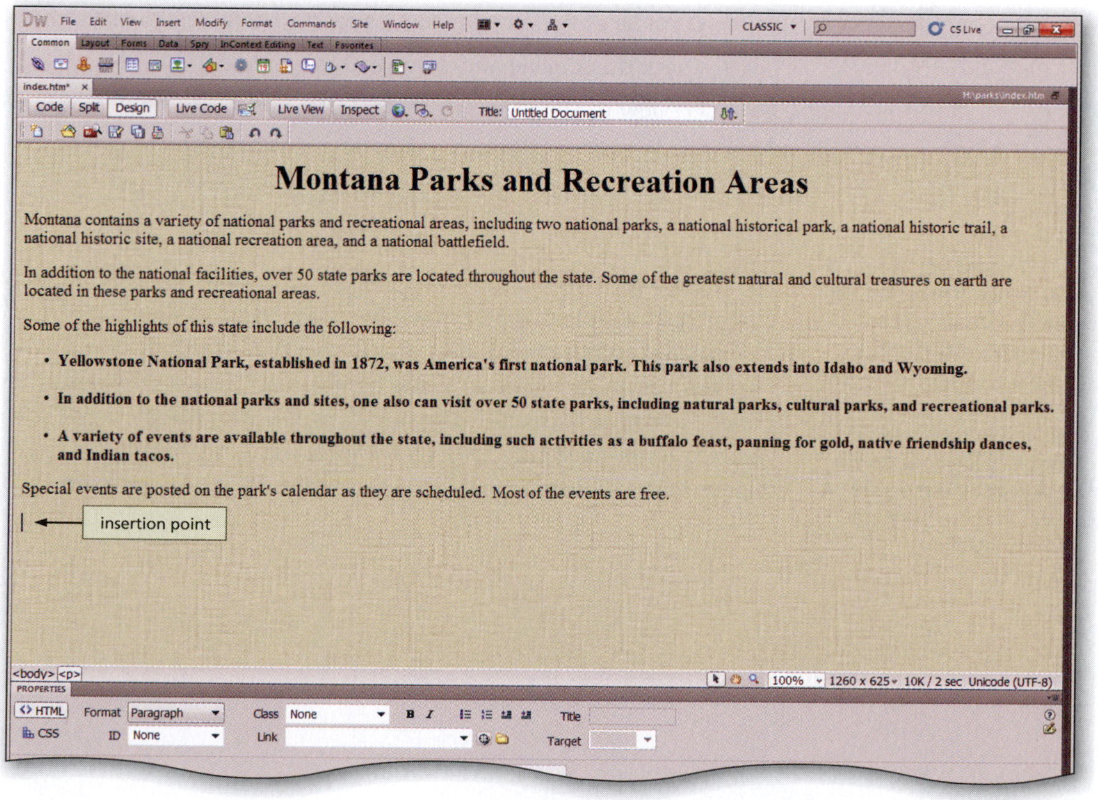

Figure 1–57

2

- Type your name and then press the SHIFT+ENTER keys to insert a line break.

- Type the current date and then press the ENTER key to add your name and the current date to the Web page (Figure 1–58).

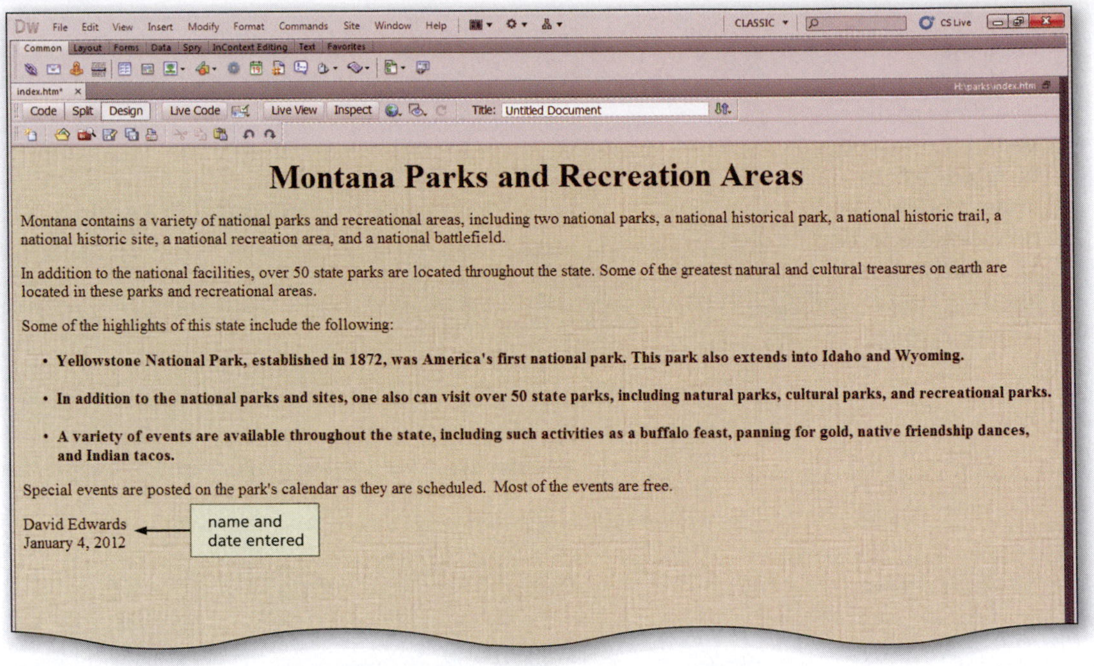

Figure 1–58

Plan Ahead

Review final tasks.

Before completing a Web page, perform the following tasks to make sure it is ready for others to view:

- Give your Web page a title.
- Consider enhancements such as special characters to make the page look professional.
- Check the spelling and proofread the text.
- Preview the page in one or more browsers to see how it looks when others open it.

BTW

Keep Data Confidential
Web pages reach a global audience. Therefore, to limit access to certain kinds of information, avoid including any confidential data on your Web pages. In particular, do not include your home address, telephone number, or other personal information.

Web Page Titles

A **Web page title** helps Web site visitors keep track of what they are viewing as they browse. It is important to give your Web page an appropriate title. When visitors to your Web page create bookmarks or add the Web page to their Favorites lists, they use the title for reference. If you do not title a page, the browser displays the page in the browser window, Favorites lists, and history lists as Untitled Document. Because many search engines use the Web page title, use a descriptive and meaningful name. Giving the document a file name when saving it is not the same as giving the page a title.

To Change the Web Page Title

The following steps show how to change the name of the Web page to Montana Parks and Recreation Areas.

1
- Drag to select the text, Untitled Document, in the Title text box on the Document toolbar to prepare for replacing the text.

- Type **Montana Parks and Recreation Areas** in the Title text box and then press the ENTER key to enter a descriptive title for the Web page (Figure 1–59).

2
- Click the Save button on the Standard toolbar to save the document.

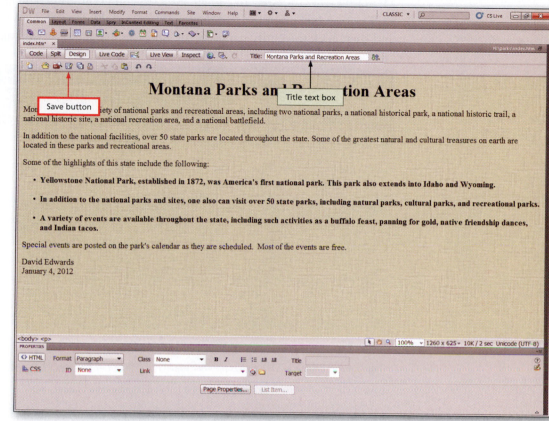

Figure 1–59

Other Web Page Enhancements

Dreamweaver includes many other features that you can use to enhance your Web page. Some of the more commonly used enhancements that you may want to apply to a Web page are special characters.

Special Characters

Sometimes you need to enter special characters such as quotation marks and ampersands as well as non-keyboard symbols like trademarks and registrations into a Web page. To have the browser display these special characters requires a character code. **Character entities**, another name for character codes, allow a browser to show special characters. HTML represents these codes by a name (named entity) or a number (numbered entity). Both types of entities begin with an ampersand (&) and end with a semicolon (;). HTML includes entity names for characters such as the copyright symbol (©), the ampersand (&), and the registered trademark symbol (®). Some entities, such as the left and right quotation marks, include a number sign (#) and a numeric equivalent (such as —). Table 1–2 lists the HTML entities that Dreamweaver supports. To add an entity to your Web page, you click Insert on the Application bar, point to HTML, point to Special Characters on the HTML submenu, and then click the entity name on the Special Characters submenu.

Table 1–2 Character Entities		
Name	Description	HTML Tags and Character Entities
Nonbreaking Space	Places a nonbreaking space at the insertion point	&#nbsp;
Left Quote	Places an opening, curved double quotation mark at the insertion point	$#147;
Right Quote	Places a closing, curved double quotation mark at the insertion point	$#148;
Em Dash	Places an em dash at the insertion point	$#151;
Pound	Places a pound (currency) symbol at the insertion point	&pound;
Euro	Places a euro (currency) symbol at the insertion point	&euro;
Yen	Places a yen (currency) symbol at the insertion point	&yen;
Copyright	Places a copyright symbol at the insertion point	&copy;
Registered Trademark	Places a registered trademark symbol at the insertion point	&reg;
Trademark	Places a trademark symbol at the insertion point	&#153;
Other Characters	Provides a set of special characters from which to select	Other ASCII characters

Check Spelling

After you create a Web page, you should check it visually for spelling errors. In addition, you can use Dreamweaver's Check Spelling command to identify possible misspellings. The Check Spelling command ignores HTML tags and attributes. Recall from the Introduction that attributes are additional information contained within an HTML tag.

To Check Spelling

The following steps show how to use the Check Spelling command to spell check your entire document. Your Web page may contain different misspelled words depending on the accuracy of your typing.

1
- In the second bullet, select the word-92cultural, and then type **cultral** to insert a deliberately misspelled word in the document.
- Click at the beginning of the document to position the insertion point.
- Click Commands on the Application bar and then point to Check Spelling to highlight the command (Figure 1–60).

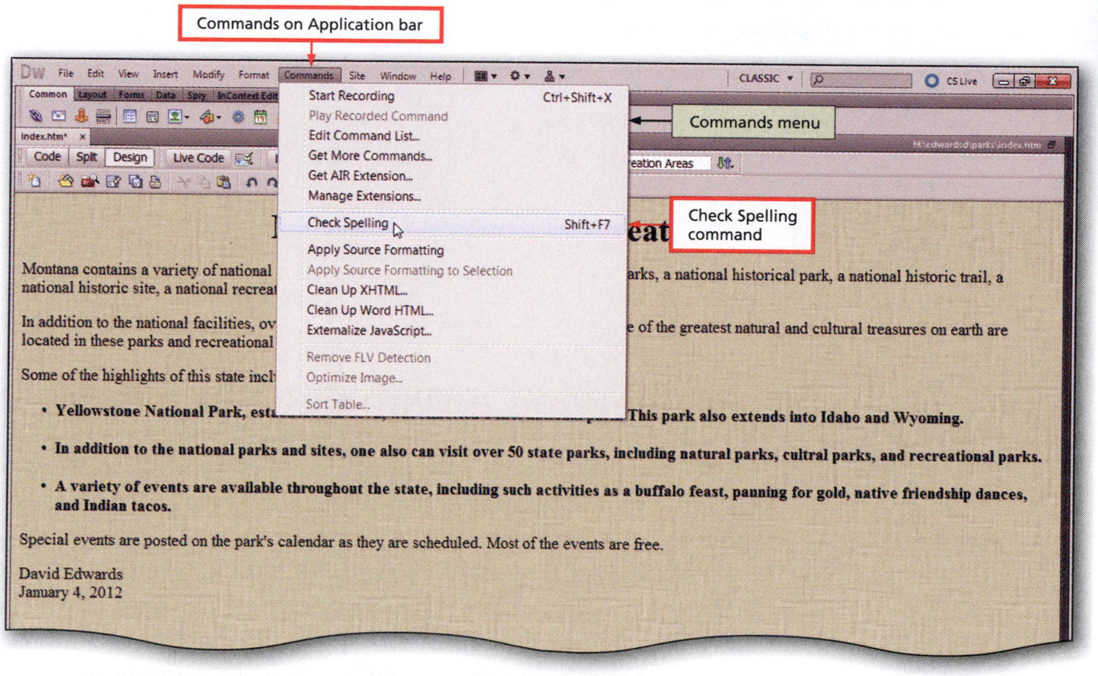

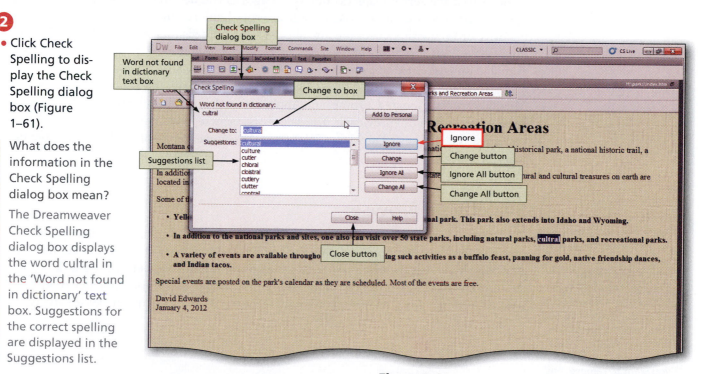

Figure 1–60

2
- Click Check Spelling to display the Check Spelling dialog box (Figure 1–61).

Q&A

What does the information in the Check Spelling dialog box mean?

The Dreamweaver Check Spelling dialog box displays the word cultral in the 'Word not found in dictionary' text box. Suggestions for the correct spelling are displayed in the Suggestions list.

Figure 1–61

Q&A

Does Dreamweaver contain a dictionary with American/British spelling options?

Yes. Dreamweaver contains 15 different spelling option dictionaries, including English (British) and English (Canadian). Access the dictionaries by clicking the Preferences command on the Edit menu, selecting the General category, and then clicking the Spelling dictionary pop-up menu arrow.

3

- The word displayed in the Change to text box shows the correct spelling of the word, so click the Change button to change cultral to cultural and continue with the spell checking.

- Continue to check the spelling and, as necessary, correct any misspelled word by accepting the suggested replacement, by clicking the Change or Change All buttons, or by typing the correct word in the Change to text box. Click Ignore if proper names are displayed as errors.

- Click the OK button to close the Check Spelling dialog box.

- Press the CTRL+S keys to save any changes.

Other Ways

1. Press SHIFT+F7

Previewing a Web Page in a Browser

After you have created a Web page, it is a good practice to test your Web page by previewing it in Web browsers to ensure that it is displayed correctly. Using this strategy helps you catch errors so you will not copy or repeat them.

As you create your Web page, you should be aware of the variety of available Web browsers. More than 25 Web browsers are in use, most of which have been released in more than one version. Each browser might display text, images, and other Web page elements differently. For this reason, you want to preview your Web pages in more than one browser to make sure it displays your Web pages as you designed them. Most Web developers target recent versions of Microsoft Internet Explorer and Mozilla Firefox, which the majority of Web visitors use. You also should know that visitors viewing your Web page might have earlier versions of these browsers. Free browser compatibility checkers also are available online (*http://browsershots.org* and *https://browserlab.adobe.com*).

You can define up to 20 browsers for previewing, including Internet Explorer, Mozilla Firefox, Google Chrome, and Apple Safari. A browser must be installed on your system before you can preview it. You select one browser as the primary browser. When you press the F12 key to preview a Web page, Dreamweaver displays the page in the primary browser.

Selecting a Browser

BTW

Remove a Browser
Just as you can specify a primary and secondary browser, you can remove a browser from the list of target browsers. Click Edit on the Application bar, click Preferences, and then click the Preview in Browser category. Select the name of the browser you want to remove, and then click the minus (–) button.

You select browser preferences in the Preferences dialog box. This dialog box provides options to select and define the settings for a primary and a secondary browser. Additionally, a Preview using temporary file option is available. Select the check box for this option to preview a page without saving it. Although it is a good practice to save before previewing in a browser, you might want to view a page quickly before saving it.

To Select Primary and Secondary Target Browsers

The following steps show how to select your target browsers — Internet Explorer and Firefox. To complete these steps requires that you have both Internet Explorer and Firefox installed on your computer. Note, however, that it is not necessary to install a secondary browser. If your choice is to use just one browser, you can choose to install only the one you would like to use. Or, you can choose to install additional browsers as well.

1
- Click Edit on the Application bar and then click Preferences to open the Preferences dialog box.

- If necessary, click the Preview in Browser category in the Preferences dialog box to select the Preview in Browser category (Figure 1–62).

Q&A What is the primary browser?

The primary browser was selected when Dreamweaver was installed on your computer. In this book, the primary browser is Internet Explorer. The browser name, IExplore, was selected automatically during the Dreamweaver installation. The browser name on your computer may be different.

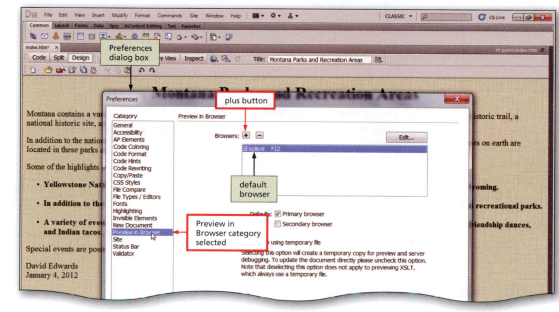

Figure 1–62

2
- Click the plus (+) button in the Preview in Browser area to display the Add Browser dialog box (Figure 1–63).

Q&A What should I do if the Preview in Browser dialog box already lists Firefox and IExplore?

Skip Steps 2 through 5. Click Firefox in the Preview in Browser dialog box, and then click the Secondary browser check box. Click IExplore in the Preview in Browser dialog box, and then click the Primary browser check box. Then click the OK button.

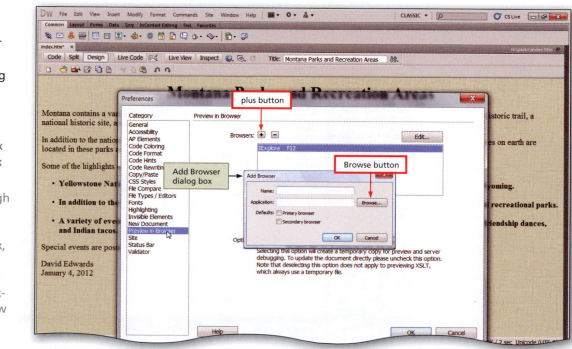

Figure 1–63

3

- Click the Browse button and then locate and click the Firefox program file to select the file.

Q&A Where can I find the Firefox program file?

Most likely this file is located on Local Drive (C:). Use the following path to locate the file: C:\Program Files\ Mozilla Firefox\ firefox. The path and file name on your computer may be different.

- Click the Open button to add the browser name and path to the Add Browser dialog box (Figure 1–64).

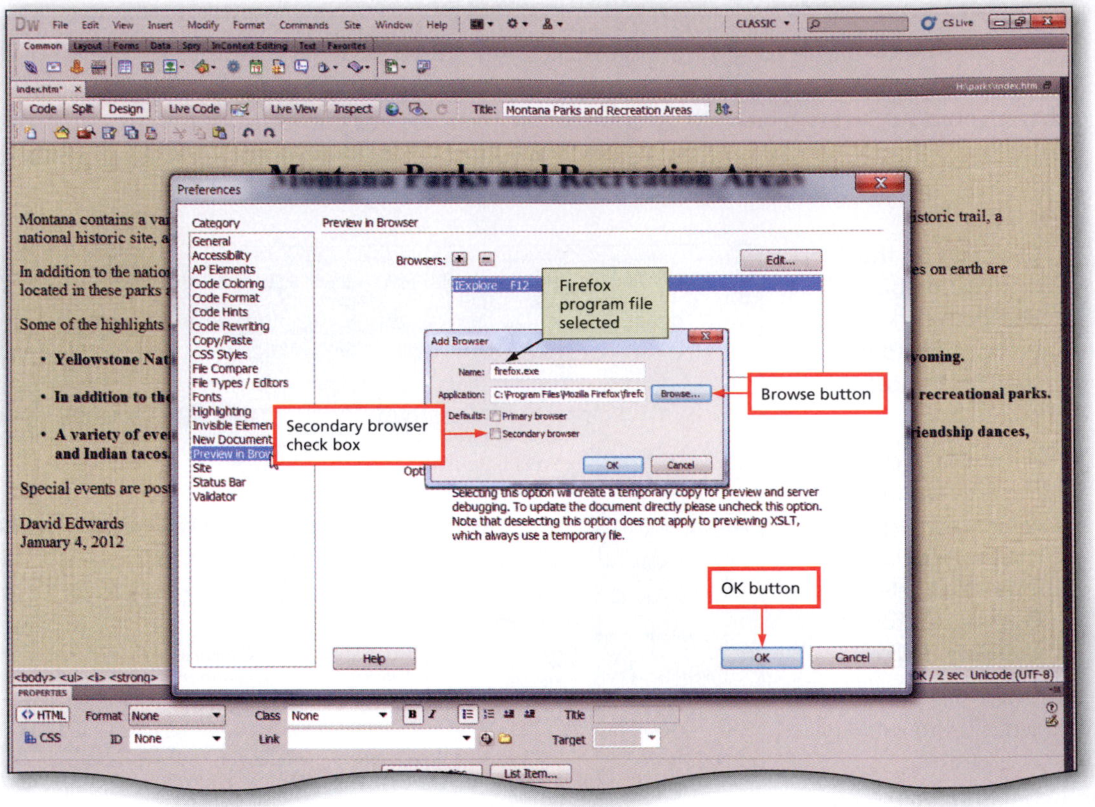

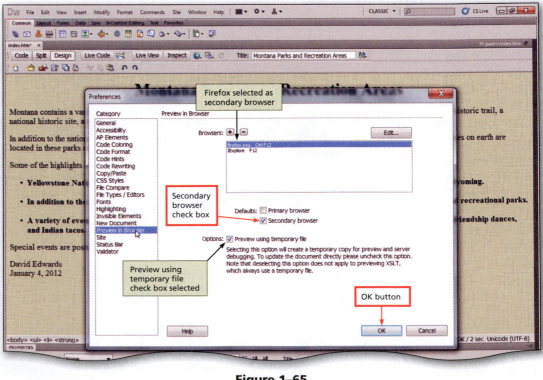

Figure 1–64

4

- If necessary, click the Secondary browser check box to select it.

Q&A What does the information in the Add Browser dialog box mean?

The Name text box displays firefox. exe, the name of the Firefox program file. The Application text box displays the path and file name. The path and spelling of Firefox on your computer may be different from those shown in Figure 1–64.

- Click the OK button to add Firefox as the secondary browser.

Figure 1–65

- If necessary, click the 'Preview using temporary file' check box to select it (Figure 1–65).

5
- Click the OK button to select Internet Explorer and Firefox as the preview browsers.
- If a Dreamweaver CS5 dialog box appears, click the OK button to confirm your selections and close the dialog box.
- Click the Save button on the Standard toolbar to save your work.

To Preview the Web Page

With the target browsers set up, you are ready to preview a Web page. To select the browser you want to use for the preview, you use the Preview in Browser command on the File menu. The following steps illustrate how to preview the Montana Parks and Recreation Areas Web page using Internet Explorer and Firefox.

1
- Click File on the Application bar, point to Preview in Browser, and then click IExplore to display the Montana Parks and Recreation Areas Web page in the Internet Explorer browser.
- If necessary, maximize your browser window to display the entire Web page (Figure 1–66).

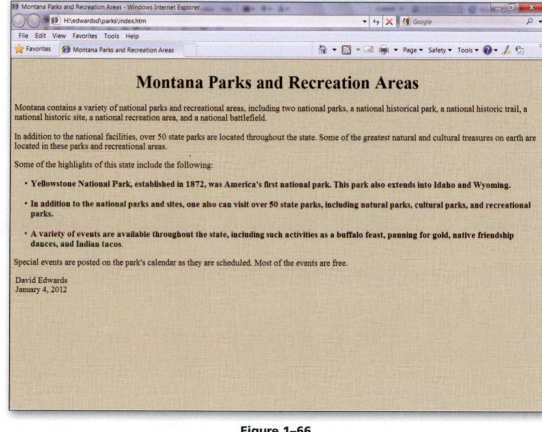

2
- Click the Internet Explorer Close button to close the browser.
- Click File on the Application bar and then point to Preview in Browser to prepare for changing browsers.

Figure 1–66

- Click Firefox.exe on the Preview in Browser submenu to display the Web page in the Firefox browser.
- Click the Firefox Close button to close the browser.

Other Ways

1. Press F12 to display primary browser
2. Press CTRL+F12 to display secondary browser

Printing a Web Page

You may want to print a Web page for a variety of reasons. Dreamweaver provides an option to print code, but does not provide an option to print Design view. To print a Web page, you first must preview it in a browser. Printing a page from your browser is similar to printing a word-processing document.

To Print a Web Page

The following steps illustrate how to print a Web page in a browser.

1
- Press the F12 key to display the page in your primary browser.
- Click the Print button arrow on the Internet Explorer toolbar to display the Print commands (Figure 1–67).

2
- Click Print to display the Print dialog box.
- Select an appropriate printer and click the Print button to send your Web page to the printer.
- Retrieve your printout.
- Close Internet Explorer.

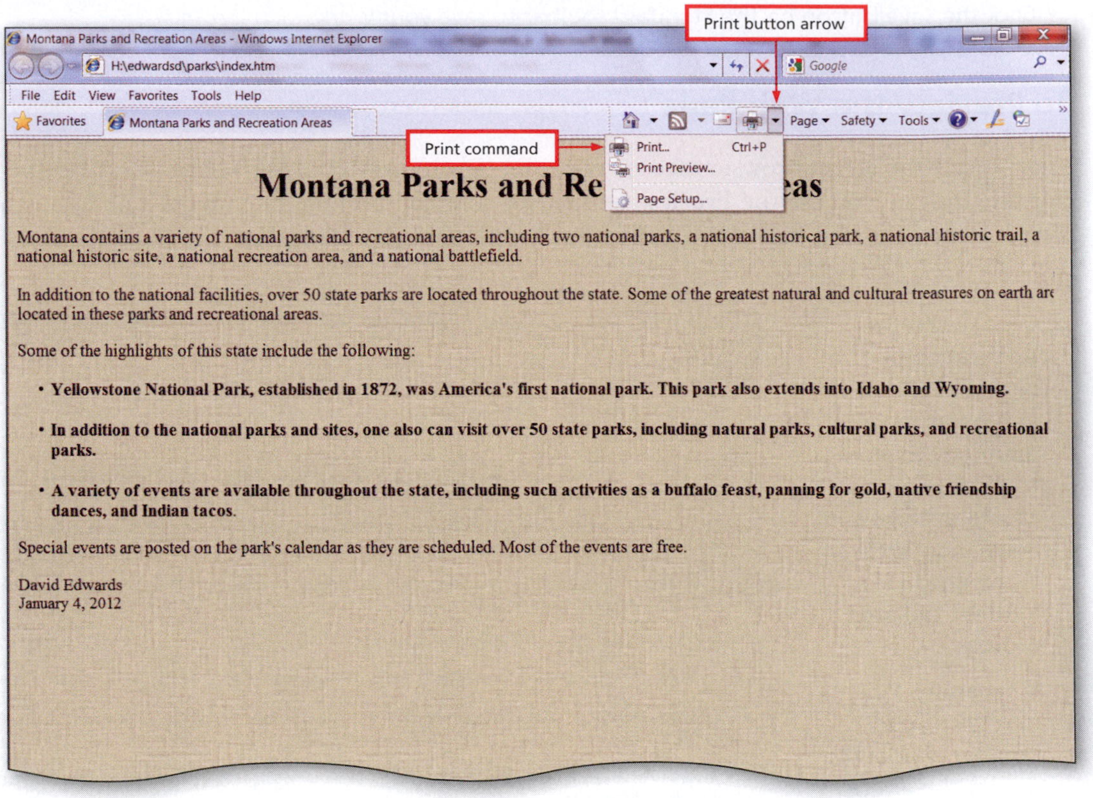

Figure 1–67

Dreamweaver Help System

Reference materials and other forms of assistance are available using the Dreamweaver Help system. You can display these documents, print them, or download them as a PDF file. All of the Dreamweaver CS5 Help is available online. Click Help on the Application bar, and then select one of the commands listed in Table 1–3, or press the F1 key. The main Help page opens connected to the Adobe Web site. Appendix A provides detailed instructions on using Dreamweaver Help.

Table 1–3 Dreamweaver Help System	
Command	**Description**
Dreamweaver Help	Displays the Dreamweaver online help system, which is connected to the Adobe Web site by default. You can search for help or download a PDF file containing the program's documentation.
Reference	Opens the Reference panel, a searchable guide to HTML tags, Cascading Style Sheets, and JavaScript commands.
Dreamweaver Support Center	Opens the online Dreamweaver Help and Support Web page. This page is part of the Adobe Web site and offers links to tutorials and the Dreamweaver Help system, troubleshooting suggestions, videos showing how to perform typical tasks, and access to online forums.

Disabling the Welcome Screen and Quitting Dreamweaver

After you create, save, preview, and print the Montana Parks and Recreation Areas Web page and review how to use Help, your work in Chapter 1 is complete.

To Disable the Welcome Screen, Close the Web Site, and Quit Dreamweaver

The following steps show how to disable the Welcome screen, close the Web page, quit Dreamweaver CS5, and return control to Windows.

1

• Click Edit on the Application bar and then click Preferences to display the Preferences dialog box.

• If necessary, click General in the Category column to display the General options.

• In the Document options section, click the Show Welcome Screen check box to deselect it (Figure 1-68).

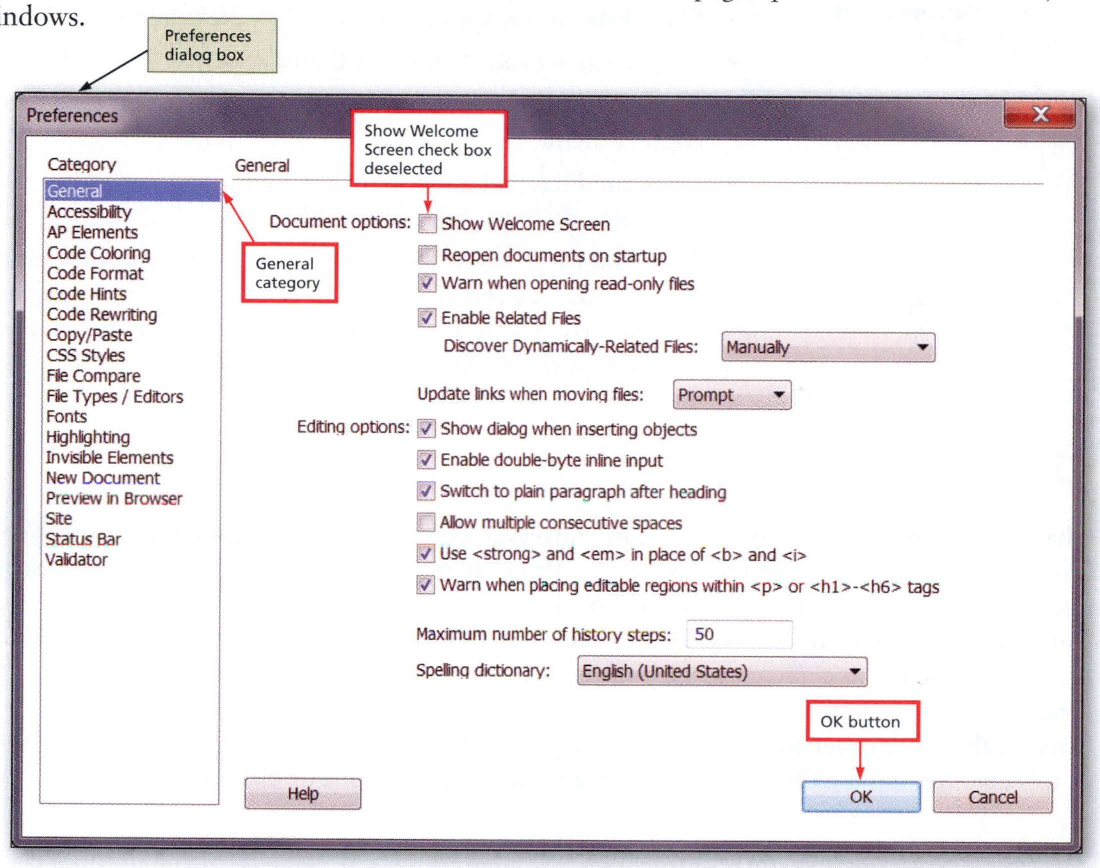

2

• Click the OK button to accept the setting change.

• Click the Close button in the upper-right corner of the Dreamweaver window to close Dreamweaver.

Preferences dialog box

Preferences

Category | General
General
Accessibility
AP Elements
Code Coloring
Code Format
Code Hints
Code Rewriting
Copy/Paste
CSS Styles
File Compare
File Types / Editors
Fonts
Highlighting
Invisible Elements
New Document
Preview in Browser
Site
Status Bar
Validator

Show Welcome Screen check box deselected

General category

Document options: ☐ Show Welcome Screen
☐ Reopen documents on startup
☑ Warn when opening read-only files
☑ Enable Related Files
Discover Dynamically-Related Files: Manually

Update links when moving files: Prompt

Editing options: ☑ Show dialog when inserting objects
☑ Enable double-byte inline input
☑ Switch to plain paragraph after heading
☐ Allow multiple consecutive spaces
☑ Use <strong> and <em> in place of <b> and <i>
☑ Warn when placing editable regions within <p> or <h1>-<h6> tags

Maximum number of history steps: 50
Spelling dictionary: English (United States)

OK button

Help | OK | Cancel

Figure 1–68

Other Ways

1. On File menu, click Exit
2. Press CTRL+Q

Starting Dreamweaver and Opening a Web Page

Opening an existing Web page in Dreamweaver is much the same as opening an existing document in most other software applications: that is, you use the File menu and Open command. In addition to this common method to open a Web page, Dreamweaver provides other options. The Dreamweaver File menu also contains the Open Recent command. Pointing to this command displays the Open Recent submenu, which contains a list of the 10 most recently opened files. Additionally, if you want to display the page on which you currently are working when you next open Dreamweaver, you can select the Reopen Documents on Startup command from the Open Recent submenu.

If the page you want to open is part of a Dreamweaver Web site, you can open the file from the Files panel. To open a Web page from the Files panel, you first must select the appropriate Web site. The Sites pop-up menu button in the Files panel lists sites you have defined. When you open the site, a list of the pages and subfolders within the site is displayed. To open the page you want, double-click the file name. After opening the page, you can modify text, images, tables, and any other elements.

Because you disabled the Welcome screen, the next time you open Dreamweaver, the Welcome screen will not be displayed. Instead, a blank window is displayed, requiring that you open an existing document or open a new document. Dreamweaver provides four options to open a new Document window:

- Click File on the Application bar, click New, and then select Blank Page
- Press CTRL+N and then select Blank Page
- Right-click the site's root folder in the Files panel, and then click New File on the context menu
- Click the Files panel Options menu button, point to File on the pop-up menu, and then click the New File command

The first two options display the New Document dialog box. From this dialog box, you select the Blank Page category and the HTML page type and then click the Create button. When you create a new page by right-clicking the root folder in the Files panel or by using the Options menu button, a default untitled file is created in the Files panel.

Chapter Summary

Chapter 1 introduced you to starting Dreamweaver, defining a Web site, and creating a Web page. You added an image background and used Dreamweaver's Property inspector to format text. You also learned how to use an unordered list to organize information. You added line breaks and learned about special characters. Once your Web page was completed, you learned how to save the Web page and preview it in a browser. You also learned how to print using the browser. To enhance your knowledge of Dreamweaver further, you learned the basics about the Dreamweaver Help system. The following tasks are all the new Dreamweaver skills you learned in this chapter, listed in the same order they were presented in the chapter. For a list of keyboard commands for topics introduced in this chapter, see the Quick Reference for Windows at the back of this book.

1. Start Dreamweaver (DW 36)
2. Display the Standard Toolbar, Change the Icon Colors, and Close and Open Panels (DW 43)
3. Use Site Setup to Create a Local Web Site (DW 47)
4. Copy Data Files to the Local Web Site (DW 52)
5. Hide the Rulers, Change the .html Default, and Save a Document as a Web Page (DW 55)
6. Add a Background Image to the Index Page (DW 60)
7. Hide the Panel Groups (DW 62)
8. Add a Heading and Introductory Paragraph Text (DW 63)
9. Format Text with the Heading 1 Style (DW 68)
10. Center the Web Page Heading (DW 70)
11. Create an Unordered List (DW 72)
12. Bold Text (DW 73)
13. Add a Line Break (DW 74)
14. Add Your Name and Date (DW 75)
15. Change the Web Page Title (DW 77)
16. Check Spelling (DW 78)
17. Select Primary and Secondary Target Browsers (DW 81)
18. Preview the Web Page (DW 83)
19. Print a Web Page (DW 84)
20. Disable the Welcome Screen, Close the Web Site, and Quit Dreamweaver (DW 85)

Learn It Online

Test your knowledge of chapter content and key terms.

Instructions: To complete the Learn It Online exercises, start your browser, click the Address bar, and then enter the Web address `scsite.com/dwCS5/learn`. When the Dreamweaver CS5 Learn It Online page is displayed, click the link for the exercise you want to complete and then read the instructions.

Chapter Reinforcement TF, MC, and SA
A series of true/false, multiple choice, and short answer questions that test your knowledge of the chapter content.

Flash Cards
An interactive learning environment where you identify chapter key terms associated with displayed definitions.

Practice Test
A series of multiple choice questions that test your knowledge of chapter content and key terms.

Who Wants To Be a Computer Genius?
An interactive game that challenges your knowledge of chapter content in the style of a television quiz show.

Wheel of Terms
An interactive game that challenges your knowledge of chapter key terms in the style of the television show *Wheel of Fortune*.

Crossword Puzzle Challenge
A crossword puzzle that challenges your knowledge of key terms presented in the chapter.

Apply Your Knowledge

Reinforce the skills and apply the concepts you learned in this chapter.

Adding Text and Formatting a Web Page
Instructions: In this activity, you modify a Web page by adding a background image, changing the heading style, adding bullets, and centering text (Figure 1–69 on the next page). To use Dreamweaver effectively, it is necessary to create a new site for the Apply Your Knowledge exercises in this book. Make sure you have downloaded the data files for Chapter01\apply, which are available in the Data Files for Students folder. See the inside back cover of this book for instructions on downloading the Data Files for Students, or contact your instructor for information about accessing the required files.

Figure 1–69

Perform the following tasks:

1. Start Dreamweaver. Use the Site Setup dialog box to define a local site in the *your name* folder. Enter **Apply Exercises** as the name of the new site.

2. Using the Browse for folder icon next to the Local Site Folder text box, create a new subfolder in the *your name* folder. Enter **apply** as the name of the subfolder. Open the folder and then select it as the local site folder.

3. In the Advanced Settings category of the Site Setup for Apply Exercises dialog box, click the Browse for folder icon next to the Default Images folder text box. In the apply folder, create a subfolder named images. Open the images folder, and then select it as the default folder for images.

4. Make sure the path in the Default Images folder text box ends with *your name*\apply\images. Click the Site category and make sure the path in the Local site folder text box ends with *your name*\ apply. Click the Save button in the Site Setup for Apply Exercises dialog box to save the settings for the new site.

5. Using Windows Explorer or the Windows Computer tool, copy the apply.htm data file from the Chapter01\apply data files folder into the *your name*\apply folder for the Apply Exercises Web site. Copy the apply_bkg.jpg from the Chapter01\apply\images data files folder into the *your name*\ apply\images folder for the Apply Exercises Web site.

6. In the Local Files list of the Files panel, double-click apply.htm to open the apply.htm page. If necessary, expand the Property inspector. Verify that the HTML button is selected on the left side of the Property inspector.

7. Click the Page Properties button in the Property inspector and apply the apply_bkg background image to the Web page.

8. Apply the Heading 1 style to the first line of text.

9. Select the first two lines. Use the Align command on the Format menu to center the lines.

10. Select the list of items (beginning with animal training and ending with landscape design) and create an unordered list by applying bullets.

11. Click at the end of the last line and press ENTER.

12. Add your name, press SHIFT+ENTER to insert a line break, and then add the current date. Title the document **Chamberlain Academy**.

13. Save your document and then view it in your browser, comparing your Web page to Figure 1–69. Make any changes as necessary, save your changes, and then submit your work in the format specified by your instructor.

Extend Your Knowledge

Extend the skills you learned in this chapter and experiment with new skills. You may need to use Help to complete the assignment.

Adding Text and Formatting a Web Page

Instructions: In this activity, you modify a Web page by adding a background image, inserting line breaks, and centering text (Figure 1–70). To use Dreamweaver effectively, it is necessary to create a new site for the Extend Your Knowledge exercises in this book. Make sure you have downloaded the data files for Chapter01\extend, which are available in the Data Files for Students folder. See the inside back cover of this book for instructions on downloading the Data Files for Students, or contact your instructor for information about accessing the required files.

Figure 1–70

Perform the following tasks:

1. Start Dreamweaver. Use the Site Setup dialog box to define a local site in the *your name* folder. Enter **Extend Exercises** as the name of the new site.

2. Using the Browse for folder icon next to the Local Site Folder text box, create a new subfolder in the *your name* folder. Enter **extend** as the name of the subfolder. Open the folder, and then select it as the local site folder.

3. In the Advanced Settings category of the Site Setup for Extend Exercises dialog box, click the Browse for folder icon next to the Default Images folder text box. In the extend folder, create a subfolder named images. Open the images folder, and then select it as the default folder for images.

4. Make sure the path in the Default Images folder text box ends with *your name*\extend\images. Click the Site category and make sure the path in the Local site folder text box ends with *your name*\extend. Click the Save button in the Site Setup for Extend Exercises dialog box to save the settings for the new site.

5. Using Windows Explorer or the Windows Computer tool, copy the extend.htm data file from the Chapter01\extend folder into the *your name*\extend folder for the Extend Exercises Web site. Copy the extend_bkg.jpg from the Chapter01\extend\images data files folder into the *your name*\extend\images folder for the Extend Exercises Web site.

6. Open the extend.htm page. If necessary, expand the Property inspector. Verify that the HTML button on the left side of the Property inspector is selected.

7. Click the Page Properties button in the Property inspector and apply the extend_bkg background image to the Web page.

8. Type your name and the current date where indicated.

9. Apply the Heading 2 style to the first three lines.

10. On the Format menu, use the Underline command on the Style submenu to underline the third line.

11. Select the next four lines containing the names of flowers and bullet the text. Press SHIFT+ENTER at the end of the first bulleted item, and then press SHIFT+ENTER again to insert a blank, unbulleted line. Do the same to insert a blank line between each of the remaining bulleted items.

12. Center all of the text. Bold the bulleted list, your name, and the date.

13. Enter **Mary's Flower Shoppe** as the title of the document.

14. Save your document and then view it in your browser, comparing your Web page to Figure 1–70. Submit your work in the format specified by your instructor.

Make It Right

In this activity, you analyze a Web page, correct all errors, and/or improve the design.

Adding Text and Formatting a Web Page

Instructions: In this activity, you modify an existing Web page by formatting and adjusting text and adding data (Figure 1–71). To use Dreamweaver effectively, it is necessary to create a new site for the Make It Right exercises in this book. Make sure you have downloaded the data files for Chapter01\right, which are available in the Data Files for Students folder. See the inside back cover of this book for instructions on downloading the Data Files for Students, or contact your instructor for information about accessing the required files.

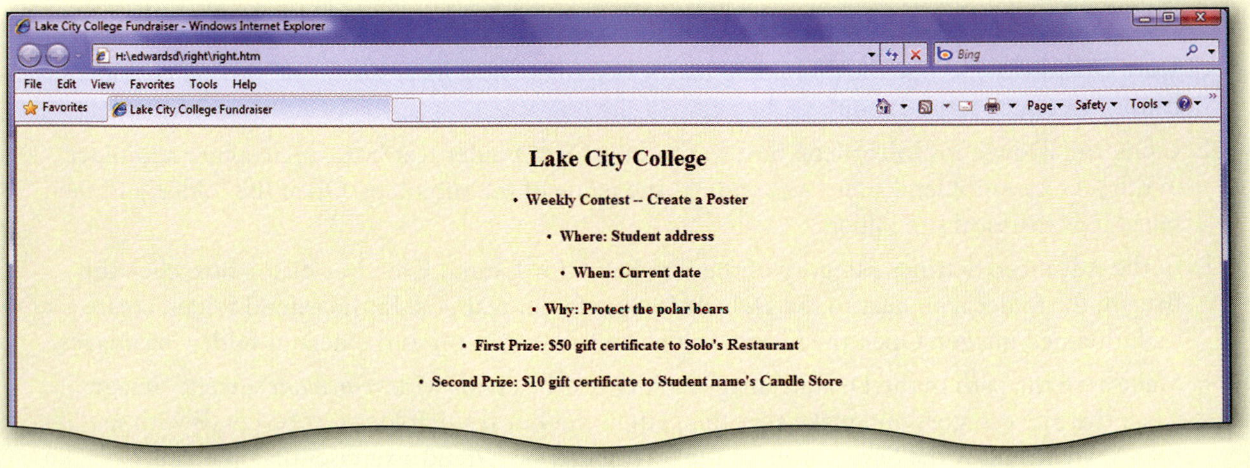

Figure 1–71

Perform the following tasks:

1. Start Dreamweaver. Use Site Setup dialog box to define a local site in the *your name* folder. Enter **Right Exercises** as the name of the new site.

2. Using the Browse for folder icon next to the Local Site Folder text box, create a new subfolder in the *your name* folder. Enter **right** as the name of the subfolder. Open the folder, and then select it as the local site folder.

3. In the Advanced Settings category of the Site Setup for Right Exercises dialog box, click the Browse for folder icon next to the Default Images folder text box. In the right folder, create a subfolder named images. Open the images folder, and then select it as the default folder for images.

4. Make sure the path in the Local Site Folder text box ends with *your name*\right and the path in the Default Images folder text box ends with *your name*\right\images, and then click the Save button in the Site Setup for Right Exercises dialog box to save the settings for the new site.

5. Using Windows Explorer or the Windows Computer tool, copy the right.htm data file from the Chapter01\right folder into the *your name*\right folder for the Right Exercises Web site. Copy the right_bkg.jpg from the Chapter01\right\images data files folder into the *your name*\right\images folder for the Right Exercises Web site.

6. Open the right.htm page. If necessary, expand the Property inspector. Verify that HTML is selected in the Property inspector.

7. Apply the right_bkg background image to the Web page. Select and center the title. Apply the Heading 2 format.

8. Select the rest of the text and add bullets. Bold the bulleted text. Center the text and add a blank, unbulleted line break between each item.

9. Insert your school's address and a date where indicated. Replace "Carole" with your name.

10. Enter **Lake City College Fundraiser** as the document title.

11. Save your document and then view it in your browser, comparing your Web page to Figure 1–71. Submit your work in the format specified by your instructor.

In the Lab

Create a Web page using the guidelines, concepts, and skills presented in this chapter. Labs are listed in order of increasing difficulty.

Lab 1: Creating a Computer Repair Services Web Site

Problem: After watching his computer repair service grow, Bryan asks for your help creating a Web page describing his services. He asks you to assist him in preparing a Web site to list his activities and promote his mission statement.

Define a Web site and create and format a Web page for Bryan's Computer Repair Services. The Web page as it is displayed in a browser is shown in Figure 1–72 on the next page. The text for the Web site is shown in Table 1–4 on the next page.

Software and hardware settings determine how a Web page is displayed in a browser. Your Web pages may be displayed differently in your browser than the pages shown in the figure.

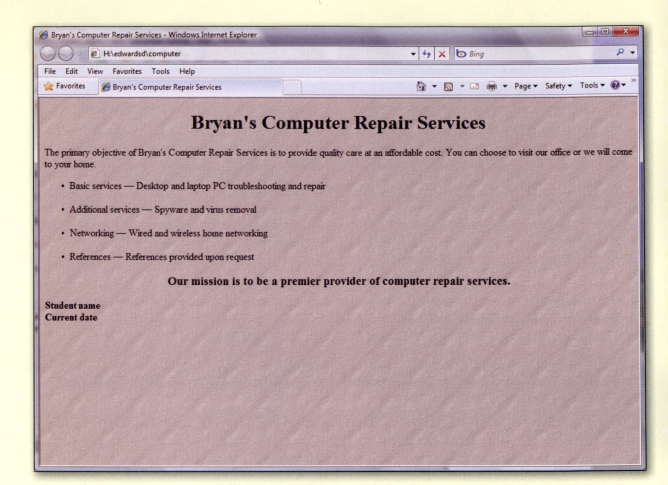

Figure 1–72

Table 1–4 Bryan's Computer Repair Services	
Section	**Text**
Heading	Bryan's Computer Repair Services
Introductory paragraph	The primary objective of Bryan's Computer Repair Services is to provide quality care at an affordable cost. You can choose to visit our office or we will come to your home.
List item 1	Basic services — Desktop and laptop PC troubleshooting and repair
List Item 2	Additional services — Spyware and virus removal
List Item 3	Networking — Wired and wireless home networking
List Item 4	References — References provided upon request
Closing	Our mission is to be a premier provider of computer repair services.

Perform the following tasks:

1. In Dreamweaver, click Site on the Application bar, click New Site, and then use the Site Setup dialog box to create a local Web site in the *your name* folder. In the Site Name text box, enter **Computer Repair Services** as the name of the site.

2. Using the Browse for folder icon next to the Local Site Folder text box, create a new subfolder in the *your name* folder. Enter **computers** as the name of the subfolder. Open the folder, and then select it as the local site folder. The path will be H:*your name*\computers (substitute your name and the drive letter of the drive on which you are saving your files).

3. In the Advanced Settings category of the Site Setup for Computer Repair Services dialog box, click the Browse for folder icon next to the Default Images folder text box. In the computers folder, create a new subfolder. Enter `images` as the name of the subfolder. Open the images folder, and then select it as the default images folder. The path will be H:*your name*\\computers\\images.

4. Click the Save button in the Site Setup for Computer Repair Services dialog box to save the settings for the new site.

5. Using Windows Explorer or the Windows Computer tool, copy the repair_bkg.jpg from the Chapter01\\lab01\\images data files folder into the *your name*\\computer\\images folder for the Computer Repair Services Web site.

6. Click File on the Application bar and then click New. Click Blank Page and HTML, verify that <none> is selected under Layout, and then click Create. Use the Save As command on the File menu to save the page with the name index.

7. Click Modify on the Application bar, and then click Page Properties. Apply the repair_bkg background image (located in the images folder) to the index page.

8. Type the Web page text shown in Table 1–4 on the previous page. Press the ENTER key after typing the text in each section and after each one of the list items in the table. The em dash, used in the four list items, is an HTML object. To insert the em dash, click the Insert menu, point to HTML, point to Special Characters, and then click Em-Dash.

9. Select the heading text and then apply the Heading 1 format. Use the Format menu to center the heading.

10. Select the four list items. Click the Unordered List button in the Property inspector to create a bulleted list with these four items.

11. Click at the end of the first bulleted item. Press the SHIFT+ENTER keys twice to insert a blank line between the first and second items, press the SHIFT+ENTER keys twice to insert a blank line between the second and third items, and then press the SHIFT+ENTER keys twice to insert a blank line between the third and the fourth items.

12. Select the closing paragraph. Center the sentence and then click the Bold button in the Property inspector. When this is complete, do not deselect the sentence.

13. Click the Format button in the Property inspector and apply Heading 3 to the sentence.

14. In the Title text box on the Document toolbar, enter `Bryan's Computer Repair Services` as the title of the Web page.

15. Click at the end of the closing paragraph and then press the ENTER key. Point to Align on the Format menu and then click Left. Type your name, insert a line break, and then type the current date.

16. Select your name and the current date, and then apply bold to the text.

17. Click at the beginning of the document, click Commands on the Application bar, and then click Check Spelling. Spell check your document and correct any errors.

18. Click File on the Application bar and then click Save.

19. Press the F12 key to view the Web page in the primary browser. Compare the Web page to Figure 1–72 on the previous page and make additional changes as necessary. Submit your work in the format specified by your instructor.

In the Lab

Lab 2: Creating a Gift Baskets Web Site

Problem: Putting together gift baskets has long been a hobby of Carole Wells, a friend of yours. She enjoys the hobby so much that she has decided to start her own online business. She has asked you to assist her in preparing a Web site to help her understand how to share her knowledge and her work with others and how to turn her hobby into a business (Figure 1–73). Software and hardware settings determine how a Web page is displayed in a browser. Your Web pages may be displayed differently in your browser than the one shown in the figure.

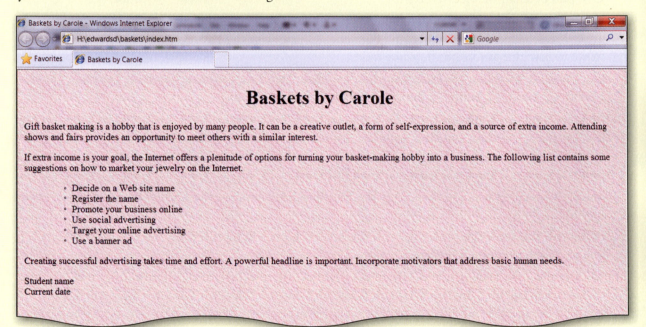

Figure 1–73

Define a Web site and create and format a Web page for Baskets by Carole. The text for the Web page is shown in Table 1–5.

Section	Web Page Text
Table 1–5 Baskets by Carole Web Page	
Heading	Baskets by Carole
Introductory paragraph	Gift basket making is a hobby that is enjoyed by many people. It can be a creative outlet, a form of self-expression, and a source of extra income. Attending shows and fairs provides an opportunity to meet others with a similar interest.
Second paragraph	If extra income is your goal, the Internet offers a plenitude of options for turning your basket-making hobby into a business. The following list contains some suggestions on how to market your baskets on the Internet.
List item 1	Decide on a Web site name
List item 2	Register the name
List item 3	Promote your business online
List item 4	Use social advertising
List item 5	Target your online advertising
List item 6	Use a banner ad
Closing	Creating successful advertising takes time and effort. A powerful headline is important. Incorporate motivators that address basic human needs.

Perform the following tasks:

1. In Dreamweaver, use the Site Setup dialog box to create a local Web site in the *your name* folder. Enter `Gift Basket Designs` as the name of the new site.

2. Using the Browse for folder icon next to the Local Site Folder text box, create a new subfolder in the *your name* folder. Enter `baskets` as the name of the subfolder. Open the folder, and then select it as the local site folder.

3. Using the Advanced Settings category of the Site Setup for Gift Basket Designs dialog box, create and then select the *your name*\baskets\images folder as the default folder for images.

4. Make sure the path in the Default Images folder text box ends with *your name*\baskets\images and make sure the path in the Local site folder text box ends with *your name*\baskets. Click the Save button in the Site Setup for Gift Baskets Designs dialog box to save the settings for the new site.

5. Using Windows Explorer or the Windows Computer tool, copy the baskets_bkg.jpg from the Chapter01\lab02\images data files folder into the *your name*\baskets\images folder for the Gift Basket Designs Web site.

6. Click File on the Application bar, and then click New. Click Blank Page, verify that HTML and <none> are selected, and then click Create. Use the Save As command on the File menu to save the page with the name index.

7. Click the Modify menu and then click Page Properties. Apply the baskets_bkg background image to the index page.

8. Click in the Document window and then type the Web page text shown in Table 1–5. Press the ENTER key after typing each section and after each list item in the table.

9. Apply the Heading 1 format to the heading and then center the heading.

10. Create an unordered list for the list items. With these items still selected, click the Indent button in the Property inspector to increase the indent.

11. Enter `Baskets by Carole` as the Web page title.

12. Click at the end of the closing line and then press the ENTER key. Type your name. Insert a line break and then type the current date.

13. Check the spelling of your document and correct any errors.

14. Save your document and then view it in your browser, comparing your Web page to Figure 1–73. Submit your work in the format specified by your instructor.

In the Lab

Lab 3: Creating a Credit Protection Web Site

Problem: Identity theft is a growing issue and one of the major concerns facing people today. Recently, you learned that two fellow employees became victims of identity theft; you have decided to create a Web site (Figure 1–74) that will provide some information on how to prevent becoming a victim.

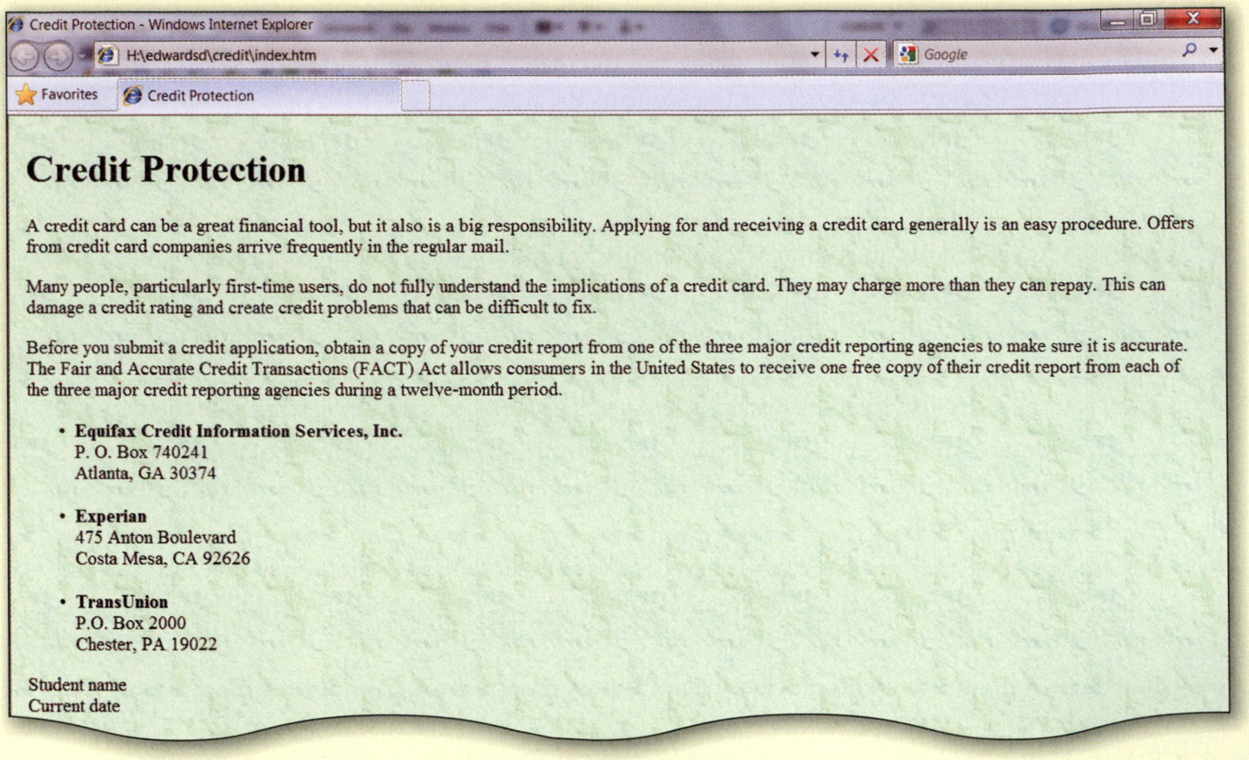

Credit Protection - Windows Internet Explorer

H:\edwardsd\credit\index.htm

Google

Favorites   Credit Protection

Credit Protection

A credit card can be a great financial tool, but it also is a big responsibility. Applying for and receiving a credit card generally is an easy procedure. Offers from credit card companies arrive frequently in the regular mail.

Many people, particularly first-time users, do not fully understand the implications of a credit card. They may charge more than they can repay. This can damage a credit rating and create credit problems that can be difficult to fix.

Before you submit a credit application, obtain a copy of your credit report from one of the three major credit reporting agencies to make sure it is accurate. The Fair and Accurate Credit Transactions (FACT) Act allows consumers in the United States to receive one free copy of their credit report from each of the three major credit reporting agencies during a twelve-month period.

- **Equifax Credit Information Services, Inc.**
  P. O. Box 740241
  Atlanta, GA 30374

- **Experian**
  475 Anton Boulevard
  Costa Mesa, CA 92626

- **TransUnion**
  P.O. Box 2000
  Chester, PA 19022

Student name
Current date

Figure 1–74

Table 1–6 Credit Protection Web Page	
Section	**Web Page Text**
Heading	Credit Protection
Introductory paragraph	A credit card can be a great financial tool, but it also is a big responsibility. Applying for and receiving a credit card generally is an easy procedure. Offers from credit card companies arrive frequently in the regular mail.
Second paragraph	Many people, particularly first-time users, do not fully understand the implications of a credit card. They may charge more than they can repay. This can damage a credit rating and create credit problems that can be difficult to fix.
Third paragraph	Before you submit a credit application, obtain a copy of your credit report from one of the three major credit reporting agencies to make sure it is accurate. The Fair and Accurate Credit Transactions (FACT) Act allows consumers in the United States to receive one free copy of their credit report from each of the three major credit reporting agencies during a twelve-month period.
List item 1	Equifax Credit Information Services, Inc. P. O. Box 740241 Atlanta, GA 30374
List item 2	Experian 475 Anton Boulevard Costa Mesa, CA 92626
List item 3	TransUnion P.O. Box 2000 Chester, PA 19022

Perform the following tasks:

1. In Dreamweaver, define a local Web site in the *your name* folder. Enter **Credit Protection** as the name of the site. Create a new subfolder in the *your name* folder and name the new subfolder **credit**. Select the *your name*\credit folder as the local site folder.

2. Create a subfolder in the credit folder and name it **images**. Select the *your name*\credit\images folder as the default folder for images.

3. Copy the image data file (credit_bkg.jpg) into the *your name*\credit\images folder.

4. Open a new Document window and use the Save As command to save the page with the name index. Apply the background image to the index page.

5. Type the heading and first three paragraphs of the Web page text shown in Table 1–6. Press the ENTER key after typing each section of the text in the table. Insert line breaks where shown in Figure 1–74.

6. Type List item 1 as shown in Table 1–6. Insert a line break after the company name and after the address. Press the ENTER key after the city, state, and zip code. Type List items 2 and 3 in the same fashion.

7. Apply the Heading 1 style to the heading text. Align the heading to the left (to ensure it is displayed properly in the browser).

8. Select the three list items (companies and addresses) and create an unordered list. Insert two line breaks between item 1 and item 2, and between item 2 and item 3.

9. Bold the company name of the first item in the bulleted list (Equifax Credit Information Services, Inc.). Bold the names of the other two companies.

10. Title the Web page Credit Protection.

11. Click at the end of the last line of text and then press the ENTER key. If a bullet is displayed, click the Unordered List button in the Property inspector to remove the bullet. Type your name, add a line break, and then type the current date.

12. Check the spelling of your document and correct any errors.

13. Save your document and then view it in your browser, comparing your Web page to Figure 1–74. Submit your work in the format specified by your instructor.

Cases and Places

Apply your creative thinking and problem-solving skills to design and implement a solution.

• EASIER ••MORE DIFFICULT

• 1: Create the Favorite Sports Web Site

Define a Web site named Favorite Sports with a local root folder named sports (stored in the *your name* folder). Prepare a Web page listing your favorite sports and favorite teams. Include a title for your Web page. Bold and center the title, and then apply the Heading 1 style. Include a sentence or two explaining why you like the sport and why you like the teams. Bold and italicize the names of the teams and the sports. Give the Web page a meaningful title. Apply a background image to your Web page. Check the spelling in the document. Use the concepts and techniques presented in the chapter to format the text. Save the file in the sports folder. For a selection of images and backgrounds, visit the Dreamweaver CS5 Media Web page (scsite.com/dwcs5/media).

• 2: Create the Hobbies Web Site

Your instructor has asked you to create a Web page about one of your hobbies. Define the Web site using Hobbies for the site name and hobby for the local root folder name. Store the hobby folder in the *your name* folder. Italicize and center the title, and then apply the Heading 1 style. Type a paragraph of three or four sentences explaining why you selected the subject. Select and center the paragraph. Add a list of five items and create an ordered list from the five items. Include line breaks between each numbered item. Title the Web page the name of the hobby you selected. Check the spelling in your document. Use the concepts and techniques presented in the chapter to format the text. For a selection of images and backgrounds, visit the Dreamweaver CS5 Media Web page (scsite.com/dwcs5/media).

•• 3: Create the Politics Web Site

Assume you are running for office in your city's local government. Define a Web site using the name of the city in which you live and a local root folder named government. Include the following information in your Web page: your name, centered, with Heading 1 and a font color of your choice; the name of the office for which you are running, bold and italicized; and a paragraph about the duties of the office. Create a bulleted list within your Web page. Change the title of the Web page from Untitled to your name. Use the concepts and techniques presented in the chapter to format the text. For a selection of images and backgrounds, visit the Dreamweaver CS5 Media Web page (scsite.com/dwcs5/media).

•• 4: Create the Favorite Baseball Player Web Site

Make It Personal

Define a Web site and create a Web page that gives a description and information about your favorite baseball player. Name the Web site Favorite Player and the local root folder player. Apply a background image to the Web page. Include a center-aligned heading formatted with the Heading 1 style. Include a subheading formatted with Heading 3. List four facts about why you selected this baseball player. Include informational facts regarding a) the team for which he plays, b) his position, and c) his batting average. Bold and italicize each of the facts and apply a font color of your choice. Create an ordered list from the three facts. Title the Web page Favorite Player. Use the concepts and techniques presented in the chapter to format the text. Save the file as index in the baseball folder. For a selection of images and backgrounds, visit the Dreamweaver CS5 Media Web page (scsite.com/dwcs5/media).

•• 5: Create the Student Trips Web Site

Working Together

Your school has a budget for student celebrations and dances. Your assignment and that of your teammates is to put together a Web site and Web page that lists various information about these two topics. Save the site in a local root folder named celebrations. Apply an appropriate background image. Include a title, formatted with Heading 1, and a subtitle, formatted with Heading 2. Add a bullet to each item and include information about the location for each item. Title the page Student Celebrations. Use the concepts and techniques presented in the chapter to format the text. For a selection of images and backgrounds, visit the Dreamweaver CS5 Media Web page (scsite.com/dwcs5/media).

2 | Adding Web Pages, Links, and Images

Objectives

You will have mastered the material in this chapter when you can:

- Add pages to a Web site
- Describe Dreamweaver's image accessibility features
- Describe image file formats
- Insert, resize, and align images within a Web page
- Describe the different types of links
- Create relative, absolute, and e-mail links

- Describe how to change the color of links
- Edit and delete links
- Check spelling
- Describe Code view, Split view, and Design view
- Display Code view
- Use Live view

2 | Adding Web Pages, Links, and Images

Introduction

The majority of Web sites consist of several pages with links between the pages. The pages in a site generally are linked and contain shared attributes, such as related topics, a similar design, or a shared purpose. Dreamweaver contains a site structure feature that provides a way to maintain and organize your files within a site. Most Web site developers also enhance a Web site by including images on their Web pages.

Project — Two New Pages, Links, and Images

When creating a Web site, you should follow a standard format or style for all pages contained within the site. The content, which is the information provided on the Web site, should be engaging, relevant, and appropriate to the audience. Accessibility issues should be addressed when developing the site. Experience level of the users, the types of tasks that will be performed on the site, and required connection speeds are important components.

In this chapter, you continue building the Montana Parks Web site. You create two additional Web pages, add image backgrounds to the two new pages, add images to the two new pages and to the index page, add links to and from the index page, and add absolute links to the national preserves and historic sites highlighted in the two new pages.

Each new page contains a link to the home (index) page, and the index page contains links to each new page. This arrangement presents the information to the users in a logical order, making it easy to always return to the home page from any point within the Web site. The two new pages and the home page also follow Web site design guidelines that address accessibility principles (Figures 2–1a, 2–1b, and 2–1c on the next page).

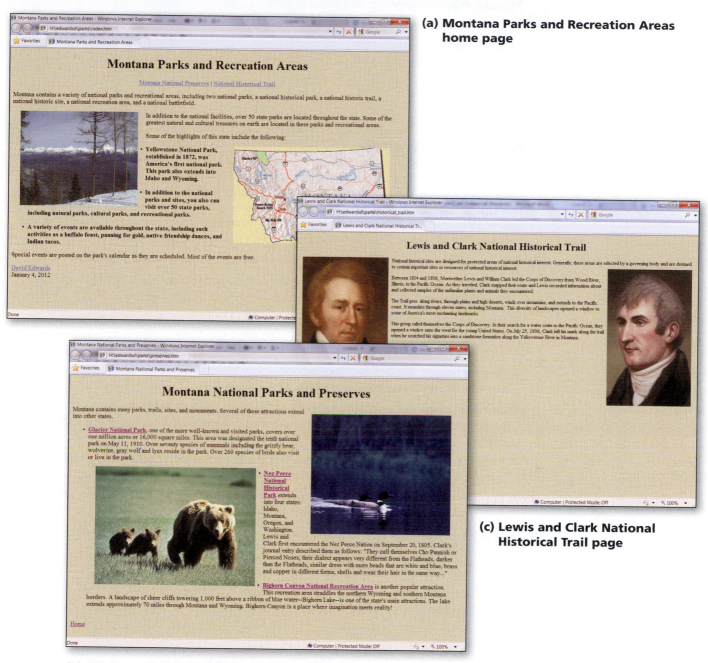

(a) **Montana Parks and Recreation Areas home page**

(c) **Lewis and Clark National Historical Trail page**

(b) **Montana National Parks and Preserves page**

Figure 2–1

Overview

As you read this chapter, you will learn how to add pages to the Montana Parks Web site to create and modify the documents shown in Figure 2–1 and how to use Dreamweaver to perform the following tasks:

- Copy data files to the Web site folder.
- Add pages to a Web site.
- Use Dreamweaver's image accessibility features.
- Insert, resize, and align images within a Web page.

- Create relative, absolute, and e-mail links.
- Edit, change color, and delete links.
- Check spelling.
- Use Live view.
- Display a page in Code view.

General Project Guidelines

When creating a Web site, the organization of the site and how different users will approach the site is of paramount importance. Most Web sites have a home page or index page, but that does not necessarily mean that all visitors enter the Web site through the home page. Generally, with most Web sites, considering that the visitor has a Web page address, they can enter the site at any point. As you modify the home page and add the pages shown in Figures 2–1a, b, and c, you should follow these guidelines.

1. **Organize your content**. Create and organize the content for the two new pages.

2. **Identify links**. Consider the content of each new page and how it will link to and from the home page.

3. **Include standard links for navigation**. Visitors to your Web site will use links to navigate the site, and expect to find links to the home page and to main topics. They also expect descriptive links and links for sending e-mail to someone in charge of the Web site.

4. **Prepare images**. Acquire and then organize your images within the Assets panel. Determine which one goes with which Web page.

5. **Consider image placement**. Consider where you will place the images on each of the pages. Determine how much vertical and horizontal space to designate around the image.

6. **Resize images as necessary**. Review each of the images regarding size and determine which ones, if any, need to be resized.

7. **Consider accessibility**. Consider accessibility issues, how they can be addressed, and which ones you need to address within the Web site.

8. **Verify browser viewing**. Use your browser to verify that the page is displayed appropriately and that the links work.

9. **Proofread and check spelling**. Proofread each page and check the spelling.

With a good understanding of the requirements, and an understanding of the necessary decisions and planning process, the next step is to copy the data files to the parks Web site.

Copying Data Files to the Local Web Site

Your data files contain images for Chapter 2. These images are in an images folder. You can use Windows Computer or Windows Explorer to copy the Chapter 2 images to your parks\images folder. See the inside back cover of this book for instructions for downloading the data files, or see your instructor for information about accessing the files required for this book.

The folder containing the data files for this chapter is stored on Removable Disk (H:). The location on your computer may be different. If necessary, verify the location of the data files folder with your instructor.

To Copy Data Files to the Parks Web Site

The following steps show how to copy the files to the parks local root folder using Windows Computer. Before you start enhancing and adding to your Web site, you need to copy the data files into the site's folder hierarchy.

1 Click the Start button on the Windows taskbar and then click Computer to display the Computer window.

2 Navigate to the location of the downloaded data files for Chapter 2, double-click the folder containing your data files, double-click the Chapter02 folder to open it, double-click the parks folder to display the data files, and then double-click the images folder to display the image data files.

3 Click the clark01 image file, or the first file in the list, hold down the SHIFT key, and then click the montana_map image file, or the last file in the list.

4 Right-click the selected files to display the context menu, click the Copy command, and then navigate to the *your name* folder, which contains the folders and files for the Montana Parks Web site.

5 Double-click the *your name* folder, double-click the parks folder, and then double-click the images folder.

6 Right-click anywhere in the open window to display the context menu, and then click the Paste command to copy the images into the Montana Parks Web site images folder. Verify that the folder now contains seven images, including the parks_bkg image (Figure 2–2).

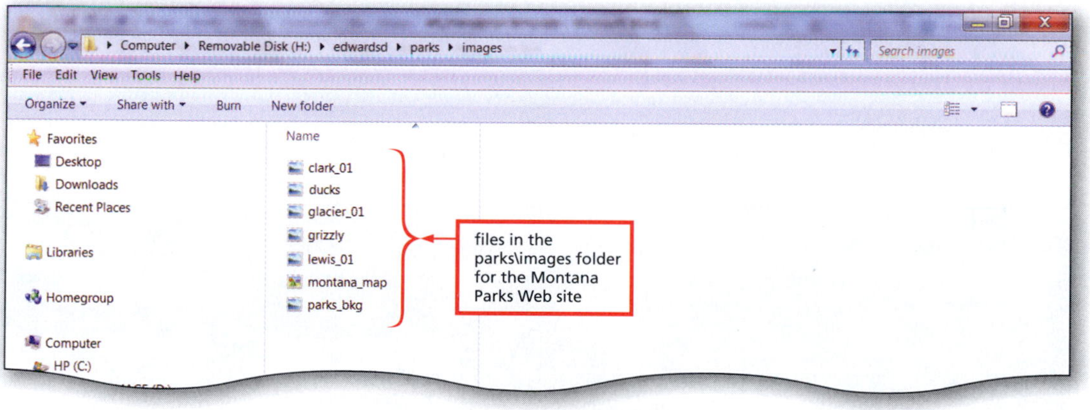

Figure 2–2

Is it necessary to create a folder for images within the Web site?

The hierarchy of folders and files in a Web site is critical to Web development. Even for the simplest of sites, you should create a separate folder for the images. The folder name can be any name you choose, but it is best to use a descriptive, meaningful name.

Starting Dreamweaver and Opening a Web Site

Each time you start Dreamweaver, it opens to the last site displayed when you closed the program. You might therefore need to open the parks Web site. Clicking the **Site pop-up menu button** on the Files panel lists the sites you have defined. When you open the site, a list of pages and subfolders within the site is displayed.

To Start Dreamweaver and Open the Montana Parks Web Site

The following steps illustrate how to start Dreamweaver and open the Montana Parks Web site.

1

• Click the Start button on the Windows taskbar.

• Click Adobe Dreamweaver CS5 on the Start menu or point to All Programs on the Start menu, and then click Adobe Dreamweaver CS5 on the All Programs list to start Dreamweaver.

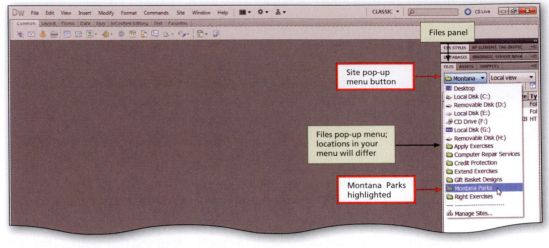

Figure 2–3

• If necessary, display the panel groups.

• If the Montana Parks hierarchy is not displayed, click the Site pop-up menu button in the Files panel to display the drives on your computer and Web sites created with Dreamweaver (Figure 2–3).

Q&A My Dreamweaver window appears in a different size from the one shown in Figure 2–3. Is that a problem?

No. Make sure your Dreamweaver window is maximized. The figures in this book show the Dreamweaver window using a 1024 x 768 resolution. The window might still appear in a different size depending on the type of monitor you are using.

2

• Click Montana Parks to display the Montana Parks Web site hierarchy (Figure 2–4).

Q&A What type of Web structure does this chapter use for the Montana Parks Web pages?

The Introduction chapter illustrates four types of Web

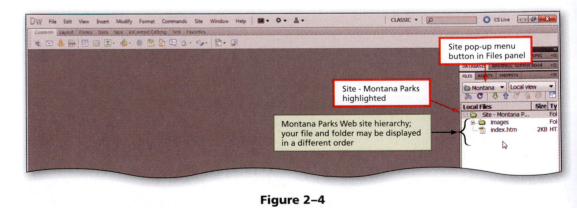

Figure 2–4

structures: linear, hierarchical, web (or random), and grid. This chapter uses a hierarchical structure. The index page is the home page, or entrance to the Web site. From this page, the visitor to this site can link to a page about Montana National Parks and Preserves or to a page about the Lewis and Clark National Historical Trail.

Q&A My Files panel is open, but the Montana Parks files are not displayed. How can I display them?

Refresh the Files panel. To do so, click the Refresh button on the Files panel toolbar or press the F5 key.

Managing a Web Site

Organization is a key element of Web design. Dreamweaver works best with entire sites rather than individual Web pages and has many built-in tools, such as checking links and organizing files, to make site creation easy. You defined the Montana Parks Web site in Chapter 1 and created the index page. You can add pages to your site by creating a new page and saving it as part of the site, or by opening an existing page from another source and saving it as part of the site. In this chapter, you will create two new pages.

Almost all Web sites have a home page. Compare the home page to your front door. Generally, the front door is the first thing guests see when they visit you. The same applies to a Web site's home page. When someone visits a Web site, he or she usually enters through the home page.

The home page normally is named **index.htm** or **index.html**. Recall that this file name has special significance. Most Web servers recognize index.htm (or index.html) as the default home page and automatically display this page without requiring that the user type the full Uniform Resource Locator (URL), or Web address. For example, if you type *nps.gov* into a Web browser's Address box to access the National Park Services Web site, what you see is http://www.nps.gov/index.htm — the actual file name of the site's home page — even though you did not type it that way.

Organizing your Web site and using Dreamweaver's site management features can assure you that the media within your Web page will be displayed correctly. Bringing all of these elements together will start you on your way to becoming a successful Web site developer.

The Files Panel

Organization is one of the keys to a successful Web site. Creating documents without considering where they belong in the folder hierarchy generally creates a difficult-to-manage Web site. The Dreamweaver **Files panel** provides a view of the devices and folders on your computer and shows how these devices and folders are organized. You can create new folders and files for your site through the Files panel, which is similar to organizing files in Windows. You also can use the Files panel to drag or copy and paste files from one folder to another on your computer or from one Web site to another. You cannot, however, copy a file from a Windows folder and paste it into a site in the Dreamweaver Files panel.

In Windows, the main directory of a disk is called the **root directory** or the **top-level directory**. A small device icon or folder icon is displayed next to each object in the list. The **device icon** represents a device such as the desktop or a disk drive, and the **folder icon** represents a folder. Many of these icons have an expand or collapse icon next to them, which indicates whether the device or folder contains additional folders or files. Windows arranges all of these objects — root directory, folders, subfolders, and files — in a hierarchy. The expand and collapse icons are controls that you can click to expand or collapse the view of the file hierarchy. In the Files panel, Dreamweaver uses the same hierarchy arrangement, but site folders and other file icons appear in a different color than non-site folders and files so that you easily can distinguish between the two.

The Home Page

Most Web sites have a starting point, called a home page. In a personal home page within a Web site, for example, you probably would list your name, your e-mail address, some personal information, and links to other information on your Web site. The index page you created in Chapter 1 is the home page for the Montana Parks Web site.

Adding Pages to a Web Site

You copied the data files necessary and pasted them in the parks local root folder in the Files panel. It is time to start building and enhancing your site. You will create two additional pages for the Web site: the Montana National Parks and Preserves page and the Lewis and Clark National Historical Trail page. You will add links and Web page images to the index (or home) page and add links, a background image, and Web page images to the two new pages.

To Open a New Document Window

The first task is to open a new Document window. This will become the Montana National Parks and Preserves Web page. The following steps illustrate how to open a new Document window and save the page as preserves.htm.

1
- Click File on the Application bar and then point to New (Figure 2–5).

Q&A

What are other ways to add a Web page to a site?

If you have already created a document that you can use as a Web page, store it in the root folder for your site, and then use the Open command on the File menu (or the Open button on the Standard toolbar). You can then edit the page in Dreamweaver. You also can insert the contents of a document such as a Microsoft Word or Excel file into a new or existing Web page. To do this, use the Import command on the File menu.

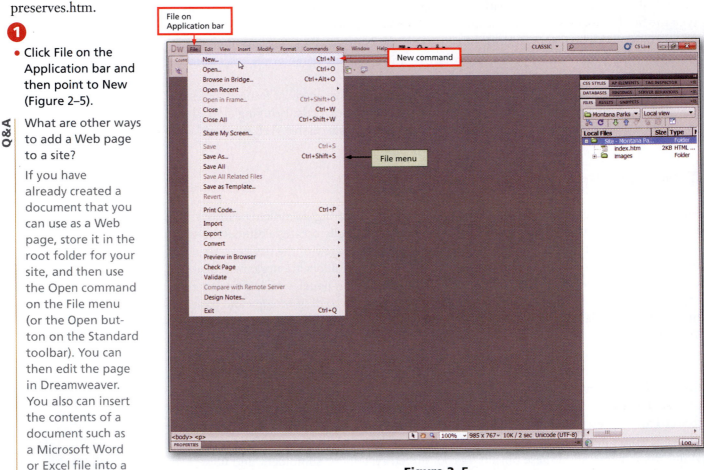

Figure 2–5

2
- Click New to display the New Document dialog box. If necessary, click Blank Page.

- If necessary, click HTML in the Page Type column to specify the type of Web page you are creating.

- If necessary, click <none> in the Layout column to specify no layout. Verify that XHTML 1.0 Transitional is selected on the DocType pop-up menu button (Figure 2–6).

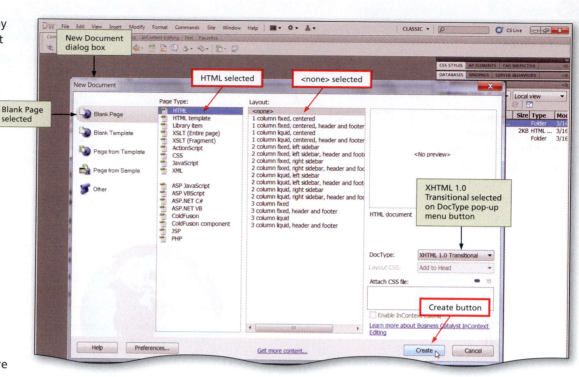

Figure 2–6

Q&A

What is XHTML and why is it important?

XHTML is an authoring language that defines the structure and layout of a document so that it is displayed as a Web page and is compatible with most Web browsers.

3
- Click the Create button to create and display a new Untitled-1 document.

- If necessary, click View on the Application bar, point to Toolbars, and then click Standard to display the Standard toolbar (Figure 2–7).

Q&A

Is it a problem if my new Web page is named Untitled-2?

No. Dreamweaver increments the number for untitled Web pages. You save the page with a more descriptive name in the next step.

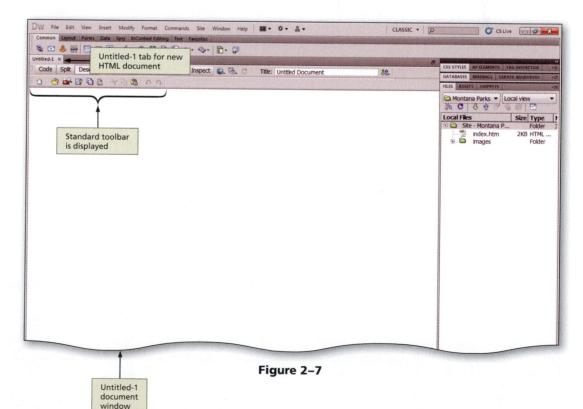

Figure 2–7

4

- Click the Save button on the Standard toolbar to display the Save As dialog box.

- Type **preserves** in the File name text box to provide a descriptive name for the Web page (Figure 2–8).

Q&A

Do I need to specify the path or folder for the new Web page?

No. Dreamweaver assumes you want to save the new Web page in the root local folder, which is parks for the preserves page.

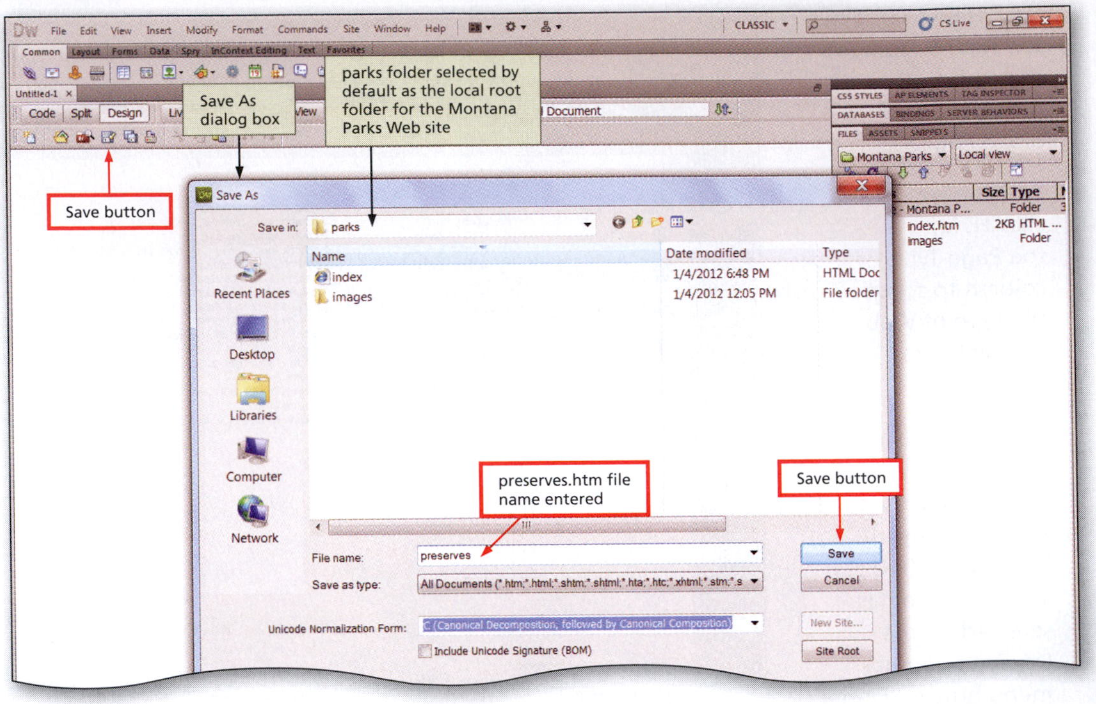

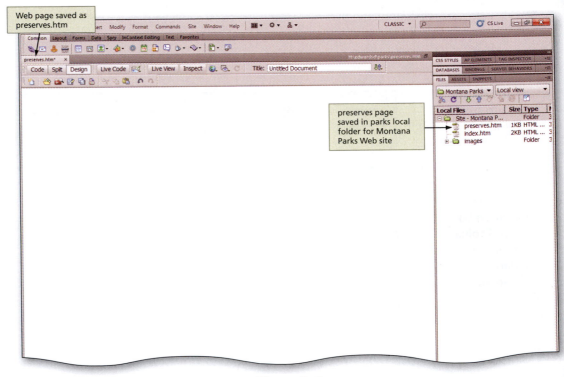

Figure 2–8

5

- Click the Save button in the Save As dialog box to save the preserves page in the parks local folder (Figure 2–9).

Figure 2–9

Other Ways

1. Click New button on Standard toolbar

2. Press CTRL+N

Creating the Montana National Parks and Preserves Web Page

To create the Montana National Parks and Preserves Web page, you type its text in the Document window. Table 2–1 includes the text for the Montana National Parks and Preserves Web page. Press the ENTER key after typing each section as indicated in Table 2–1.

Table 2–1 Montana National Parks and Preserves Web Page Text	
Section	**Text to Add**
Main heading	Montana National Parks and Preserves < ENTER >
Introduction	Montana contains many parks, trails, sites, and monuments. Several of these attractions extend into other states. < ENTER >
Part 1	Glacier National Park, one of the more well-known and visited parks, covers over one million acres or 16,000 square miles. This area was designated the tenth national park on May 11, 1910. Over seventy species of mammals including the grizzly bear, wolverine, gray wolf and lynx reside in the park. Over 260 species of birds also visit or live in the park.< ENTER >
Part 2	Nez Perce National Historical Park extends into four states: Idaho, Montana, Oregon, and Washington. Lewis and Clark first encountered the Nez Perce Nation on September 20, 1805. Clark's journal entry described them as follows: "They call themselves Cho Punnish or Pierced Noses; their dialect appears very different from the Flatheads, darker than the Flatheads, similar dress with more beads that are white and blue, brass and copper in different forms, shells and wear their hair in the same way..." < ENTER >
Part 3	Bighorn Canyon National Recreation Area is another popular attraction. This recreation area straddles the northern Wyoming and southern Montana borders. A landscape of sheer cliffs towering 1,000 feet above a ribbon of blue water—Bighorn Lake—is one of the state's main attractions. The lake extends approximately 70 miles through Montana and Wyoming. Bighorn Canyon is a place where imagination meets reality! < ENTER >
Closing	Home < ENTER >

To Create the Montana National Parks and Preserves Web Page

The following steps show how to create the first new Web page.

1
• Type the heading for the Montana National Parks and Preserves Web page as shown in Table 2–1. Press the ENTER key to create a new paragraph.

2
• Type the rest of the text as shown in Table 2–1. Press the ENTER key as indicated in the table to add blank lines between the paragraphs (Figure 2–10).

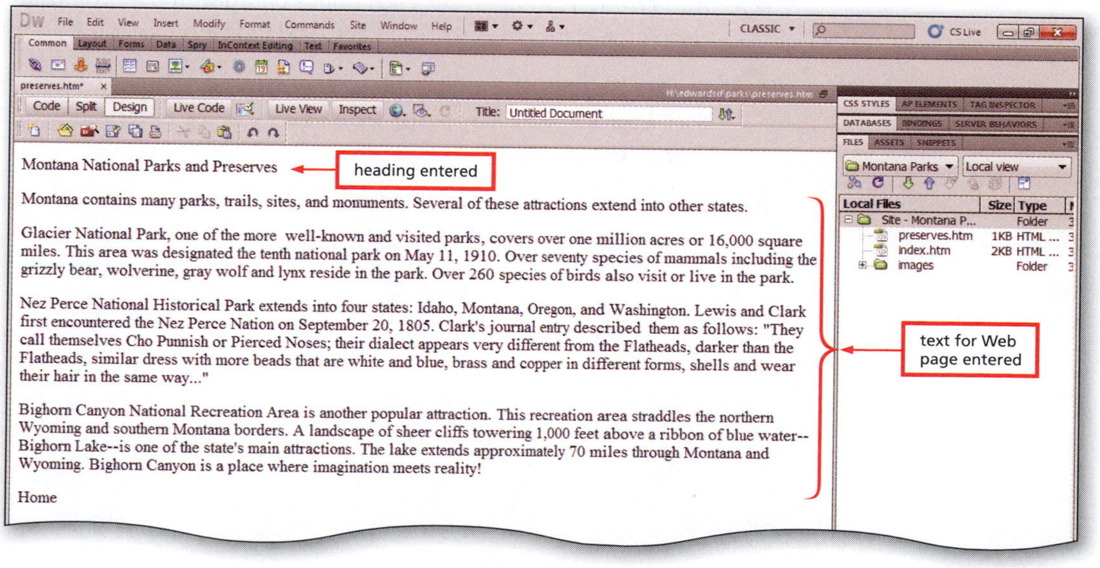

Figure 2–10

To Format the Montana National Parks and Preserves Web Page

In Chapter 1, you formatted the index page by adding headings and bullets and by centering and bolding text. The following steps show how to apply similar formatting to the Montana National Parks and Preserves page.

1 If necessary, scroll up to the top of the Web page, apply Heading 1 to the heading text, and then center the heading.

2 Select and then add bullets to the following three paragraphs that begin: Glacier National Park, Nez Perce National Historical Park, and Bighorn Canyon National Recreation Area (Figure 2–11).

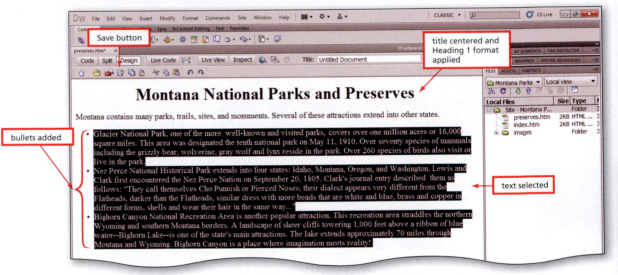

Figure 2–11

3 Click anywhere on the page to deselect the bulleted items.

4 Bold the names of the parks and preserves at the beginning of each of the three paragraphs: Glacier National Park, Nez Perce National Historical Park, and Bighorn Canyon National Recreation Area.

5 Add two line breaks after each bullet paragraph describing the Glacier National Park, Nez Perce National Historical Park, and Bighorn Canyon National Recreation Area.

6 On the Document toolbar, select the text in the Title text box, type `Montana National Parks and Preserves` to enter a descriptive title for the page, and then press ENTER.

7 Click the Save button on the Standard toolbar to save your changes to the preserves.htm Web page (Figure 2–12).

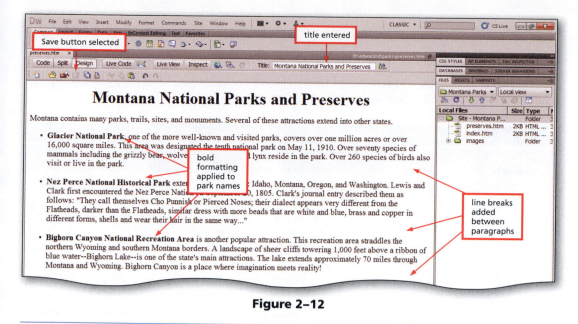

Figure 2–12

Creating the Lewis and Clark National Historical Trail Web Page

You create the Lewis and Clark National Historical Trail Web page by entering text the same way you entered the text for the Montana National Parks and Preserves page. Start by opening a new Document window, add the text, and then format it.

To Open a New Document Window

The following steps show how to open a new Document window for the third Web page for the Montana Parks Web site — the Lewis and Clark National Historical Trail page.

1 Click File on the Application bar, click New, and then, if necessary, click Blank Page.

2 If necessary, click HTML in the Page Type column to select the page type for the Web page.

3 If necessary, click <none> in the Layout column to specify no predefined layout.

4 Click the Create button to create and display the new blank Web page.

5 Save the Web page as historical_trail in the parks folder (Figure 2–13).

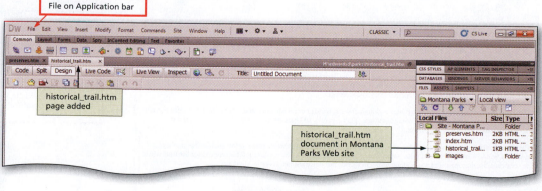

Figure 2–13

Entering Text for the Lewis and Clark National Historical Trail Web Page

Type the text for the Lewis and Clark National Historical Trail Web page using Table 2–2 and the following steps. Press the ENTER key as indicated in the table.

Table 2-2 Lewis and Clark National Historical Trail Web Page Text	
Section	**Text to Add**
Main Heading	Lewis and Clark National Historical Trail < ENTER >
Introduction	National historical sites are designated for protected areas of national historical interest. Generally, these areas are selected by a governing body and are deemed to contain important sites or resources of national historical interest. < ENTER >
Part 1	Between 1804 and 1806, Meriwether Lewis and William Clark led the Corps of Discovery from Wood River, Illinois, to the Pacific Ocean. As they traveled, Clark mapped their route and Lewis recorded information about and collected samples of the unfamiliar plants and animals they encountered. < ENTER >
Part 2	The Trail goes along rivers, through plains and high deserts, winds over mountains, and extends to the Pacific coast. It meanders through eleven states, including Montana. This diversity of landscapes opened a window to some of America's most enchanting landmarks. < ENTER >
Part 3	This group called themselves the Corps of Discovery. In their search for a water route to the Pacific Ocean, they opened a window onto the west for the young United States. On July 25, 1806, Clark left his mark along the trail when he scratched his signature into a sandstone formation along the Yellowstone River in Montana. < ENTER >
Closing	Home < ENTER >

To Create the Lewis and Clark National Historical Trail Web Page

The next task is to add text to the Web page and then format it. The following steps show how to enter and then format text for the Lewis and Clark National Historical Trail Web page.

1 Type the text of the Web page as shown in Table 2–2, and then click the Save button to save your changes (Figure 2–14).

Q&A If I have already entered text in another document, how can I add it to a new Web page?

You can copy and paste the text just as you do in a word processing document. Copy text from another application, switch to Dreamweaver, position the insertion point in the Design view of the Document window, and then press CTRL+V to paste the text.

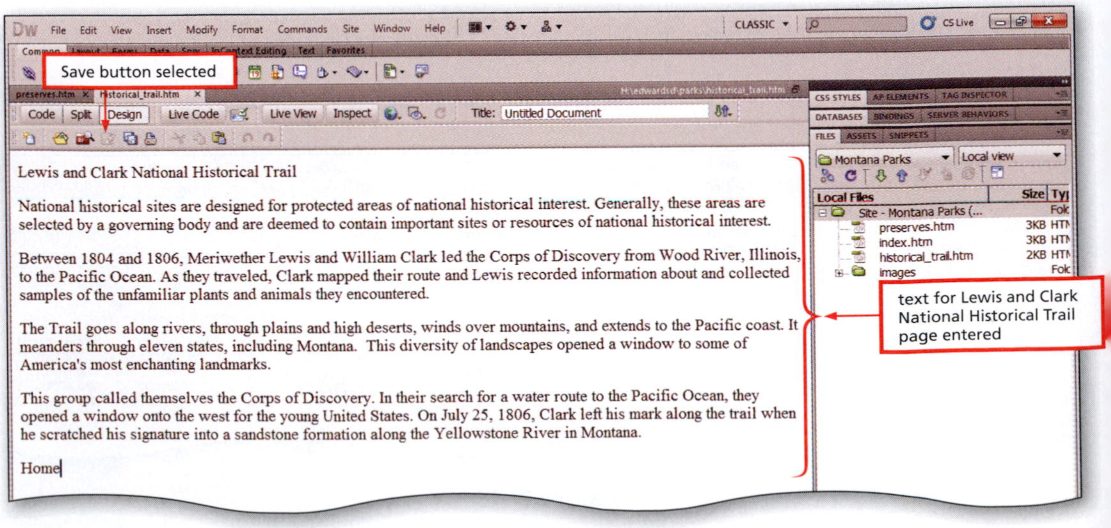

Figure 2–14

2 If necessary, scroll to the top of the Web page, apply Heading 1 to the title, and then center the title.

3 Type `Lewis and Clark National Historical Trail` as the Web page title.

4 Click the Save button on the Standard toolbar to save your work (Figure 2–15).

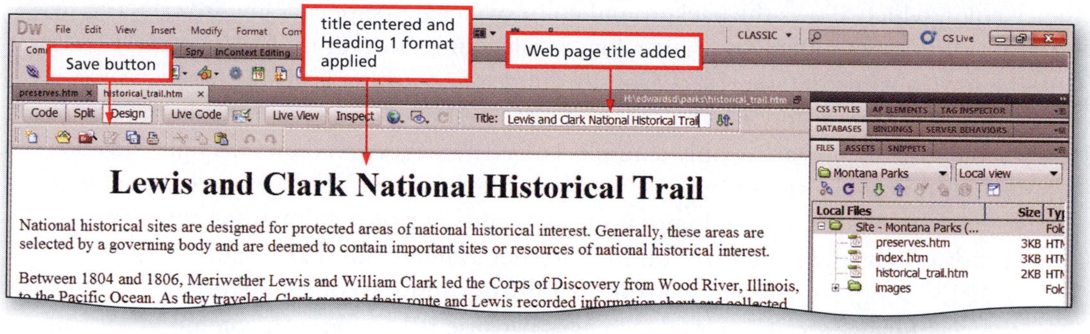

Figure 2–15

Images

You have finished entering and formatting the text for the two new pages and copied the images to the images folder for the Montana Parks Web site. It is time to add other enhancements to your site. In Chapter 1, you added a background image to the index page. In this chapter, you learn more about images. You will add the same background image to the two new pages, and then add images and links to all three pages.

If used correctly and with an understanding of the Web site audience, images add excitement and interest to a Web page. When you are selecting images for a Web site, you should understand that the size and type of image or images used within a Web page affect how fast the Web page downloads and is displayed in the viewer's Web browser. A Web page that downloads too slowly will turn away visitors.

Image File Formats

Graphical images used on the Web are in one of two broad categories: vector and bitmap. **Vector images** are composed of key points and paths, which define shapes and coloring instructions, such as line and fill colors. The vector file contains a mathematical description of the image. The file describes the image to the computer, and the computer draws it. This type of image generally is associated with Adobe Flash or LiveMotion animation programs. One of the benefits of vector images is the small file size, particularly compared to the larger file size of bitmap images.

Bitmap images are the more common type of image file. A bitmap file maps out or plots an image pixel by pixel. A **pixel**, or **picture element**, is the smallest point in a graphical image. Computer monitors display images by dividing the display screen into thousands (or millions) of pixels, arranged in a **grid** of rows and columns. The pixels appear connected because they are so close together. This grid of pixels is a **bitmap**. The **bit-resolution** of an image is the number of bits used to represent each pixel. There are 8-bit images as well as 24- or 32-bit images, where each bit represents a pixel. An 8-bit image supports up to 256 colors, and a 24- or 32-bit image supports up to 16.7 million colors.

Web browsers currently support three bitmap image file types: GIF, JPEG, and PNG.

GIF (.gif) is an acronym for **Graphics Interchange Format**. The GIF format uses 8-bit resolution, supports up to a maximum of 256 colors, and uses combinations of these 256 colors to simulate colors beyond that range. The GIF format is best for displaying images such as logos, icons, buttons, and other images with even colors and tones. GIF images come in two different versions: GIF87 format and GIF89a format. The GIF89a format contains three features not available in the GIF87 or JPEG formats: transparency, interlacing, and animation. Using the **transparency** feature, you can specify a transparency color, which allows the background color or image to appear. The **interlacing** feature lets the browser begin to build a low-resolution version of the full-sized GIF picture on the screen while the file is still downloading, so something is visible to the visitor as the Web page downloads. The **animation** feature allows you to include moving images. Animated GIF images are simply a number of GIF images saved into a single file and looped, or repeated, over and over. A number of shareware GIF editors are available to create animated GIFs. If you do not want to create your own animations, you can find thousands of free animated GIFs on the Internet available for downloading.

JPEG (.jpg) is an acronym for **Joint Photographic Experts Group**. JPEG files are the best format for photographic images because JPEG files can contain up to 16.7 million colors. **Progressive JPEG** is a new variation of the JPEG image format. This image format supports a gradually built display similar to the interlaced GIFs. Older browsers do not support progressive JPEG files.

PNG (.png) stands for **Portable Network Graphics**. PNG, which is the native file format of Adobe Fireworks, is a GIF competitor, and is used mostly for Web site images. Some older browsers do not support this format without a special plug-in. Generally, it still is better to use GIF or JPEG images in your Web pages.

When developing a Web site that consists of many pages, you should maintain a consistent, professional layout and design throughout all of the pages. The pages in a single site, for example, should use similar features such as background colors or images, margins, and headings.

Plan Ahead

Prepare images.
Nearly every Web site displays images such as photographs, drawings, and background textures. Before you add images to a Web site, prepare them using the following guidelines:

- **Acquire the images.** To create your own images, you can take photos with a digital camera and store them in the JPEG format, use a scanner to scan your drawings and photos, or use a graphics editor such as Adobe Photoshop to design images. You also can download images from public domain Web sites, use clip art, or purchase images from stock photo collections. Be sure you have permission to reproduce the images you acquire from Web sites, unless the images are clearly marked as in the public domain.

- **Choose the right format.** Use JPEG files for photographic images and complicated graphics that contain color gradients and shadowing. Use GIF files for basic graphics, especially when you want to take advantage of transparency. You also can use PNG for basic graphics, but not for photos.

- **Keep image file size small.** Images with small file sizes appear in a browser faster than larger images. Use a graphics editor such as Adobe Photoshop to compress image files and reduce their file size without affecting quality. Background images in particular should have a small file size because they often appear on every page.

- **Check the dimensions.** Determine the dimensions of an image file in pixels. You can reduce the dimensions on the Web page by changing the width and height or by cropping the image. Enlarging images generally produces poor results.

Background Colors and Background Images

Many Web pages are displayed with a default white or gray background. Generally, the browser used to display the Web page determines the default background. Recall that you can enhance your Web page by adding a background image or background color.

If you use a background color, be sure to use Web-safe colors. This means the colors will be displayed correctly on the computer screen when someone is viewing your Web page.

Background images add texture and interesting color to a Web page and set the overall appearance of the document. Most browsers support background images. A background image can be a large image, but more frequently it is a smaller image. The image tiles to fill the screen in the Dreamweaver Document window and in the browser window.

To Add a Background Image to the Lewis and Clark National Historical Trail Web Page

In Chapter 1, you added a background image to the index page. Now you use the Page Properties dialog box to add the same image to the Lewis and Clark National Historical Trail Web page and the Montana National Parks and Preserves page. The following steps show how to add a background image to the Lewis and Clark National Historical Trail page.

1 If necessary, click the historical_trail.htm tab to display the page in the Document window.

2 Click Modify on the Application bar and then click Page Properties to open the Page Properties dialog box.

3 Click Appearance (HTML) in the Category column.

4 Click the Browse button to the right of the Background image text box to navigate to the images folder.

5 If necessary, navigate to and then open the images folder.

6 Click parks_bkg and then click the OK button in the Select Image Source dialog box to select the image.

7 Click the OK button in the Page Properties dialog box to apply the background image.

8 Click the Save button on the Standard toolbar to save your work (Figure 2–16 on the next page).

Q&A Is it necessary to add a background image to a Web page?

No, you do not need to add a background image. If you do add a background image to your Web page, however, select an image that does not clash with the text and other content. The background image should not overwhelm the Web page.

Q&A How can I apply a background color instead of a background image?

To apply a background color to a Web page, you can click the Page Properties button in the Property inspector, click the Appearance (HTML) category, and then click the Background icon to display a color picker, which provides a palette of Web-safe colors. Click a color in the palette, and then click the OK button to apply the color to the Web page background.

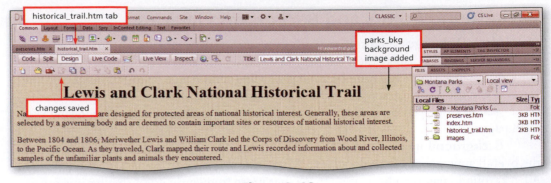

Figure 2–16

To Add a Background Image to the Montana National Parks and Preserves Web Page

The following steps illustrate how to add a background image to the Montana National Parks and Preserves page.

1. Click the preserves.htm tab to display the page in the Document window.

2. Click Modify on the Application bar and then click Page Properties to open the Page Properties dialog box.

3. Click Appearance (HTML) in the Category column.

4. Click the Browse button to the right of the Background image box to navigate to the images folder.

5. Click parks_bkg and then click the OK button in the Select Image Source dialog box.

6. Click the OK button in the Page Properties dialog box to apply the background image.

7. Click the Save button on the Standard toolbar (Figure 2–17).

Figure 2–17

Assets Panel

Besides adding background images, you also can add images such as photos to your Web pages. To enhance your index.htm Web page, you will add two images. One image will be displayed in the upper-left part of the page, and the second image will be displayed to the right of the bulleted list. Dreamweaver has features to assist with placing and enhancing images. The Assets panel provides visual cues for your images, the invisible element feature provides placement control for the images, and the accessibility tools provide information for individuals with disabilities.

Assets are elements, such as images or Flash files, that you use in building a page or a site. The **Assets panel**, which is grouped with the Files panel, helps you manage and organize your Web site's assets (Figure 2–18). This panel contains a list of all the asset types (images, colors, URLs, Flash and Shockwave files, movies, scripts, templates, and library items) within the selected local root folder. The Site option shows the assets in your site. The Favorites list shows only the assets you have selected and added to the list. The Assets panel in Figure 2–18 is resized to show all options.

You can insert most asset types into a document by dragging them into the Document window, using the Insert button at the bottom of the Assets panel, or using the Media command on the Insert menu. Also, you can either insert colors and URLs or apply them to selected text in Design view. Additionally, you can apply URLs to other elements in Design view, such as images. When an image file name is selected, a thumbnail of the image is displayed at the top of the Assets panel. You will use the Assets panel to insert the images into the Montana Parks Web pages.

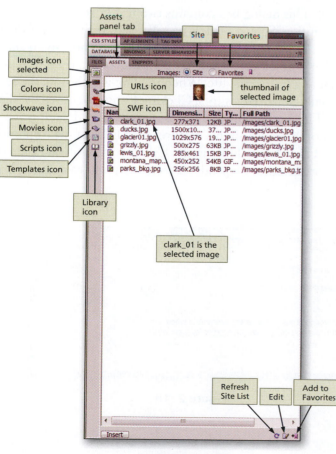

Figure 2–18

Accessibility

When developing a Web page, the Web page developer needs to consider the full spectrum of visitors who might access the site. Dreamweaver provides accessibility tools that allow the Web site developer to create pages to meet the needs of all visitors, including those with disabilities. The four accessibility object tools included in Dreamweaver are form objects, frames, media, and images. This chapter includes accessibility information relative to images. The three other objects are covered in later chapters.

Plan Ahead

Consider accessibility.

Accessibility features let people with visual, auditory, motor, and other disabilities use Web sites easily. Prepare for providing accessible content on your Web pages by using the following guidelines:

- **Set up the workspace for accessible page design.** Make sure that Dreamweaver reminds you to enter accessibility information for objects such as images. Use the Accessibility category in the Preferences dialog box to select the Show Attributes When Inserting option.

- **Enter accessibility attributes.** When you insert an image, Dreamweaver prompts you to enter accessibility attributes such as text equivalents for the image. Electronic screen readers can then recite the text equivalents. Be sure to enter text that describes the image briefly but thoroughly.

When you insert an image, the Image Tag Accessibility Attributes dialog box is displayed (Figure 2–19). This dialog box contains two text boxes — one for Alternate text and one for Long description. Screen readers translate and recite the information you enter in both text boxes. You should limit your Alternate text entry to 50 characters or less so it is easy to remember. For a more detailed description of the image, create and save a text file and then add it as a link to the file. When the link is activated, the screen reader recites the text for visually impaired visitors. Clicking Cancel removes the dialog box and inserts the image. The Accessibility feature is turned on by default when you install Dreamweaver. To turn off the Accessibility feature, click Edit on the Application bar and then click Preferences. Click Accessibility in the Category column and then deselect the check boxes for the four attributes. Appendix B contains a full overview of Dreamweaver's accessibility features.

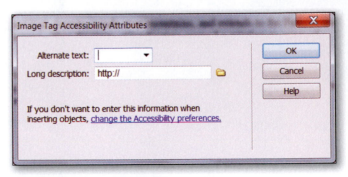

Figure 2–19

Invisible Elements

Dreamweaver's Document window displays basically what you see in a Web browser window. It sometimes is helpful, however, when designing a Web page to see the placement of certain code elements. For example, viewing the Line Break code <br/> provides a visual cue regarding the layout. Dreamweaver lets you control the visibility of 13 different codes, including those for image placement, through the Preferences dialog box.

When you insert and then align an image in a Document window, Dreamweaver can display an **invisible element marker** that shows the location of the inserted image within the HTML code. This visual aid is displayed as a small yellow icon. When you select the icon, you can use it to cut and paste or drag and drop the image. When using invisible elements with images, however, the invisible element marker is not displayed if the image is aligned to the left. Dreamweaver provides the invisible element marker for 12 other elements, including tables, ActiveX objects, plug-ins, and applets. To hide all invisible elements temporarily, select Hide All on the View menu Visual Aids submenu or use CTRL+SHIFT+I.

BTW

Invisible Elements and Precision Layout
Displaying invisible elements can change the layout of a page slightly, so for precision layout, when moving elements by a few pixels might change the entire page, hide the invisible elements.

To Set Invisible Element Preferences and Turn on Visual Aids

The following steps illustrate how to display the invisible element marker for aligned elements such as images and how to turn on invisible elements through the Visual Aids submenu command.

1
• Click Edit on the Application bar and then click Preferences to display the Preferences dialog box (Figure 2–20).

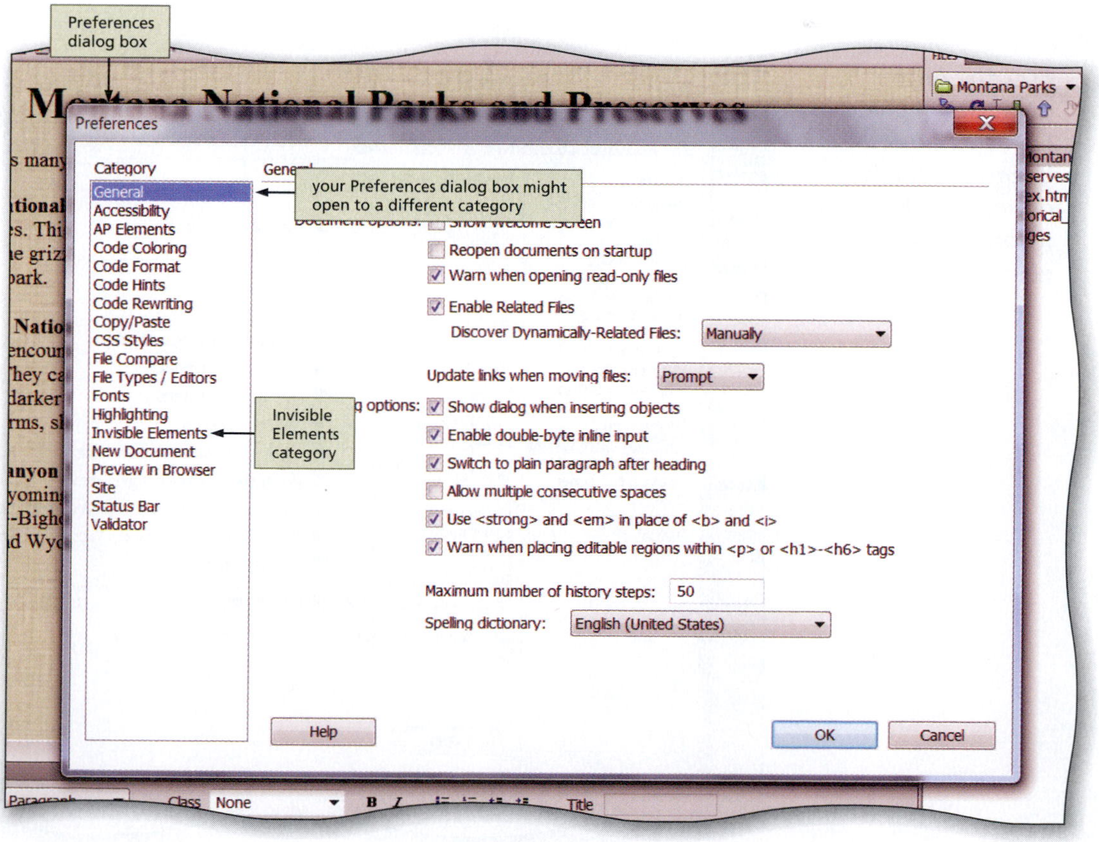

Figure 2–20

2

- Click Invisible Elements in the Category list to display the Invisible Elements options in the Preferences dialog box (Figure 2–21).

Q&A

Is it necessary for me to display the invisible element markers when working with images?

No. You can work with images without displaying the invisible element markers. However, the markers help you locate and work with images on a Web page in Design view.

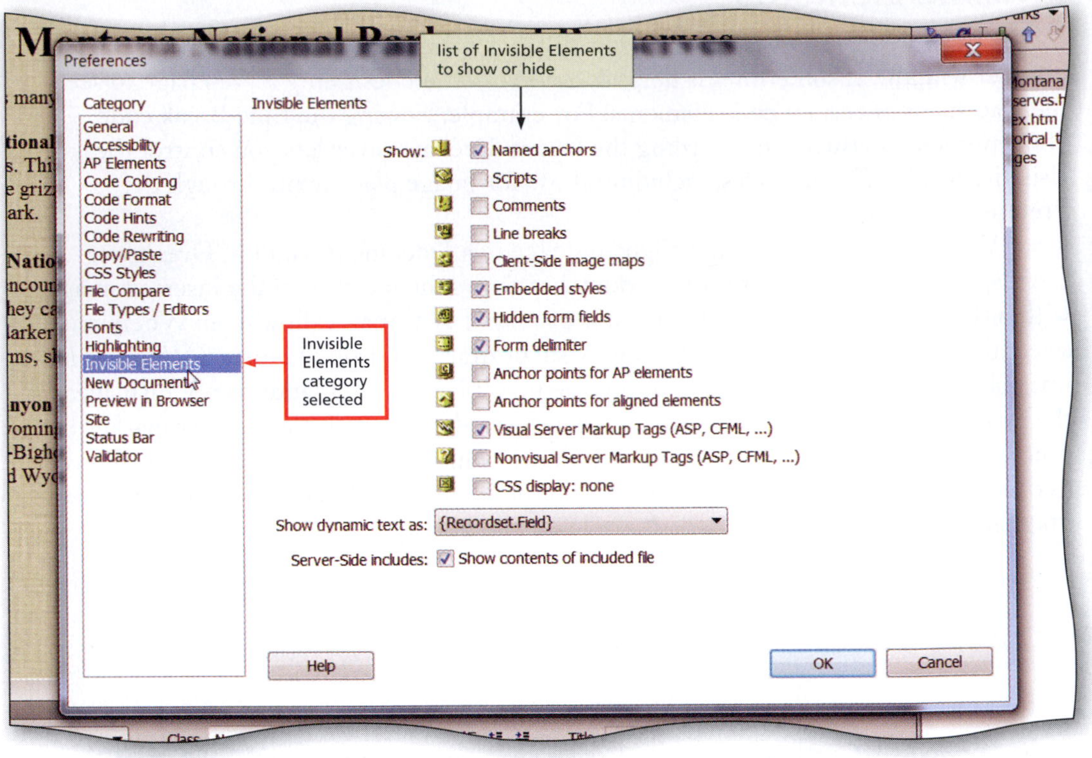

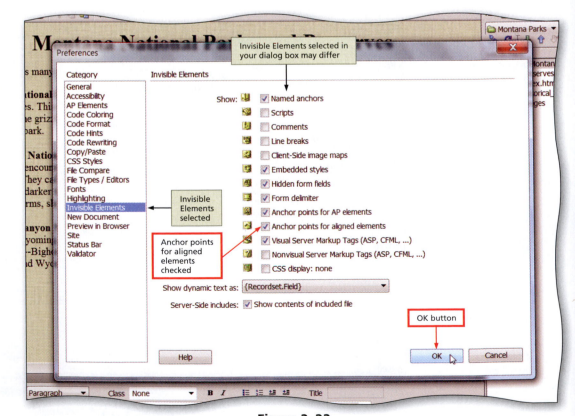

Figure 2–21

3

- Click the Anchor points for aligned elements check box to select this option, which makes it easier to align elements (Figure 2–22).

Figure 2–22

4

- Click the OK button in the Preferences dialog box to confirm the new setting and close the Preferences dialog box.

- Click View on the Application bar, point to Visual Aids, and then point to Invisible Elements on the Visual Aids submenu to highlight the command (Figure 2–23).

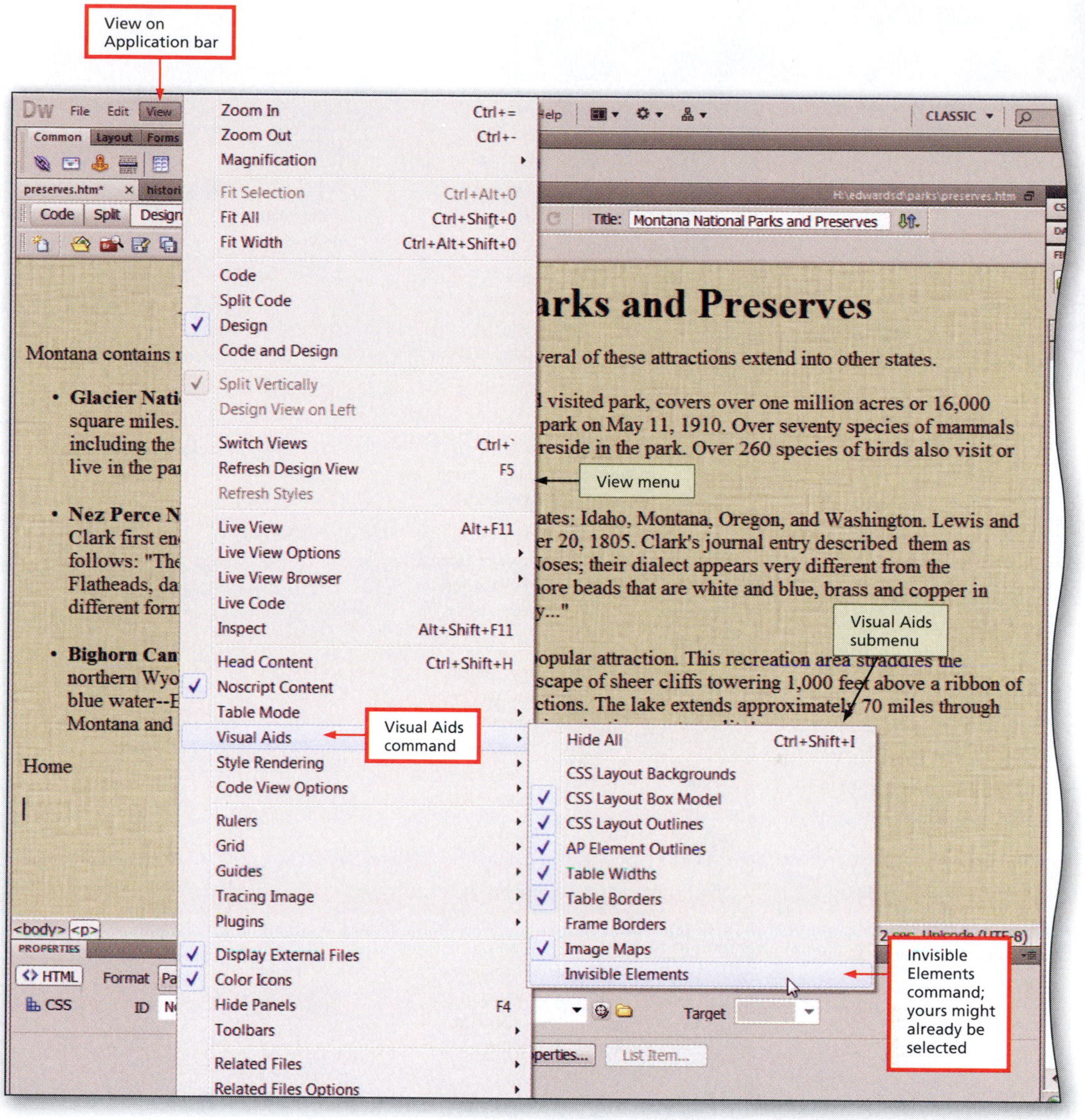

View on Application bar

View menu

Visual Aids submenu

Visual Aids command

Invisible Elements command; yours might already be selected

Figure 2–23

5

• If necessary, click Invisible Elements to add a check mark to the Invisible Elements command (Figure 2–24).

Q&A

What if the Invisible Elements command is already checked?

Do not complete Step 5 — the Invisible Elements command already is selected. Click the Document window to close the View menu.

Q&A

Should I notice a change in the Document window after displaying the visual aids?

No. No visible changes are displayed in the Document window.

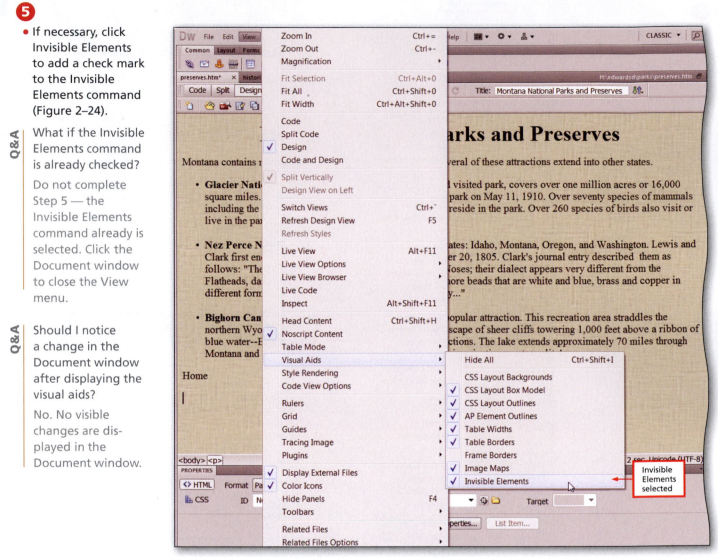

Figure 2–24

Other Ways

1. Click Visual Aids button on Document toolbar, click Invisible Elements

Opening a Web Page

Once you have created and saved a Web page or copied a Web page to a Web site, you often need to retrieve it from a disk. Opening an existing Web page in Dreamweaver is much the same as opening an existing document in most other software applications; that is, you use the File menu and Open command or Open Recent command, or you can click the Open button on the Standard toolbar. If, however, the page is part of a Web site created with Dreamweaver, you also can open the file from the Files panel. After opening the page, you can modify text, images, tables, and any other elements.

To Open a Web Page from a Local Web Site

The following step illustrates how to open a Web page from a local site in the Files panel.

1

- Double-click index.htm in the Files panel to open the index page.

- If the Standard toolbar is not displayed, click View on the Application bar, point to Toolbars, and then click Standard to display the Standard toolbar (Figure 2–25).

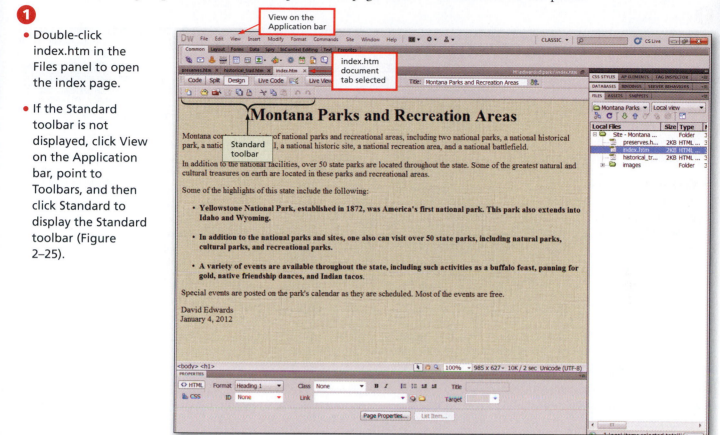

Figure 2–25

Other Ways

1. On File menu, click Open, select file
2. Press CTRL+O, select file

Inserting an Image into a Web Page

Inserting images into your Web page is easy and quick with Dreamweaver — you drag and drop the image from the Files panel or the Assets panel. Image placement, however, can be more complex. When you view the Web page in a browser, the image might be displayed differently than in the Document window. If the images are not displayed correctly, you can select and modify the placement of the images in the Document window by dragging the invisible element marker to move the image.

To Insert an Image into the Index Page

In the following steps, you add an image of a map of Montana to the index.htm Web page.

1

- If necessary, scroll to the top of the page.

- Click the Assets panel tab to display the Assets panel. Verify that the Images icon is selected.

- Click montana_map .gif in the Assets panel to select the image file (Figure 2–26).

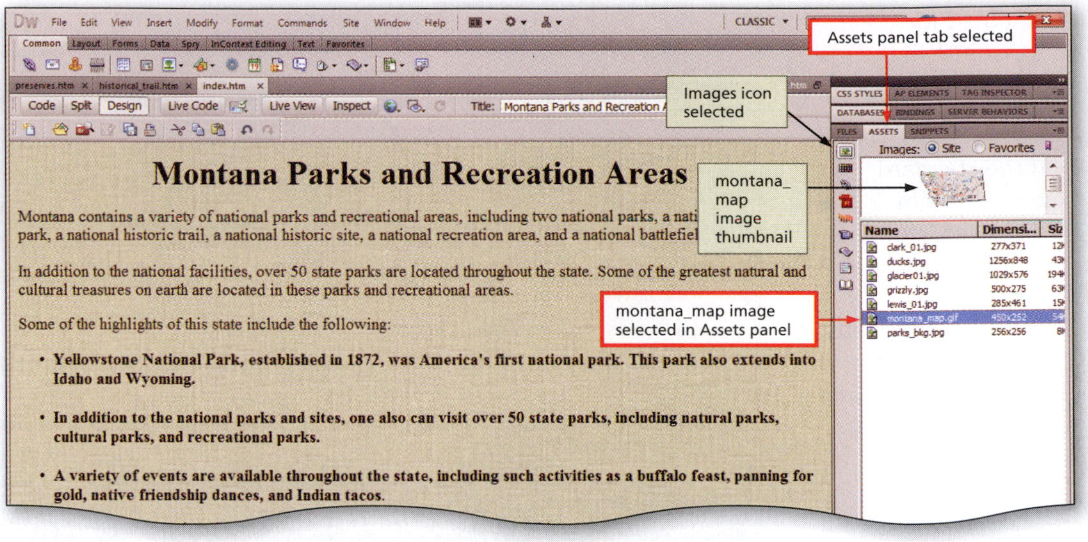

Q&A

How do I resize the Assets panel?

You resize panels by pointing to the panel's vertical bar until it changes to a two-headed arrow, and then you hold down the mouse button and drag.

Figure 2–26

Q&A

How do I add an asset to the Favorites list?

To add an asset to the Favorites list, select the item in the Site list and then click the Add to Favorites button. Remove an item from the list by selecting the Favorites option button, selecting the item, and then clicking the Remove from Favorites button.

2

- Drag montana_map from the Assets panel to the left of the first bulleted line. The Image Tag Accessibility Attributes dialog box is displayed (Figure 2–27).

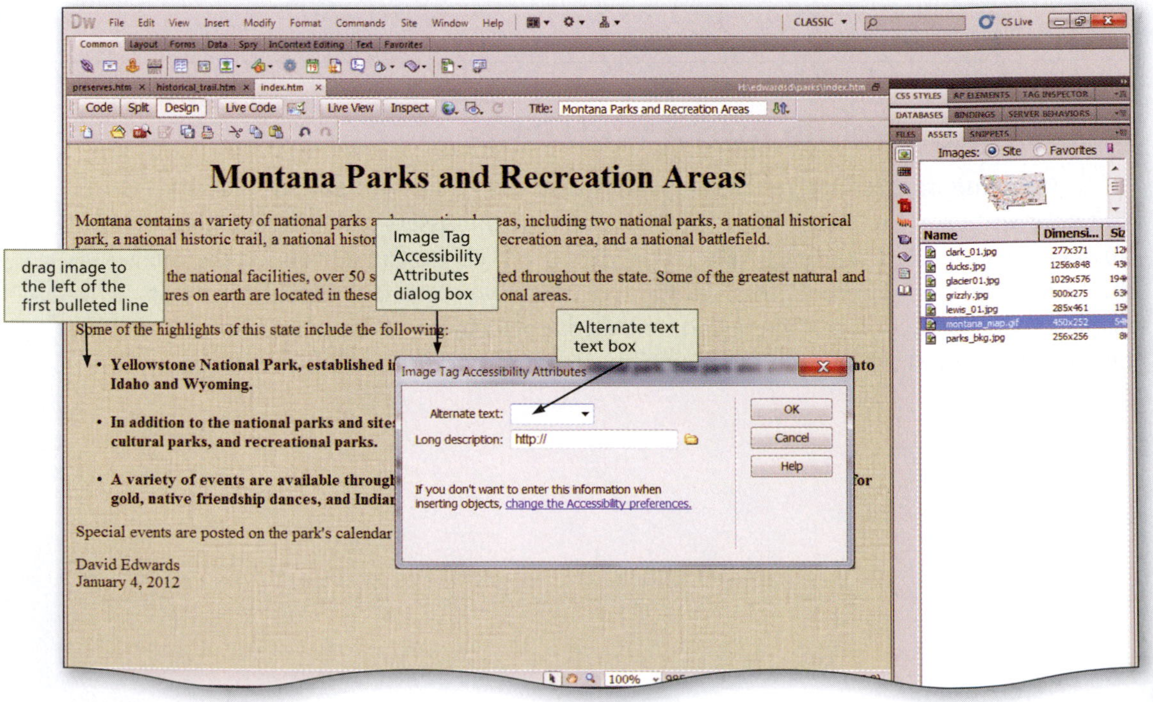

Figure 2–27

3

- Type **Montana map** in the Alternate text text box to provide alternate text for the montana_map image (Figure 2–28).

Q&A

Am I required to enter text in the Alternate text or Long description text box?

No. It is not required that you enter text in either text box. For images in this chapter and other chapters, however, instructions are included to add alternate text.

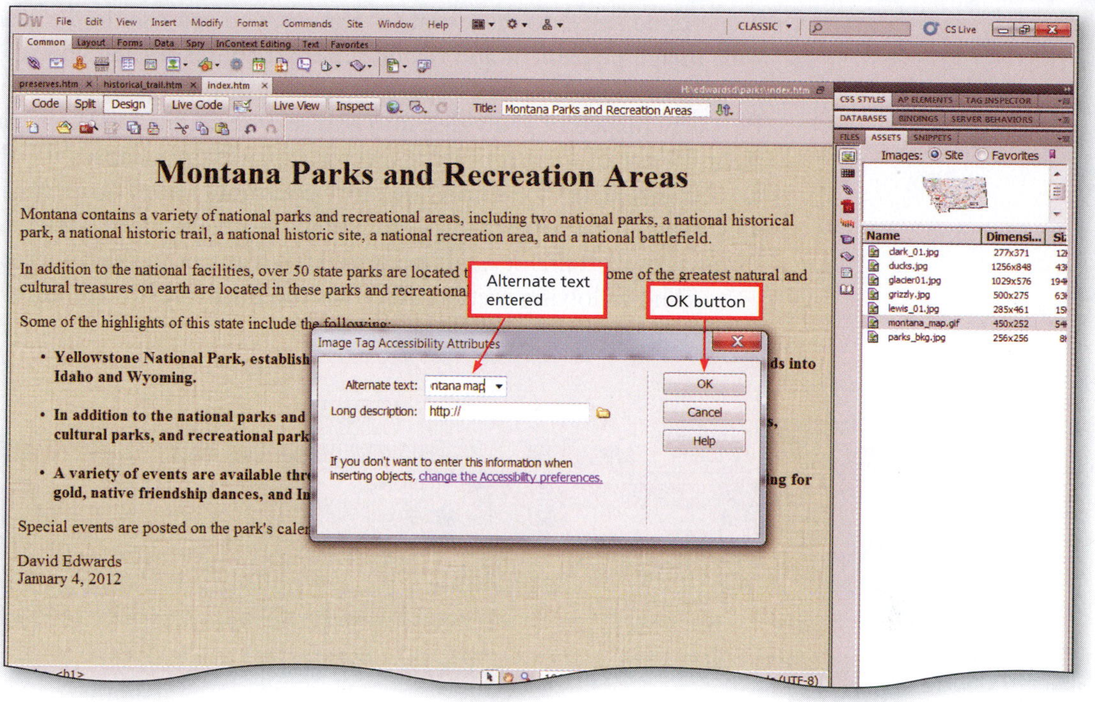

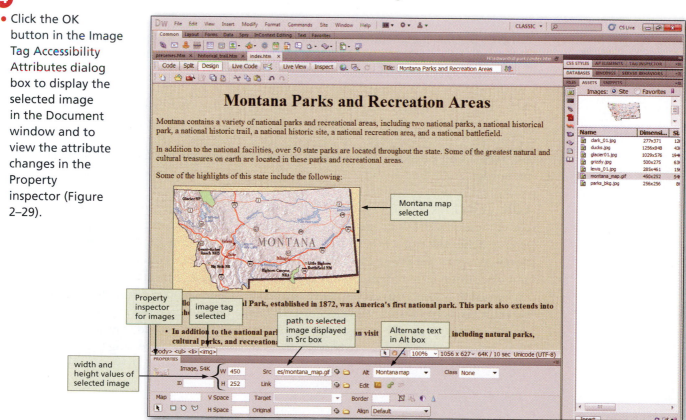

Figure 2–28

4

- Click the OK button in the Image Tag Accessibility Attributes dialog box to display the selected image in the Document window and to view the attribute changes in the Property inspector (Figure 2–29).

Figure 2–29

Other Ways

1. Drag image from Files panel

2. On Insert menu, click Image, select file

3. In Assets panel, right-click image file, click Insert

4. Press CTRL+ALT+I, select file

Property Inspector Image Tools

In addition to the visual aid feature, you can use the Property inspector to help with image placement and to add other attributes. When you select an image within the Document window, the Property inspector displays properties specific to that image. The Property inspector is divided into two sections. Clicking the expander arrow in the lower-right corner of the Property inspector expands or collapses the Property inspector. When it is collapsed, it shows only the more commonly used properties for the selected element. The expanded Property inspector shows more advanced options. The Property inspector for images contains several image-related features in the upper and lower sections.

The following section describes the image-related features of the Property inspector (Figure 2–30).

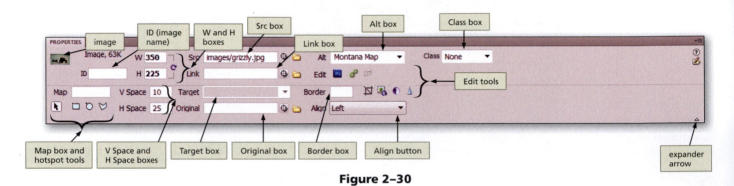

Figure 2–30

Align   Set the alignment of an image in relation to other elements in the same paragraph, table, or line with the **Align button**. This property option is discussed in more detail later in this chapter.

Alt   Use Alt to specify alternate text for the image. For visually impaired users who use speech synthesizers with text-only browsers, the text is spoken aloud.

Border   The **Border** is the width, in pixels, of the image's border. The default is no border.

Edit   The **Edit** section contains the following editing option tools: (a) **Edit** opens the computer's default image editor, such as Adobe Fireworks or Photoshop; the Edit icon matches the icon of the default image editor on your computer; (b) **Edit Image Settings** opens the Image Preview dialog box, which contains options to remove colors, add smoothing to the edges, modify colors, and other image formatting choices; (c) update from original; (d) crop (reduce the area of the image); (e) resample (add or subtract pixels from a resized JPEG or GIF image file to match the appearance of the original image as closely as possible); (f) modify the brightness and contrast of pixels in an image; and (g) sharpen (adjust the focus of an image by increasing the contrast of edges found within the image).

ID   Specifies the image name that is contained in the source code.

Link   The **Link** box allows you to make the selected image a hyperlink to a specified URL or Web page. To create a relative link, you can click the Point to File or Browse for File icons to the right of the Link box to browse to a page in your Web site, or you can drag a file from the Files panel into the Link box. For an external link, you can type the URL directly into the Link box or use copy and paste.

Map and Hotspot Tools   Use the **Map** box and the **Hotspot tools** to label and create an image map.

Original   The path to an image file stored outside of the current Web site.

Reset Size   If you change an image size, the **Reset Size** tool is displayed next to the W and H text boxes after an image size has been changed. Use this tool to reset the W and H values to the original size of the image.

Src   The path to an image file stored in the current Web site.

Target   Use **Target** to specify the frame or window in which the linked page should load. This option is not available when the image is linked to another file.

V Space and H Space   Use V Space and H Space to add space, in pixels, along the sides of the image. **V Space** adds space along the top and bottom of an image. **H Space** adds space along the left and right of an image.

W and H   The W and H boxes indicate the width and height of the image, in pixels. Dreamweaver automatically displays the dimensions when an image is inserted into a page. You can specify the image size in the following units: pc (picas), pt (points), in (inches), mm (millimeters), cm (centimeters), and combinations, such as 2in+5mm. Dreamweaver converts the values to pixels in the source code.

Aligning the Image and Adjusting the Image Size

After you insert the image into the Web page and then select it, the Property inspector displays features specific to the image. As discussed earlier, alignment is one of these features. **Alignment** determines where on the page the image is displayed and if and how text wraps around the image.

You also can adjust the image size easily through the W and H text boxes in the Property inspector or by dragging the handles surrounding the image. Additionally, when you insert an image into a Web page that contains text, by default, the text around the image aligns to the right and bottom of the image. The image alignment options on the Align button pop-up menu in the Property inspector let you set the alignment for the image in relation to other page content. Dreamweaver provides 10 alignment options for images. Table 2–3 describes these image alignment options.

Table 2–3 Image Alignment Options	
Alignment Option	**Description**
Default	Aligns the image with the baseline of the text in most browser default settings
Baseline	Aligns the image with the baseline of the text regardless of the browser setting
Top	Aligns the image with the top of the item; an item can be text or another object
Middle	Aligns the image with the baseline of the text or object at the vertical middle of the image
Bottom	Aligns the image with the baseline of the text or the bottom of another image regardless of the browser setting
TextTop	Aligns the image with the top of the tallest character in a line of text
Absolute Middle	Aligns the image with the middle of the current line of text
Absolute Bottom	Aligns the image with the bottom of the current line of text or another object
Left	Aligns the image at the left margin
Right	Aligns the image at the right margin

To Align an Image

The following steps show how to align the Montana map image to the right and wrap text to the left of the image. To have a better overview of how the page will be displayed in a browser, you start by collapsing the panel groups.

1

- Click the panel groups Collapse to Icons arrow to collapse the panel groups.

- If necessary, click the montana_map image in the Document window to select the image.

- Click the Align button in the Property inspector to display the alignment options.

- Point to Right on the pop-up menu to highlight the Right command (Figure 2–31).

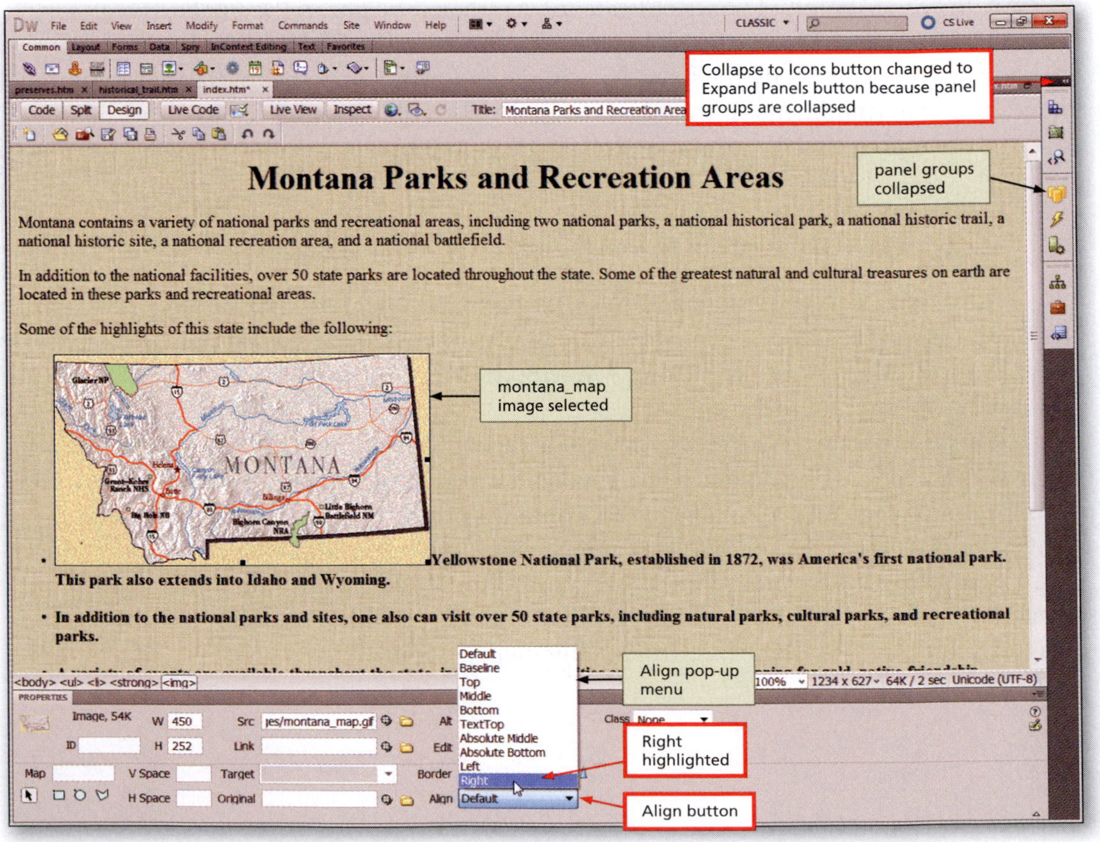

Q&A

What are the most widely used Align options?

The most widely used options are Left and Right.

Figure 2–31

2

- Click Right to move the selected image to the right side of the Document window and to display the element marker (Figure 2–32).

Q&A

What should I do if the element marker is not displayed?

First, open the Preferences dialog box, click the Invisible Elements category, and then make sure the Anchor points for aligned elements box is checked. Next, click View on the Application bar, point to Visual Aids, and make sure the Invisible Elements command is checked.

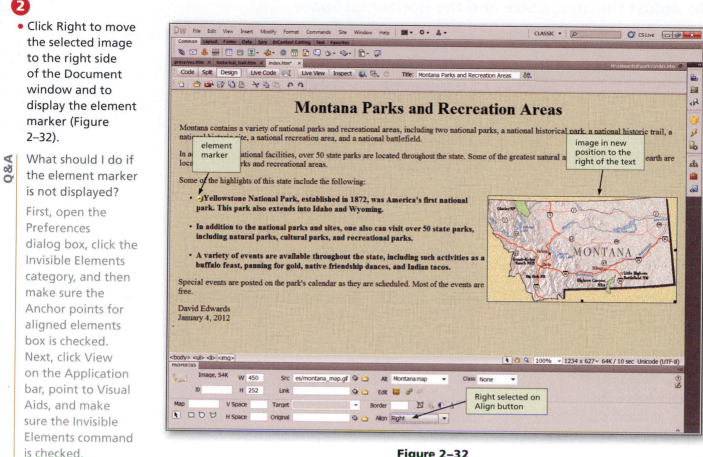

Figure 2–32

Adjusting Space Around Images

When aligning an image, by default, only about three pixels of space are inserted between the image and adjacent text. You can adjust the amount of vertical and horizontal space between the image and text by using the V Space and H Space settings in the Property inspector. The V Space setting controls the vertical space above and below an image. The H Space setting controls the horizontal space to the left and right side of the image.

To Adjust the Image Size and the Horizontal Space

The following steps show how to resize an image and add horizontal space around an image.

1

• If necessary, click to select the image.

• Double-click the W text box in the Property inspector to select the current width value, and then type **400** to adjust the width of the image.

• Press the TAB key and type **245** in the H text box to adjust the height of the image.

• Press the ENTER key.

• Click the H Space text box and type **25** to adjust the horizontal space between the image and the text.

• Press the TAB key to apply the horizontal space setting to the image (Figure 2–33).

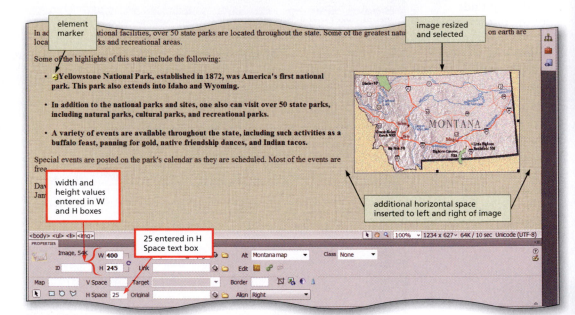

Figure 2–33

2

• Click outside the image to remove the selection box and to view the added space and the reduced size (Figure 2–34).

Q&A Why do I need to adjust the width and height of the image?

In many instances, adjusting the image size creates a better balance on the page.

Q&A How do the V Space and H Space settings change the placement of the image?

Figure 2–34

V Space adds space along the top and bottom of an image. H Space adds space along the left and right of an image.

Other Ways

1. Select image, drag sizing handle

To Insert the Second Image

To enhance your index Web page further, you will add a second image. This image will appear on the left side of the page, below the first paragraph. The following steps show how to insert a second image on the Montana Parks and Recreation Areas page.

1 If necessary, scroll up and position the insertion point to the left of the second paragraph, which begins "In addition to the national facilities."

2 Expand the panel groups, and then click the Assets tab, if necessary, to display the images in the Assets panel (Figure 2–35).

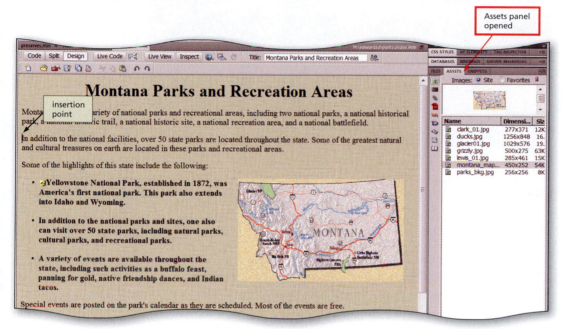

Figure 2–35

3 Drag the glacier01.jpg image from the Assets panel to the insertion point to add the image to the Web page and to display the Image Tag Accessibility Attributes dialog box.

4 Type **Montana glacier** in the Alternate text text box, and then click the OK button to insert the glacier01 image into the Web page (Figure 2–36 on the next page).

Q&A How does the Alternate text make my Web page more accessible?

For visually impaired users who use speech synthesizers with text-only browsers, the Alternate text is spoken aloud.

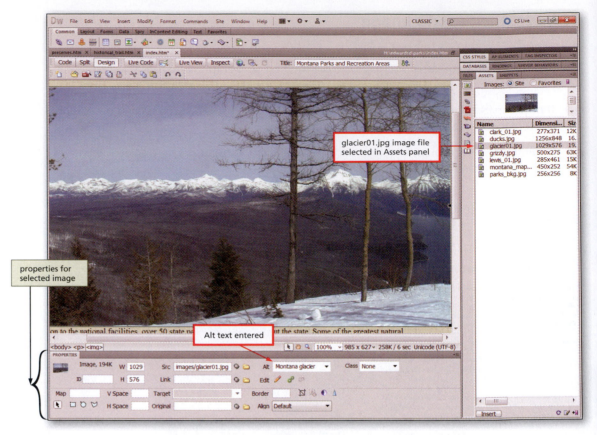

glacier01.jpg image file
selected in Assets panel

properties for
selected image

Alt text entered

Figure 2–36

5 In the Property inspector, click the Align button, and then click Left in the Align pop-up menu to move the image to the left side of the window (Figure 2–37).

Q&A

How can I tell that the image is now left-aligned?

It is difficult to see the alignment of the figure because it is so large. The alignment will be clear when you resize the image in the next step.

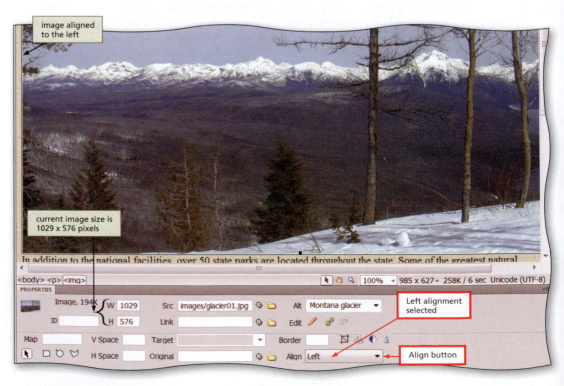

image aligned
to the left

current image size is
1029 x 576 pixels

Left alignment
selected

Align button

Figure 2–37

6 In the Property inspector, change the W value to 300 and the H value to 240.

7 Click the H Space box, type **2 0** as the horizontal space, and then press the ENTER key to apply the setting changes to the glacier01 image (Figure 2-38).

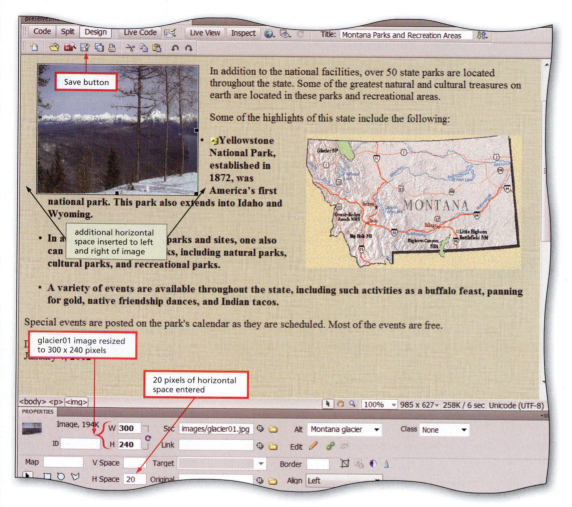

Figure 2–38

8 Click the Save button on the Standard toolbar to save the index.htm page.

9 Press the F12 key to view the Web page in your browser (Figure 2–39).

10 Close the browser to return to Dreamweaver.

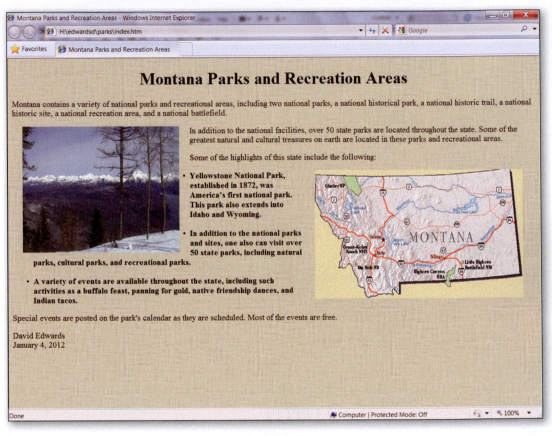

Figure 2–39

To Insert and Align an Image in the Montana National Parks and Preserves Web Page

The next page in your Web site is the Montana National Parks and Preserves page. The following steps show how to further develop this Web page by adding an image to it.

1 Click the preserves.htm document tab to display the page in the Document window.

2 Position the insertion point to the left of the first sentence after the heading, and then drag the ducks.jpg image file from the Assets panel to the insertion point.

3 Type `Montana ducks` in the Alternate text text box and then click the OK button to display the image.

4 Enter `430` in the W box to change the width, enter `360` in the H box to change the height, and then press the ENTER key to display the resized image in the Document window.

5 Enter `15` in the V Space box and `20` in the H Space box to add space around the ducks image.

6 Click the Align button in the Property inspector, and then click Right to align the image to the right side of the window.

7 If necessary, scroll up to display the entire ducks image (Figure 2–40).

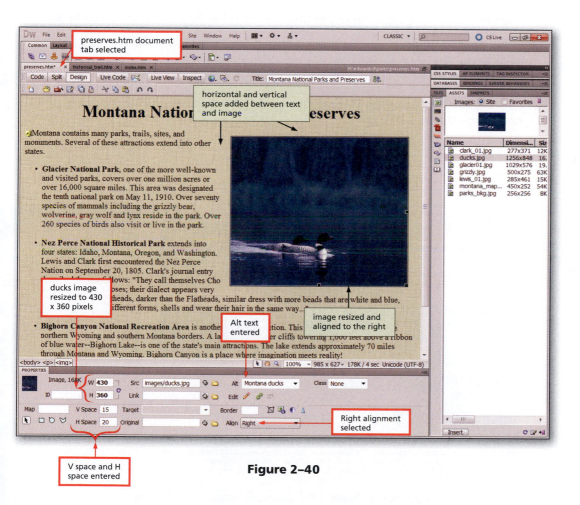

Figure 2–40

To Insert and Align a Second Image in the Montana National Parks and Preserves Web Page

The following steps show how to add a second image to the Montana National Parks and Preserves Web page.

① Drag the grizzly.jpg image from the Assets panel to the end of the second paragraph (the "Glacier National Park" bullet).

② Type **Montana Grizzly** in the Alternate text text box and then click the OK button to enter Alt text for this image.

③ Click the Align button in the Property inspector, and then click Left to align the image to the left.

④ Change the width value in the W box to 300 and the height value in the H box to 300.

⑤ Enter 15 as the vertical space value in the V Space box, enter 20 as the horizontal space value in the H Space box, and then press the ENTER key to add the space around the grizzly image.

⑥ Click the Save button on the Standard toolbar to save the preserves.htm page with the new image (Figure 2–41).

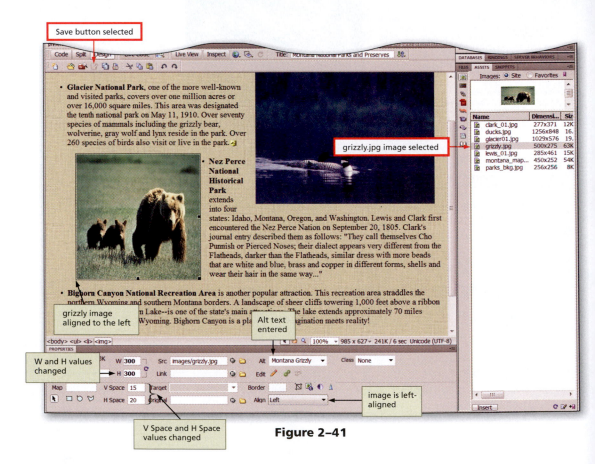

Figure 2–41

7 Press the F12 key to display the Montana National Parks and Preserves page in the browser (Figure 2–42).

8 Close the browser to return to Dreamweaver.

Figure 2–42

To Insert and Align an Image in the Lewis and Clark National Historical Trail Web Page

The third page in your Web site is the Lewis and Clark National Historical Trail page. The following steps illustrate how to add the first of two images to the Lewis and Clark National Historical Trail Web page.

1 Click the historical_trail.htm Web page tab to display that page in the Document window.

2 Click the clark_01.jpg file in the Assets panel, and then position the insertion point to the left of the first sentence (Figure 2–43).

Figure 2–43

3 Drag the clark_01.jpg file from the Assets panel to the insertion point to display the Image Tag Accessibility Attributes dialog box.

4 Type `William Clark` in the Alternate text text box and then click the OK button to enter Alt text for this image and to insert the image in the page.

5 Click the Align button in the Property inspector and then click Left on the Align pop-up menu to align the image to the left side of the page (Figure 2–44).

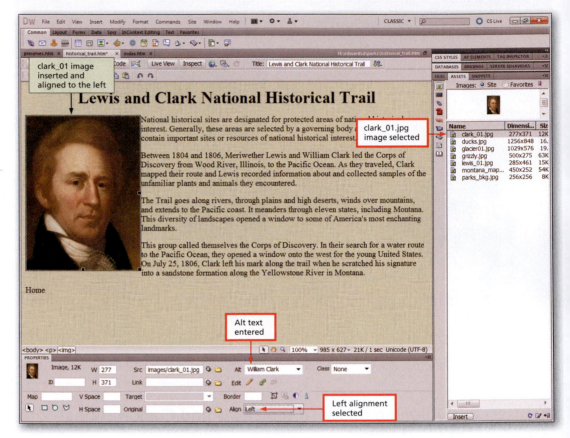

Figure 2–44

6 In Property inspector, click the H Space box, type `10` as the horizontal space, and then press the ENTER key to add the space (Figure 2–45).

Q&A When I add horizontal and vertical space, what are the measurement units?

The measurement units are in pixels, so when you enter 10 in the H Space box, you are specifying 10 pixels of horizontal space around the image.

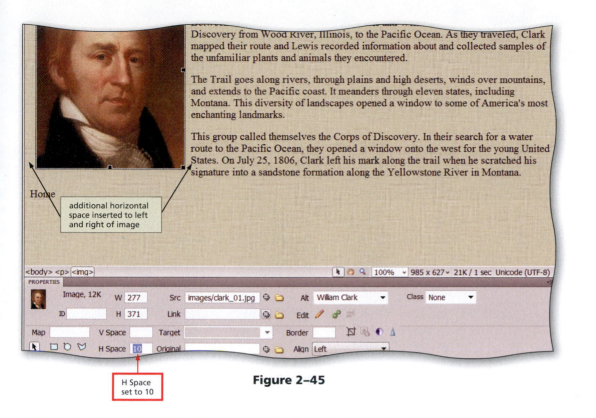

Figure 2–45

To Insert and Align a Second Image in the Lewis and Clark National Historical Trail Web Page

The following steps illustrate how to add the second of two images to the Lewis and Clark National Historical Trail Web page.

1 Position the insertion point to the right of the first paragraph to prepare for adding the second image to the page (Figure 2–46).

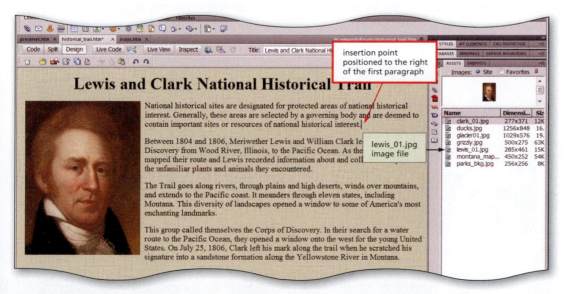

Figure 2–46

2 Drag the lewis01.jpg image from the Assets panel to the insertion point to display the Image Tag Accessibility Attributes dialog box.

3 Type **Meriwether Lewis** in the Alternate text box and then press the ENTER key to enter Alt text for this image and to insert the image in the page. If necessary, scroll down to view the image (Figure 2–47).

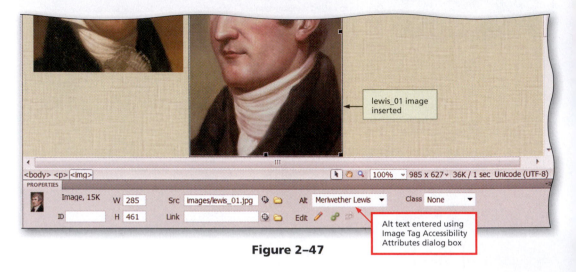

Figure 2–47

4 In the Property inspector, click the Align button and then click Right on the Align pop-up menu to align this image to the right side of the page.

5 Change the width value in the W box to **265** and change the height value in the H box to **435**.

6 In the V Space box, enter **10** as the vertical space, and in the H Space box, enter **10** as the horizontal space.

7 Press the ENTER key to resize and position the image, and then click anywhere on the page to deselect the image.

8 Click the Save button on the Standard toolbar to save the changes to the historical_trail.htm page (Figure 2–48).

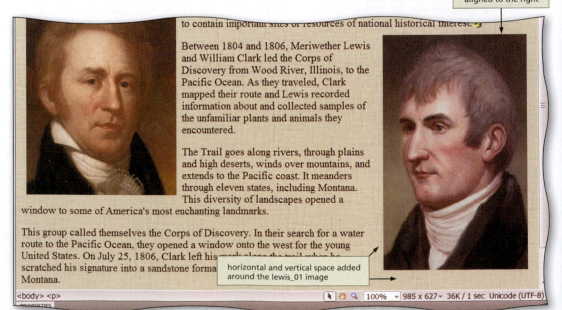

Figure 2–48

9 Press the F12 key to view the Lewis and Clark National Historical Trail page in your browser (Figure 2–49).

10 Close the browser.

Figure 2–49

Image Editing Tools

Dreamweaver provides several basic image editing tools in the Property inspector to modify and enhance an image.

- Use an external image editor: Adobe Photoshop is the default image editor if it is installed on your computer, but you can specify which external editor should start for a specified file type. To select an external editor, click Edit on the Application bar and display the Preferences dialog box. Select File Types/Editors from the Category list to display the Preferences File Types/Editors dialog box. Select the image extension and then browse for the External Code Editor executable file.

- Crop an image: **Cropping** lets you edit an image by reducing the area of the image and allows you to eliminate unwanted portions of the image. When you crop an image and then save the page, the source image file is changed on the disk. Prior to saving, make a backup copy of the image file in case you need to revert to the original image.

- Resample an image: **Resampling** adds or subtracts pixels to or from a resized JPEG or GIF image file to match the appearance of the original image as closely as possible. Resampling an image also reduces an image's file size, resulting in improved download performance. When you resize an image in Dreamweaver, you can resample it to accommodate its new dimensions. To resample a resized image, first resize the image and then click the Resample button in the Property inspector.

BTW

Resizing Images Visually
Besides using the W and H boxes in the Property inspector, you can click an image and then drag a selection handle to visually resize the image. Whether you resize by dragging or by using the Property inspector, you are not changing the size of the original image file, only the appearance of the image on the Web page.

- Adjust brightness and contrast: The **Brightness and Contrast** tool modifies the contrast or brightness of the pixels in an image. Recall that a pixel is the smallest point in a graphical image. Brightness makes the pixels in the image lighter or darker overall, while Contrast either emphasizes or de-emphasizes the difference between lighter and darker regions. This affects the highlights, shadows, and midtones of an image.

- Sharpen an image: **Sharpening** adjusts the focus of an image by increasing the contrast of edges found within the image.

To Crop and Modify the Brightness/Contrast of an Image

The ducks image in the Montana National Parks and Preserves page needs some modification. Cropping the image and emphasizing a better view of the ducks in the image will enhance the page. The following steps show how to crop the image, and then modify the brightness and contrast.

1

- Click the preserves .htm document tab to open the preserves.htm page.

- Select the ducks image to prepare for cropping it.

- Collapse the panel groups so you have more room to work.

- Click the Crop tool in the Property inspector to apply the bounding box (Figure 2–50).

Q&A What should I do if a Dreamweaver dialog box is displayed warning that cropping permanently alters the image?

Click the 'Don't show me this message again' check box, and then click the OK button.

Figure 2–50

Q&A When is cropping an image effective?

Cropping can be very effective for improving the appearance of a photo by highlighting the main point of interest in an image.

2

- Click the crop handle in the lower-right corner of the ducks image and adjust the handles until the bounding box surrounds the area of the image similar to that shown in Figure 2–51. The W value should be approximately 360 and the H value approximately 305.

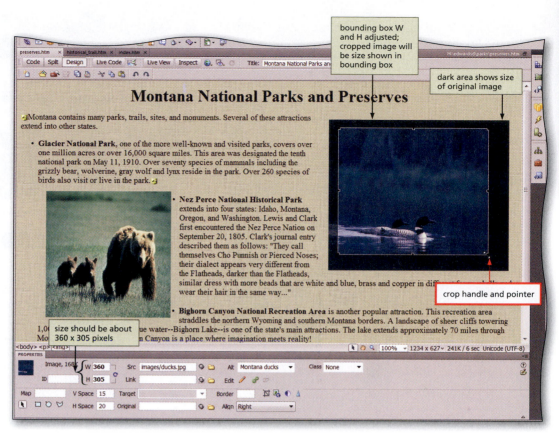

Figure 2–51

3

- Double-click inside the bounding box to apply the cropping by resizing the image to match the size of the bounding box.

- If necessary, click the ducks image to select it and to verify that the size after cropping is about 360 x 305 pixels (Figure 2–52).

Q&A

How can I make changes after I apply the cropping?

If you need to make changes, click the Undo button on the Standard toolbar and repeat Steps 1 – 3.

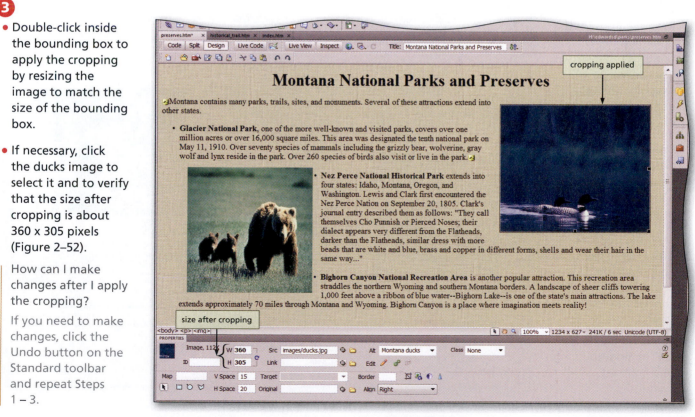

Figure 2–52

4

• Click the Brightness and Contrast tool in the Property inspector to display the Brightness/ Contrast dialog box (Figure 2–53).

Q&A

What should I do if a Dreamweaver dialog box is displayed warning that adjusting the brightness and contrast permanently alters the image?

Click the 'Don't show me this message again' check box, and then click the OK button.

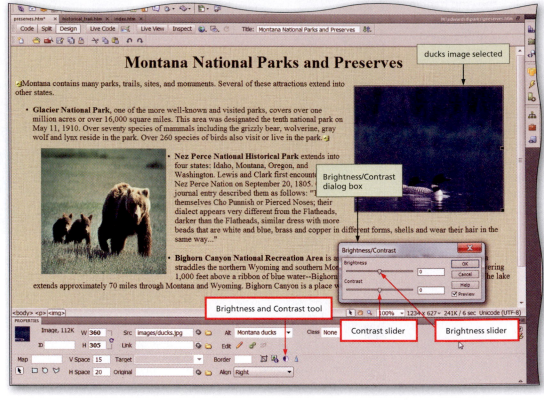

Figure 2–53

5

🔍 **Experiment**

• Drag the Brightness slider and the Contrast slider so you can see how changing the value of each affects the ducks image.

• Drag the Brightness slider to the left and adjust the setting to −10 to change the brightness level.

• Drag the Contrast slider to the right and adjust the setting to 20 to change the contrast level (Figure 2–54).

Q&A

What are the ranges for the Brightness and Contrast settings?

The values for the Brightness and Contrast settings range from −100 to 100.

Figure 2–54

6

- Click the OK button to accept the Brightness and Contrast settings.

- Click the Save button on the Standard toolbar to save the changes to the preserves.htm page.

- Press the F12 key to view the preserves .htm page in your browser (Figure 2–55).

7

- Close the browser to return to the Dreamweaver window.

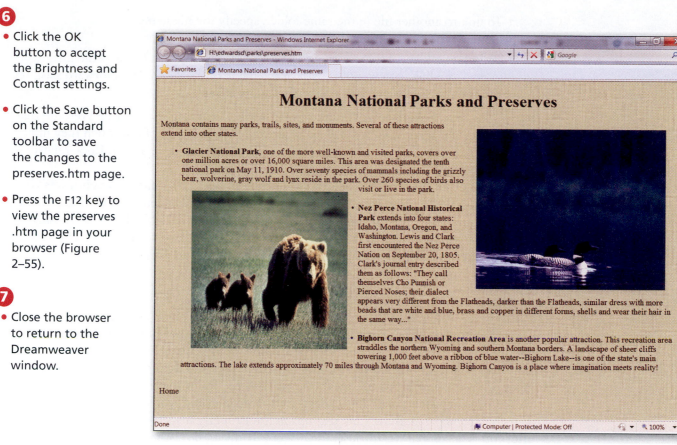

Figure 2–55

Other Ways

1. On Modify menu, point to Image, click Crop

2. On Modify menu, point to Image, click Brightness/Contrast

Understanding Different Types of Links

To connect the pages within the Web site, you create links. Links are the distinguishing feature of the World Wide Web. A link, also referred to as a hyperlink, is the path to another document, to another part of the same document, or to other media such as an image or a movie. Most links are displayed as colored and/or underlined text, although you also can link from an image or other object. Clicking a link accesses the corresponding document, other media, or another place within the same document. If you place the mouse pointer over the link in the browser, the Web address of the link, or path, usually appears at the bottom of the window, on the status bar.

Three types of link paths are available: absolute, relative, and root-relative. An **absolute link** provides the complete URL of the document. This type of link also is referred to as an **external link**. Absolute links generally contain a protocol (such as http://) and primarily are used to link to documents on other servers.

You use **relative links** for local links. This type of link also is referred to as a **document-relative link**, or an **internal link**. If the linked documents are in the same folder, such as those in your parks folder, this is the best type of link to use. You also can use a relative link to link to a document in another folder, such as the images folder. All the files you see in the Files panel in the Local Files list are internal files and are referenced as relative links. You link to a document in another folder on your Web site by specifying the path through the folder hierarchy from the current document to the linked document. Consider the following examples.

- To link to another file in the same folder, specify the file name. Example: preserves.htm.
- To link to a file in a subfolder of the current Web site folder (such as the images folder), the link path would consist of the name of the subfolder, a forward slash (/), and then the file name. Example: images/ducks.jpg.

You use the **root-relative link** primarily when working with a large Web site that requires several servers. Web developers generally use this type of link when they must move HTML files from one folder or server to another folder or server. Root-relative links are beyond the scope of this book.

Two other types of links are named anchor and e-mail. A **named anchor** lets you link to a specific location within a document. To create a named anchor, click the Named Anchor command on the Insert menu. An **e-mail link** creates a blank e-mail message containing the recipient's address. Another type of link is a **null**, or **script**, **link**. This type of link provides for attaching behaviors to an object or executes JavaScript code.

Relative Links

Dreamweaver offers a variety of ways to create a relative link. Three common methods are point to file, drag-and-drop, and browse for file. The point to file and drag-and-drop methods require that the Property inspector and the Files or Assets panels be open. To use the **point to file method**, you drag the Point to File icon to the file or image in the Files or Assets panel. In the **drag-and-drop method**, you drag the file from the Files or Assets panel to the Link text box in the Property inspector. The **browse for file method** is accomplished through the Select File dialog box, which is accessed through the Make Link command on the Modify menu. A fourth method is to use the context menu. To do this, you select the text for the link, right-click to display the context menu, and then select the Make Link command.

Plan Ahead

Identify links.
Before you use links to create connections from one document to another on your Web site or within a document, keep the following guidelines in mind:

- **Prepare for links**. Some Web designers create links first, before creating the associated page. Others prefer to create all the files and pages first, and then create links. Choose a method that suits your work style, but be sure to test all your links before publishing your Web site.

- **Link to text or images**. You can select any text or image on a page to create a link. When you do, visitors to your Web site can click the text or image to open another document or move to another place on the page.

- **Know the path or address**. To create relative links, the files need to be stored in the same root folder or a subfolder in the root folder. To create absolute links, you need to know the URL to the Web page. To create e-mail links, you need to know the e-mail address.

- **Test the links**. Test all the links on a Web page when you preview the page in a browser. Fix any broken links before publishing the page.

To Add Text for Relative Links

To create relative links from the index page, you add text to the index page and use the text to create the links to the other two Web pages in your Web site. You will center the text directly below the Montana National Parks and Recreation Areas heading. The following steps show how to add the text for the links.

1

• Expand the panel groups, and then click the Files tab to display the Files panel.

• Click the index.htm tab in the Document window. If necessary, scroll to the top of the page and then position the insertion point at the end of the title, Montana National Parks and Recreation Areas.

• Press the ENTER key to move the insertion point to the next line. If necessary, click the Align command on the Format menu and select Center to center the insertion point (Figure 2–56).

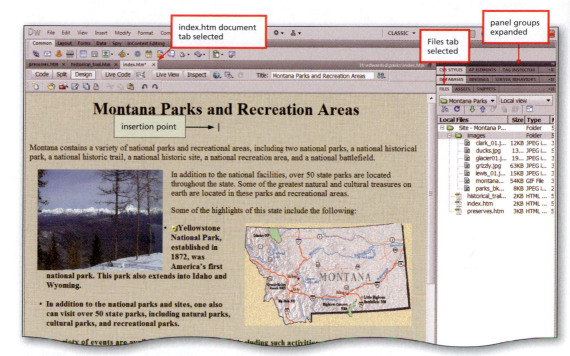

Figure 2–56

2

• Type **Montana National Preserves** and then press the SPACEBAR to enter the text for the first link.

• Hold down the SHIFT key and then press the vertical line key (|) to insert a vertical line.

• Press the SPACEBAR and then type **National Historical Trail** to add the text for the second link (Figure 2–57).

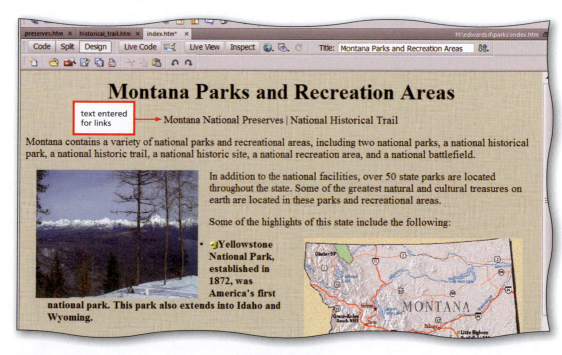

Figure 2–57

To Create a Relative Link Using Point to File

You will use the Montana National Preserves text to create a link to the preserves.htm page and the National Historical Trail text to create a link to the historical_trail.htm page. The following steps illustrate how to use the point to file method to create a relative link from the Montana Parks home page to the Montana National Parks and Preserves Web page.

- Drag to select the text Montana National Preserves (Figure 2–58).

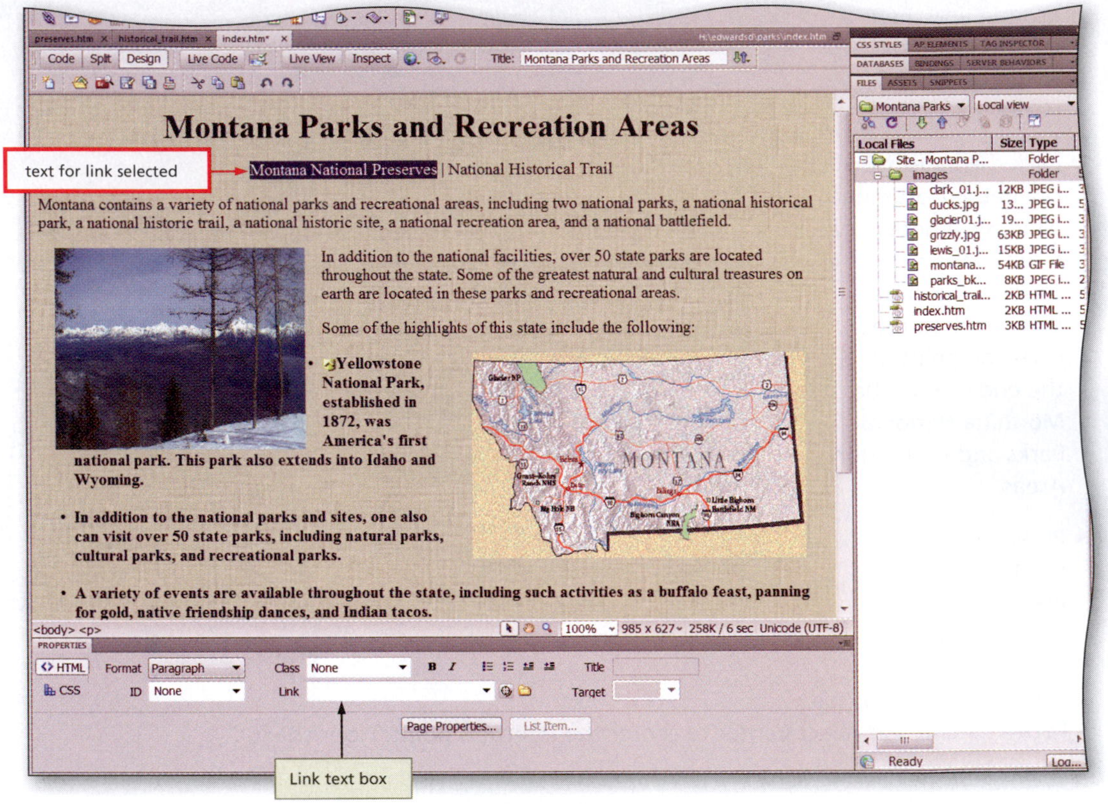

Figure 2–58

2

• Click the Point to File tool next to the Link text box in the Property inspector, and then drag the pointer to the preserves.htm file in the Files panel (Figure 2-59).

3

• When the pointer is over the preserves.htm file in the Files panel, release the mouse button to display the linked text in the Property inspector Link box.

Q&A

Why am I inserting a relative link?

You use relative links when the linked documents are in the same folder, such as those in your parks folder.

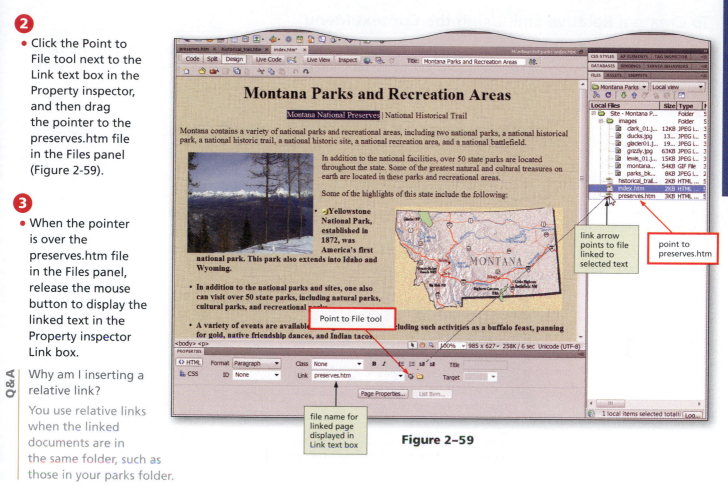

Figure 2–59

Other Ways

1. Hold down SHIFT key, drag to file

To Create a Relative Link Using the Context Menu

The context menu is a second way to create a link. Using this method, you select the file name in the Select File dialog box. The following steps illustrate how to use the context menu to create a link to the Lewis and Clark National Historical Trail page.

1

- Drag to select the text National Historical Trail on the index.htm page, and then right-click the selected text to display the context menu.

- Point to Make Link to highlight the command (Figure 2–60).

Q&A How can I create a link from an image?

Use the same techniques as you do for creating a link from text. Select the image, and then use the context menu to select the Web page file. You can also type or drag the file name into the Property inspector Link box.

Q&A Can I create links on a new page that doesn't contain any text or images yet?

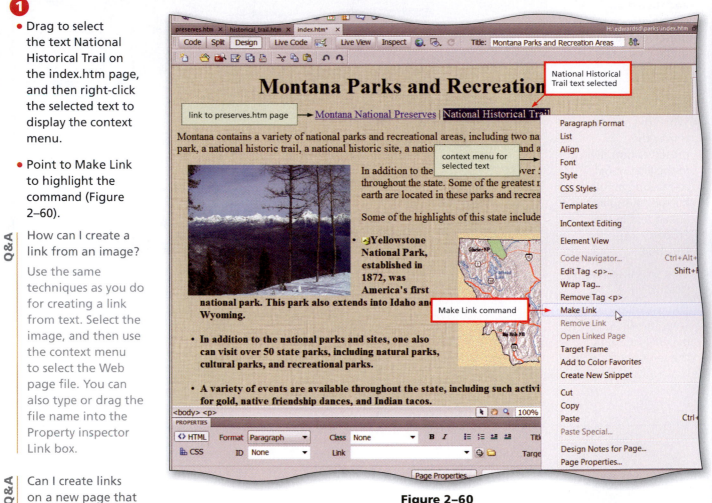

Figure 2–60

No. You must select something on a page that becomes the link to another location, so you need to add text or images before creating links. If you want to create links on a new page, it's a good idea to save the page before making the links.

2

• Click the Make Link command and then click historical_trail in the Select File dialog box to indicate you want to link to the Lewis and Clark National Historical Trail page (Figure 2–61).

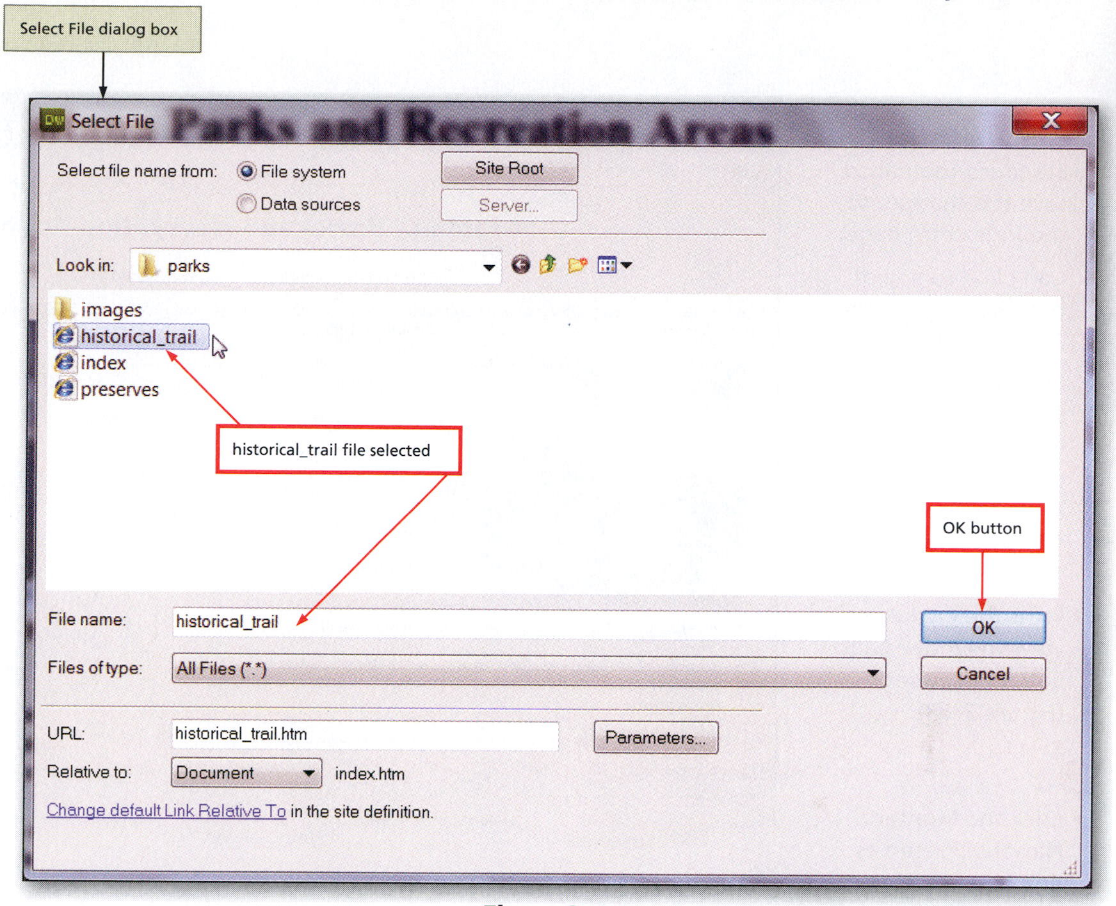

Select File dialog box

historical_trail file selected

OK button

Figure 2–61

3

• Click the OK button in the Select File dialog box, and then click the selected text, National Historical Trail, to display the underlined link (Figure 2–62).

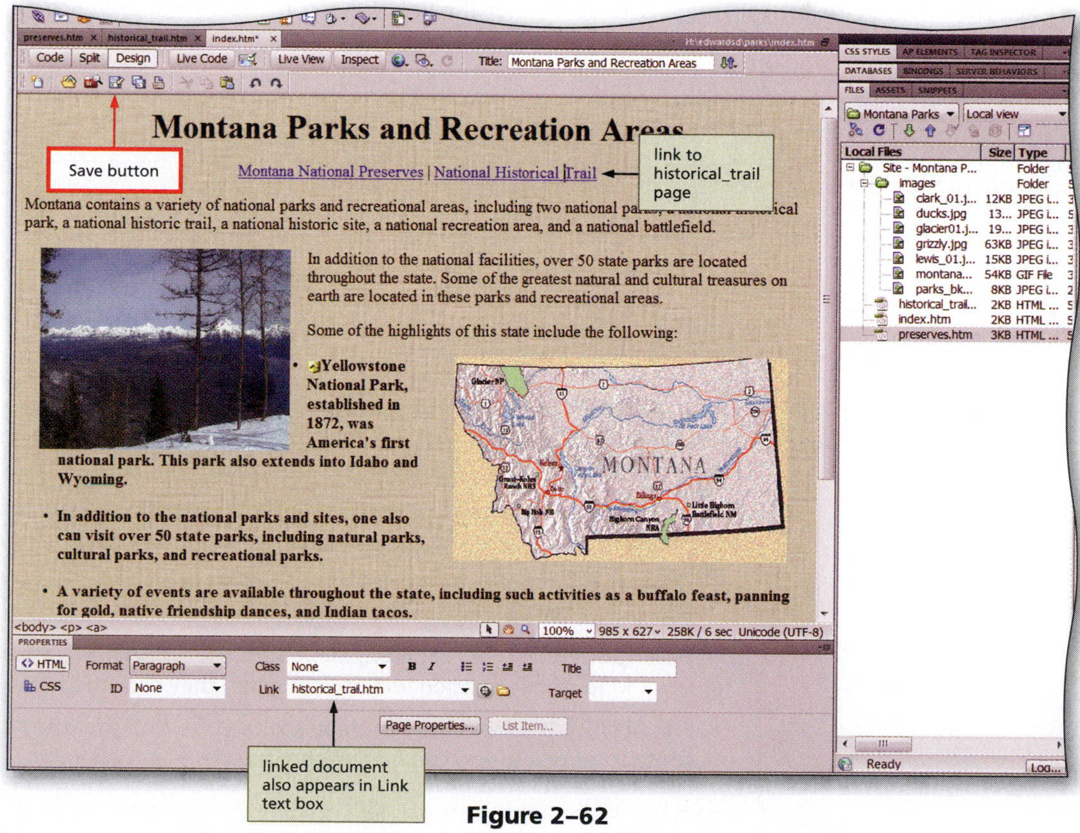

Save button

link to historical_trail page

Montana Parks and Recreation Areas

linked document also appears in Link text box

Figure 2–62

4

• Click the Save button on the Standard toolbar to save the changes to the index.htm page.

Q&A

Can I link to any of the files listed in the Files panel?

Yes. All the files you see in the Files panel in the Local Files list are internal files and are referenced as relative links.

• Press the F12 key to view the index page in your browser (Figure 2–63).

5

• Click the Montana National Preserves link to verify that the link displays the

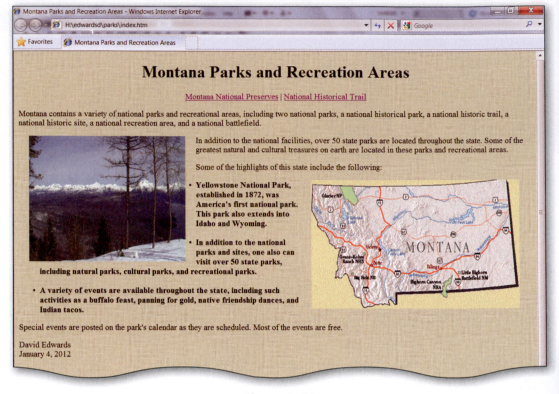

Figure 2–63

preserves.htm page (titled Montana National Parks and Preserves), and then click the browser Back button to return to the index page.

• Click the National Historical Trail link to verify that the link displays the historical_trail.htm page (titled Lewis and Clark National Historical Trail).

• Close the browser.

Other Ways

1. On Insert menu, click Hyperlink, enter link text, enter file name

2. In Common category of Insert panel, click Hyperlink, enter link text, enter file name

Plan Ahead

Include standard links for navigation.

Visitors to your Web site will use links to navigate the site, and expect to find the following types of links:

• **Links to the home page**. If your site is organized around a home page, include a link to the home page on every page in your site so visitors easily can return to it.

• **Links to main topics**. For each Web page that discusses a main topic, include links to other main-topic Web pages.

• **Descriptive links**. For text links, make sure the text is descriptive so that visitors know what kind of information will appear when they click the link.

• **E-mail links**. If visitors have problems with your Web site, they expect to be able to contact someone who can help them. Include an e-mail link to the appropriate person.

To Create a Relative Link to the Home Page

Visitors can enter a Web site at any point, so you should always include a link from each page within the site to the index page. To accomplish this for the Montana Parks Web site, you create a relative link to the index page from the Lewis and Clark National Historical Trail page and from the Montana National Parks and Preserves page, as shown in the following steps.

1

- Click the preserves .htm tab to display that page in the Document window, and then scroll to the bottom of the page. Drag to select the text Home.

- Drag the index. htm file name from the Files panel to the Link box in the Property inspector, and then click in the Document window to deselect the text.

- Click the Save button on the Standard toolbar to save your changes to the preserves.htm page.

- Press the F12 key to view the Montana National Parks and Preserves page in your browser (Figure 2–64).

Figure 2–64

Q&A Do I need to specify the complete path to the index.htm page?

No. When you link to another file in the same folder, you only need to specify the file name.

Q&A Can I make a linked Web page open in a new browser window?

Yes. By default, when you click a link, the linked Web page opens in the current browser window. However, you can specify that a linked Web page opens in a new browser window. To do this, first select the item and create the link. Next, in the Property inspector, click the Target box arrow and then click _blank on the Target pop-up menu. When you view the page in a browser and click the link, it is displayed in a new window.

2

• Click the Home link to display the index page (Figure 2–65).

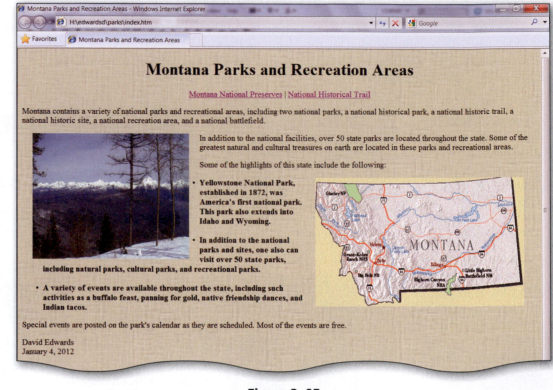

Figure 2–65

3

• Close the browser to redisplay Dreamweaver.

• Click the historical_trail.htm tab to display that page in the Document window. If necessary, scroll to the end of the document and then drag to select the text Home.

• Drag the index .htm file name from the Files panel to the Link box in the Property inspector to create the link, and then click anywhere in the Document window to deselect the text.

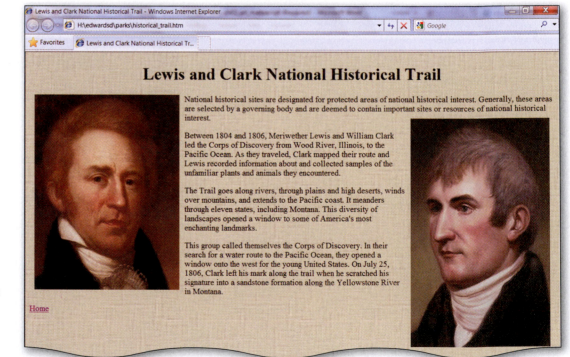

Figure 2–66

• Click the Save button on the Standard toolbar to save your changes to the historical_trail.htm page.

• Press the F12 key to view the Lewis and Clark National Historical Trail page in your browser (Figure 2–66).

4

- Click the Home link to verify that it works.

- Close the browser.

Creating an Absolute Link

Recall that an absolute link (also called an external link) contains the complete Web site address of a document. You create absolute links the same way you create relative links — select the text and paste or type the Web site address.

To Create Absolute Links

You now will create three absolute links in the Montana National Parks and Preserves page and two absolute links in the Lewis and Clark National Historical Trail page. The links in the Montana National Parks and Preserves page are to Web pages about the selected preserve. In the Lewis and Clark National Historical Trail page, the links are to Web pages about Lewis and Clark. The following steps show how to create these links. Keep in mind that Web site addresses change. If the absolute links do not work, check the Dreamweaver CS5 companion site at *www.scsite.com/dwcs5/* for updates.

1

- Select the Montana National Parks and Preserves page (preserves.htm). Drag to select the text Glacier National Park in the first bulleted item.

- Click the Link box in the Property inspector and then type `http:// www.nps.gov/ glac/index. htm` as the link. Press the ENTER key.

- Drag to select the text Nez Perce National Historical Park. Click the Link box and then type `http://www. nps.gov/nepe/ index.htm` as the link. Press the ENTER key.

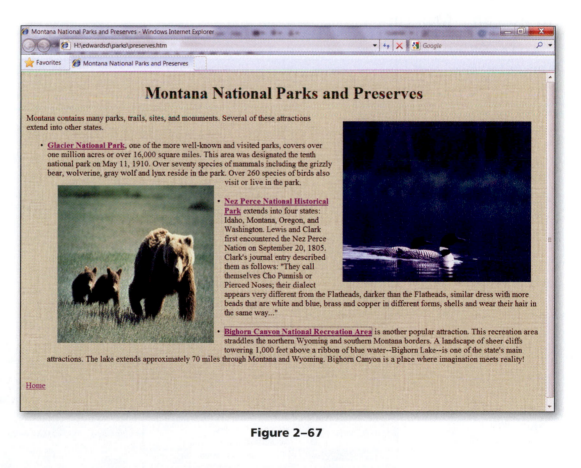

Figure 2–67

- Drag to select the text Bighorn Canyon National Recreation Area. Click the Link box and then type `http://www.nps.gov/bica/index.htm` as the link. Press the ENTER key.

- Save the preserves.htm page.

- Press the F12 key and then click each link to verify that they work (Figure 2–67).

Q&A How do I return to the Montana National Parks and Preserves page after clicking each link?

Click the Back button in your browser.

2

● Close the browser to return to the Dreamweaver window.

Other Ways

1. Start browser, open Web page, select URL, copy URL, close browser, paste in Link box

E-Mail Links

An **e-mail link** is one of the foundation elements of any successful Web site. Visitors must be able to contact you for additional information or to comment on the Web page or Web site. When visitors click an e-mail link, their default e-mail program opens a new e-mail message. The e-mail address you specify is inserted automatically in the To box of the e-mail message header.

To Add an E-Mail Link

The following steps show how to use the Insert menu to create an e-mail link for your home page using your name as the linked text.

1

● Click the index.htm tab, scroll down to the end of the page, and then drag to select your name.

● Click Insert on the Application bar and then point to Email Link to highlight it (Figure 2–68).

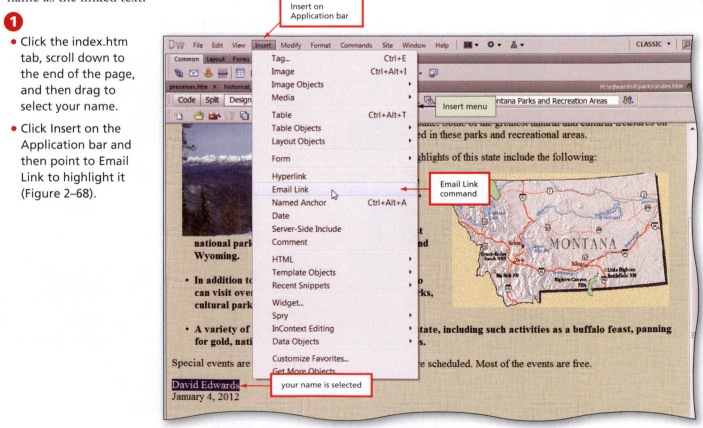

Figure 2–68

2

• Click Email Link to display the Email Link dialog box (Figure 2–69).

Q&A

What happens if I change the name in the Text box?

The text that you selected to create the e-mail link is also changed.

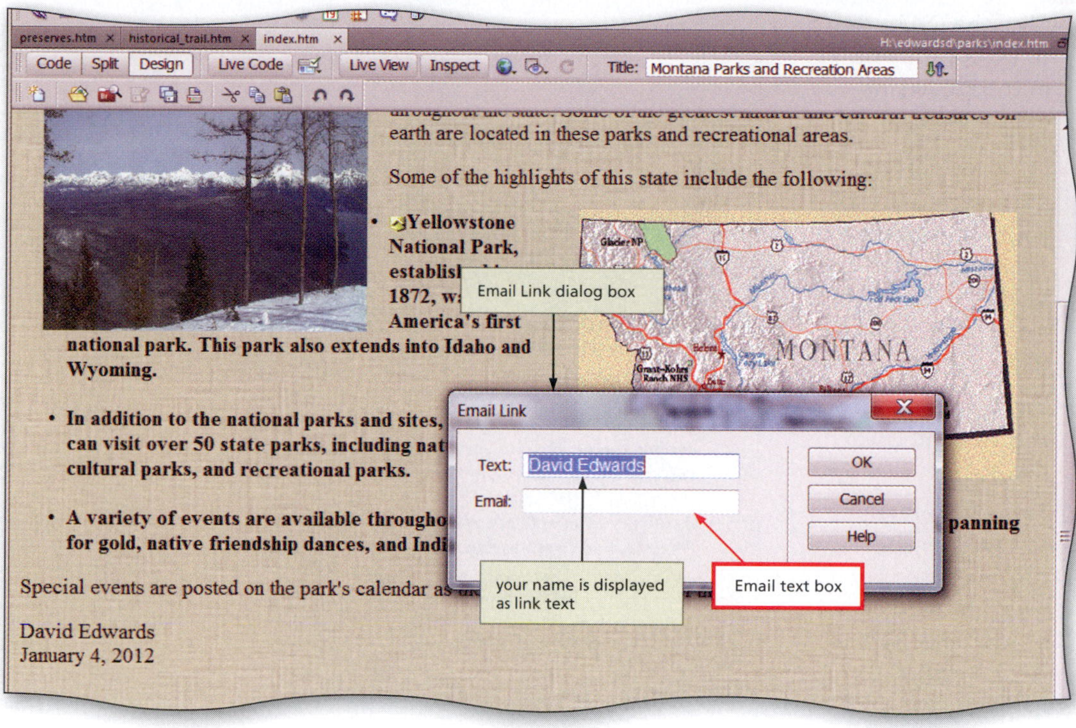

Figure 2–69

3

• Click the Email text box and then type your e-mail address (Figure 2–70).

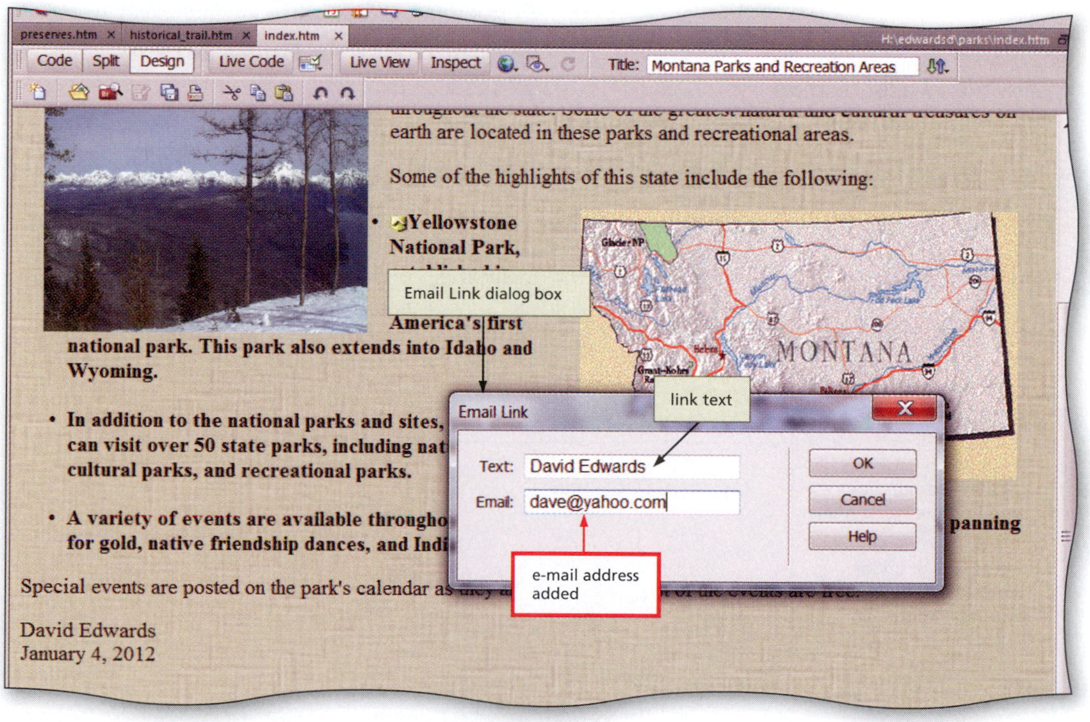

Figure 2–70

4

- Click the OK button to accept the entries in the Email Link dialog box.

- Click anywhere in the selected text of your name to view your e-mail address in the Property inspector Link box (Figure 2–71).

Q&A

What does mailto mean in the Link box?

This text refers to the Internet protocol used to send electronic mail. E-mail links start with "mailto" to indicate that the Web page should use this protocol when linking to the e-mail address in the Link box.

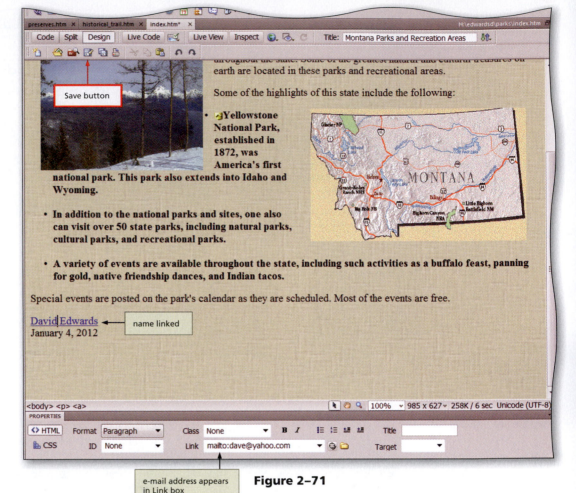

Figure 2–71

5

- Click the Save button on the Standard toolbar to save the changes to the index.htm page.

- Press the F12 key to view the page in your browser.

- Click your name to open your e-mail program.

- Send a message to yourself and one of your classmates.

- Close your e-mail program and then close the browser.

Other Ways

1. In Common category of Insert panel, click Email Link, enter e-mail address

2. Select text or image, type mailto: followed by e-mail address in Link box

Changing the Color of Links

The Page Properties HTML dialog box provides three options for link colors: Link (the link has not been clicked), Active Link (the link changes color when the user clicks it), and Visited Link (the link has been visited). The default color for a link is blue and a visited link is purple. You easily can make changes to these default settings and select colors that complement the background and other colors you are using on your Web pages. This is accomplished through the Page Properties dialog box. You display the Page Properties dialog box by clicking Modify on the Application bar or by clicking the Page Properties button in the Property inspector and then selecting the Appearance (HTML) option. You then can click the box that corresponds to one of the three types of links (Links, Visited links, and Active links) and select a color to match your color scheme.

Editing and Deleting Links

Web development is a never-ending process. At some point, it will be necessary to edit or delete a link. For instance, an e-mail address may change, a URL to an external link may change, or an existing link may contain an error.

Dreamweaver makes it easy to edit or delete a link. First, select the link or click the link you want to change. The linked document name is displayed in the Link box in the Property inspector. To delete the link without deleting the text on the Web page, delete the text from the Link box in the Property inspector. To edit the link, make the change in the Link box.

A second method to edit or delete a link is to use the context menu. Right-click the link you want to change, and then click Remove Link on the context menu to eliminate the link or click Change Link on the context menu to edit the link. Clicking the URLs icon in the Assets panel displays a list of all absolute and e-mail links within the Web site.

Dreamweaver Views

Dreamweaver provides several ways to look at a document: **Design view**, **Code view**, **Split view**, and **Live view**. Thus far, you have been working in Design view. As you create and work with documents, Dreamweaver automatically generates the underlying source code. Recall that the source code defines the structure and layout of a Web document by using a variety of tags and attributes. Even though Dreamweaver generates the code, occasions occur that necessitate the tweaking or modifying of code.

Dreamweaver provides several options for viewing and working with source code. You can use Split view to split the Document window so that it displays both Code view and Design view. You can display only Code view in the Document window, or you can open the Code inspector.

Using Code View and Design View

In Split view, you work in a split-screen environment. You can see the design and the code at the same time. When you make a change in Design view, the HTML code also is changed but is not visible in the Document window. You can set word wrapping, display line numbers for the code, highlight invalid HTML code, set syntax coloring for code elements, and set indenting through the View menu's Code View Options submenu. Viewing the code at this early stage may not seem important, but the more code you learn, the more productive you will become.

BTW

Using the Quick Tag Editor
If you are familiar with HTML, you can use the Dreamweaver Quick Tag Editor to quickly review, insert, and edit HTML tags without leaving Design view. To use the Quick Tag Editor, select the text or image associated with the code you want to view, and then press CTRL+T. The Quick Tag Editor window opens displaying the HTML code, if appropriate, so you can examine or edit the code. If you type invalid HTML in the Quick Tag Editor, Dreamweaver attempts to correct it by inserting quotation marks or angle brackets where needed.

Within the HTML source code, tags can be entered in uppercase, lowercase, or a combination of upper- and lowercase. The case of the tags has no effect on how the browser displays the output.

If the code is XHTML compliant, however, all tags are lowercase. In this book, if you use the instructions provided in Chapter 1 to create a new Web page, then your page is XHTML compliant. XHTML was discussed in the Introduction chapter. Therefore, when describing source code tags, this book uses lowercase letters for tags and attributes to make it easier to differentiate them from the other text and to coordinate with the XHTML standard.

To Use Design View and Code View Simultaneously

The following steps show how to use the Split button to display Code view and Design view at the same time.

1

- Click the preserves .htm tab to display that page in the Document window.

- Collapse the panel groups to provide room for Split view.

- Position the insertion point to the left of the heading, Montana National Parks and Preserves.

- Click the Split button on the Document toolbar to display Code view in the left pane and Design view in the right pane (Figure 2–72).

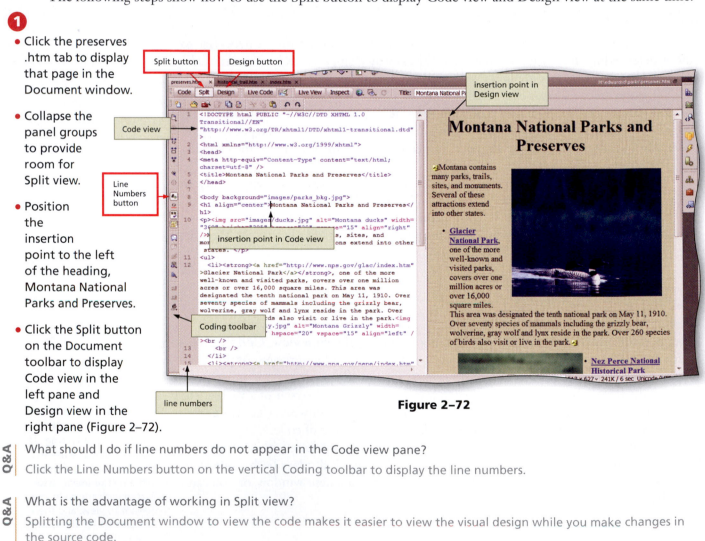

Figure 2–72

Q&A | What should I do if line numbers do not appear in the Code view pane?
Click the Line Numbers button on the vertical Coding toolbar to display the line numbers.

Q&A | What is the advantage of working in Split view?
Splitting the Document window to view the code makes it easier to view the visual design while you make changes in the source code.

2

- Click the Design button on the Document toolbar to return to Design view.

Other Ways

1. On View menu, click Code and Design

Modifying Source Code

One of the more common problems within Dreamweaver and the source code relates to line breaks and paragraphs. Occasionally, you inadvertently press the ENTER key or insert a line break and need to remove the tag. Or, you may copy and paste or open a text file that contains unneeded paragraphs or line breaks.

Pressing the BACKSPACE key or DELETE key may return you to the previous line, but does not always delete the line break or paragraph tag within the source code. The deletion of these tags is determined by the position of the insertion point when you press the BACKSPACE or DELETE keys. If the insertion point is still inside the source code, pressing the BACKSPACE key will not delete these tags and your page will not be displayed correctly. When this occurs, the best solution is to delete the tag through Code view.

Live View

Generally, to view a Web page in a browser such as Internet Explorer or Firefox requires that you leave Dreamweaver and open the browser in another window. If the Web designer wants to view the source code, an additional window also needs to be opened. Dreamweaver's **Live view** feature, however, allows you to preview how the page will look in a browser without leaving Dreamweaver. If you want to view and modify code, you can do so through a split screen; and the changes to the code are reflected instantly in the rendered display.

To Use Live View

In the following steps, you switch to Live view.

1

• Click the Live View button on the Document toolbar to view the page as it would appear in the browser and to verify that the line spacing is correct and that the document is properly formatted (Figure 2–73).

Q&A

What should I do if an Information bar appears explaining a Flash plug-in was not found?

Click the Close link in the Information bar, and then install the Flash plug-in from the Adobe Web site at *www.adobe.com*.

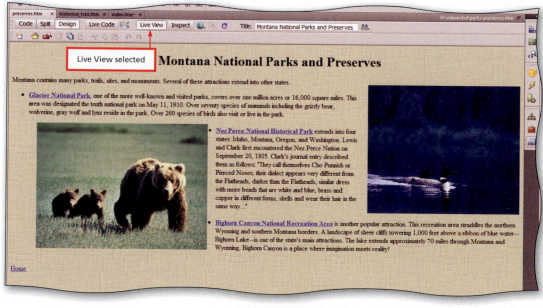

Figure 2–73

2

• Click the Live View button to return to Design view and make any necessary corrections. If necessary, click the Save button.

BTW

Quick Reference
For a table that lists how to complete tasks covered in this book using the keyboard, see the Quick Reference at the end of this book.

Quitting Dreamweaver

After you add pages to your Web site, including images and links, and then view your pages in a browser, Chapter 2 is complete.

To Close the Web Site and Quit Dreamweaver

The following steps show how to close the Web site, quit Dreamweaver, and return control to Windows.

1 Click the Close button on the right corner of the Dreamweaver title bar to close the Dreamweaver window, the Document window, and the Montana Parks Web site.

2 Click the Yes button if a prompt is displayed indicating that you need to save changes.

Chapter Summary

Chapter 2 introduced you to images and links, and discussed how to view source code and use Live view. You began the chapter by copying data files to the local site. You added two new pages, one for Lewis and Clark National Historical Trail and one for Montana National Parks and Preserves, to the Web site you started in Chapter 1. Next, you added images to the index page. Following that, you added a background image and page images to the two new pages. Then, you added relative links to all three pages. You added an e-mail link to the index page and absolute links to the Montana National Parks and Preserves and Lewis and Clark National Historical Trail pages. Finally, you learned how to view source code. The items listed below include all the new Dreamweaver skills you have learned in this chapter.

1. Create the Montana National Parks and Preserves Web Page (DW 109)
2. Create the Lewis and Clark National Historical Trail Web Page (DW 112)
3. Set Invisible Element Preferences and Turn on Visual Aids (DW 119)
4. Open a Web Page from a Local Web Site (DW 123)
5. Insert an Image into the Index Page (DW 124)
6. Align an Image (DW 128)
7. Adjust the Image Size and the Horizontal Space (DW 130)
8. To Insert the Second Image (DW 131)
10. Crop and Modify the Brightness/Contrast of an Image (DW 142)
11. Add Text for Relative Links (DW 147)
12. Create a Relative Link Using Point to File (DW 148)
13. Create a Relative Link Using the Context Menu (DW 150)
14. Create a Relative Link to the Home Page (DW 153)
15. Create Absolute Links (DW 155)
16. Add an E-Mail Link (DW 156)
17. Use Design View and Code View Simultaneously (DW 160)
18. Use Live View (DW 161)

Learn It Online

Test your knowledge of chapter content and key terms.

Instructions: To complete the Learn It Online exercises, start your browser, click the Address bar, and then enter the Web address `scsite.com/dwCS5/learn`. When the Dreamweaver CS5 Learn It Online page is displayed, click the link for the exercise you want to complete and then read the instructions.

Chapter Reinforcement TF, MC, and SA

A series of true/false, multiple choice, and short answer questions that test your knowledge of the chapter content.

Flash Cards

An interactive learning environment where you identify chapter key terms associated with displayed definitions.

Practice Test

A series of multiple choice questions that test your knowledge of chapter content and key terms.

Who Wants to Be a Computer Genius?

An interactive game that challenges your knowledge of chapter content in the style of a television quiz show.

Wheel of Terms

An interactive game that challenges your knowledge of chapter key terms in the style of the television show *Wheel of Fortune*.

Crossword Puzzle Challenge

A crossword puzzle that challenges your knowledge of key terms presented in the chapter.

Apply Your Knowledge

Reinforce the skills and apply the concepts you learned in this chapter.

Adding, Aligning, and Resizing an Image on a Web Page

Instructions: In this activity, you modify a Web page by adding, aligning, and resizing an image (Figure 2–74). Make sure you have downloaded the data files for Chapter02\apply, which are available in the Data Files for Students folder. See the inside back cover of this book for instructions on downloading the Data Files for Students, or contact your instructor for information about accessing the required files.

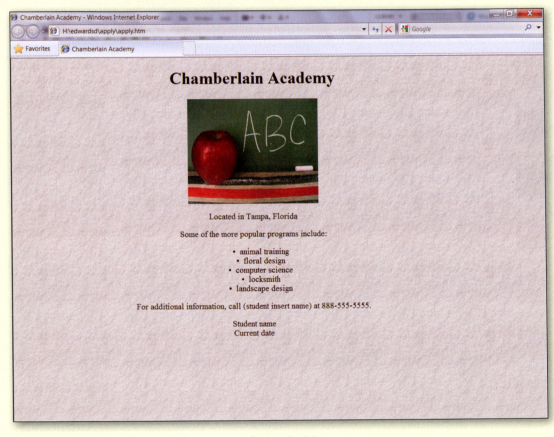

Figure 2–74

Perform the following tasks:

1. Use Windows Computer or Windows Explorer to copy the school_house.jpg image from the Chapter02\apply data files folder into the images folder for your Apply Exercises local Web site. (For example, the images folder might be stored on H:\edwardsd\apply\images.)

2. Start Dreamweaver, and then open the Apply Exercises site.

3. Open the apply.htm file (the page you created for the Apply Your Knowledge exercise in Chapter 1).

4. Insert a new blank line after the "Chamberlain Academy" heading by clicking at the end of the heading and then pressing the ENTER key.

5. Display the Assets panel, and then click the Refresh Site List button at the bottom of the panel, if necessary, to display the images. Select the school_house.jpg image, and then drag it to the insertion point on the new blank line.

6. Type the following text in the Image Tag Accessibility Attributes text box: `school`. Click the OK button.

7. If necessary, select the image. Double-click the W text box and type `250`. Double-click the H text box, type `200`, and then press the ENTER key.

8. Use the Align button to align the image to the middle of the line.

9. Use the Format menu to center all of the text on the page.

10. Save your document and then view it in your browser. Submit it in the format specified by your instructor.

Extend Your Knowledge

Extend the skills you learned in this chapter and experiment with new skills. You may need to use Help to complete the assignment.

Adding, Aligning, and Resizing Images on a Web Page

Instructions: In this activity, you modify a Web page by adding, aligning, and resizing images (Figure 2–75). Make sure you have downloaded the data files for Chapter02\extend, which are available in the Data Files for Students folder. See the inside back cover of this book for instructions on downloading the Data Files for Students, or contact your instructor for information about accessing the required files.

Figure 2–75

Perform the following tasks:

1. Copy the data files from the Chapter02\extend data files folder into the images folder for your Extend Exercises local Web site. (For example, the images folder might be stored on H:\edwardsd\extend\images.)

2. Start Dreamweaver, and open the Extend Exercises site.

3. Open the extend.htm file (the page you created for the Extend Your Knowledge exercise in Chapter 1).

4. Remove the bold from the bulleted list, your name, and the date.

4. Drag the flower01 image to the top of the page and to the left of the second line, which begins, "Choose from among".

5. Type flower01 in the Alternate text text box.

6. Resize the image width to 165 and the height to 185.

7. Type 25 in both the V Space box and the H Space box.

8. Align the image to the left.

9. Click after the second line (which begins, "Choose from among"). Drag the flower02 image to the insertion point. Type flower02 in the Alternate text text box.

10. Resize the image width to 165 and the height to 185.

11. Enter 25 for both the V Space and the H Space.

12. Align the image to the right.

13. Move the sentence that begins with "Choose from among" after the bulleted list. Make sure you do not move the element marker. Also make sure the sentence remains centered and does not have a bullet. Bold the sentence if it is not already bolded.

14. Save your document and then view it in your browser. Submit it in the format specified by your instructor.

Make It Right

Analyze a document and then correct all errors and/or improve the design.

Adding an Image to a Web Page

Instructions: In this activity, you modify an existing Web page by adding an image (Figure 2–76). Make sure you have downloaded the data files for Chapter02\right, which are available in the Data Files for Students folder. See the inside back cover of this book for instructions on downloading the Data Files for Students, or contact your instructor for information about accessing the required files.

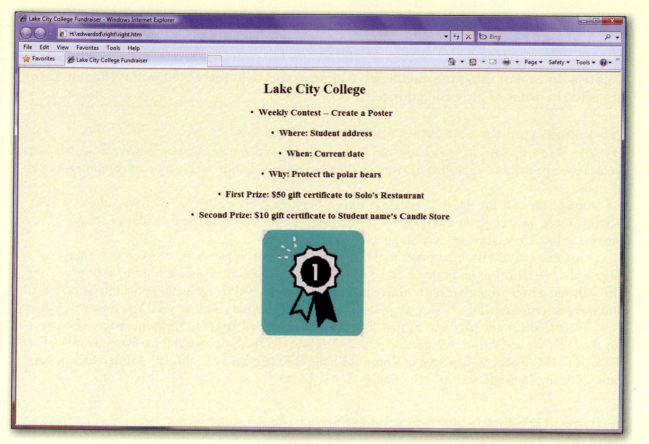

Figure 2–76

Perform the following tasks:

1. Copy the data file from the Chapter02\right data files folder into the images folder for your Right Exercises local Web site. (For example, the images folder might be stored on H:\edwardsd\right\ images.)

2. Start Dreamweaver, open the Right Exercises site, and then open the right.htm page. If necessary, open the Local Files panel and the Property inspector. Verify that HTML is selected.

3. Insert a new line after the last item in the list. If a bullet is displayed, click the Unordered List button in the Property inspector. Center the line, if necessary.

4. Drag the ribbon01 image to the insertion point. Type `ribbon` for the alternate text.

5. Adjust the image width to 177 and the height to 183.

6. Make any other adjustments as necessary to make your Web page match the one shown in Figure 2–76.

7. Save your document and then view it in your browser.

8. Submit your Web page in the format specified by your instructor.

In the Lab

Create a document using the guidelines, concepts, and skills presented in this chapter. Labs are listed in order of increasing difficulty.

Lab 1: Modifying the Computer Repair Services Web Site

Problem: Now that Bryan has a basic Web page for his Computer Repair Services Web site, he wants to make the page more appealing to visitors. He asks you to help him add images of computers to his Web page.

Image files for the Bryan's Computer Repair Services Web site are included with the data files. See the inside back cover of this book for instructions for downloading the data files or see your instructor for information on accessing the files in this book.

You need to add two new pages to the Bryan's Computer Repair Services Web site: a services page and a references page. In this exercise, you will add relative and absolute links to each page. You also will add a background image to the new pages. Next, you will insert images on all three pages and use the settings in Table 2–4 to align the images and enter the alternate text. You then will add an e-mail link to the home page and relative links from the two new pages to the home page. The pages for the Web site are shown in Figures 2–77a, 2–77b, and 2–77c. (Software and hardware settings determine how a Web page is displayed in a browser. Your Web pages may be displayed differently in your browser from the pages shown in the figures.)

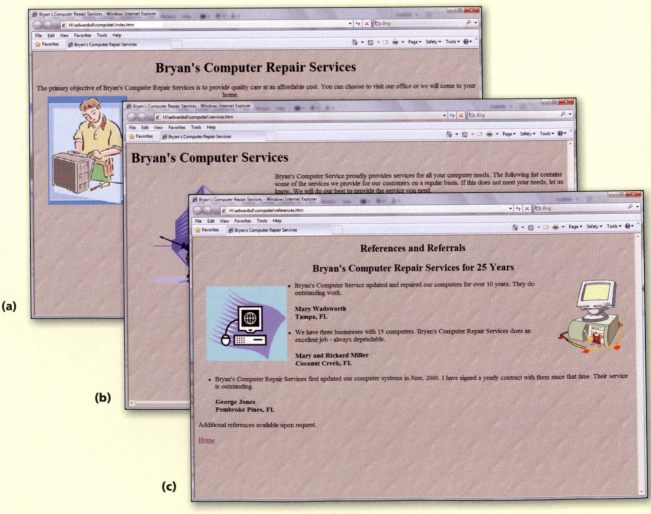

(a)

(b)

(c)

Figure 2–77

Table 2–4 Image Property Settings for the Bryan's Computer Repair Services Web Site

Image Name	W	H	V Space	H Space	Align	Alt
computer_repair01	191	253	10	25	left	repairs
computer_repair02	239	235	25	50	left	desktop computer
computer_repair03	150	174	20	20	right	disk drive
computer_repair04	190	175	10	20	left	monitor
hard_drive	260	260	20	50	right	hard drive

Perform the following tasks:

1. Copy the services and references data files from the Chapter02\computers data files folder into the root folder for your Computer Repair Services local Web site. (For example, the root folder might be stored on H:\edwardsd\computers.) Copy the image data files from the Chapter02\computers\ images data files folder into the images folder for your Computer Repair Services local Web site. (For example, the images folder might be stored on H:\edwardsd\computers\images.)

2. Start Dreamweaver and display the panel groups. Open the Computer Repair Services site, and then open the index.htm file (which you created in Chapter 1).

3. If necessary, click the expander arrow to expand the Property inspector and display the Standard toolbar.

4. Open the Assets panel to display the contents of the images folder. Position the insertion point at the end of the first sentence. Drag the computer_repair01 image to the insertion point, add the alternate text as indicated in Table 2–4, and then apply the settings shown in Table 2–4 to resize and align the image.

5. Position the insertion point at the end of the first sentence again. Drag the hard_drive image to the insertion point and then apply the settings shown in Table 2–4.

6. Select the text Basic services in the first bulleted item. Click the Files tab in the panels group, and then use the drag-and-drop file method to create a link to the services page. Repeat this process to add a link from the References text to the references page.

7. Select your name. Use the Insert menu to create an e-mail link using your name. Center the first sentence, if necessary. Save the index page (Figure 2–77a).

8. Open the services page. Click Modify on the Application bar and then click Page Properties. Apply the repair_bkg background image (located in the images folder) to the services page.

9. Position the insertion point to the left of the first sentence. Open the Assets panel, drag the computer_repair02 image to the insertion point, and then apply the settings shown in Table 2–4.

10. If necessary, scroll down. Select Home, click the Files tab in the panels group, and then create a relative link to the index page. Save the services page (Figure 2–77b).

11. Open the references page. Apply the repair_bkg background image (located in the images folder) as you did in Step 8 for the services page.

12. Position the insertion point to the right of the second heading and then drag the computer_repair03 image to the insertion point. Apply the settings shown in Table 2–4 to the image.

13. Insert a blank line before the first bulleted item in the list. Remove the bullet, if necessary. Drag the computer_repair04 image to the insertion point. Apply the settings shown in Table 2–4 to the image.

14. Scroll to the bottom of the page. Select Home and then create a relative link to the index page. Save the references page (Figure 2–77c).

15. View the Web site in your browser. Check each link to verify that it works. Submit the documents in the format specified by your instructor.

In the Lab

Lab 2: Modifying the Baskets Web Site

Problem: Carole Wells, for whom you created the Baskets by Carole Web site and Web page, is very pleased with the response she has received. She asks you to add two images to the index page and to create a second page with links and images. Carole wants the new page to include information about her company's history.

Add a second Web page to the Baskets by Carole Web site. The revised Web site is shown in Figures 2–78a and 2–78b. Table 2–5 includes the settings and alternate text for the images. Software and hardware settings determine how a Web page displays in a browser. Your Web pages may be displayed differently in your browser from those in the figures.

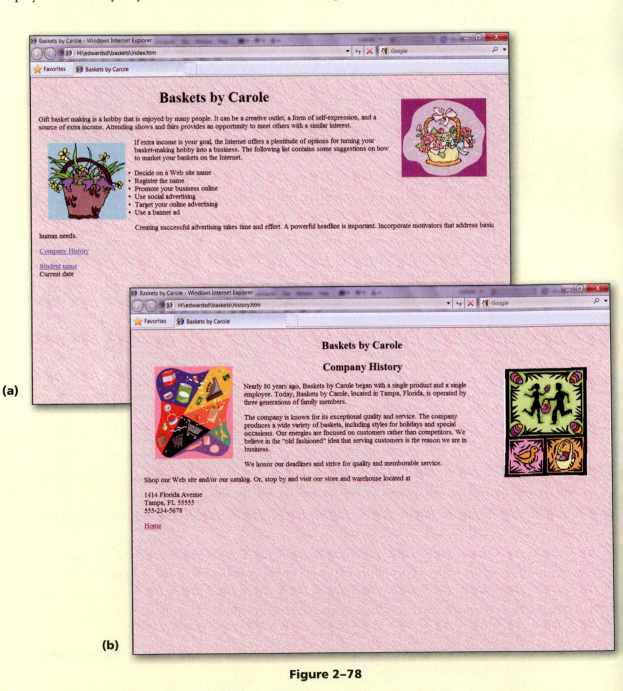

(a)

(b)

Figure 2–78

Table 2–5 Image Property Settings for the Baskets by Carole Web Site						
Image Name	**W**	**H**	**V Space**	**H Space**	**Align**	**Alt**
basket01	190	174	25	25	right	rose basket
basket02	174	170	10	20	left	daisy basket
basket03	183	239	20	50	right	baskets
basket04	174	204	10	25	left	shopping

Perform the following tasks:

1. Copy the history data file from the Chapter02\baskets data files folder into the root folder for your Gift Basket Designs local Web site. (For example, the root folder might be stored on H:\edwardsd\baskets.) Copy the image data files from the Chapter02\baskets\images data files folder into the images folder for your Gift Basket Designs local Web site. (For example, the images folder might be stored on H:\edwardsd\baskets\images.)

2. Start Dreamweaver and display the panel groups. Open the Gift Basket Designs site, and then open the index.htm file (which you created in Chapter 1).

3. If necessary, click the expander arrow to expand the Property inspector and display the Standard toolbar.

4. Position the insertion point to the right of the heading and then drag the basket01 image to the insertion point. Enter the Alt text, and then apply the settings shown in Table 2–5 to resize and align the image.

5. Position the insertion point to the left of the paragraph that begins "If extra income is your goal", and then drag the basket02 image to the insertion point. Apply the settings shown in Table 2–5.

6. Position the insertion point to the right of the last sentence and then press the ENTER key.

7. Type the following text: **Company History**. Select the Company History text and use the drag-and-drop method to create a link to the history page. Select your name. Use the Insert menu to create an e-mail link using your e-mail address. Save the index page.

8. Open the history page. Open the Page Properties dialog box, and then add the background image (baskets_bkg) to the history page.

9. Position the insertion point at the end of subhead, Company History, and then drag the basket03 image to the insertion point. Apply the settings shown in Table 2–5.

10. Position the insertion point at the end of the Company History subhead again. Drag the basket04 image to the insertion point. Apply the settings shown in Table 2–5.

11. Select Home and then create a relative link to the index page. Save the history page.

12. Check the spelling of your document and correct any errors.

13. Save the file.

14. View the Web site in your browser. Check each link to verify that it works. Submit the documents in the format specified by your instructor.

In the Lab

Lab 3: Modifying the Credit Protection Web Site

Problem: Jessica Minnick has received favorable comments about the Web page and site you created on credit information. Her bank wants to use the Web site to provide additional information to its customers. Jessica has asked you and another intern at the bank to work with her to create two more Web pages to add to the site. They want one of the pages to discuss credit protection and the other page to contain information about identity theft.

Revise the Credit Protection Web site. The revised pages for the Web site are shown in Figures 2–79a, 2–79b, and 2–79c. Table 2–6 on the next page includes the settings and Alt text for the images. Software and hardware settings determine how a Web page displays in a browser. Your Web pages may be displayed differently in your browser from those in the figures.

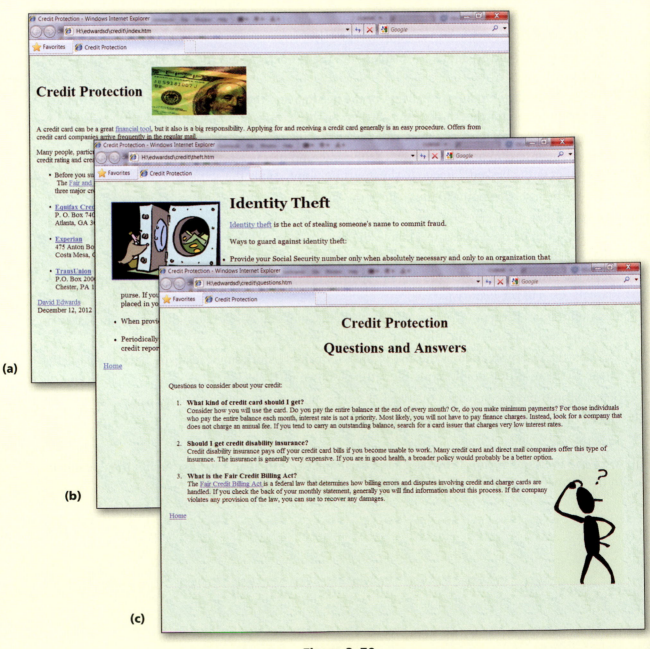

(a)

(b)

(c)

Figure 2–79

Table 2–6 Image Property Settings for the Credit Protection Web Site

Image Name	W	H	V Space	H Space	Align	Alt
money	211	107	none	20	absolute middle	Money
protection	240	170	14	20	left	Identity theft
question	150	300	none	none	right	Questions?
theft	188	193	none	100	right	Protect personal information

Perform the following tasks:

1. Copy the questions and theft data files from the Chapter02\credit data files folder into the root folder for your Credit Protection local Web site. (For example, the root folder might be stored on H:\edwardsd\credit.) Copy the image data files from the Chapter02\credit\images data files folder into the images folder for your Credit Protection local Web site. (For example, the images folder might be stored on H:\edwardsd\credit\images.)

2. Start Dreamweaver and display the panel groups. Open the Credit Protection site, and then open index.htm (which you created in Chapter 1).

3. If necessary, display the Property inspector and the Standard toolbar. Expand the Property inspector.

4. Position the insertion point to the right of the heading and then drag the money image to the insertion point. Apply the settings shown in Table 2–6.

5. Select the text financial tool, located in the first sentence of the first paragraph. Create a relative link from the selected text to the questions page. Select the text Fair and Accurate Credit Transactions (FACT), located in the second sentence of the third paragraph. Create an absolute link to http://www.annualcreditreport.com. Select the name of the company in the first bulleted list item (Equifax Credit Information Services, Inc.) and create an absolute link using http://www .equifax.com. Create absolute links from the other two company names, using http://www.experian .com and http://www.transunion.com, respectively.

6. Position the insertion point at the end of the second paragraph (after the word fix). Press the SPACEBAR. Type the following text: `Credit card and identity theft can be a major issue when applying for credit.` Select the text you just typed and then create a relative link to the theft page. Add an e-mail link to your name. Save the index page (Figure 2–79a on the previous page). Position the insertion point at the end of the second line in the second bulleted point, and then drag the theft image to the insertion point. Apply the settings shown in Table 2–6.

7. Open the theft page and apply the background image (credit_bkg) to the page.

8. Position the insertion point to the left of the second line and then drag the protection image to the insertion point. Apply the settings shown in Table 2–6.

9. Drag to select the text Identity theft at the beginning of the first sentence, and then create an absolute link using http://www.consumer.gov/idtheft as the URL. Create an absolute link from the protection image using the same URL. Select the image and then type the URL in the Link box. Select Home and then create a relative link to the index.htm page. Save the theft page (Figure 2–79b).

10. Open the questions page. Apply the background image that you added to the theft page in Step 7. Use the text, Home, at the bottom of the page to create a relative link to the index page.

11. Position the insertion point to the right of question 3, What is the Fair Credit Billing Act? Drag the question image to the insertion point. Apply the settings in Table 2–6.

12. Create an absolute link from the Fair Credit Billing Act text in the answer to question 3. In this link, use the following as the URL: http://www.ftc.gov/bcp/edu/pubs/consumer/credit/cre16.shtm. Save the questions page (Figure 2–79c).

13. View the Web site in your browser and verify that your external and relative links work. *Hint*: Remember to check the link for the image on the theft.htm page. Submit the documents in the format specified by your instructor.

Cases and Places

Apply your creative thinking and problem solving skills to design and implement a solution.

● Easier ●●More Difficult

● 1: Modify the Favorite Sports Web Site

In Chapter 1, you created a Web site named Favorite Sports with a Web page listing your favorite sports and teams. Now, you want to add another page to the site. Create and format the new page, which should include general information about a selected sport. Create a relative link from the home page to the new page and from the new page to the home page. Add a background image to the new page and insert an image on one of the pages. Include an appropriate title for the page. Save the page in the sports subfolder. For a selection of images and backgrounds, visit the Dreamweaver CS5 Media Web page (scsite.com/dwcs5/media).

● 2: Modify the Hobbies Web Site

Several of your friends were impressed with the Web page and Web site you created about your favorite hobby in Chapter 1. They have given you some topics they think you should include on the site. You decide to create an additional page that will consist of details about your hobby and the topics your friends suggested. Format the page. Add an absolute link to a related Web site and a relative link from the home page to the new page and from the new page to the home page. Add a background image to the new page. Create an e-mail link on the index page. Title the page with the name of the selected hobby. Save the page in the hobby subfolder. For a selection of images and backgrounds, visit the Dreamweaver CS5 Media Web page (scsite.com/dwcs5/media).

● ● 3: Modify the Politics Web Site

In Chapter 1, you created a Web site and a Web page to publicize your campaign for public office. Develop two additional pages to add to the site. Apply a background image to the new pages. Apply appropriate formatting to the two new pages. Scan a picture of yourself or take a picture with a digital camera and include the picture on the index page. Add a second image illustrating one of your campaign promises. Include at least two images on one of the new pages and one image on the other new page. Add alternate text for all images, and then add appropriate H Space and V Space property features to position the images. Create e-mail links on all three pages and create relative links from the home page to both pages and from each of the pages to the home page. Create an absolute link to a related site on one of the pages. Give each page a meaningful title and then save the pages in the government subfolder. For a selection of images and backgrounds, visit the Dreamweaver CS5 Media Web page (scsite.com/dwcs5/media).

•• 4: Modify the Favorite Music Web Site

Make It Personal

Modify the music Web site you created in Chapter 1 by creating a new page. Format the page. Discuss your favorite artist or band on the new page. Add a background image to the new page. On the index page, add an image and align the image to the right, and on the new page, add a different image and align the image to the left. Add appropriate alternate text for each image. Position each image appropriately on the page by using the H Space and V Space property features. Add an e-mail link on the index page, and add text and a relative link from the new page to the index page. View your Web pages in your browser. Give the page a meaningful title and then save the page in your music subfolder. For a selection of images and backgrounds, visit the Dreamweaver CS5 Media Web page (scsite.com/dwcs5/media).

•• 5: Create the Student Trips Web Site

Working Together

The student trips Web site you and your classmates created in Chapter 1 is a success. Everyone loves it. The dean is so impressed that she asks the group to continue with the project. Your team creates and formats three additional Web pages, one for each of three possible locations for the trip. Add a background image to all new pages. Add two images to each of the pages, including the index page. Resize one of the images. Add the Alt text for each image, and then position each image appropriately using the H Space and V Space property features. Create a link from the index page to each of the three new pages and a link from each page to the index page. Create an absolute link to a related informational Web site on each of the three new pages. Add an appropriate title to each page. Preview in a browser to verify the links. Save the pages in your trips subfolder. For a selection of images and backgrounds, visit the Dreamweaver CS5 Media Web page (scsite.com/dwcs5/media).

3 | Tables and Page Layout

Objectives

You will have mastered the material in this chapter when you can:

- Understand page layout
- Design a Web page using tables
- Create a table structure
- Modify a table structure
- Describe HTML table tags
- Add content to a table
- Add a border to a table
- Format table content
- Format a table
- Add borders to images
- Create head content

3 | Tables and Page Layout

Introduction

Chapter 3 introduces you to using tables for page layout and adding head content elements. Page layout is an important part of Web design because it determines the way your page will be displayed in a browser, which is one of the major challenges for any Web designer.

Dreamweaver's table feature is a great tool for designing a Web page. One reason is that it is very similar to the table feature in word-processing programs such as Microsoft Office Word. A table allows you to add vertical and horizontal structure to a Web page. Using a table, you can put just about anything on your page and have it be displayed in a specific location. Using tables in Dreamweaver, you can create columns of text or navigation bars and lay out tabular data. You can delete, split, and merge rows and columns; modify table, row, or cell properties to add color and adjust alignment; and copy, paste, and delete cells in the table structure.

Project — Formatted Tables with Images

In this chapter, you continue creating the Montana Parks Web site. You use tables to create two new Web pages focusing on two of Montana's more popular parks — Nez Perce National Historic Trail and Glacier National Park. You then add these new pages to the park's Web site and link to them from the index.htm Web page. When you complete your Web page additions, you add keywords and a description as the head content. Figures 3–1a and 3–1b show the two new pages in their final form.

In the second part of this chapter, you learn the value of head content and how to add it to a Web page. When you create a Web page, the underlying source code is organized into two main sections: the head section and the body section. In Chapters 1 and 2, you created Web pages in the body section, which contains the page content that is displayed in the browser. The head section contains a variety of information, including keywords that search engines use. With the exception of the page title, all head content is invisible when viewed in the Dreamweaver Document window or in a browser. Some head content is accessed by other programs, such as search engines, and some content is accessed by the browser. This chapter discusses the head content options and the importance of adding this content to all Web pages.

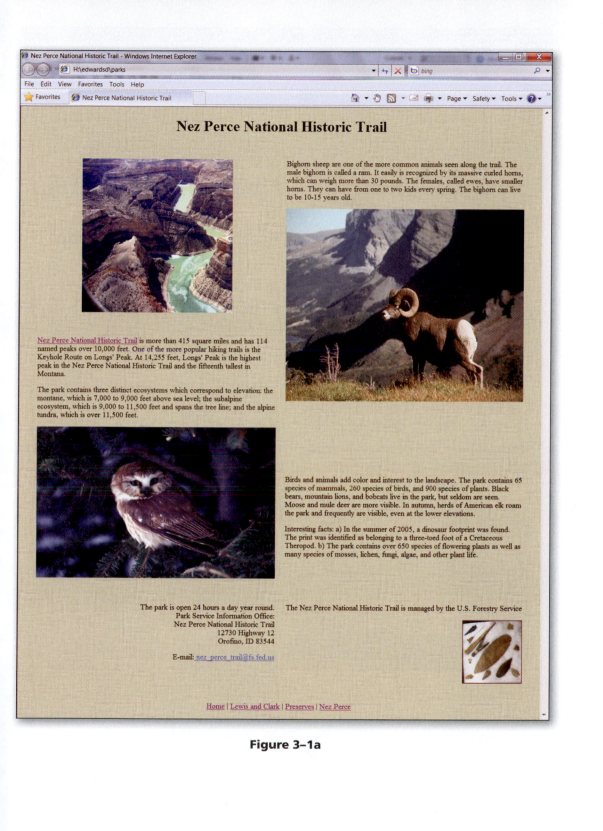

Figure 3–1a

Figure 3–1b

Overview

As you read this chapter, you learn how to add to your Web site the pages shown in Figures 3–1a and 3–1b by performing these general tasks:

- Insert a table into a Dreamweaver Web page.
- Center the table.
- Change vertical alignment within the table.
- Specify column width.
- Merge cells.
- Add accessibility attributes.
- Add text and images to a table.
- Add links.
- Add borders to tables and images.

General Project Guidelines

When adding pages to a Web site, consider the appearance and characteristics of the completed site. As you create and add the two Web pages to the Montana Parks Web site shown in Figure 3–1a and Figure 3–1b, you should follow these general guidelines:

1. **Plan the Web pages.** Determine how the pages will fit into the Web site.

2. **Determine when to insert tables.** Create and organize the new content for the Web pages on your site. Consider whether you can organize and format some content in tables.

3. **Lay out Web pages with tables.** Insert Web page elements in a specific order — tables, text, and then images — as you create and enhance each page.

4. **Determine when to add borders.** Consider when and where to add borders to tables and images. Determine the number of pixels that should be added for these elements.

5. **Identify cells to merge.** Determine whether cells within the table need to be merged to provide a better layout. If so, determine which cells need to be merged to provide a more attractive Web page.

6. **Plan head content.** Select the keywords and descriptions to add to the head content for each page so that search engines and Web users can find your pages easily.

When necessary, more specific details concerning the above guidelines are presented at appropriate points in the chapter. The chapter also will identify the actions performed and decisions made regarding these guidelines during the creation of the Web pages shown in Figures 3–1a and 3–1b on pages DW 179 and DW 180.

Plan Ahead

Starting Dreamweaver and Opening a Web Site

Each time you start Dreamweaver, it opens to the last site displayed when you closed the program. It therefore may be necessary for you to open the parks Web site.

To Start Dreamweaver and Open the Montana Parks Web Site

With a good understanding of the requirements, the necessary decisions, and the planning process, the next step is to start Dreamweaver and open the Montana Parks Web site.

1 Click the Start button on the Windows taskbar.

2 Click Adobe Dreamweaver CS5 on the Start menu or point to All Programs on the Start menu, click Adobe Design Premium CS5 if necessary, and then click Adobe Dreamweaver CS5 on the All Programs list.

3 If necessary, display the panel groups.

4 If the Montana Parks hierarchy is not displayed, click the Sites pop-up menu button on the Files panel and point to Montana Parks to highlight it (Figure 3–2).

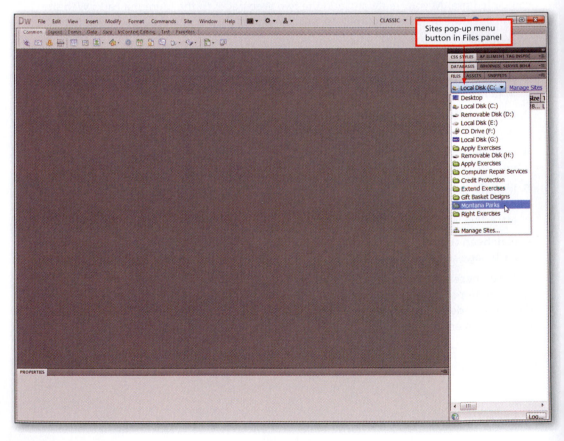

Figure 3–2

Q&A

How can I see a list of the sites I have defined in Dreamweaver?

Clicking the **Sites pop-up menu button** in the Files panel lists the sites you have defined. When you open the site, a list of pages and subfolders within the site is displayed.

5 If necessary, click Montana Parks to display the Montana Parks Web site in the Files panel.

Copying Data Files to the Local Web Site

In the following steps, the data files for this chapter are stored on drive H:. The location on your computer may be different. If necessary, verify the location of the data files with your instructor.

To Copy Data Files to the Parks Web Site

Your data files contain images for Chapter 3. In Chapters 1 and 2, you copied the data files using the Windows Computer tool. Now that you are more familiar with the Files panel, you can use it to copy the data files for Chapter 3 into the images folder for your Montana Parks Web site. In the following steps, you copy the data files for Chapter 3 from the Chapter03 folder on a USB drive to the parks\images folder stored in the *your name* folder on the same USB drive.

1 Click the Sites pop-up menu button in the Files panel, and then click the name of the drive containing your data files, such as Removable Disk (H:).

2 If necessary, click the plus sign (**+**) next to the folder containing your data files to expand that folder, and then click the plus sign (**+**) next to the Chapter03 folder to expand it.

3 Expand the parks folder to display the data files.

4 Click the first file in the list, which is the arrowheads image file, to select the file.

5 Hold down the SHIFT key and then click the last file in the list, which is the sunset image, to select all the data files.

6 Press CTRL+C to copy the files.

7 If necessary, click the Sites pop-up menu button, and then click the drive containing the Montana Parks Web site. Expand the *your name* folder and the parks folder, and then click the images folder to select it.

8 Press CTRL+V to paste the files in the images folder (Figure 3–3).

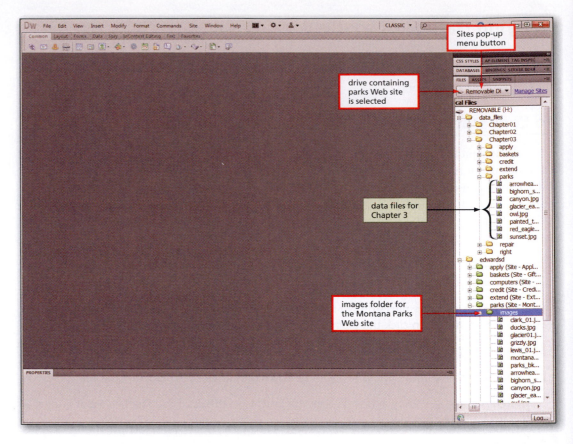

Figure 3–3

Q&A Is there another method for copying data files into the Web site folder?

Yes, you can copy the files using Windows Explorer or the Windows Computer tool.

Q&A What if my Files panel doesn't match the one in Figure 3–3?

In Figure 3–3, the Files panel displays the contents of the USB drive, Removable Disk (H:), which includes both the data files for Chapter 3 and the *your name* folder for the Web sites you create in this book. If your Montana Parks Web site is stored on a drive other than Removable Disk (H:), the name of the drive appears in the Sites pop-up menu button, and the data files for Chapter 3 are listed on your designated drive.

Adding Pages to a Web Site

You copied the images necessary to begin creating your new Web pages in the Montana Parks local root folder in the Files panel. You will add two pages to the Web site: a page for the Nez Perce National Historic Trail and a page for Glacier National Park. You first create the Nez Perce National Historic Trail Web page. You add the background image and a heading to each new page. Next, you insert a table on each page and add text, images, and links into the cells within the table.

To Open a New Document Window

The following steps illustrate how to open a new Document window, which will become the Nez Perce National Historic Trail page, and then save the page.

1 Click the Sites pop-up menu button on the Files panel, and then click Montana Parks to display the files for the Montana Parks Web site.

2 Click File on the Application bar, and then click New to display the New Document dialog box.

3 If necessary, click Blank Page to indicate you are creating a new page.

4 If necessary, click HTML in the Page Type list to indicate the page is a standard HTML page.

5 If necessary, click <none> in the Layout list to indicate you are not using a predefined layout.

6 Click the Create button to create the page.

7 Click the Save button on the Standard toolbar to display the Save As dialog box.

8 Type `nez_perce` as the file name.

9 Click the Save button in the Save As dialog box to display the new, blank nez_perce.htm page in the Document window (Figure 3–4).

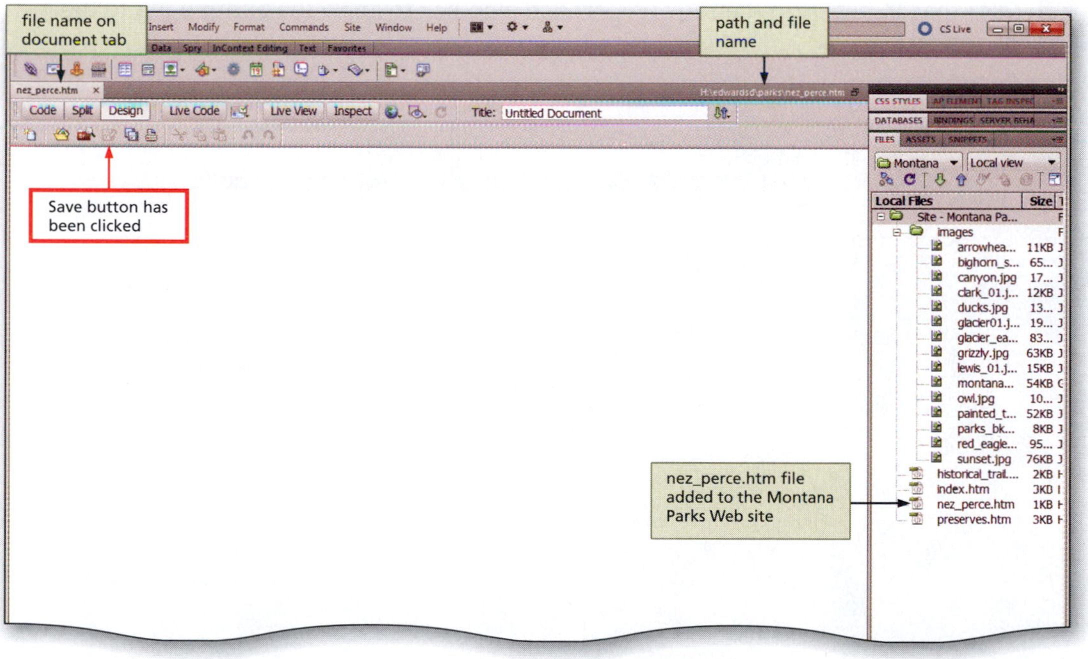

Figure 3–4

Creating the Nez Perce National Historic Trail Web Page

You start creating the Nez Perce National Historic Trail page by applying a background image. This is the same background image you used for the Montana Parks Web site pages in Chapters 1 and 2.

To Add a Background Image to the Nez Perce National Historic Trail Web Page

To provide additional space in the Document window and to create a better overview of the layout, collapse the panel groups. Next, expand the Property inspector to display the additional table options. The following steps also illustrate how to apply the background image.

1 Click the Collapse to Icons button to collapse the panel groups. If necessary, drag the vertical bar between the Document window and the panel groups to resize the panel groups so they display icons only.

2 If necessary, click the Property inspector expander arrow to display both the upper and lower sections of the Property inspector.

3 Click the Page Properties button in the Property inspector to display the Page Properties dialog box.

4 Click Appearance (HTML) in the Category column.

5 Click the Browse button to the right of the Background image box to display the Select Image Source dialog box.

6 If necessary, navigate to and open the parks\images folder.

7 Click parks_bkg and then click the OK button to select the background image.

8 Click the OK button in the Page Properties dialog box to apply the background to the page (Figure 3–5).

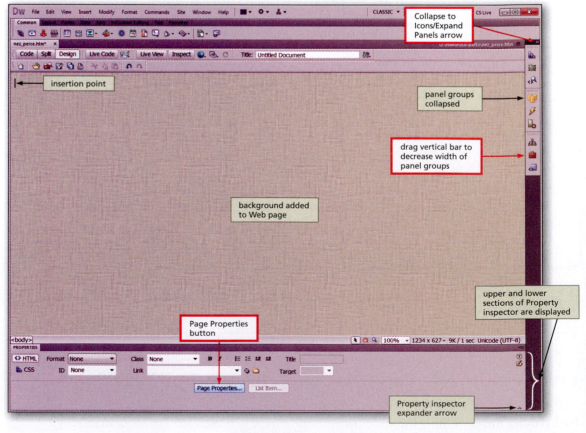

Figure 3–5

To Insert and Format the Heading

Next, you insert and format the heading. You apply the same heading format you applied to the heading in the index page. The following steps show how to add the heading and apply the Heading 1 format.

1 Type `Nez Perce National Historic Trail` as the page heading.

2 Click the Format button in the Property inspector, and then click Heading 1 to apply Heading 1 to the text.

3 Click Format on the Application bar, point to Align, and then click Center to center the heading.

4 Select the text in the Title box on the Document toolbar, and then type `Nez Perce National Historic Trail` as the page title.

5 Click at the end of the heading in the Document window, and then press the ENTER key to move the insertion point to the next line.

6 Click the Save button on the Standard toolbar to save the page with the centered and formatted heading (Figure 3–6).

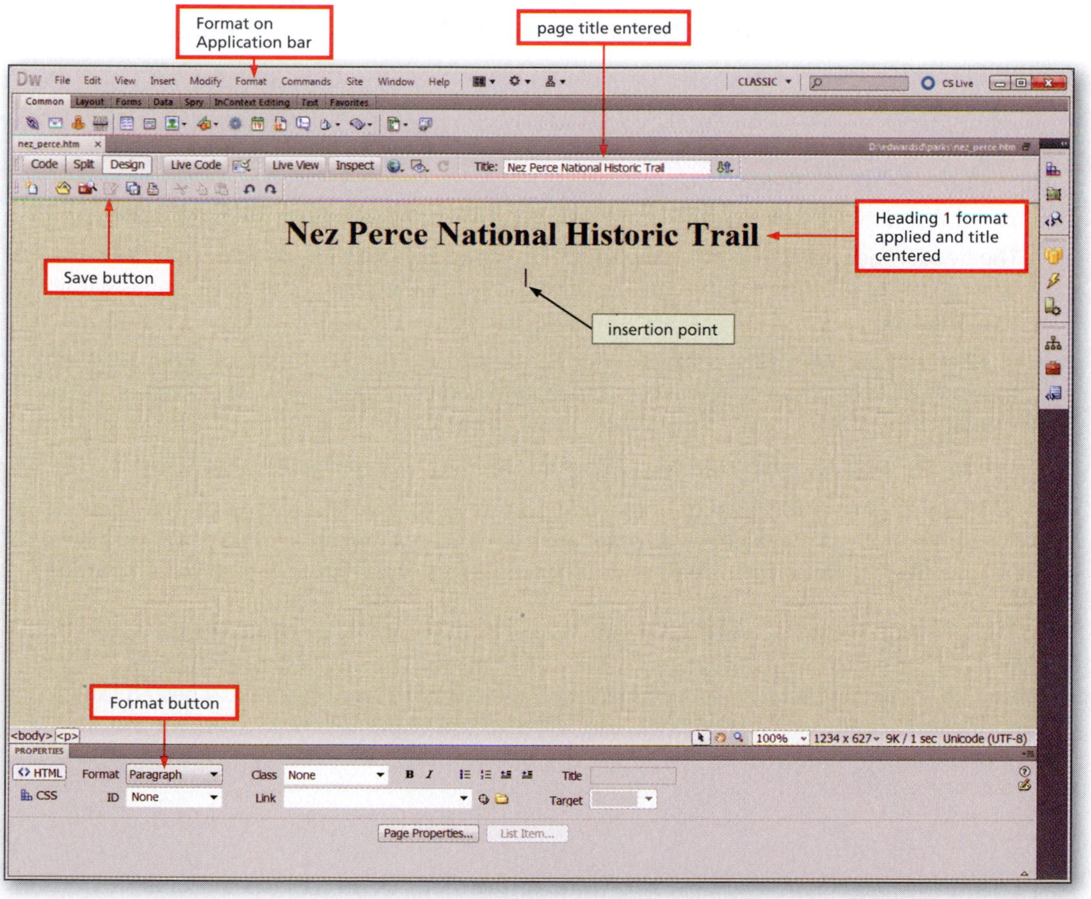

Figure 3–6

Understanding Tables and Page Layout

Tables have many uses in HTML design. The most obvious is a table of data, but, as already mentioned, tables also are used for page layout, such as placing text and graphics on a page at just the right location. **Tables** also provide Web designers with a method to add vertical and horizontal structure to a page. ClassicA table consists of three basic components: rows, columns, and cells. A **row** is a horizontal collection of cells and a **column** is a vertical collection of cells. A **cell** is the container created when the row and column intersect. Each cell within the table can contain any standard element you use on a Web page. This includes text, images, and other objects.

Page layout is the process of arranging the text, images, and other elements on the page. The basic rules of page layout are that your site should be easy to navigate, easy to read, and quick to download. Studies indicate that visitors lose interest in your Web site if the majority of a page does not download within 15 seconds. One popular design element that downloads quickly is tables.

Tables download quickly because they are created with HTML code. They can be used anywhere — for the home page, menus, images, navigation bars, frames, and so on. Tables originally were intended for presenting data arranged by rows and columns, such as tabular data within a spreadsheet. Web designers, however, quickly seized upon the use of tables to produce specific layout effects. You can produce good designs by using tables creatively. Tables allow you to position elements on a Web page with much greater accuracy. Using tables for layout provides the Web page author with endless design possibilities.

Plan Ahead

> **Determine when to insert tables.**
> A typical Web page is composed of three sections: the header, the body, and the footer.
>
> - The **header**, generally located at the top of the page, can contain logos, images, or text that identifies the Web site. The header also can contain hyperlinks to other pages within the Web site.
>
> - The **body** of the Web page contains information about your site. This content may be in the form of text, graphics, animation, video, and audio, or a combination of any of these elements.
>
> - The **footer** provides hyperlinks for contact information and navigational controls.
>
> The controls in the footer might be in addition to the navigation controls in the header. Other common items contained in a footer are the name and e-mail address of the author or the Webmaster. Sometimes, hyperlinks to other resources or to Help information are part of the footer.
>
> Tables make it easy to create this header/body/footer structure or to create any other layout structure that meets your specific Web page needs. The entire structure can be contained within one table or a combination of multiple and nested tables. A nested table is a table inside another table. You will use tables to create the two new pages for the Montana Parks Web site.

To insert a table, you can use the Table button on the Insert bar or the Table command on the Insert menu. Both the Common category and the Layout category on the Insert bar contain a Table button that works the same way in either category. However, the Layout category includes the Standard and Expanded Tables mode buttons. In Expanded Tables mode, Dreamweaver temporarily adds cell padding and spacing to all the tables in a document and expands the tables' borders to make detailed editing easier. Some operations, such as resizing tables and images, work unpredictably in Expanded

Tables mode and are better performed in Standard mode. In this chapter, you work in Standard mode only because you do not need to perform the types of precise selections that Expanded Tables mode makes possible.

If you have a table created in another application, such as Microsoft Word or Excel, you can import the data. To do so, click File on the Application bar, point to Import, and then click Tabular Data. (You also can click Insert on the Application bar, point to Table Objects, and then click Import Tabular Data.) Select the file you want to import, specify settings such as table width, border, cell padding, and cell spacing, and then click OK.

Inserting a Table into the Nez Perce National Historic Trail Page

You will add two tables to the Nez Perce National Historic Trail page and then add text and images to the cells within the tables. The first table will consist of three rows and two columns, with a cell padding of 5 and cell spacing of 10. **Cell padding** is the amount of space between the edge of a cell and its contents, whereas **cell spacing** is the amount of space between cells. The border will be set to 0, which is the default. When the table is displayed in Dreamweaver, a border outline appears around the table. When the table's border is set to 0 and the table is viewed in a browser; however, this outline is not displayed.

The table width is 90 percent. When specifying the width, you can select percent or pixels. A table with the width specified as a **percent** expands with the width of the window and the monitor size in which it is being viewed. A table with the width specified as **pixels** will remain the same size regardless of the window and monitor size. If you select percent and an image is larger than the selected percentage, the cell and table will expand to accommodate the image. Likewise, if the **No wrap** property is enabled and the text will not fit within the cell, the cell and table will expand to accommodate the text. It is not necessary to declare a table width. When no value is specified, the table is displayed as small as possible and then expands as content is added. If modifications are necessary to the original specified table values, you can change these values in the Property inspector.

The second table for the Nez Perce National Historic Trail page is a one-cell table, consisting of one row and one column. This table will contain links to the Home page and to other pages in the Web site. You use the Layout category on the Insert bar and the Property inspector to control and format the tables.

Using the Insert Bar

By default, the Classic workspace shows the Insert bar at the top of the window below the Application bar. This toolbar contains several categories, or tabs, and is fully customizable through the Favorites tab. The Insert bar contains buttons for creating and inserting objects such as tables and advanced elements such as div tags, frames, the Spry Menu Bar, and other Spry options.

You can hide, customize, or display the Insert bar as necessary. All selections within the categories also are available through the Application bar and many of the selections also are available through the Property inspectors. The Table button command also can be accessed through the Insert menu on the Application bar.

BTW

Inserting Content with the Insert Bar
Besides inserting tables, you can insert other types of content using the Insert bar, including images, video, and widgets such as calendars and tabbed panels.

To Display the Insert Bar and Select the Layout Tab

You use the Table buttons on the Layout tab of the Insert bar to assist with page design. The following steps illustrate how to display the Insert bar if necessary and select the Layout tab.

1
• If necessary, click Window on the Application bar and then click Insert to display the Insert bar.

Q&A
What should I do if the Insert bar is displayed as a pane instead of a bar?

Drag the title bar of the Insert pane below the Application bar to display it as a bar.

• Point to the Layout tab on the Insert bar (Figure 3–7).

Figure 3–7

2
• Click the Layout tab to display the Insert bar Layout category (Figure 3–8).

Q&A
What kinds of options are available on the Layout tab of the Insert bar?

The Layout tab contains options for working with tables, div tags, and panels.

Q&A
What are the dimmed buttons to the right of the Table button?

When any part of a table is selected, the four dimmed buttons are displayed so you can format the table.

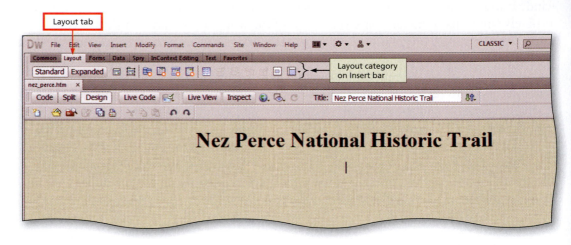

Figure 3–8

Layout Tab

You use the Layout tab (Figure 3–9 on the next page) to work with tables and table features. Dreamweaver provides two modes, or ways, to use the table feature: Standard mode and Expanded Tables mode. Standard mode uses the Table dialog box. When you create a table, the Table dialog box opens in Standard mode by default so you can set the basic structure of the table. It then is displayed as a grid and expands as you add text and images.

As mentioned earlier, you use the Expanded button on the Layout tab to switch to Expanded Tables mode. This mode temporarily enlarges your view of the cells so you can select items easily and place the insertion point precisely. Use this mode as a temporary visual aid for selection and insertion point placement. After placing the insertion point, return to Standard mode to make your edits and to provide a better visualization of your changes. Other buttons on the Layout tab are for working with Spry objects, which don't apply to tables.

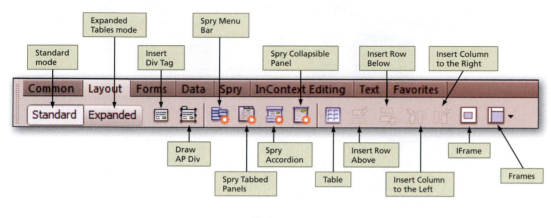

Figure 3–9

Table 3–1 lists the button names and descriptions available in the Insert bar Layout category.

Table 3–1 Buttons on the Layout tab of the Insert Bar	
Button Name	**Description**
Standard mode	Displays a table as a grid of lines
Expanded Tables mode	Temporarily adds cell padding and spacing
Insert Div Tag	Inserts a <div> tag
Draw AP Div	Inserts a <div> tag at a fixed absolute point within a Web document
Spry Tabbed Panels	Inserts a tabbed panel widget directly into the Web page
Spry Menu Bar	Inserts an AJAX predefined control
Spry Accordion	Creates horizontal regions on a Web page that can be expanded or collapsed
Spry Collapsible Panel	Displays collapsible panels that have a clickable tab
Table	Places a table at the insertion point
Insert Row Above	Inserts a row above the selected row
Insert Row Below	Inserts a row below the selected row
Insert Column to the Left	Inserts a column to the left of the selected column
Insert Column to the Right	Inserts a column to the right of the selected column
IFrame	Displays data (text and image) that is stored in a separate page
Frames	Displays Frames pop-up menu

Table Defaults and Accessibility

When you insert a table, the Table dialog box is displayed and contains default settings for each of the table attributes (Figure 3–10 on the next page). After you create a table and change these defaults, the settings that are displayed remain until you change them for the next table. Table 3–2 lists and describes the defaults for each table attribute.

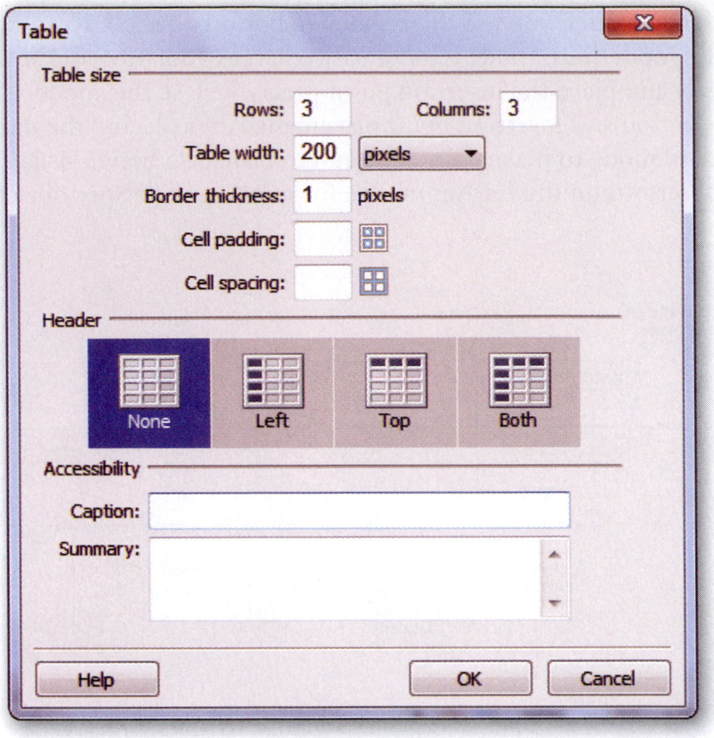

Figure 3–10

Table 3–2 Table Dialog Box Default Values		
Attribute	**Default**	**Description**
Rows	3	Determines the number of rows in the table
Columns	3	Determines the number of columns in the table
Table width	200 pixels	Specifies the width of the table in pixels or as a percentage of the browser window's width
Border thickness	1	Specifies the border width in pixels
Cell padding	None	Specifies the number of pixels between a cell's border and its contents
Cell spacing	None	Specifies the number of pixels between adjacent table cells
Header	None	Specifies whether the top row and/or column is designated as a header cell
Caption	None	Provides a table heading
Summary	None	Provides a table description; used by screen readers

It is advisable to use headers for tables when the table presents tabular information. Screen readers scan table headings and help screen-reader users keep track of table information. Additionally, the Caption option provides a table title that is displayed outside of the table. If a Caption is specified, the Align Caption option indicates where the table caption appears in relation to the table. The Summary option provides a table description. Summary text is similar to the Alt text you added for images in Chapter 2. You add Summary text to the tables you create in this chapter. Screen readers read the summary text, but the text does not appear in the user's browser.

Table Layout

As indicated previously, the Header and Caption options are important when a table displays tabular data. When using a table for layout, however, other options apply. Structurally and graphically, the elements in a table used for layout should be invisible in the browser. For instance, when using a table for layout, use the None option for Headers. The None option prevents the header tags <th> and </th> from being added to the table. Because the table does not contain tabular data, a header would be of no benefit to the screen-reader user. Screen readers, however, read table content from left to right and top to bottom. Therefore, it is important to structure the table content in a linear arrangement.

Plan Ahead

Lay out Web pages with tables.

Tables help you lay out Web pages that contain text and images. After creating a Web page and setting its properties, add tables, text, and images in the following order:

1. **Table:** Insert a table before entering any text other than the page heading. Set table properties such as size, cell padding, and cell spacing.

2. **Text:** Add text to the table cells. You can apply formats to the text such as Heading 1 and bold text to emphasize it, for example.

3. **Images:** Insert images after you enter text to balance the images and the rest of the table content. Then you can resize each image, align it, and set other image properties.

To Insert a Table

The following steps illustrate how to insert a table with three rows and two columns into the Nez Perce National Historic Trail Web page.

1

- Click the Table button on the Layout tab to display the Table dialog box (Figure 3–11).

Q&A Should the settings in my Table dialog box match those in the figure?

The settings displayed are the settings from the last table created, so your dialog box might contain different values.

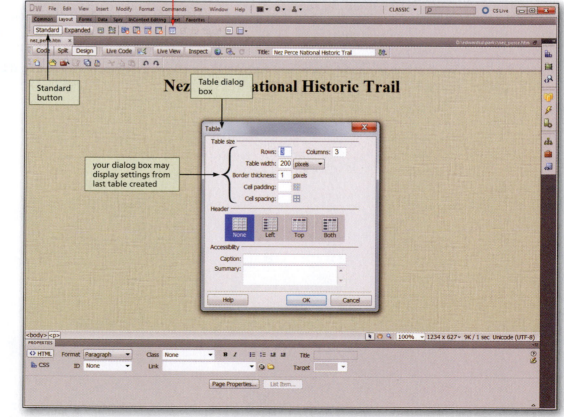

Figure 3–11

2

- If necessary, type 3 in the Rows box to create a table with three rows, and then press the TAB key to move to the Columns box.

- Type 2 to create a table with two columns, and then press the TAB key to move to the Table width box.

- Type 90 to set the table width, and then click the Table width button to display the Table width options.

- Click percent to specify the table width as a percentage, and then press the TAB key to move to the Border thickness box.

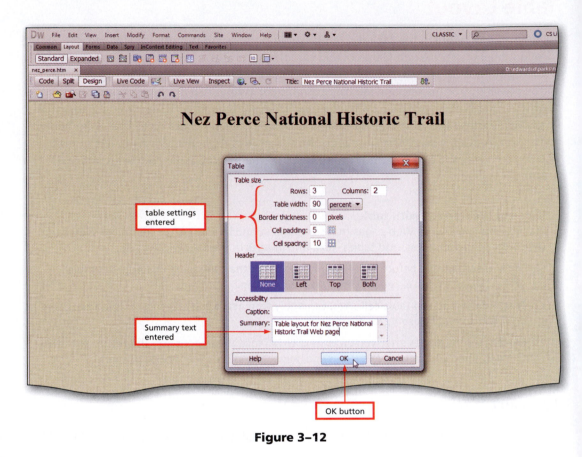

Figure 3–12

- Type 0 to set the border thickness, and then press the TAB key to move to the Cell padding box.

- Type 5 to add 5 pixels of cell padding, and then press the TAB key to move to the Cell spacing box.

- Type 10 to add 10 pixels of space between adjacent table cells.

- Click the Summary text box and type `Table layout for Nez Perce National Historic Trail Web page` (Figure 3–12).

3

- Click the OK button to insert the table into the Document window (Figure 3–13).

Why does a border appear around the table if the Border thickness is set to 0?

Although the border thickness is set to 0, it appears as an outline in the Document window. The border will not appear when displayed in the browser.

Can I add rows after I create a table?

Yes. Right-click a row to display the context menu, point to Table, and then click Insert Row to add a row after the current one.

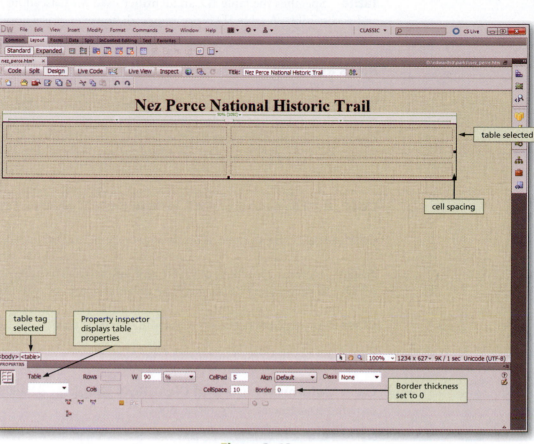

Figure 3–13

Property Inspector Table Features

As you have seen, the Property inspector options change depending on the selected object. You use the Property inspector to modify and add table attributes. When a table is selected, the Property inspector displays table properties in both panels. When another table element — a row, column, or cell — is selected, the displayed properties change and are determined by the selected element. The following section describes the table-related features of the Property inspector shown in Figure 3–14.

Other Ways

1. On Insert menu, click Table, select table properties, click OK button
2. Press CTRL+ALT+T

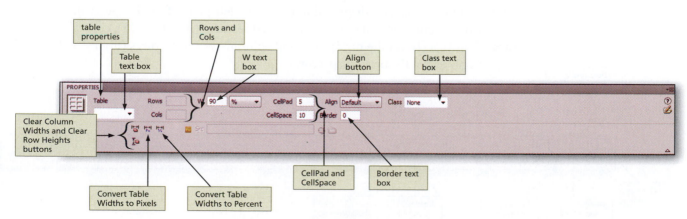

Figure 3–14

Table   Specifies the table ID, an identifier used for Cascading Style Sheets, scripting, and accessibility. A table ID is not required; however, it is a good idea always to add this identifier.

Rows and Cols   The number of rows and columns in the table.

W   Specifies the minimum width of the table in either pixels or percent. If a size is not specified, the size can vary depending on the monitor and browser settings. A table width specified in pixels is displayed as the same size in all browsers. A table width specified in percent is altered in appearance based on the user's monitor resolution and browser window size.

CellPad   The number of pixels between the cell border and the cell content.

CellSpace   The number of pixels between adjacent table cells.

Align   Determines where the table appears, relative to other elements in the same paragraph such as text or images. The default alignment is to the left.

Class   An attribute used with Cascading Style Sheets.

Border   Specifies the border width in pixels.

Clear Column Widths and Clear Row Heights   Deletes all specified row height or column width values from the table.

Convert Table Widths to Pixels   Sets the width of each column in the table to its current width expressed as pixels.

Convert Table Widths to Percent   Sets the width of the table and each column in the table to their current widths expressed as percentages of the Document window's width.

Cell, Row, and Column Properties

When a cell, row, or column is selected, the properties in the upper pane of the Property inspector are the same as the standard properties for text. You can use these properties to include standard HTML formatting tags within a cell, row, or column. The part of the table selected determines which properties are displayed in the lower pane of the Property inspector. The properties for cells, rows, and columns are the same, except for one element — the icon displayed in the lower-left pane of the Property inspector. The following section describes the row-related features (Figure 3–15), cell-related features (Figure 3–16 on the next page), and column-related features (Figure 3–17 on the next page) of the Property inspector.

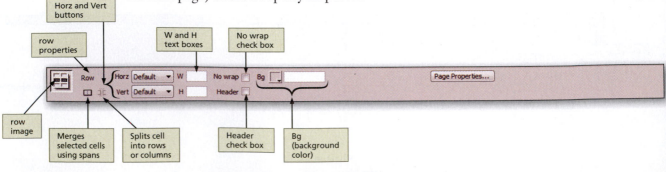

Figure 3–15

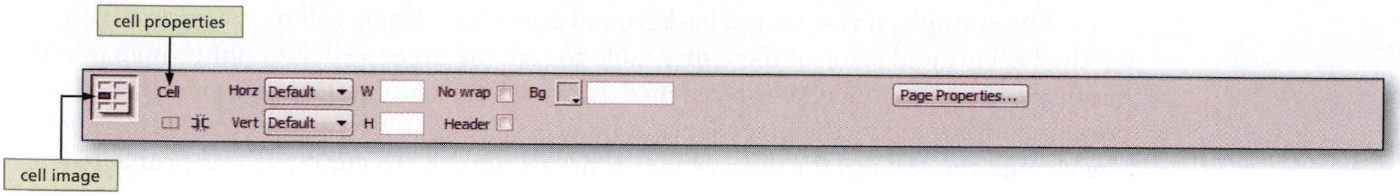

cell properties

Figure 3–16

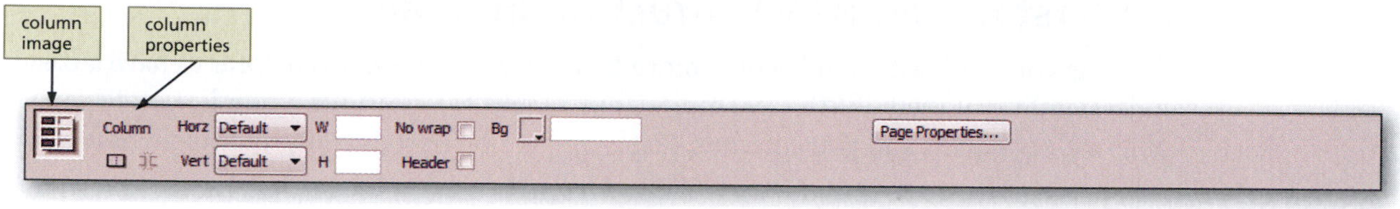

cell image

column image

column properties

Figure 3–17

Horz   Specifies the horizontal alignment of the contents of a cell, row, or column. The contents can be aligned to the left, right, or center of the cells.

Vert   Specifies the vertical alignment of the contents of a cell, row, or column. The contents can be aligned to the top, middle, bottom, or baseline of the cells.

W and H   Specifies the width and height of selected cells in pixels or as a percentage of the entire table's width or height.

No wrap   Prevents line wrapping, keeping all text in a given cell on a single line. If No Wrap is enabled, cells widen to accommodate all data as it is typed or pasted into a cell.

Bg (background color)   Sets the background color of a cell, row, or column selected from the color picker (use the Bg icon) or specified as a hexadecimal number (use the Bg text box).

Header   Formats the selected cells as table header cells. The contents of table header cells are bold and centered by default.

Merges selected cells using spans   Combines selected cells, rows, or columns into one cell (available when two or more cells, rows, or columns are selected).

Splits cell into rows or columns   Divides a cell, creating two or more cells (available when a single cell is selected).

Table Formatting Conflicts

When formatting tables in Standard mode, you can set properties for the entire table or for selected rows, columns, or cells in the table. Applying these properties, however, introduces a potential for conflict. To prevent conflicts, HTML assigns levels of precedence. The order of precedence for table formatting is cells, rows, and table. When a property, such as background color or alignment, is set to one value for the whole table and another value for individual cells, cell formatting takes precedence over row formatting, which in turn takes precedence over table formatting.

For example, if you set the background color for a single cell to green, and then set the background color of the entire table to red, the green cell does not change to red, because cell formatting takes precedence over table formatting. Dreamweaver, however, does not always follow the precedence. The program will override the settings for a cell if you change the settings for the row that contains the cell. To eliminate this problem, you should change the cell settings last.

Understanding HTML Structure in a Table

As you work with and become more familiar with tables, it is helpful to have a basic understanding of the HTML structure within a table. Suppose, for example, you have a table with two rows and two columns, displaying a total of four cells, such as the following:

First cell	Second cell
Third cell	Fourth cell

The general syntax of the table is:
<table>
<tr>
 <td> First cell </td>
 <td> Second cell </td>
</tr>
<tr>
 <td> Third cell </td>
 <td> Fourth cell </td>
</tr>
</table>

In Dreamweaver, the tag selector displays the <table>, <td>, and <tr> tags. The <table> tag indicates the whole table. Clicking the <table> tag in the tag selector selects the whole table. The <td> tag indicates table data. Clicking the <td> tag in the tag selector selects the cell containing the insertion point. The <tr> tag indicates table row. Clicking the <tr> tag in the tag selector selects the row containing the insertion point.

Selecting the Table and Selecting Cells

The Property inspector displays table attributes only if the entire table is selected. To select the entire table, click the upper-left corner of the table, click anywhere on the top or bottom edge of the table, or click in a cell and then click <table> in the tag selector. When selected, the table is displayed with a dark border and selection handles on the table's lower and right edges (Figure 3–18 on the next page).

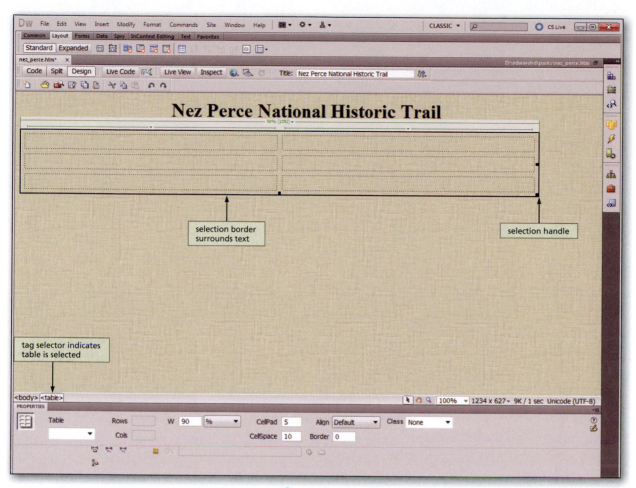

Figure 3–18

Selecting a cell, row, or column is easier than selecting the entire table. When a cell, row, or column is selected, the selected item has a dark border. To select a cell, click inside the cell. When you click inside the cell, the <td> tag is displayed as selected on the status bar. To select a row or column, click inside one of the cells in the row or column and drag to select the other cells. When you select a row, the <tr> tag is displayed on the status bar. In Figure 3–19 on the next page, a row is selected.

A second method for selecting a row or column is to point to the left edge of a row or the top edge of a column. When the pointer changes to a selection arrow, click to select the row or column. In Figure 3–20 on the next page, a column is selected.

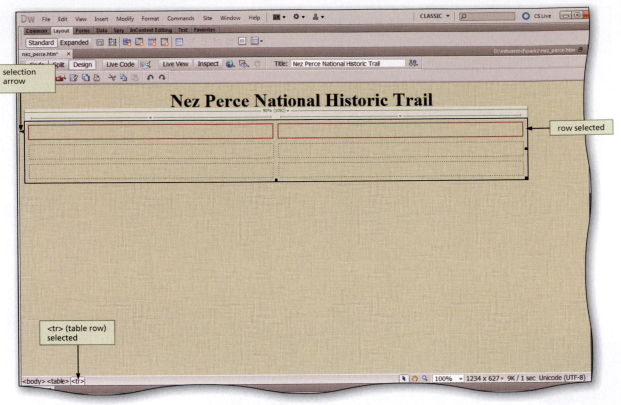

Figure 3–19

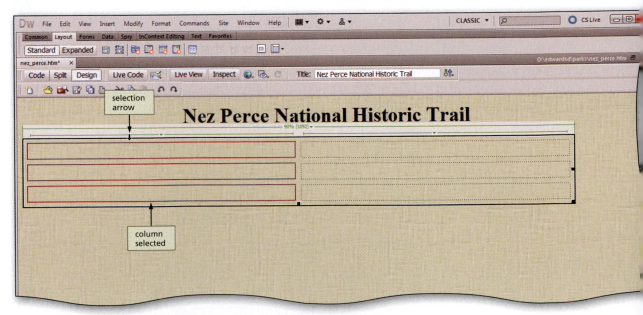

Figure 3–20

Centering a Table

When a table is inserted into the Document window with a specified width, it aligns to the left by default. Using the Property inspector, you can center the table by selecting it and then applying the Center command.

To Select and Center a Table

The following steps illustrate how to select and center the table using the Property inspector.

1

• Click in row 1, column 1 to place the insertion point in the first cell of the table (Figure 3–21).

2

• Click <table> in the tag selector to select the table and to display handles on the lower and right borders of the table.

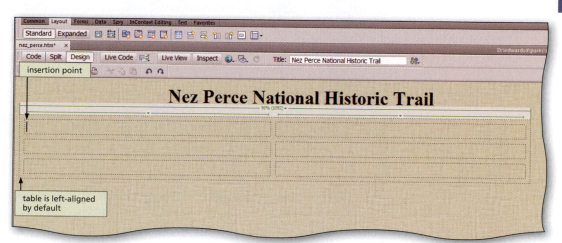

Figure 3–21

• Click the Align button in the Property inspector and then point to Center (Figure 3–22).

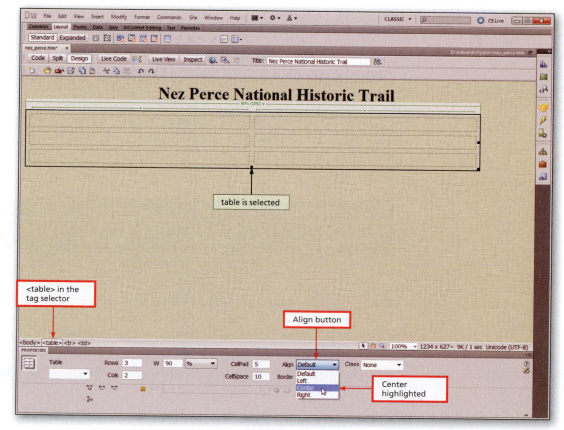

Figure 3–22

3
- Click Center to center the table on the page (Figure 3–23).

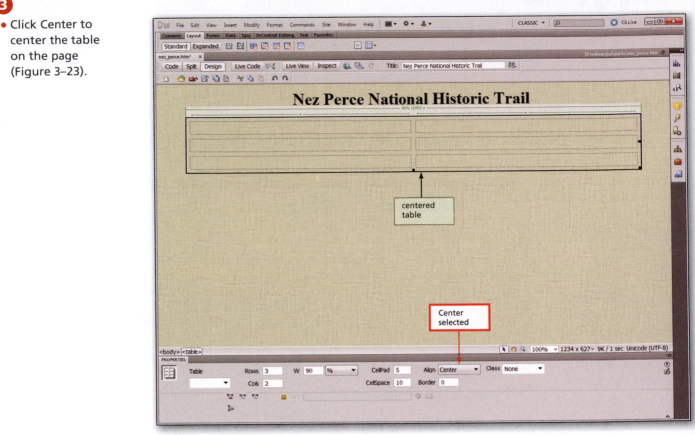

Figure 3–23

Changing the Default Cell Alignment for Text

The default horizontal cell alignment for text is left. When you enter text in a cell, it defaults to the left margin of the cell. You can change the horizontal alignment through the Property inspector Align button pop-up menu by clicking the cell and then changing the default to Center or Right. The default vertical cell alignment is Middle, which aligns the cell content in the middle of the cell. Table 3–3 describes the cell alignment options.

Table 3–3 Cell Alignment Options	
Alignment	**Description**
Default	Specifies a baseline alignment; default may vary depending on the user's browser
Baseline	Aligns the cell content at the bottom of the cell (same as Bottom)
Top	Aligns the cell content at the top of the cell
Bottom	Aligns the cell content at the bottom of the cell
TextTop	Aligns the top of the image with the top of the tallest character in the text line
Absolute Middle	Aligns the middle of the image with the middle of the text in the current line
Absolute Bottom	Aligns the bottom of the image with the bottom of the line of text

Alignment	Description
Left	Places the selected image on the left margin, wrapping text around it to the right; if left-aligned text precedes the object on the line, it generally forces left-aligned objects to wrap to a new line
Middle	Aligns the middle of the image with the baseline of the current line
Right	Places the image on the right margin, wrapping text around the object to the left; if right-aligned text precedes the object on the line, it generally forces right-aligned objects to wrap to a new line

Table 3–3 Cell Alignment Options (*continued*)

You can change the alignment using the Align button in the Property inspector by clicking the cell and then selecting another alignment option. These properties can be applied to a single cell, to multiple cells, or to the entire table.

To Change Vertical Alignment from Middle to Top

The following steps show how to select all of the cells and change the default alignment from middle to top.

1

- Click in row 1, column 1 and then drag to the right and down to select the three rows and two columns in the table.

- Click the Vert button in the Property inspector to display the Vert pop-up menu and then point to Top (Figure 3–24).

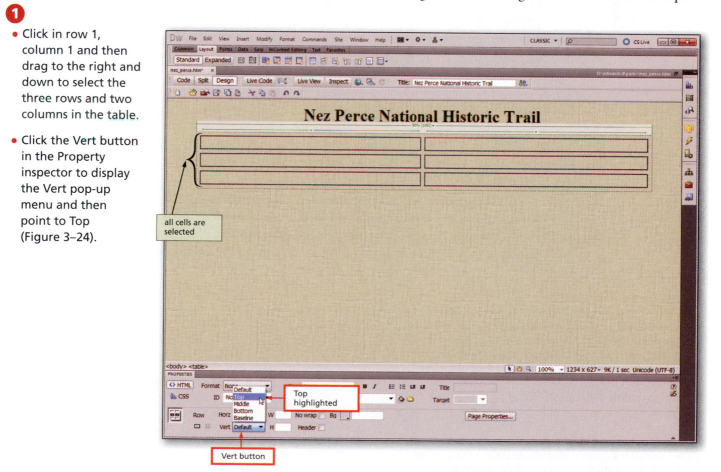

Figure 3–24

2

- Click Top to change the vertical alignment from Middle to Top (Figure 3–25).

Q&A

Should the appearance of the table change after applying a new vertical alignment? The change is not visible in the Document window yet — the new alignment is noticeable when the cells contain text or images.

Nez Perce National Historic Trail

no visible changes to the blank table

Top selected

Figure 3–25

Specifying Column Width

When a table width is specified as a percentage, each column's width expands to accommodate the text or image. When you add content to the table, this expansion can distort the table appearance and make it difficult to visualize how the final page will be displayed. You can control this expansion by setting the column width.

BTW

Changing Column Width
In addition to using the Property inspector to change the width or height of a column, you can drag the right border of a column to resize it. To change a column width without affecting other columns in the table, hold down the SHIFT key as you drag. If you are familiar with HTML, you can change cell widths and heights directly in the HTML code.

BTW

Clearing Column Widths and Row Heights
To clear all the column widths you set in a table, select the table, and then click the Clear Column Widths button in the Property inspector. To clear all the row heights you set, select the table, and then click the Clear Row Heights button.

To Specify Column Width

The objective for the Nez Perce National Historic Trail page is to display the page in two columns — column 1 at 45% and column 2 at 35%. The following steps show how to specify column width.

1

- Click the cell in row 1, column 1 and then drag to select all cells in column 1.

- Click the W box in the Property inspector, type **45%**, and then press the ENTER key to set the width for column 1 at 45%.

- Click the cell in row 1, column 2 and then drag to select all cells in column 2.

- Click the W box in the Property inspector, type **35%**, then press the ENTER key to set the width for column 2 at 35% (Figure 3–26).

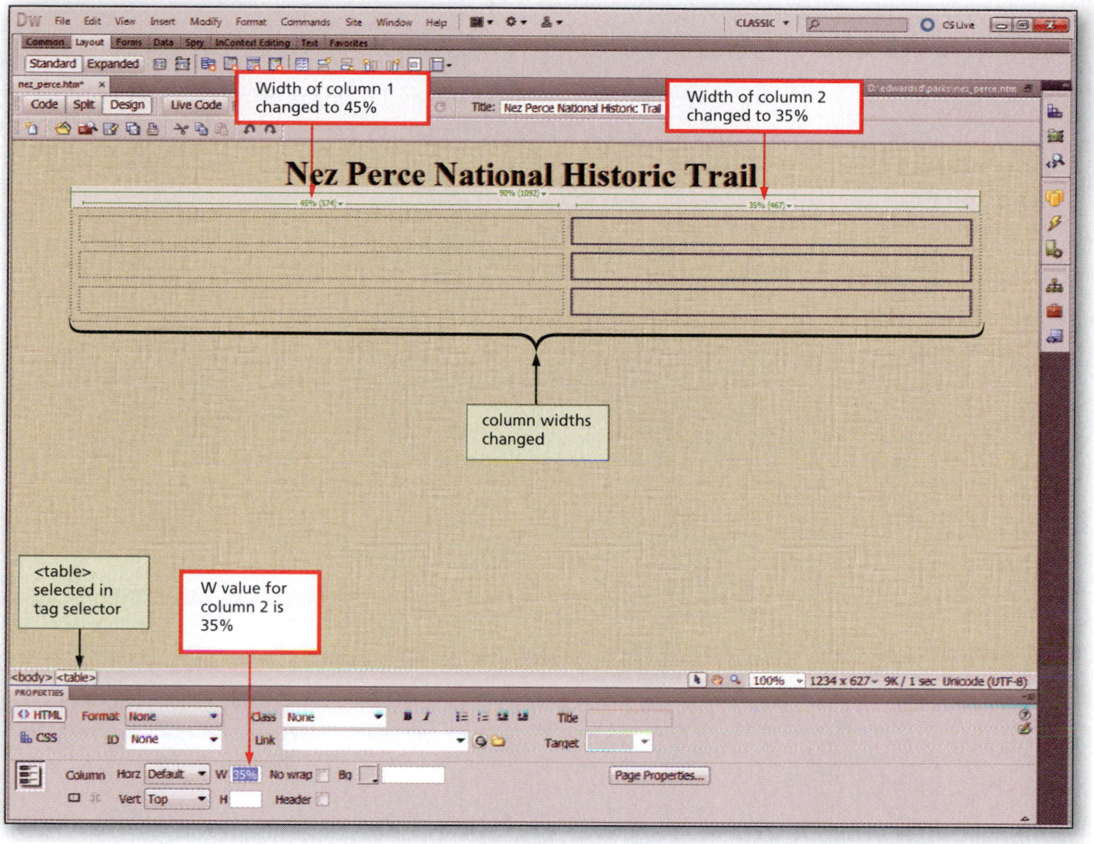

2

- Click anywhere in the table to deselect the column.

Figure 3–26

Adding an ID

Tables, images, and other Web site elements can be assigned a name through the Table field located in the Property inspector. This ID identifies the content of an object within the HTML code. Spaces and characters cannot be used except for the dash or underscore.

To Add a Table ID to the Nez Perce National Historic Trail Table

The following step illustrates how to select the table and add a table ID to the Nez Perce National Historic Trail feature table.

1

- Click <table> in the tag selector to select the table.

- Click the Table text box and then type **nez_perce** as the ID text.

- Press the ENTER key to add the table ID (Figure 3–27). 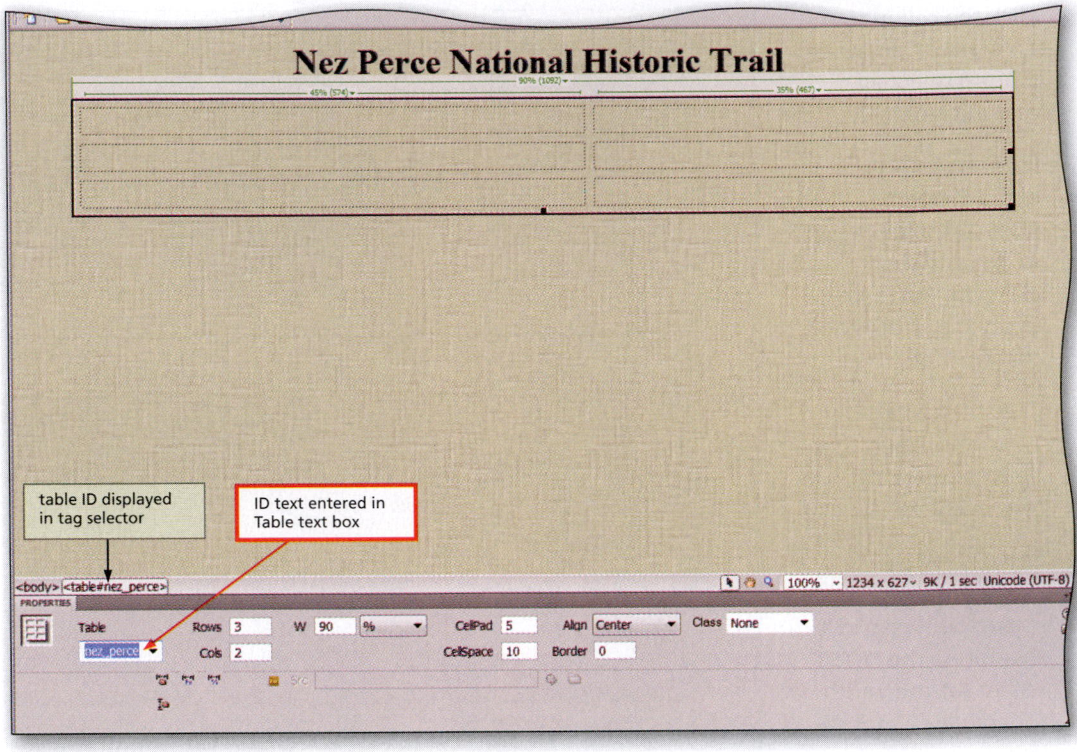

Figure 3–27

Adding Text to the Nez Perce National Historic Trail Web Page

Next, you enter and format the text for the Nez Perce National Historic Trail Web page. Table 3–4 on the next page includes the text for the first table. The text is entered into the table cells. If you have not set the width and height of a cell, when you begin to enter text into a table cell, the cell expands to accommodate the text. The other cells may appear to shrink, but they also will expand when you type in the cells or add an image to the cells.

Table 3–4 Nez Perce National Historic Trail Text

Section	Text
Part 1	Nez Perce National Historic Trail is more than 415 square miles and has 114 named peaks over 10,000 feet. One of the more popular hiking trails is the Keyhole Route on Longs' Peak. At 14,255 feet, Longs' Peak is the highest peak in the Nez Perce National Historic Trail and the fifteenth tallest in Montana. <ENTER> The park contains three distinct ecosystems which correspond to elevation: the montane, which is 7,000 to 9,000 feet above sea level; the subalpine ecosystem, which is 9,000 to 11,500 feet and spans the tree line; and the alpine tundra, at the top, which is over 11,500 feet.
Part 2	Birds and animals add color and interest to the landscape. The park contains 65 species of mammals, 260 species of birds, and 900 species of plants. Black bears, mountain lions, and bobcats live in the park, but seldom are seen. Moose and mule deer are more visible. In autumn, herds of American elk roam the park and frequently are visible, even at the lower elevations. <ENTER> Interesting facts: a) In the summer of 2005, a dinosaur footprint was found. The print was identified as belonging to a three-toed foot of a Cretaceous Theropod. b) The park contains over 650 species of flowering plants as well as many species of mosses, lichens, fungi, algae, and other plant life.
Part 3	The park is open 24 hours a day year round.< br /> Park Service Information Office: Nez Perce National Historic Trail 12730 Highway 12 Orofino, ID 83544<ENTER> E-mail: nez_perce_trail@fs.fed.us
Bighorn sheep text	Bighorn sheep are one of the more common animals seen along the trail. The male bighorn is called a ram. It easily is recognized by its massive curled horns, which can weigh more than 30 pounds. The females, called ewes, have smaller horns. They can have from one to two kids every spring. The bighorn can live to be 10–15 years old.

To Add Text to the Nez Perce National Historic Trail Web Page

The following steps show how to add text to the Nez Perce National Historic Trail page. Press the ENTER key when indicated or press SHIFT+ENTER to insert a line break, <br />, as specified in Table 3–4 on the previous page. Press the TAB key to move from cell to cell.

1

- Type the two paragraphs of Part 1 in Table 3–4 in row 1, column 1 of the table in the Document window, pressing the ENTER key as indicated in the table (Figure 3–28).

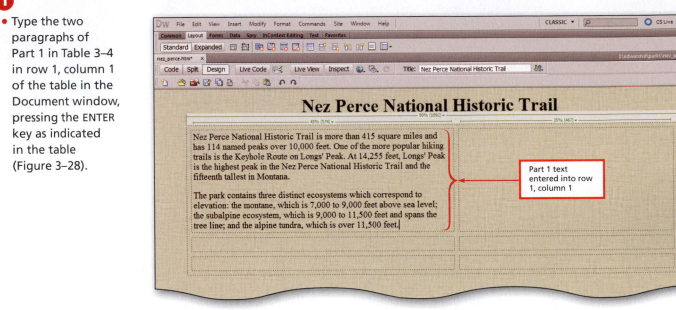

Figure 3–28

2

- Type the two paragraphs of Part 2, as shown in Table 3–4, into row 2, column 2 of the table.

- Type the text of Part 3, as shown in Table 3–4, into row 3, column 1 of the Document window (Figure 3–29).

Q&A How do I enter the line breaks?

Press SHIFT+ENTER to insert the line breaks.

Q&A Where is the insertion point after I insert a line break?

The insertion point is within the cell below the last line and may not be visible.

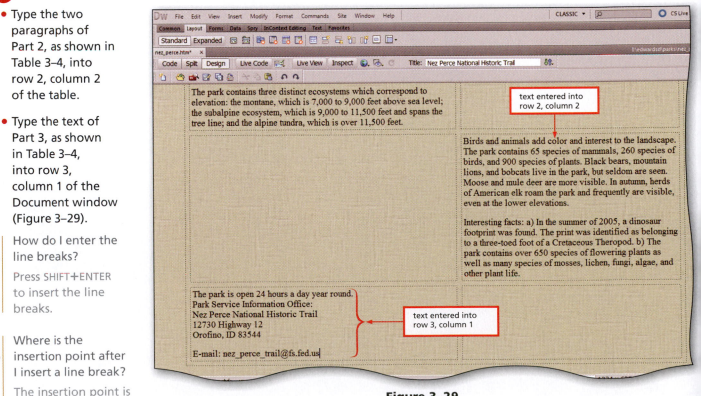

Figure 3–29

3

- Select the text in row 3, column 1 to prepare for aligning the text.
- Click the Horz button in the Property inspector, and then click Right to align the text to the right.
- Click anywhere on the page to deselect the text (Figure 3–30).

4

- Click the Save button to save the page.

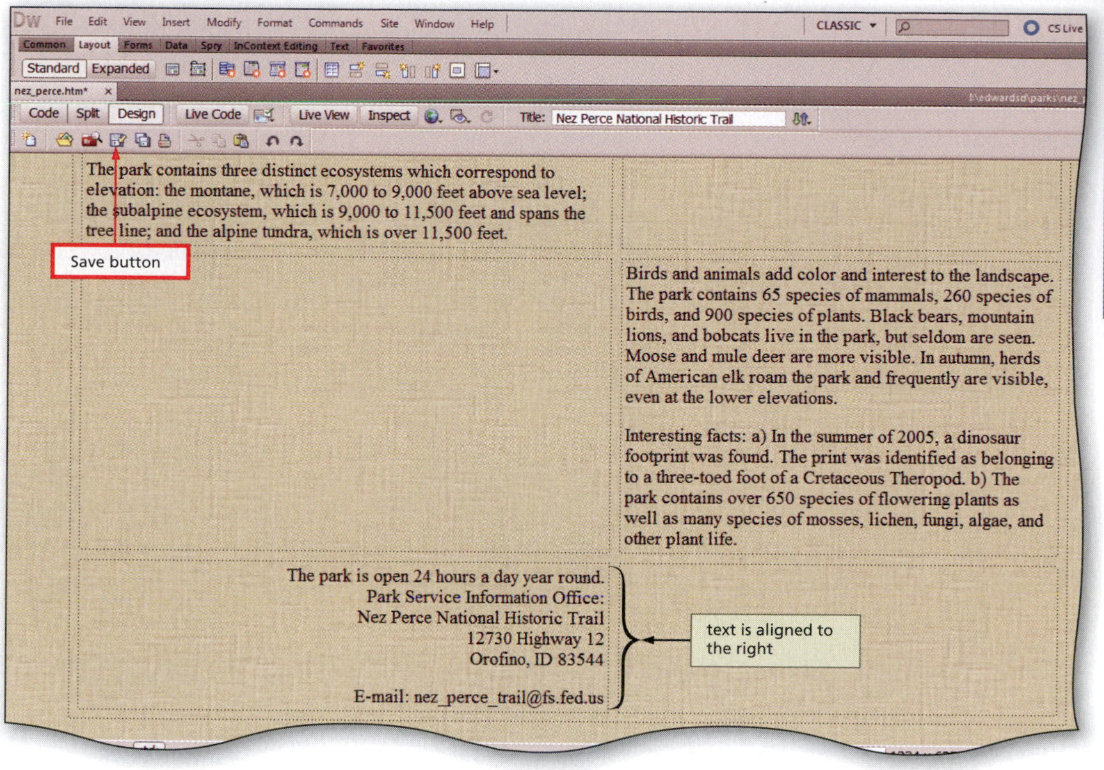

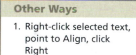

Figure 3–30

Other Ways

1. Right-click selected text, point to Align, click Right

Adding a Second Table to the Nez Perce National Historic Trail Web Page

Next, you add a second table to the Nez Perce National Historic Trail Web page. This table will contain one row and one column and will serve as the footer for your Web page.

To Add a Second Table to the Nez Perce National Historic Trail Web Page

The text for the footer should be centered in the cell and contain links to the home page and to the other pages within the Web site. When you create the page for the Nez Perce National Historic Trail, you can copy and paste these links into that page. The following steps show how to add the second table using the Layout tab on the Insert bar.

1

- Click outside the right border of the existing table to position the insertion point outside the table (Figure 3–31).

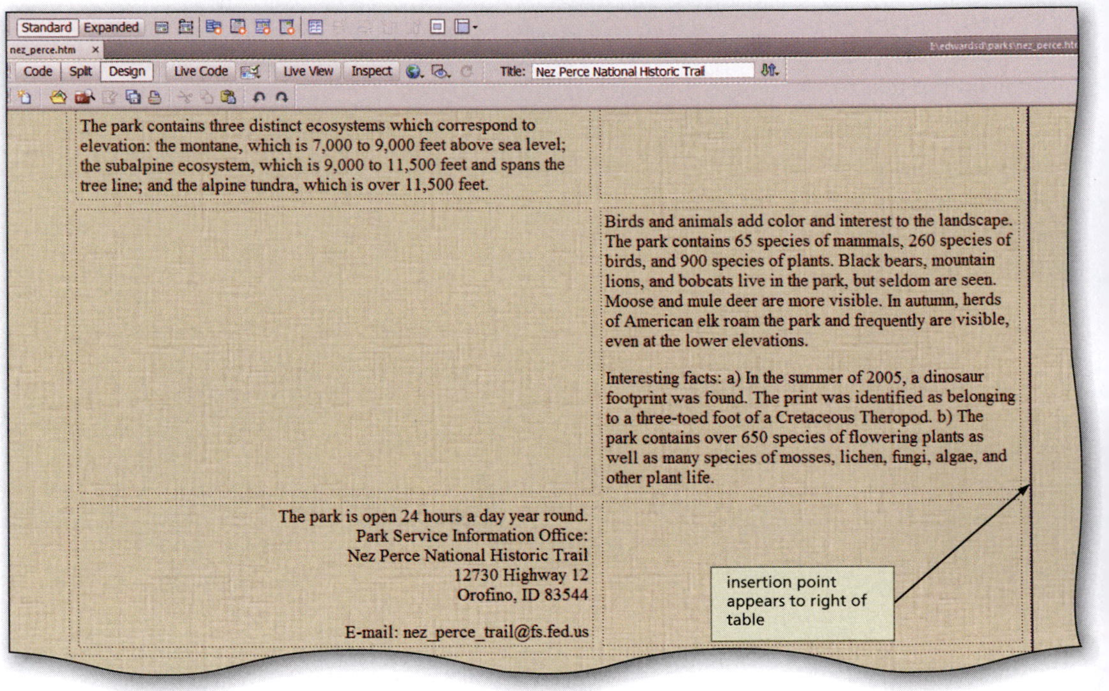

Figure 3–31

2

- Press the ENTER key to move the insertion point below the table.

- Click the Table button on the Layout tab on the Insert bar to display the Table dialog box (Figure 3–32).

Q&A

Should the settings in my Table dialog box match those in Figure 3–32?

Not necessarily. The dialog box on your computer may show different settings.

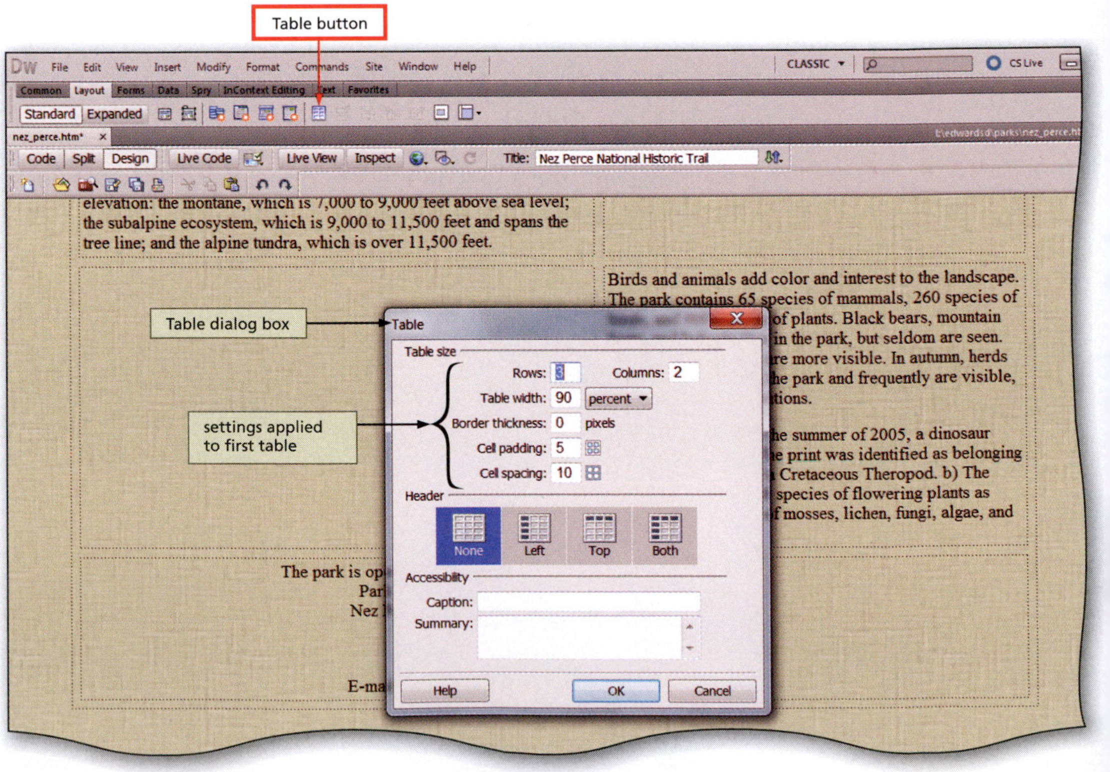

Figure 3–32

3

- Change the number of rows to 1, the number of columns to 1, the width to 75 percent, the border thickness to 0, the cell padding to 0, and the cell spacing to 10 to set the properties for the table.

- Type **Footer table for links** in the Summary text box to add the table description.

- If necessary, change other settings to match the settings shown in Figure 3–33.

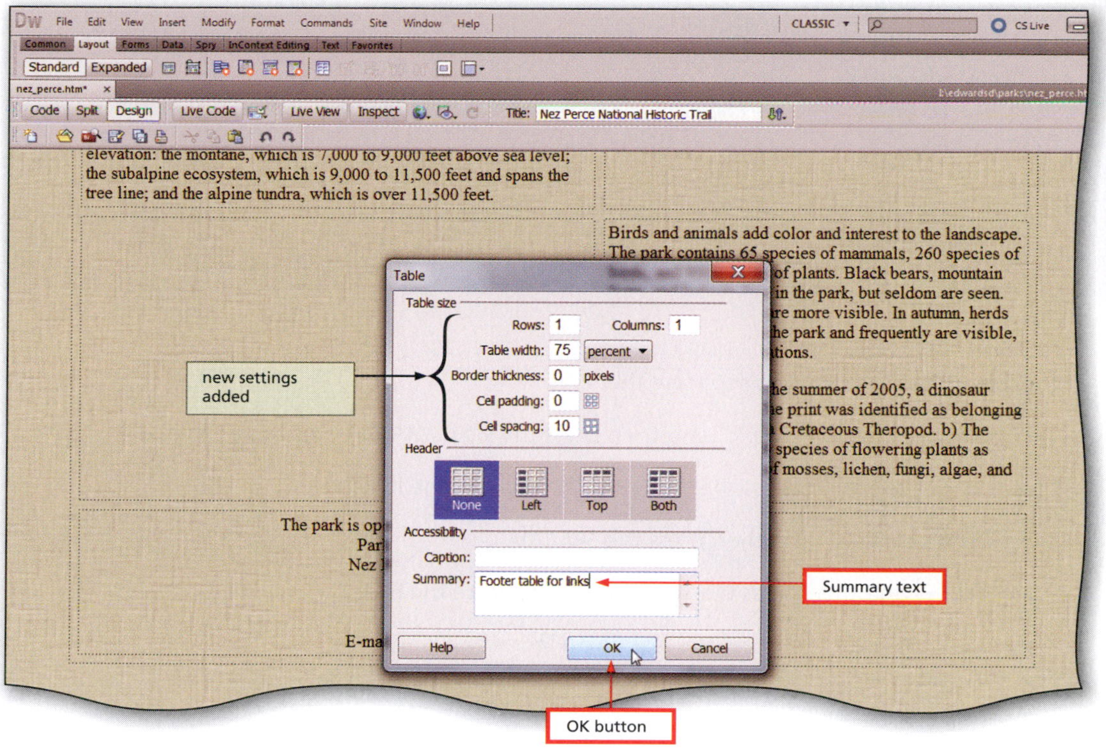

Figure 3–33

4

- Click the OK button to insert the one-cell table.

- Click the Align button and then click Center to center the one-cell table (Figure 3–34).

Q&A

Why does the table have a dark border and handles?

The dark border and handles indicate that the table is selected.

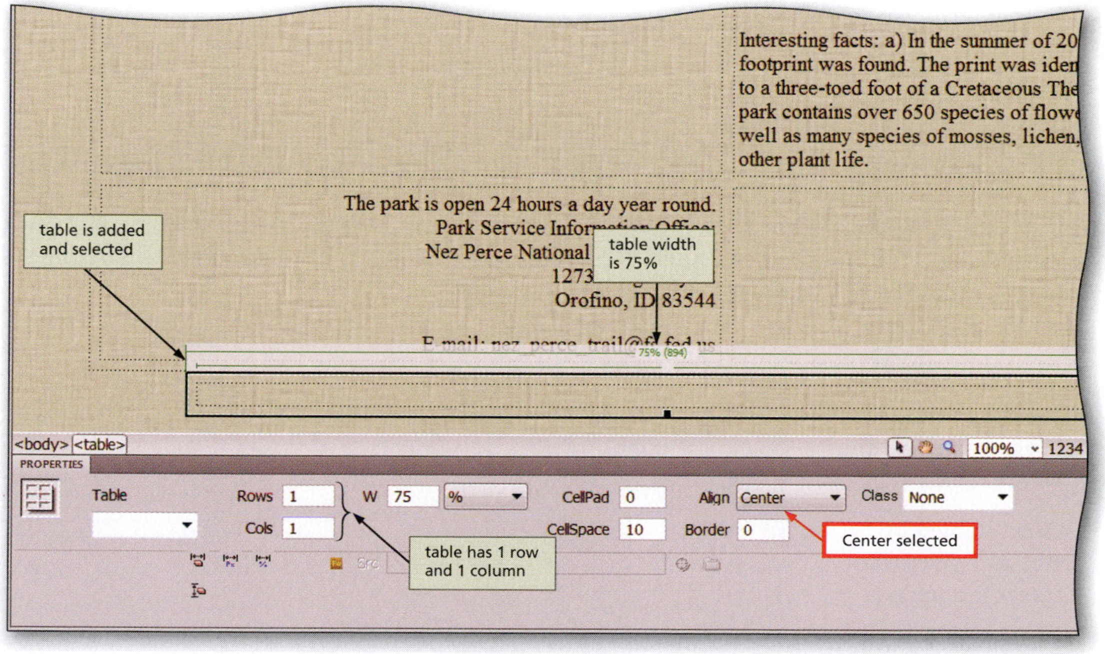

Figure 3–34

5
- Click the cell in the table. Type **Home** and then press the SPACEBAR to enter the first link.

links text added to table

Figure 3–35

- Press SHIFT+| (vertical bar) and then press the SPACEBAR to separate the links.

- Type **Lewis and Clark** and then press the SPACEBAR to enter the next link.

- Press SHIFT+| and then press the SPACEBAR to separate the links.

- Type **Preserves** and then press the SPACEBAR.

- Press SHIFT+| and then press the SPACEBAR to separate the links.

- Type **Nez Perce** to enter the last link (Figure 3–35).

BTW

Hiding the Table Width Bar
You can hide the bar that shows the column and table widths by clicking the down-pointing arrow next to the table width indicator and then clicking Hide Table Widths.

Adjusting the Table Width

If you overestimate or underestimate the table width when first inserting a table into the Document window, it is easy to make adjustments to the table width through the Property inspector.

To Adjust the Table Width, Center the Text, and Add the Table ID

The links table is too wide for the text it contains and needs to be adjusted. You adjust the table width by selecting the table and then changing the width in the Property inspector. The following steps illustrate how to adjust the width and add the table ID to the links table.

1
- If necessary, click in the cell in the links table to make it the active table.

- Click <table> in the tag selector to select the table.

- Double-click the W box in the Property inspector to select the width value.

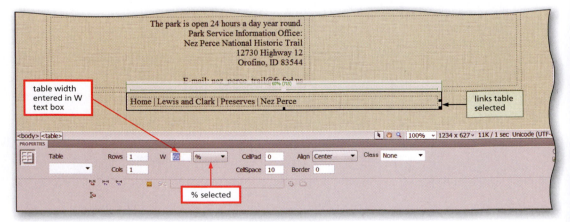

table width entered in W text box

links table selected

% selected

Figure 3–36

- Type 60 and then press the ENTER key to decrease the table width.

- If necessary, click the W button arrow and select % (the percent sign) (Figure 3–36).

2

- Click the cell in the table to select the cell.

- Click the Horz button, and then click Center to center the text.

- Click <table> in the tag selector to select the table.

- Click the Table text box, type **Montana_ parks_links**, and then press the ENTER key to name the table (Figure 3–37). 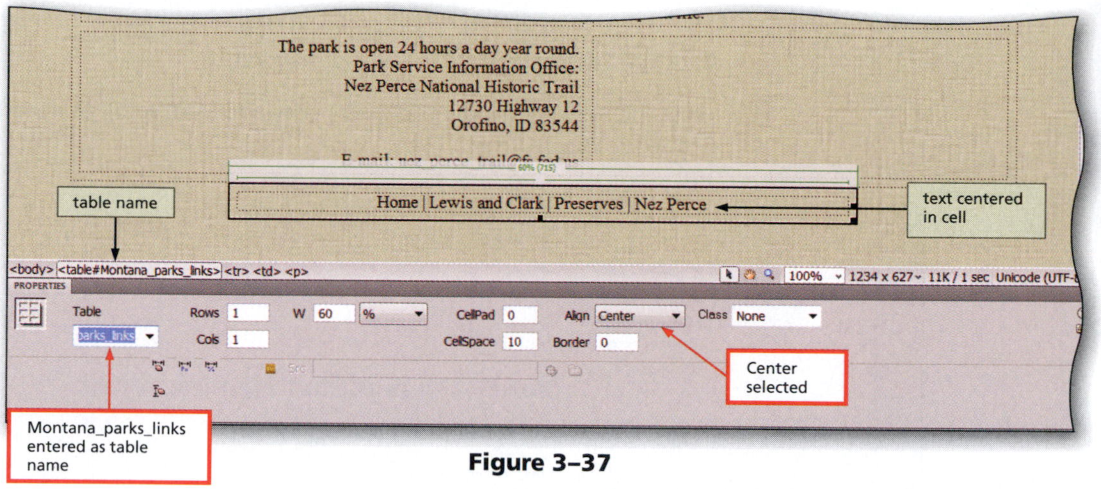

The park is open 24 hours a day year round.
Park Service Information Office:
Nez Perce National Historic Trail
12730 Highway 12
Orofino, ID 83544

Home | Lewis and Clark | Preserves | Nez Perce

table name

text centered in cell

<body> <table#Montana_parks_links> <tr> <td> <p>

| Table | Rows | 1 | W | 60 | % | CellPad | 0 | Align | Center | Class | None |
| parks_links | Cols | 1 | | | | CellSpace | 10 | Border | 0 | | |

Montana_parks_links entered as table name

Center selected

Figure 3–37

3

- Click anywhere in the Document window to deselect the table.

To Add Links to the Nez Perce National Historic Trail Web Page

Next, you add absolute, e-mail, and relative links to the Nez Perce National Historic Trail page. The following steps show how to add the links. You add relative links to the index, historical_trail, preserves, and nez_perce pages. You include a link to the nez_perce page so you can copy all the links to other pages for consistency.

1 Select the first instance of Nez Perce National Historic Trail located in the first table in row 1, column 1. In the Link box, type **http://www.nps.gov/nepe/index.htm** and then press ENTER to create an absolute link.

2 Select nez_perce_trail@fs.fed.us located in the first table in row 3, column 1. Click Insert on the Application bar and then click Email Link to display the Email Link dialog box.

3 Make sure the Email text box contains nez_perce_trail@fs.fed.us as the e-mail address, and then click the OK button to enter the e-mail link.

4 Select Home in the second table, click the Link box, type **index.htm,** and then press ENTER to enter a relative link to the home page for the Montana Parks Web site.

5 Select Lewis and Clark in the second table, click the Link box, type **historical_ trail.htm,** and then press ENTER to create the relative link to the Lewis and Clark Web page.

6 Select Preserves in the second table, click the Link box, type **preserves.htm,** and then press ENTER to create the relative link to the Montana National Parks and Preserves page.

7 Select Nez Perce in the second table, click the Link box, type `nez_perce.htm,` and then press ENTER to create the relative link to the Nez Perce National Historic Trail page.

Q&A Why are we creating a link to the current page?

The links table serves as the footer, and will be repeated on each page in the site.

8 Click the Save button on the Standard toolbar.

9 Press the F12 key to view the Web page, and then scroll as necessary to view the links (Figure 3–38).

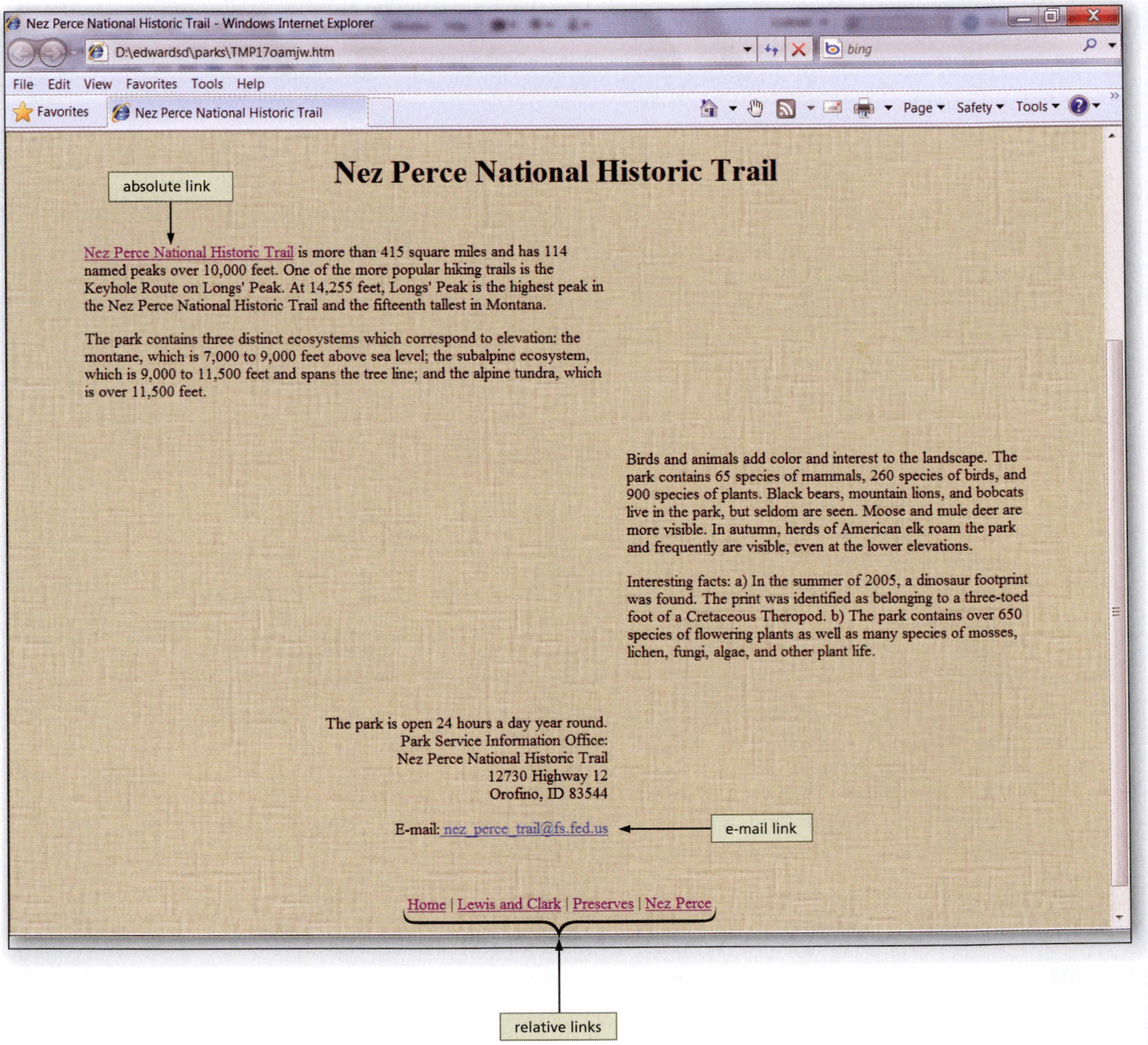

Figure 3–38

10 Click the Home link to display the index.htm page, and then click the browser Back button and test each of the links, including the e-mail link.

11 Close the browser and return to the Dreamweaver window.

Editing and Modifying Table Structure

Thus far, you have created two tables and made adjustments in Dreamweaver for the Nez Perce National Historic Trail Web page. For various reasons, as you create and develop Web sites, you will need to edit and modify a table, change the dimensions of a table, add rows and columns, or delete the table and start over. The following section describes how to edit, modify, and delete table elements within the structure. Several options are available to accomplish the same task.

Delete a Row or Column   Select a row or column and then press the DELETE key. You also can delete a row or column by clicking a cell within the row or column, clicking Modify on the Application bar, pointing to Table, and then clicking Delete Row or Delete Column on the submenu. Or click a cell within a row or column, right-click to display the context menu, point to Table, and then click Delete Row or Delete Column.

Insert a Row or Column   Click in a cell. Right-click to display the context menu, point to Table, and then click Insert Row or Insert Column on the Table submenu. Click Modify on the Application bar, point to Table, and then click Insert Row or Insert Column on the submenu. To insert more than one row or column and to control the row or column insertion point, click in a cell, right-click to display the context menu, point to Table, and then click Insert Rows or Columns on the Table submenu to display the Insert Rows or Columns dialog box (Figure 3–39). Make your selection and then click the OK button. To add a row automatically, press the TAB key in the last cell of a table.

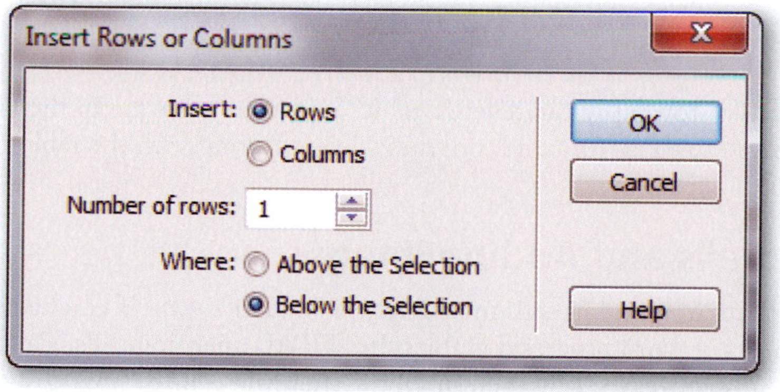

BTW

Deleting Cells
If you delete a cell, the content also is deleted. Dreamweaver does not caution you that this will occur. If you accidentally remove content, click the Undo button on the Standard toolbar, or, on the Edit menu, click the Undo command.

Figure 3–39

Merge and Split Cells   By merging and splitting cells, you can set alignments that are more complex than straight rows and columns. To merge two or more cells, select the cells and then click Merge Cells in the Property inspector. The selected cells must be contiguous and in the shape of a line or a rectangle. You can merge any number of adjacent cells as long as the entire selection is a line or a rectangle. To split a cell, click the cell and then click Split Cells in the Property inspector to display the Split Cell dialog box (Figure 3–40 on the next page). In the Split Cell dialog box, specify how to split the cell and then click the OK button. You can split a cell into any number of rows or columns, regardless of whether it was merged previously. When you split a cell into two rows, the other cells in the same row as the split cell are not split. If you split a cell into two or more columns, the other cells in the same column are not split. To select a cell quickly, click in the cell and then click the <td> tag on the tag selector.

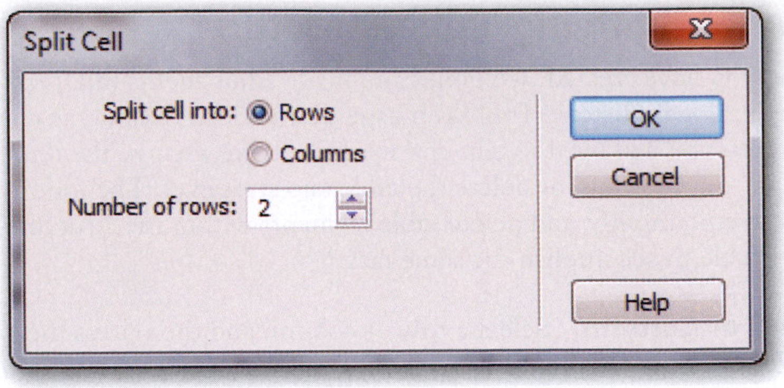

Figure 3–40

Resize a Table, Columns, and Rows   You can resize an entire table or resize individual rows and columns. To resize the table, select the table and change the W (width) in the Property inspector. A second method is to select the table and then drag one of the table selection handles. When you resize an entire table, all of the cells in the table change size proportionately. If you have assigned explicit widths or heights to a cell or cells within the table, resizing the table changes the visual size of the cells in the Document window but does not change the specified widths and heights of the cells. To resize a column or row, select the column or row and change the W or H numbers in the Property inspector. A second method to resize a column is to click the column border and then drag the border right or left. A second method to resize a row is to click the row border and then drag up or down.

Delete a Table   You easily can delete a table. Select the table tag in the tag selector and then press the DELETE key. All table content is deleted along with the table.

BTW

Splitting and Merging Cells
An alternative approach to merging and splitting cells is to increase or decrease the number of rows or columns spanned by a cell.

Merging Cells and Adding Images

The concept of merging cells most likely is familiar to you if you have worked with spreadsheets or word processing tables. In HTML, merging cells is a more complicated process. Dreamweaver, however, simplifies merging cells by hiding some complex HTML table restructuring code behind an easy-to-use interface in the Property inspector. Dreamweaver also makes it easy to add images to a table. When you add and then select an image in a table cell, the Property inspector displays the same properties as were displayed when you added and selected an image in the Document window in Chapter 2. When the image in the cell is not selected, the Property inspector displays the same properties as it does for any cell. These properties were described earlier in this chapter.

To Merge Two Cells in a Table

You will merge two cells (rows 1 and 2, column 1) so you can add four images to the Nez Perce National Historic Trail page. The following steps show how to merge two cells.

1
- If necessary, scroll up and then click in row 1, column 1 in the first table.
- Drag to select the cells in rows 1 and 2 in column 1 (Figure 3–41).

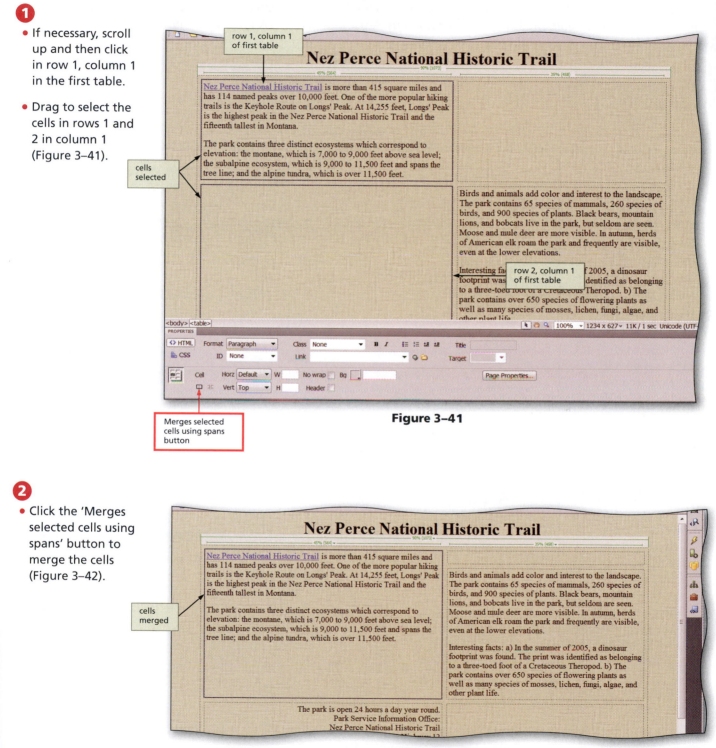

Figure 3–41

2
- Click the 'Merges selected cells using spans' button to merge the cells (Figure 3–42).

Figure 3–42

To Disable the Image Tag Accessibility Attributes Dialog Box

Recall from Chapter 2 that when you inserted an image, the default Image Tag Accessibility Attributes dialog box was displayed. In this dialog box, you can add Alternate text or create a link to a text file with a long description. For images in this chapter and the other chapters in this book, you insert alternate text using the Property inspector. Therefore, you can disable the Image Tag Accessibility Attributes dialog box now. The following steps show how to disable the Image Tag Accessibility Attributes dialog box.

1

• Click Edit on the Application bar, and then click Preferences to display the Preferences dialog box.

• Click Accessibility in the Category list to display the accessibility options.

Q&A

Where can I find more information on accessibility?

For additional information on making Web content accessible for people with disabilities, search for *Accessibility* using the Dreamweaver CS5 Help system.

• If necessary, click the check boxes to deselect Form objects, Frames, Media, and Images, which disables the Image Tag Accessibility Attributes dialog box (Figure 3–43).

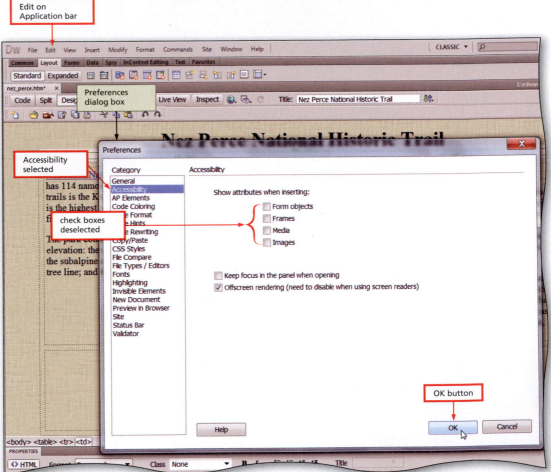

Figure 3–43

2

• Click the OK button.

To Add Images to a Table

Next, you add four images to the table. You then align the four images within the table cells and modify the size of the images. The following steps illustrate how to display the images in the Assets panel and then add, align, and modify images in a table using Standard mode.

1

• Click the Expand Panels button to expand the panel groups, and then click the Assets tab to display the assets for this Web site.

• If necessary, click the Images button and the Site option button in the Assets panel to display the images for this Web site.

Q&A

What should I do if the Assets panel does not display all my images?

Click the Refresh Site List button to view the images.

• Click at the beginning of row 1, column 1 in the first table, and then press the ENTER key to insert a blank line.

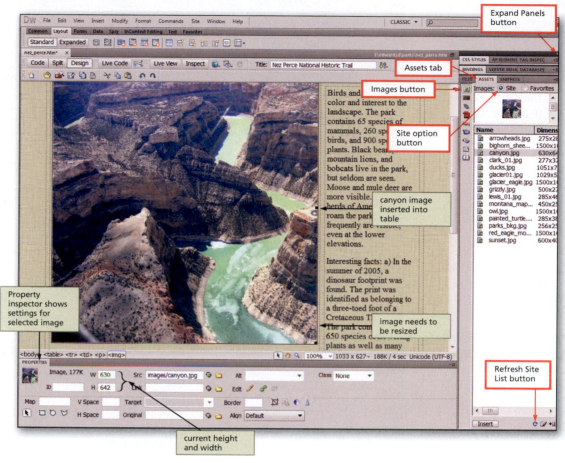

Figure 3–44

• Click the new blank line in row 1, column 1.

• Drag the canyon.jpg image from the Assets panel to the insertion point in the merged cell (Figure 3–44).

2

- With the image still selected, double-click the W box and change the width to 315.

- Double-click the H box, change the height to 320, and then press the ENTER key (Figure 3–45).

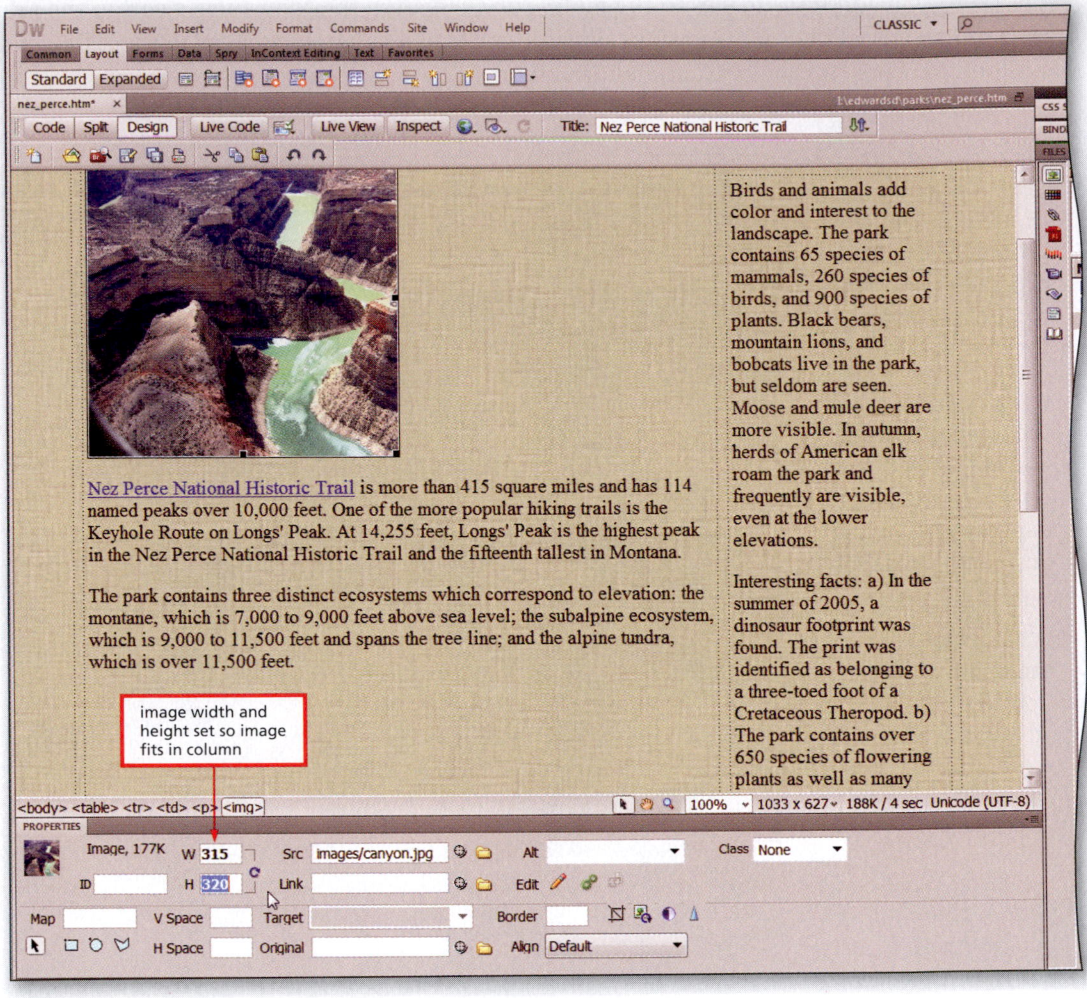

Figure 3–45

3

- Click the ID text box in the Property inspector and type **nez_perce** as the image ID.

- Click the Alt box, type **Nez Perce Canyon**, and then press the ENTER key to add the Alt text.

- Scroll as necessary to display the completed image (Figure 3–46).

Q&A

The left column of the table is still widened, even after resizing the image. What should I do?
If the table column isn't resized when you resize the image, move the insertion point above the column, and then click to select the column, click anywhere outside the cell containing the image, or press the F5 key to refresh the page.

4

- Click to the right of the image to deselect the canyon image.

- Press the ENTER key to insert a blank line after the canyon image (Figure 3–47).

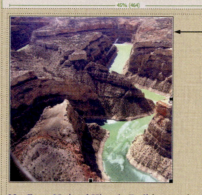

canyon image in row 1, column 1

Figure 3–46

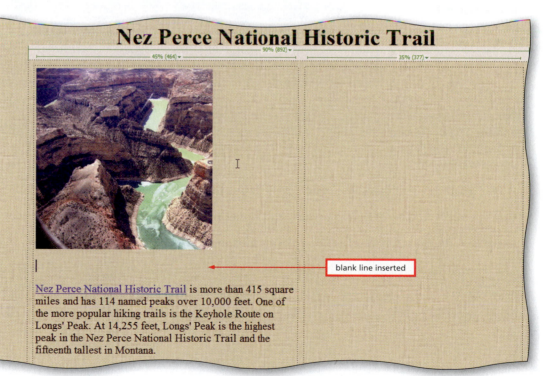

blank line inserted

Figure 3–47

5

- Click the canyon image, click the Align button in the Property inspector, and then click Middle to align the image in the middle of the line.

- Click row 1, column 2 and then type the Bighorn sheep text as indicated in Table 3–4 on page DW 207.

- Press the ENTER key, and then drag the bighorn_sheep image from the Assets panel to the insertion point to insert the image in the table.

- Verify that the bighorn_sheep image is selected, click the ID box in the Property inspector, and then type **bighorn** to name the image.

- Press the TAB key and then type **500** in the W box to set the image width.

Figure 3–48

- Press the TAB key and then type **400** in the H box to set the image height.

- Click the Alt box, type **Bighorn sheep** as the Alt text, and then press the ENTER key.

- Click the Align button and select Top to align the top of the image at the top of the line.

- Click Format on the Application bar, point to Align, and then click Center to center the resized image in the cell.

- Press the F5 key to refresh the page, and then scroll as necessary to display the sheep image (Figure 3–48).

Q&A

The width of the table and its columns changed after resizing the image. What should I do?

Press the F5 key to refresh the page.

Q&A

How are the alignment options in the Property inspector different from those on the Format menu?

When you are working with images, you use the options on the Align pop-up menu in the Property inspector to align the image in relation to other objects, such as the current line or table cell. You use the options on the Align submenu on the Format menu to align text or objects in relation to the page. However, when you're working in a table, the options in the Align submenu align text or objects with a column.

6

- Click at the end of row 1, column 1 and then press the ENTER key.

- Drag the owl image to the insertion point to insert the image in the table.

- Click the ID text box in the Property inspector and then type `owl` as the image ID.

- Press the TAB key and then type `500` in the W box as the image width.

- Press the TAB key and then type `315` as the image height.

- Click the Alt box, type `Nez Perce owl` as the Alt text, and then press the ENTER key.

- Click Format on the Application bar, point to Align, and then click Center to center the resized image. Scroll as necessary to display the owl image.

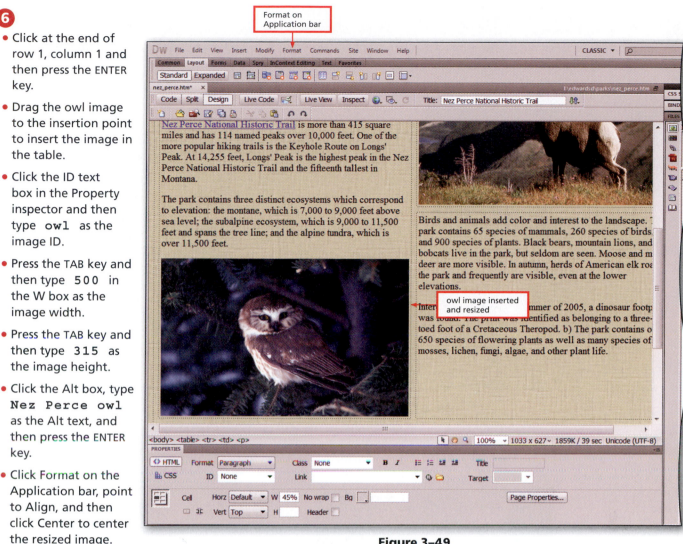

Figure 3–49

- Click the Align button in the Property inspector and then click Top.

- Click anywhere on the page to deselect the image, and then press the F5 key to refresh the page (Figure 3–49).

7

- Click row 3, column 2, type `The Nez Perce National Historic Trail is managed by the U.S. Forestry Service` and then press the ENTER key (Figure 3–50).

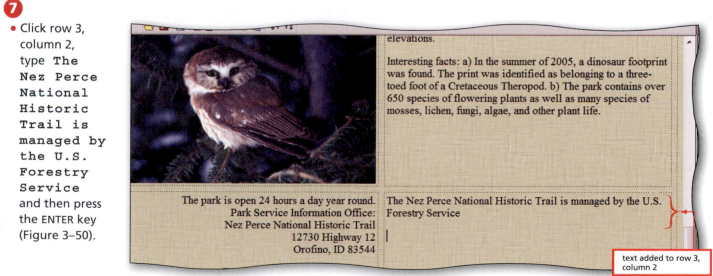

Figure 3–50

8

- Select the text, click Format on the Application bar, point to Align, and then click Right to align the text to the right (Figure 3–51).

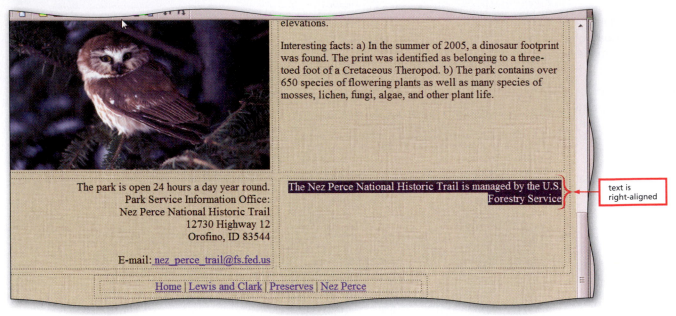

Figure 3–51

9

- Click below the text you just entered.

- Drag the arrowheads.jpg image from the Assets panel to the insertion point.

- Click the Align button in the Property inspector, and then click Right to right-align the image.

- Change the W value in the Property inspector to 125 to change the image width, and change the H value to 131 to change the image height (Figure 3–52).

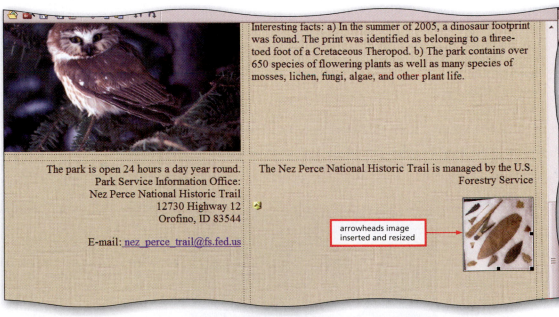

Figure 3–52

10

- Click the Save button on the Standard toolbar to save your work.

- Press the F12 key to view the page in your browser (Figure 3–53).

11

- Close the browser window to redisplay Dreamweaver.

- Close the Nez Perce National Historic Trail page.

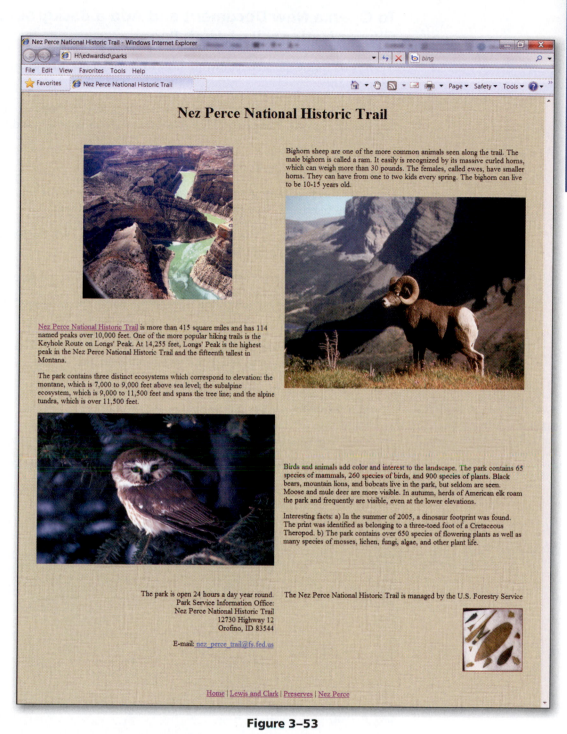

Figure 3–53

Creating the Glacier National Park Web Page

To create the Glacier National Park Web page, you open a new document. You start by applying the background image.

To Open a New Document and Add a Background Image to the Glacier National Park Web Page

The following steps illustrate how to open a new document and apply a background image.

1 Click File on the Application bar and then click New to begin creating a new Web page. If necessary, click Blank Page, click HTML in the Page Type list, and then click <none> in the Layout list.

2 Click the Create button to create the page.

3 Click the Save button on the Standard toolbar to name the file, and then type `glacier` as the file name. Save the Web page in the parks folder.

4 If necessary, display the Property inspector and then click the Page Properties button to prepare for applying the background image.

5 Click Appearance (HTML) in the Category list to display the Appearance options.

6 Click the Browse button to the right of the Background image box to find the background image.

7 If necessary, navigate to and open the parks\images folder. Click parks_bkg.jpg and then click the OK button to select the background image.

8 Click the OK button in the Page Properties dialog box to apply the background image (Figure 3–54).

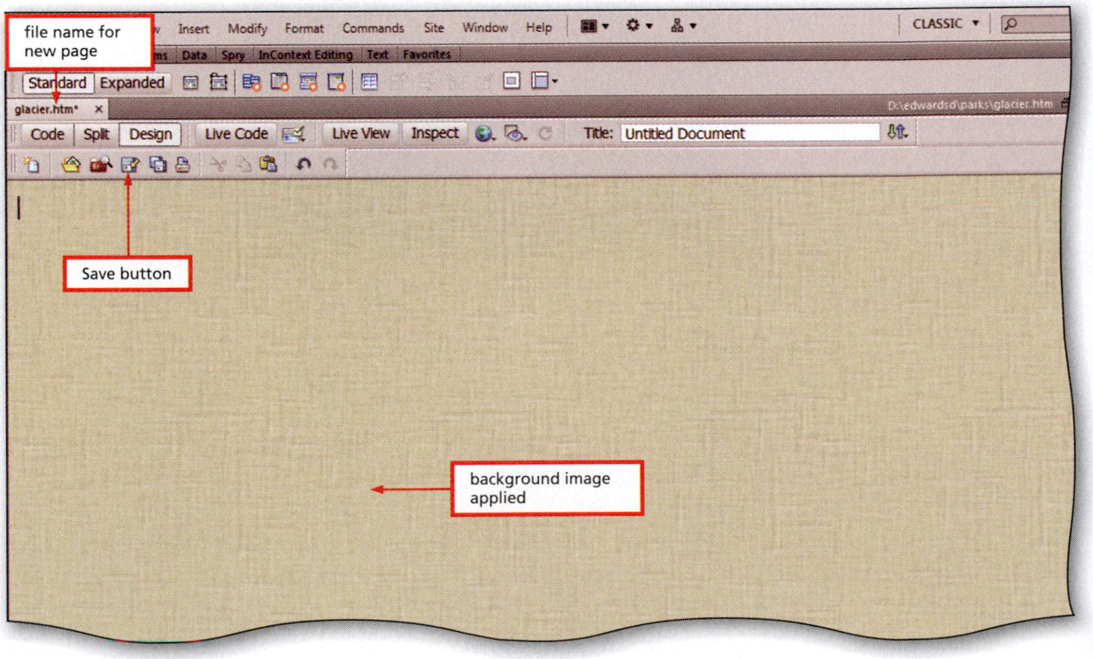

Figure 3–54

To Insert and Center a Table

Next, you enter a title, and then insert and center a four-row, two-column table. You use the table to create the Glacier National Park page by adding text and four images. You modify image placement and image size. You also add an absolute link and e-mail addresses for the park. Then you copy and paste the Links table from the Nez Perce National Historic Trail page to the Glacier National Park page.

1 Select the text in the Title box on the Document toolbar, and then type `Glacier National Park` as the page title.

2 Click the Web page and then type `Glacier National Park.` Apply Heading 1 to the text and then center it on the page. Click at the end of the heading, and then press ENTER.

3 Click the Table button on the Layout tab on the Insert bar to begin inserting a new table.

4 In the Table dialog box, change the settings as follows: Rows 4, Columns 2, Table width 90 Percent, Cell padding 5, and Cell spacing 5. (Do not enter a Border thickness value.)

5 Click the Summary text box, type `Glacier National Park feature page` as the Summary text, and then click the OK button to insert the table.

6 Click the Table text box in the Property inspector, type `glacier_01` as the ID text, and then press the ENTER key to accept the new ID.

7 Click the Align button and then click Center to center the table.

8 Click the Save button on the Standard toolbar to save the table (Figure 3–55).

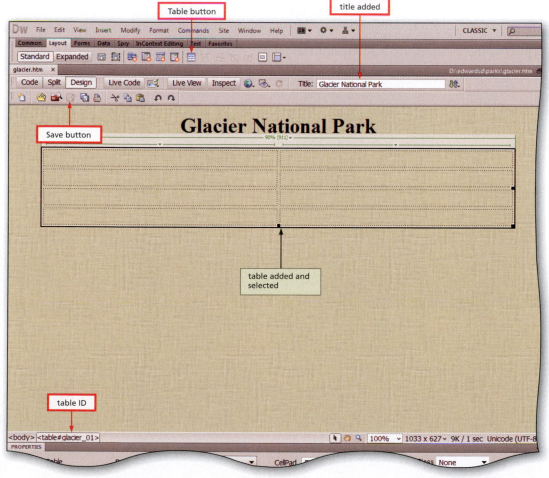

Figure 3–55

Spanning Rows and Columns

An understanding of HTML and how it relates to a table and to parts of a table provides you with the ability to use code to select a table and table components and to modify a table. Merging and varying the span of columns (as you did in the Nez Perce National Historic Trail page) and merging and varying the span of rows is helpful for grouping information, adding emphasis, creating balance, or deleting empty cells. When you merge two or more cells in a row, you are spanning a column. Continuing with the <table> example on page DW 198 and spanning the two cells in row 1, the HTML tags would be <td colspan="2">First cellSecond cell</td>. When you merge two cells in a column, you are spanning a row. The attribute rowspan would replace colspan in the above example. Understanding colspan and rowspan will help you determine when and if two columns or two rows have been merged.

To Adjust the Cell Alignment and Column Width

In the following steps, you will adjust the width for columns 1 and 2 in the Glacier National Park page, and then change the vertical alignment to Top within both columns.

1 Click in row 1, column 1, and then drag to select all the cells in the table.

2 Click the Vert button in the Property inspector, and then click Top to top-align the cells.

3 Click row 2, column 1 to adjust the width of column 1.

4 Click the W box in the Property inspector, type 60%, and then press the ENTER key to set the width of column 1.

5 Click row 2, column 2 to adjust the width of column 2.

6 Click the W box in the Property inspector, type 40%, and then press the ENTER key to set the width of column 2 (Figure 3–56 on the next page).

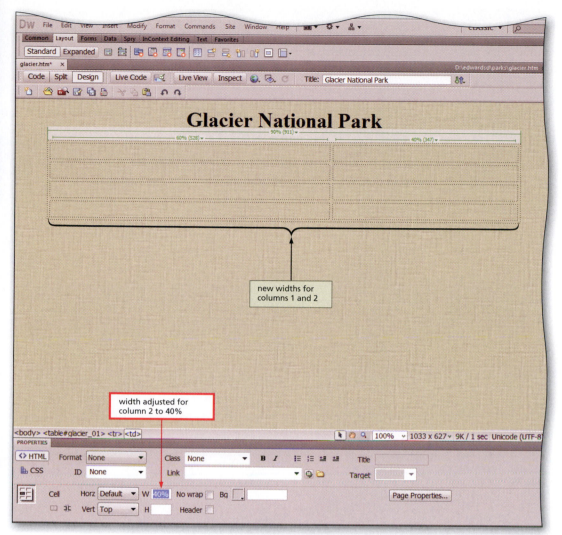

new widths for columns 1 and 2

width adjusted for column 2 to 40%

Figure 3–56

To Merge Cells in Row 1

For the Glacier National Park page, you merge columns 1 and 2 in row 1, and then merge rows 2 and 3 in column 2. The following step illustrates how to merge the cells.

1

- Click row 1, column 1 and then drag to select all of row 1.

- Click the 'Merges selected cells using spans' button in the Property inspector to merge the selected cells into one row.

- Click row 2, column 2 and then drag to select row 3, column 2.

- Click the 'Merges selected cells using spans' button in the Property inspector to merge the selected cells into one column (Figure 3–57).

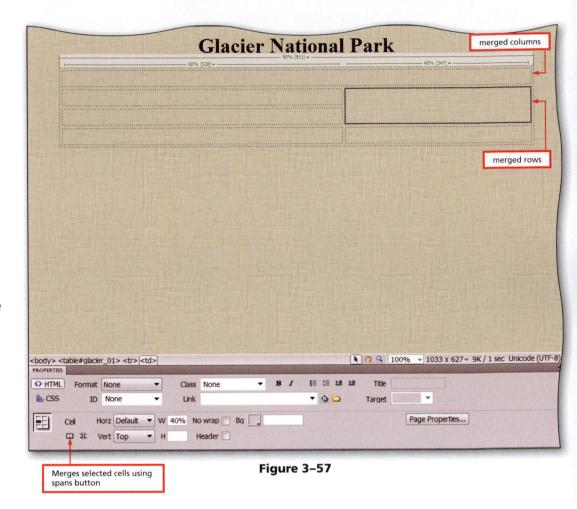

Figure 3–57

Adding Text to the Table

Now you add text to the table. Table 3–5 on the next page contains the text for the Glacier National Park Web page. You can select one of two methods to enter the text: a) copy the text from the data file and paste it into the appropriate cell in the table; or b) type the text in the appropriate cell as you did for the Nez Perce page.

To copy and paste text, open the data file in Microsoft Word or a text document. Select the text and then select Copy. Click the appropriate Dreamweaver cell and then click Paste. If the copy and paste text option is not available, use the same process you used to type the text as you did with the Nez Perce Web page.

Table 3–5 Text for the Glacier National Park Page

Section	Text
Part 1	Glacier National Park is one of the largest national parks in the lower 48 states and is one of the most beautiful of America's national parks. Native Americans referred to the park as the "Shining Mountains" and the "Backbone of the World." The park is home to over seventy species of mammals including the wolverine, grizzly bear, gray wolf, and lynx. Over 260 species of birds visit or reside in the park.
Part 2	<ENTER>Many people, when they think of Glacier, think of the grizzly bear or the brown bear. Glacier contains one of the remaining grizzly bear populations in the lower 48 states. The park, however, is home to over 60 species of other animals, including elk, gray wolf, wolverine, cougar, mountain goat, and bighorn sheep, to name a few. The lynx and grizzly are threatened species, while the gray wolf is endangered.
Part 3	A park visitor also can find a number of amphibians — some quite unusual. The tailed frog, for instance, is named for the male's inside-out reproductive opening. This is the only frog in North American that fertilizes the female's eggs internally.
Part 4	Glacier Park's cold winter is not an invitation to many reptiles. However, three species of reptiles live in the park. The Western painted turtle is one of the favorite reptiles of many visitors. Their bottom shell has bright yellow and orange markings, and the skin is streaked with yellow. They can be seen basking in the sun on logs around low elevation lakes. <ENTER>
Part 5	<ENTER>The park is open 24 hours a day year round</br> Park Service Information Office:</br> Glacier National Park</br> PO Box 128</br> West Glacier, MT 59936-0128

To Add and Format Text for the Glacier National Park Web page

Now you are ready to add text to the table. The following steps illustrate how to add and format text for the Glacier National Park Web page.

1

- Click row 1, and then type the text of Part 1 as shown in Table 3–5 (Figure 3–58).

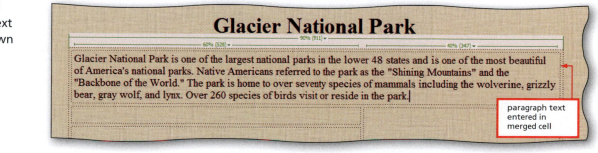

Figure 3–58

2

- Click row 2, column 1, and then type the text of Part 2 as shown in Table 3–5 on page DW 231, pressing the ENTER key as indicated (Figure 3–59).

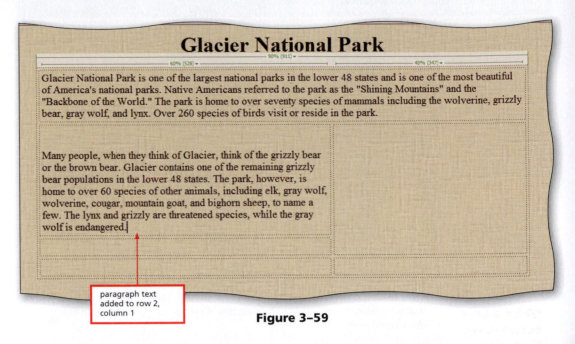

paragraph text added to row 2, column 1

Figure 3–59

3

- Click row 3, column 1, and then type the text of Part 3 as shown in Table 3–5 (Figure 3–60).

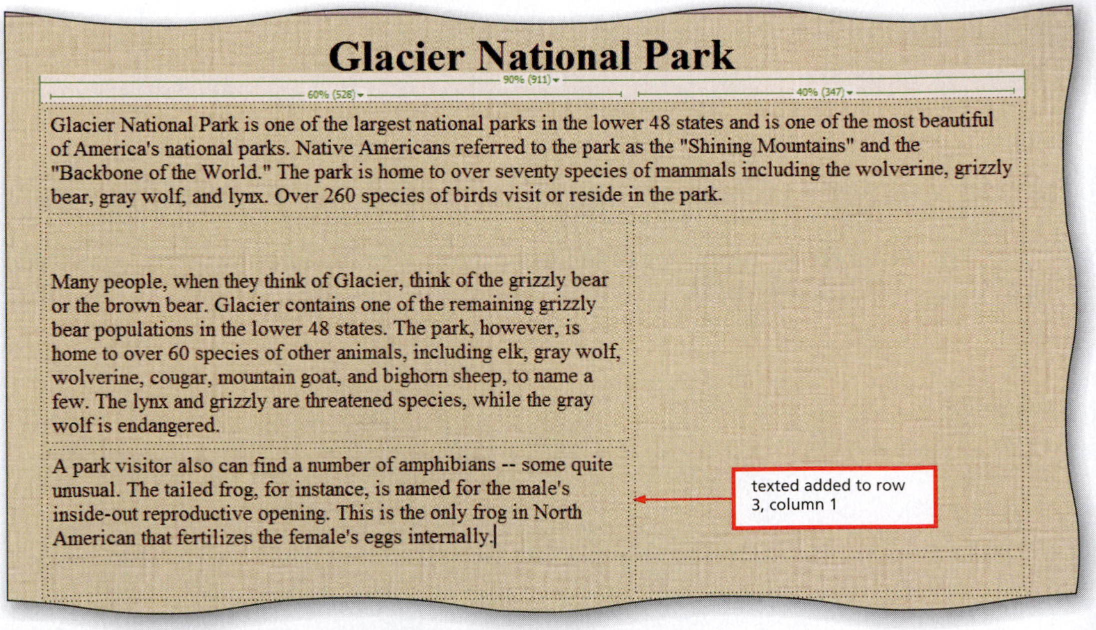

texted added to row 3, column 1

Figure 3–60

4

- Click row 4, column 1, and then type the text of Part 4 as shown in Table 3–5 on page DW 231, pressing the ENTER key as indicated (Figure 3–61).

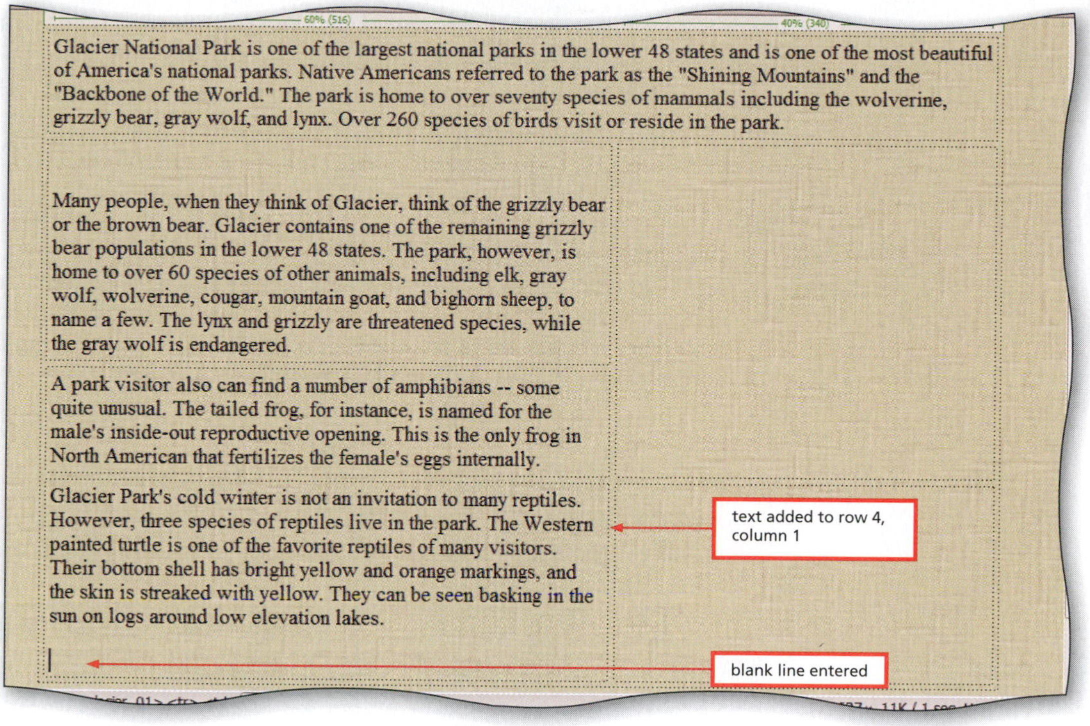

Glacier National Park is one of the largest national parks in the lower 48 states and is one of the most beautiful of America's national parks. Native Americans referred to the park as the "Shining Mountains" and the "Backbone of the World." The park is home to over seventy species of mammals including the wolverine, grizzly bear, gray wolf, and lynx. Over 260 species of birds visit or reside in the park.

Many people, when they think of Glacier, think of the grizzly bear or the brown bear. Glacier contains one of the remaining grizzly bear populations in the lower 48 states. The park, however, is home to over 60 species of other animals, including elk, gray wolf, wolverine, cougar, mountain goat, and bighorn sheep, to name a few. The lynx and grizzly are threatened species, while the gray wolf is endangered.

A park visitor also can find a number of amphibians -- some quite unusual. The tailed frog, for instance, is named for the male's inside-out reproductive opening. This is the only frog in North American that fertilizes the female's eggs internally.

Glacier Park's cold winter is not an invitation to many reptiles. However, three species of reptiles live in the park. The Western painted turtle is one of the favorite reptiles of many visitors. Their bottom shell has bright yellow and orange markings, and the skin is streaked with yellow. They can be seen basking in the sun on logs around low elevation lakes.

text added to row 4, column 1

blank line entered

Figure 3–61

5

- Click row 4, column 2, and then type the text of Part 5 as shown in Table 3–5, pressing the ENTER key and inserting line breaks as indicated in Table 3–5.

- With the insertion point in row 4, column 2, click the <td> tag in the tag selector to select the cell.

- Click Format on the Application bar, point to Align, and then click Right to right-align the text (Figure 3–62).

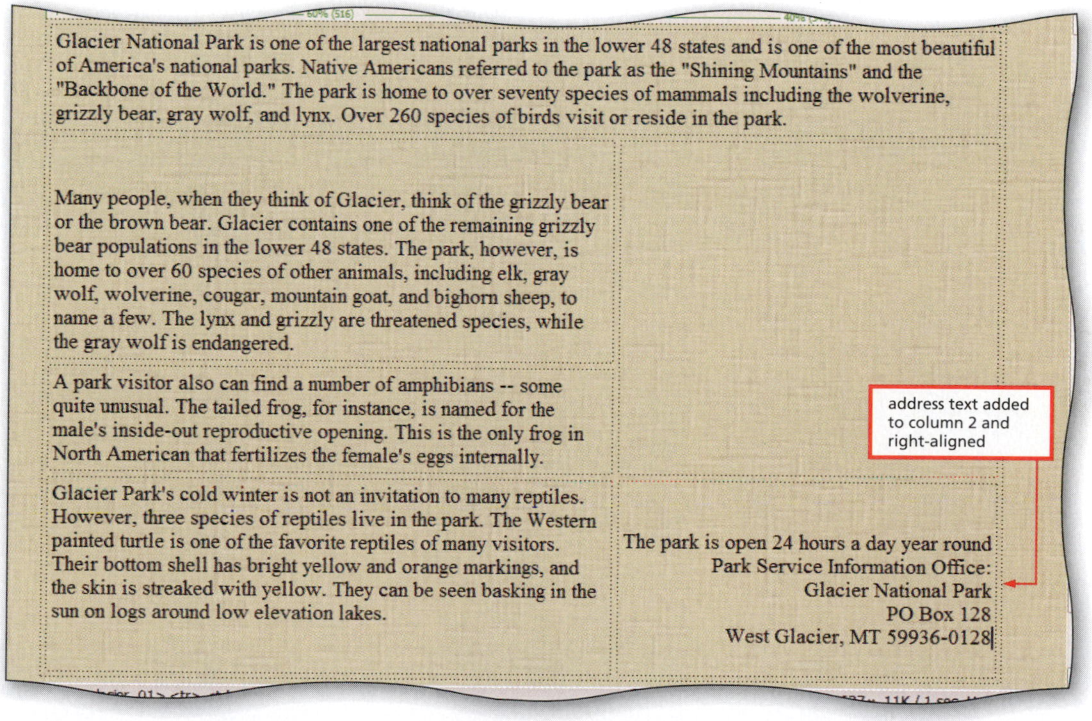

Glacier National Park is one of the largest national parks in the lower 48 states and is one of the most beautiful of America's national parks. Native Americans referred to the park as the "Shining Mountains" and the "Backbone of the World." The park is home to over seventy species of mammals including the wolverine, grizzly bear, gray wolf, and lynx. Over 260 species of birds visit or reside in the park.

Many people, when they think of Glacier, think of the grizzly bear or the brown bear. Glacier contains one of the remaining grizzly bear populations in the lower 48 states. The park, however, is home to over 60 species of other animals, including elk, gray wolf, wolverine, cougar, mountain goat, and bighorn sheep, to name a few. The lynx and grizzly are threatened species, while the gray wolf is endangered.

A park visitor also can find a number of amphibians -- some quite unusual. The tailed frog, for instance, is named for the male's inside-out reproductive opening. This is the only frog in North American that fertilizes the female's eggs internally.

Glacier Park's cold winter is not an invitation to many reptiles. However, three species of reptiles live in the park. The Western painted turtle is one of the favorite reptiles of many visitors. Their bottom shell has bright yellow and orange markings, and the skin is streaked with yellow. They can be seen basking in the sun on logs around low elevation lakes.

address text added to column 2 and right-aligned

The park is open 24 hours a day year round
Park Service Information Office:
Glacier National Park
PO Box 128
West Glacier, MT 59936-0128

Figure 3–62

Adding Images and Image Borders

The purpose of most tables in a Web page is to provide a structure for the positioning of text and images. When a table is created within Dreamweaver, therefore, the default border is 0 (zero), or no visible border. You can add a border to a table when you create the table using the Border thickness text box in the Table dialog box. When the table is selected, the table border option also is available through the Property inspector.

Plan Ahead

Determine when to add borders.
Applying a border to a table helps to structure the table content. Adding a border to an image transforms the image into a graphical element itself. Depending on the content, a table border can become a visual cue for the reader by separating content. Experiment with border thickness to achieve the effect you want to create.

You also can add borders to images. The **Border** command specifies the width, in pixels, of the line that frames the image. The alignment options for images are listed in Table 3–6. Note that these are the same as the alignment options for table cells.

Table 3–6 Image Alignment Options	
Alignment Option	**Description**
Default	Specifies a baseline alignment; default may vary depending on the user's browser
Baseline	Aligns the cell content at the bottom of the cell (same as Bottom)
Top	Aligns the cell content at the top of the cell
Bottom	Aligns the cell content at the bottom of the cell
TextTop	Aligns the top of the image with the top of the tallest character in the text line
Absolute Middle	Aligns the middle of the image with the middle of the text in the current line
Absolute Bottom	Aligns the bottom of the image with the bottom of the line of text
Left	Places the selected image on the left margin, wrapping text around it to the right; if left-aligned text precedes the object on the line, it generally forces left-aligned objects to wrap to a new line
Middle	Aligns the middle of the image with the baseline of the current line
Right	Places the image on the right margin, wrapping text around the object to the left; if right-aligned text precedes the object on the line, it generally forces right-aligned objects to wrap to a new line

To Add Images, Image Borders, and a Table Border

The next task is to add images to the Web page. In the following steps, you insert, resize, align, and add a border to the images, and then add a border to the table.

1

- Click row 2, column 1 to select the first cell in row 2, and then drag the glacier_ eagle image from the Assets panel to the insertion point.

- Click the ID text box in the Property inspector and then type `glacier_ eagle` as the image ID.

- Change the width in the W box to 335 and the height in the H box to 245 to resize the image.

- Click the H Space box and then type **50** to set the horizontal spacing.

Figure 3–63

- Click the Alt box, type `Glacier eagle,` and then press ENTER to enter the Alt text.

- Scroll to display the glacier_eagle image.

🔍 **Experiment**

- Click the Border text box, type any value from 1 to 20, and then press ENTER.

- In the Border text box, type **2** to set the border thickness.

- Click the Align button and then click Absolute Middle to align the image in the middle of the line.

- Click Format on the Application bar, point to Align, and then click Center to center the image.

- Press the F5 key to refresh the page (Figure 3–63).

2

- If necessary, scroll down and click at the beginning of the blank line at the end of row 4, column 1 to prepare for inserting the next image.

- Drag the sunset image to the insertion point in row 4, column 1 to add the sunset image to the table.

- Click the ID text box in the Property inspector and then type **evening_ sunset** as the image ID.

- Change the width in the W box to 500 and the height in the H box to 350 to resize the image.

- Click the V Space box and then type **10** to set the vertical spacing.

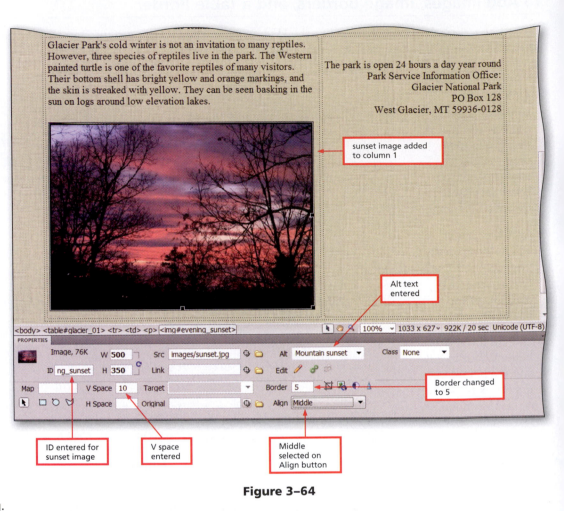

Figure 3–64

- Click the Alt box, type **Mountain sunset,** and then press ENTER to enter the Alt text.

- Click the Border text box and then type **5** to set the border thickness.

- Click the Align button and then click Middle to align the image in the middle of the line.

- Press the F5 key to refresh the page (Figure 3–64).

3

- Click the first line in row 2, column 2, and then drag the red_eagle_mountain image to the insertion point to insert the image in the cell.

- Click the ID text box in the Property inspector and then type `red_eagle_mountain` as the image ID.

- Change the width in the W box to 475 and the height in the H box to 335 to resize the image.

- Click the Alt box, type `Red Eagle Mountain` and then press ENTER to enter the Alt text for the image.

- Click the Border text box and then type 5 to set the border thickness.

- Click the Align button and then click Middle to align the image.

- Press the F5 key to refresh the page, and then scroll as necessary to display the image (Figure 3–65).

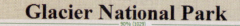

Glacier National Park

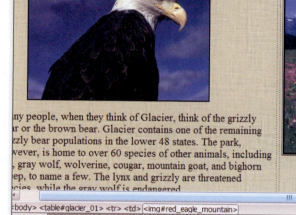

Glacier National Park is one of the largest national parks in the lower 48 states and is one of the most beautiful of America's national parks. Native Americans referred to the park as the "Shining Mountains" and the "Backbone of the World." The park is home to over seventy species of mammals including the wolverine, grizzly bear, gray wolf, and lynx. Over 260 species of birds visit or reside in the park.

Many people, when they think of Glacier, think of the grizzly bear or the brown bear. Glacier contains one of the remaining grizzly bear populations in the lower 48 states. The park, however, is home to over 60 species of other animals, including gray wolf, wolverine, cougar, mountain goat, and bighorn sheep, to name a few. The lynx and grizzly are threatened species, while the gray wolf is endangered.

<body> <table#glacier_01> <tr> <td> <img#red_eagle_mountain>

red_eagle_mountain image added to row 2, column 2

372K / 39 sec Unicode (UTF-8

Figure 3–65

4

- Click the blank line at the top of row 3, column 2, and then drag the painted_turtle image to the insertion point to insert the image in the cell.

- Click the ID box in the Property inspector, and then type **painted_turtle** as the image ID.

- Click the Alt box, type **Painted turtle** and then press ENTER to enter the Alt text.

- Click the Border box, type **5,** and then press ENTER to set the border thickness.

- Click Format on the Application bar, point to Align, and then click Center to center the image (Figure 3–66).

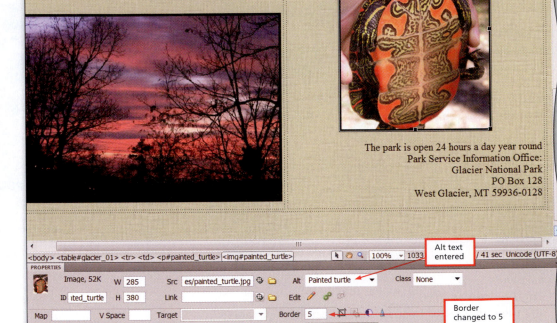

painted_turtle image added to row 3, column 2

Alt text entered

Border changed to 5

Figure 3–66

5

- Click
  <table#glacier_01>
  in the tag selector
  to select the table.

- Enter 5 in the
  Border text box,
  and then press
  ENTER to add a
  border to the table
  (Figure 3–67).

6

- Click the Save
  button to save your
  work.

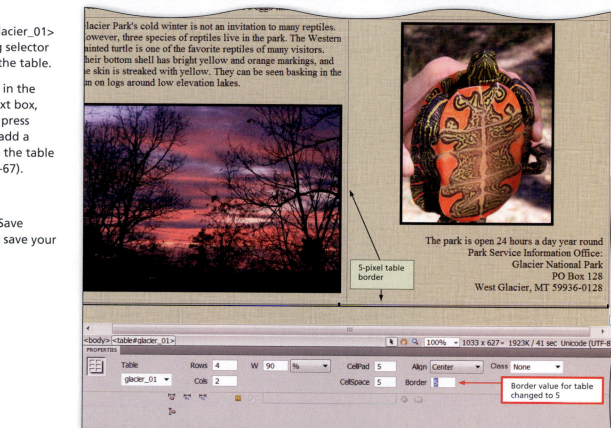

Figure 3–67

To Add Links to and Spell Check the Glacier National Park Web Page

The following steps illustrate how to add an absolute link to the Glacier National Park page, and then copy the Links table from the Nez Perce National Historic Trail page and paste it as a footer in the Glacier National Park page. You also spell check the Web page, save it, and view it in a browser.

1 If necessary, scroll down, select the text Glacier National Park in the address in row 4, column 2, type `http://www.nps.gov/glac` in the Link box, and then press ENTER to create an absolute link to the National Park Service's Web page for Glacier National Park.

2 Open the nez_perce.htm page, scroll down, and then click in the links table to set the focus on the links table.

3 Click <table#Montana_parks_links> in the tag selector to select the table, and then press CTRL+C to copy the table.

4 Click the glacier.htm document tab to return to the Glacier National Park page, click to the right of the table, press ENTER to move the insertion point to the next line, and then press CTRL+V to paste the Montana_parks_links table.

5 If necessary, select the Montana_parks_links table, click the Align button in the Property inspector, and then click Center to center the table. Click anywhere in the document to deselect the table.

6 Press the CTRL+HOME keys to move the insertion point to the beginning of the page, click Commands on the Application bar, and then click Check Spelling to begin spell checking the page. Check the spelling and make any necessary corrections.

7 Click the Save button on the Standard toolbar to save your work.

8 Press the F12 key to view the Web page in your browser (Figure 3–68).

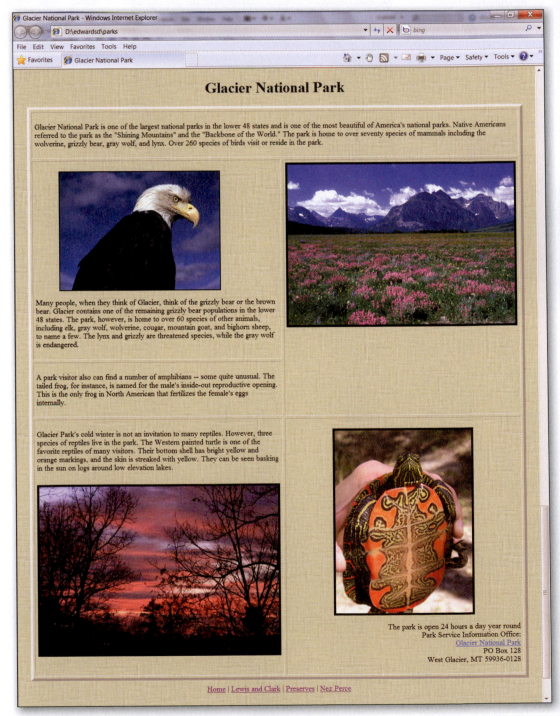

Figure 3–68

9 Close the browser.

Head Content

HTML files consist of two main sections: the head section and the body section. The head section is one of the more important sections of a Web page. A standard HTML page contains a <head> tag and a <body> tag. Contained within the head section is site and page information. With the exception of the title, the information contained in the head is not displayed in the browser. Some of the information contained in the head is accessed by the browser, and other information is accessed by other programs such as search engines and server software. You also can display the Common category on the Insert bar and then click the Head button to display a list of commands described in the next section.

Head Content Elements

Dreamweaver makes it easy to add content to the head section through the Insert menu. To access these commands, point to HTML on the Insert menu, and then point to the submenu of the command you want to select.

Meta A <meta> tag contains information about the current document. This information is used by servers, browsers, and search engines. HTML documents can have as many <meta> tags as needed. Each item uses a different set of tags.

Keywords Keywords are a list of words that someone would type into a search engine search field.

Description The description contains a sentence or two that can be used in a search engine's results page.

Refresh The <refresh> tag is processed by the browser to reload the page or load a new page after a specified amount of time has elapsed.

Base The base tag sets the base URL to provide an absolute link and/or a link target that the browser can use to resolve link conflicts.

Link The link element defines a relationship between the current document and another file. This is not the same as a link in the Document window.

Keywords, descriptions, and refresh settings are special-use cases of the meta tag.

Plan head content.
Browsers and Web search tools refer to information contained in the head section of a Web page. Although this section is not displayed in the browser window, you can set the properties of the head elements to control how your pages are identified. At a minimum, you should set properties for the following head elements:

- **Keywords:** Enter keywords you anticipate users and search engines might use to find your page. Because some search engines limit the number of keywords or characters they track, enter only a few accurate, descriptive keywords.

- **Description:** Many search engines also read the contents of the Description text. Some search engines display the Description text in the search results, so be sure to enter a meaningful description.

Plan Ahead

To Add Keywords and a Description to the Index Page

The following steps show how to add keywords and a description to the index.htm page.

1

• Open the index.htm page.

• Click Insert on the Application bar, point to HTML, point to Head Tags on the HTML submenu, and then point to Keywords on the Head Tags submenu (Figure 3–69).

Q&A

What is a keyword?

A keyword is a word or phrase that someone might type into a search engine search field.

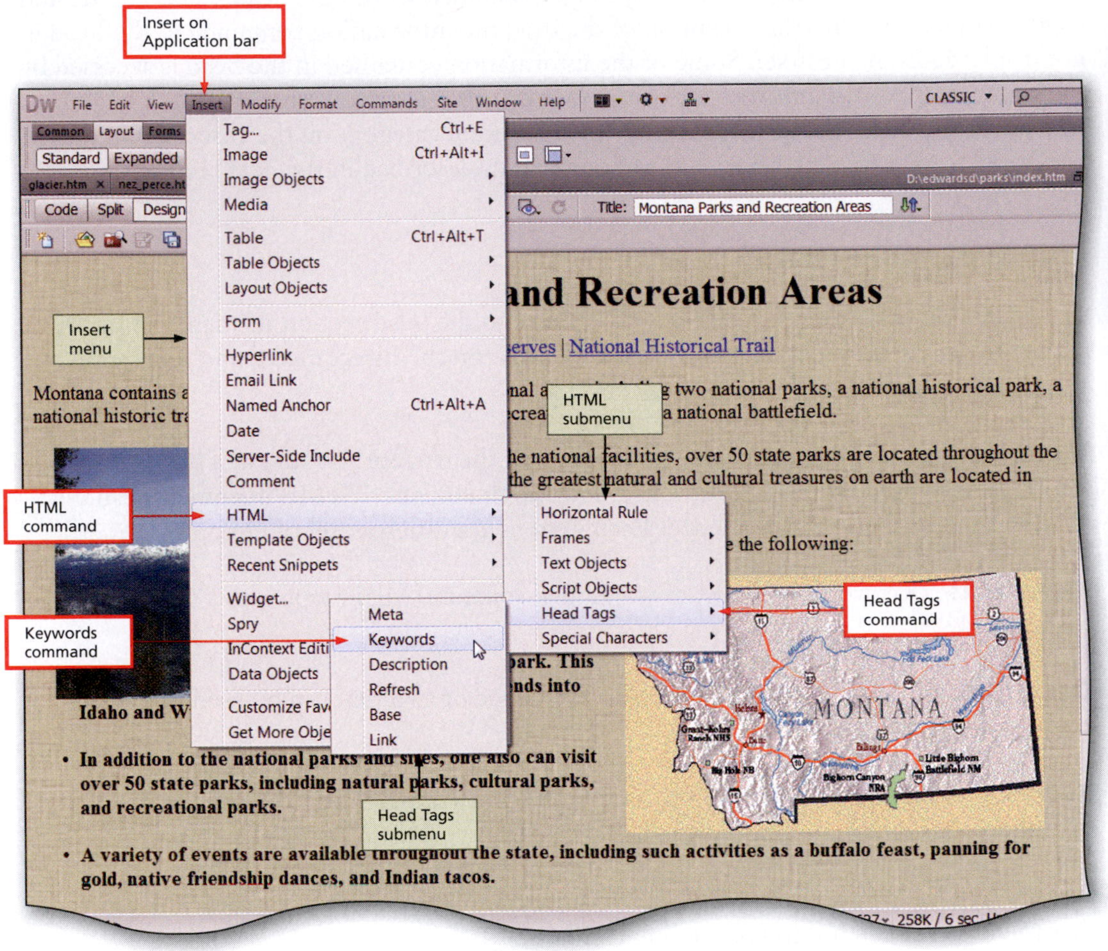

Figure 3–69

2

• Click the Keywords command to display the Keywords dialog box.

• Type **parks, Montana, national parks, national preserves** in the Keywords text box to add the keywords to the Keywords dialog box (Figure 3–70).

Q&A

What does a search engine typically do with the keywords?

When a search engine begins a search for any of the keywords, the Web site address will be displayed in the search results.

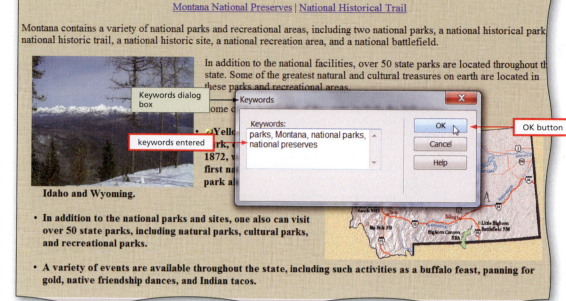

Figure 3–70

3

• Click the OK button to add the keywords to the head tag and close the Keywords dialog box.

• Click Insert on the Application bar, point to HTML, point to Head Tags on the HTML submenu, and then click Description on the Head Tags submenu to open the Description dialog box.

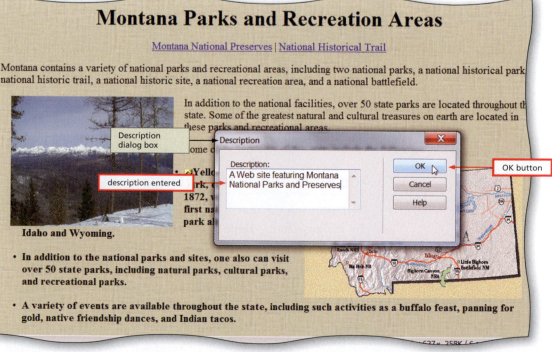

Figure 3–71

- Type **A Web site featuring Montana National Parks and Preserves** in the Description text box to describe the Web page (Figure 3–71 on the previous page).

Q&A

What is the purpose of the description?

The description contains a sentence or two that can be used in a search engine's results page.

4

- Click the OK button to close the Description dialog box.

- Click the Code button on the Document toolbar to display the page in Code view (Figure 3–72).

5

- Click the Design button on the Document tool-bar to return to Design view.

- Click the Save button on the Standard tool-bar to save your work.

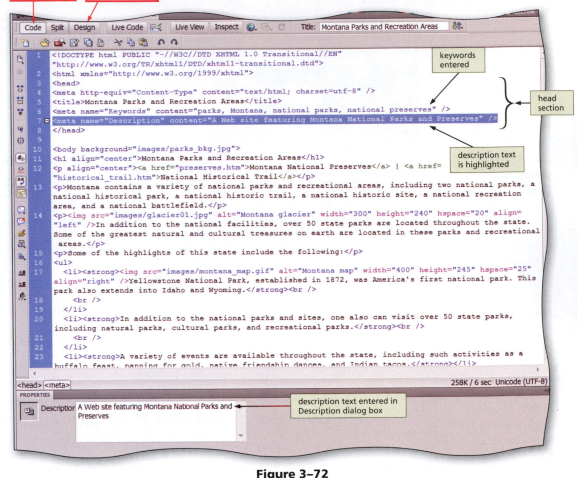

Figure 3–72

Other Ways

1. Click Code button on Document toolbar, type keywords code in code window

To Add Links to the Index Page

To integrate the two new pages in the Web site, you need to modify the index.htm page by adding a footer table at the bottom of the page. The following steps show how to delete the existing links and add a Links table.

1 Click the glacier.htm document tab to display that Web page, scroll to the bottom of the page, select the Montana_parks_links table, right-click the selection to display the context menu, and then click Copy to copy the table.

2 Click the index.htm document tab, scroll to the bottom of the page, click to the right of the last sentence (Most events are free.), and then press ENTER to move the insertion point to the next line.

3 Right-click near the insertion point to display the context menu and then click Paste to paste the Montana_parks_links table into the index page.

4 Click to the right of the Nez Perce text in the Montana_parks_links table, press the SPACEBAR, press SHIFT+| (vertical bar), press the SPACEBAR, and then type `Glacier National Park.`

5 Drag to select the space, vertical bar, and space you just entered, delete the text in the Link box in the Property inspector, click the Glacier National Park text in the Montana_ parks_links table, and then change the entry in the Link box to glacier.htm (Figure 3–73).

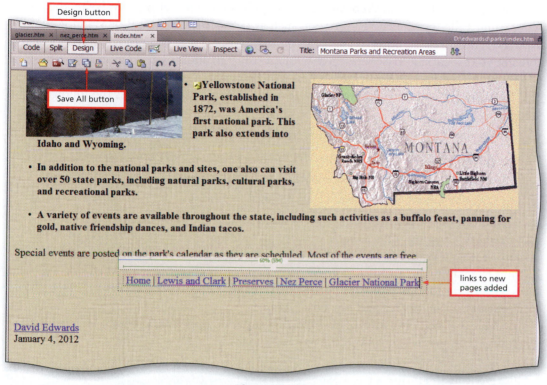

Figure 3–73

6 Scroll to the top of the index.htm page, select the two links, and then press DELETE to remove the links from the top of the page.

7 Scroll to the bottom of the page, select the space, vertical bar, space, and Glacier National Park text in the Montana_parks_links table, and then press CTRL+C to copy the linked text.

8 Click the glacier.htm document tab, click at the end of the Montana_parks_links table at the bottom of the page, and then press CTRL+V to insert the link.

9 Click the nez_perce.htm document tab, click at the end of the Montana_parks_links table at the bottom of the page, and then press CTRL+V to insert the link.

10 Click the index.htm document tab, and then click the Save All button on the Standard toolbar to save your work on the three pages.

11 Press the F12 key to preview the page in a browser, test each link to verify that it works, and then close the browser.

Publishing a Web Site

In Chapter 1 you defined a local site, and in Chapters 1, 2, and 3 you added Web pages to the local site. This local site resides on your computer's hard disk, a network drive, or possibly a USB drive. You can view the organization of all files and folders in your site through the Files panel.

To prepare a Web site and make it available for others to view requires that you publish your site by putting it on a Web server for public access. A Web server is an Internet- or intranet-connected computer that delivers, or *serves up*, Web pages. You upload files to a folder on a server and download files to a folder in the Files panel on your computer. Generally, when Web site designers publish to a folder on a Web site, they do so by using a file transfer (FTP) program such as WS_FTP, Cute FTP, or Windows Web Folders. Dreamweaver, however, includes built-in support that enables you to connect and transfer your local site to a Web server without using an additional program. To publish to a Web server requires that you have access to a Web server.

Publishing and maintaining your site using Dreamweaver involves the following steps:

1. Using the Site Setup dialog box to enter the FTP information
2. Specifying the Web server to which you want to publish your Web site
3. Connecting to the Web server and uploading the files
4. Synchronizing the local and remote sites

Your school or company may have a server that you can use to upload your Web site. Free Web hosting services such as those provided by Angelfire or Tripod are other options. These services, as well as many other hosting services, also offer low-cost Web hosting from approximately $3.95 to $9.95 a month. The FreeSite.com Web site contains a list of free and inexpensive hosting services, and FreeWebspace.net provides a PowerSearch form for free and low-cost hosting.

Table 3–7 contains a list of Web hosting services. Appendix C contains step-by-step instructions on publishing a Web site to a remote folder.

Table 3–7 Web Site Hosting Services		
Name	Web Site	Cost
Angelfire	angelfire.lycos.com	Free (ad-supported); starting at $4.95 monthly ad-free
FreeWebspace.net	freewebspace.net	A searchable guide for free Web space
The FreeSite.com	thefreesite.com/Free_Web_Space	A list of free and inexpensive hosting sites
Tripod	tripod.lycos.com	Free (ad-supported); starting at $4.95 monthly ad-free

If required by your instructor, publish the Montana Parks Web site to a remote server by following the steps in Appendix C.

Quitting Dreamweaver

After you add pages to your Web site and add the head content, Chapter 3 is complete, so you can quit Dreamweaver.

To Close the Web Site and Quit Dreamweaver

The following step illustrates how to close the Web site, quit Dreamweaver CS5, and return to Windows.

1 Click the Close button on the right corner of the Dreamweaver title bar. If prompted, click the Yes button to save any changes.

Chapter Summary

Chapter 3 introduced you to tables and to Web page design using tables. You created two Web pages. You added a border to one of the Web pages. You merged and split cells and learned how to add text and images to the tables and how to create links to other pages. Finally, you added head content to one of the Web pages. The items listed below include all the new skills you have learned in this chapter.

1. Insert a table (DW 193)
2. Select and center a table (DW 201)
3. Change vertical alignment from Middle to Top (DW 203)
4. Specify column width (DW 205)
5. Add a table ID to the Nez Perce National Historic Trail table (DW 206)
6. Add text to the Nez Perce National Historic Trail Web page (DW 208)
7. Add a second table to the Nez Perce National Historic Trail Web page (DW 210)
8. Adjust the table width, center the text, and add the table ID (DW 212)
9. Add links to the Nez Perce National Historic Trail Web page (DW 213)
10. Merge two cells in a table (DW 217)
11. Disable the Image Tag Accessibility Attributes dialog box (DW 218)
12. Add images, image borders, and a table border (DW 235)
13. Add keywords and a description to the index page (DW 242)

Learn It Online

Test your knowledge of chapter content and key terms.

Instructions: To complete the Learn It Online exercises, start your browser, click the Address bar, and then enter the Web address `scsite.com/dwcs5/learn`. When the Dreamweaver CS5 Learn It Online page is displayed, click the link for the exercise you want to complete and then read the instructions.

Chapter Reinforcement TF, MC, and SA

A series of true/false, multiple choice, and short answer questions that test your knowledge of the chapter content.

Flash Cards

An interactive learning environment where you identify chapter key terms associated with displayed definitions.

Practice Test

A series of multiple choice questions that test your knowledge of chapter content and key terms.

Who Wants to Be a Computer Genius?

An interactive game that challenges your knowledge of chapter content in the style of a television quiz show.

Wheel of Terms

An interactive game that challenges your knowledge of chapter key terms in the style of the television show *Wheel of Fortune*.

Crossword Puzzle Challenge

A crossword puzzle that challenges your knowledge of key terms presented in the chapter.

Apply Your Knowledge

Reinforce the skills and apply the concepts you learned in this chapter.

Adding a Table to a Web Page

Instructions: In this activity, you modify a Web page by adding a table and then inserting images in the table. Figure 3–74 shows the completed Web page. Make sure you have downloaded the data files for this chapter. See the inside back cover of this book for instructions for downloading the Data Files for Students, or contact your instructor for information about accessing the required files for this book.

Figure 3–74

Perform the following tasks:

1. Start Dreamweaver, and then copy the apply_ch03.htm file from the Chapter03\apply data files folder into the apply folder for your Apply Exercises local Web site. (For example, the apply folder might be stored on H:\edwardsd\apply.) Copy the three image files from the Chapter03\apply\images folder to the apply\images folder for the Apply Exercises site. (For example, the images folder might be stored on H:\edwardsd\apply\images.)

2. Open the Apply Exercises site.

3. Open the apply_ch03.htm page. Add the apply_bkg background image to the page.

4. Click to the right of the "Plants of the Week" heading and then press ENTER.

5. Insert a one-row, three-column table with a table width of 90 percent, border thickness of 3 pixels, cell padding of 5, and cell spacing of 10.

6. Click the Summary box, type **Favorite plants**, and then click OK to insert the table.

7. Center the table and type **favorite_plants** in the Table box to enter the table ID.

8. Insert the plant01 image into row 1, column 1.

9. Use the following properties for the plant01 image:

   Image ID: sunflowers

   Width: 255 pixels

   Height: 170 pixels

   Alt text: sunflowers

10. Insert the plant02 image into row 1, column 2.

11. Use the following properties for the plant02 image:

    Image ID: purple_passion

    Width: 255 pixels

    Height: 170 pixels

    Alt text: Purple passion

12. Insert the plant03 image into row 1, column 3.

13. Use the following properties for the plant03 image:

    Image ID: roses

    Width: 255 pixels

    Height: 170 pixels

    Alt text: Roses are white

14. Center each image in its table cell.

15. Save your document and then view it in your browser. Submit the Web page in the format specified by your instructor.

Extend Your Knowledge

Extend the skills you learned in this chapter and experiment with new skills. You may need to use Help to complete the assignment.

Adding, Aligning, and Resizing an Image on a Web Page

Instructions: In this activity, you create a Web page, insert text, add a table, insert images, and then align and resize the images. Figure 3–75 shows the completed Web page. Make sure you have downloaded the data files for this chapter. See the inside back cover of this book for instructions for downloading the Data Files for Students, or contact your instructor for information about accessing the required files for this book.

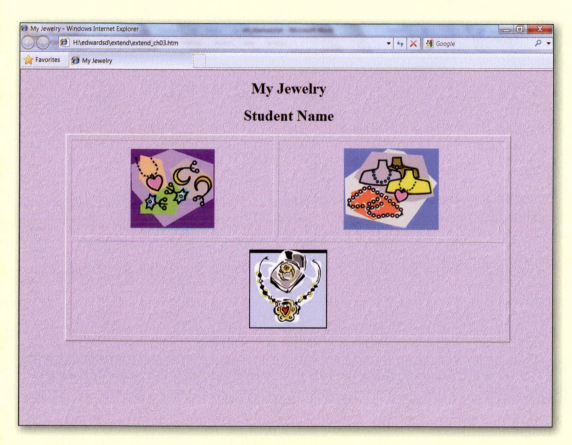

Figure 3–75

Perform the following tasks:

1. Start Dreamweaver, and then copy the three image files from the Chapter03\extend\images folder to the extend\images folder for the Extend Exercises site. (For example, the images folder might be stored on H:\edwardsd\extend\images.)

2. Open the Extend Exercises site, create a new HTML document, and then save the page as extend_ch03.htm. Apply the extend_bkg background image to the page.

3. Enter the following heading at the top of the page: My Jewelry. Press ENTER and then type your name.

4. Apply the Heading 1 format to the heading and your name, and then center both lines. Click to the right of your name and then press ENTER.

5. Insert a two-row, two-column table with a table width of 85 percent, border thickness of 3 pixels, cell padding of 15, and cell spacing of 10.

6. Use jewelry as the table ID text, and then center the table.

7. Drag the jewelry01 image to row 1, column 1. Use the following properties for the jewelry01 image:

    Image ID: purple_jewelry

    Width: 175 pixels

    Height: 165 pixels

    Alt text: purple jewelry

8. Drag the jewelry02 image to cell row 1, column 2. Use the following properties for the jewelry02 image:

    Image ID: necklaces

    Width: 200 pixels

    Height: 170 pixels

    Alt text: necklaces

9. Merge the two cells in row 2.

10. Drag the jewelry03 image to row 2. Use the following properties for the jewelry03 image:

    Image ID: jewelry_set

    Width: 163 pixels

    Height: 164 pixels

    Alt text: jewelry set

11. Align each image in the absolute middle of the cell, and then center each image.

12. Use the following text as the page title: My Jewelry.

13. Save your document and then view it in your browser. Submit the Web page in the format specified by your instructor.

Make It Right

Analyze a Web page and correct all errors and/or improve the design.

Adding an Image and E-mail Address to a Web Page

Instructions: In this activity, you modify a Web page to add a heading and a table with images. Figure 3-76 on the next page shows the completed Web page. Table 3-8 on the next page lists the properties you should use for the table and images. Make sure you have downloaded the data files for Chapter03\ right. See the inside back cover of this book for instructions for downloading the Data Files for Students, or contact your instructor for information about accessing the required files for this book.

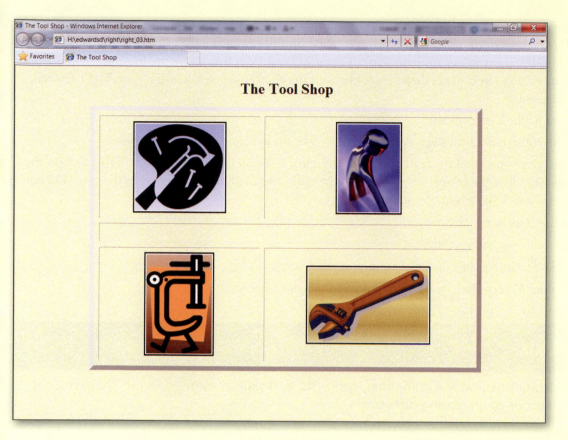

Figure 3–76

Table 3–8 Properties for Table and Images

Table Section	Image Name	Properties
Entire table	n/a	Rows: 3 Columns: 2 Width: 75 percent Border thickness: 10 Cell padding: 10 Cell spacing: 10 ID: tools Alignment: Center
Column 1, row 1	hammer01	ID: hammer_01 Alt text: regular hammer Border: 3 Alignment: Absolute Middle
Column 2, row 1	hammer02	ID: hammer_02 Alt text: special hammer Border: 3 Alignment: Absolute Middle
Column 1, row 2	blank	
Column 2, row 2	blank	
Column 1, row 3	clamp	ID: clamp Alt text: clamp Border: 3 Alignment: Middle
Column 2, row 3	wrench	ID: wrench Alt text: wrench Border: 3 Alignment: Middle

Perform the following tasks:

1. Start Dreamweaver, and then copy the right_ch03.htm file from the Chapter03\right data files folder into the right folder for your Right Exercises local Web site. Copy the four image files from the Chapter03\right\images data files folder into the right\images folder for your Right Exercises local Web site.

2. Open the Right Exercises site.

3. Open the right_ch03.htm page. Apply the right_bkg background image to the page.

4. The Web page you need to create is shown in Figure 3–76 on the previous page. Table 3–8 on the previous page lists the properties to apply to the table and the images to insert in the cells. Do not change the width or height of the images.

5. Merge the cells in row 2.

6. Center each image in its cell.

7. Save your document and then view it in your browser.

8. Submit your Web page in the format specified by your instructor.

In the Lab

Create a document using the guidelines, concepts, and skills presented in this chapter. Labs are listed in order of increasing difficulty.

Lab 1: Modifying the Computer Repair Services Web Site

Problem: Now that Bryan has a basic Web site for his Computer Repair Services business, he wants to make the site more appealing to visitors. The Web site currently contains three pages. Bryan asks you to add a fourth page with a table that includes a list of services, information about how often the services are scheduled, and the price of each service. In the table, you should merge two of the rows, add and center an image in one row, and apply a border to the entire table. You also add keywords and a description to the page. You then add a link to the home page and save the page (Figure 3–77).

Software and hardware settings determine how a Web page is displayed in a browser. Your Web page may appear different from the one shown in Figure 3–77. Appendix C contains instructions for uploading your local site to a remote site.

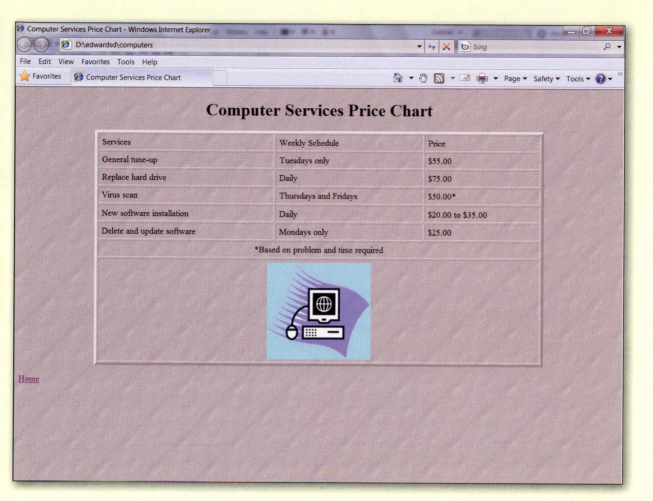

Figure 3–77

Perform the following tasks:

1. Start Dreamweaver, and then copy the price_chart data file from the Chapter03\computers data files folder into the root folder for your Computer Repair Services local Web site. (For example, the root folder might be stored on H:\edwardsd\computers.)

2. Open the Computer Repair Services site, and then open the price_chart.htm document.

3. Use the Page Properties dialog box to apply the repair_bkg background image to the page.

4. Position the insertion point after the Computer Services Price Chart heading, press the ENTER key after the heading, and then click the Layout tab on the Insert bar. Click the Table button on the Layout tab. Enter the following values in the Table dialog box and then click the OK button:

Rows: 8

Columns: 3

Table width: 75%

Border thickness: 4

Cell padding: 5

Cell spacing: 3

Summary text: Pricing chart for computer services

5. In the first six rows of the table, enter the text as shown in Table 3–9. Apply the Heading 3 format to the column title cells and center-align them. Press the TAB key to move from cell to cell.

Table 3–9 Text for Table on Prices Page

Column 1	Column 2	Column 3
Services	Weekly Schedule	Price
General tune-up	Tuesdays only	$55.00
Replace hard drive	Daily	$75.00
Virus scan	Thursdays and Fridays	$50.00*
New software installation	Daily	$20.00 to $35.00
Delete and update software	Mondays only	$25.00

6. Click anywhere in row 7 and then click the <tr> tag in the tag selector to select row 7. Click the 'Merges selected cells using spans' button. Click the Horz button arrow in the Property inspector, and then select Center. Type ***Based on problem and time required** in the merged cell.

7. Click anywhere in row 8 and then click the <tr> tag in the tag selector to select row 8. Click the 'Merges selected cells using spans' button. Click the Horz button arrow in the Property inspector, and then select Center. If necessary, display the Assets panel. With the insertion point in the middle of the merged row 8, drag the computer_repair04 image to the insertion point. With the image still selected, type **computer** in the ID text box and then type **computer repair** as the Alt text.

8. Click the <table> tag in the tag selector, click the Align button, and then click Center to center the table. Click the Table text box and then type computer_services as the ID.

9. Position the insertion point outside the table by clicking to the right of the table. Press the ENTER key. Type **Home** and then create a relative link to the index.htm file.

10. Click Insert on the Application bar, point to HTML, point to Head Tags, and then click the Keywords command. When the Keywords dialog box is displayed, type the following text in the Keywords text box: **computer repair, computer service, price schedule, your name**. Click the OK button. Click Insert on the Application bar, point to HTML, point to Head Tags, and then click the Description command. When the Description dialog box is displayed, type **Bryan's Computer Repair Services price schedule** in the Description text box. Click the OK button.

11. Check the spelling of the document, and then save the price_chart.htm Web page.

12. Open the index.htm page and then scroll to the end of the page. Click at the end of the sentence that reads, "Our mission is to be a premier…" and then press the ENTER key. Type **Check our prices**. Create a link from the words Check our prices to the price_chart.htm page. Save the index.htm Web page.

13. View the pages in your browser. Verify that your links work.

14. Submit your Web pages in the format specified by your instructor.

In the Lab

Lab 2: Adding a Page with a Table to the Baskets by Carole Web Site

Problem: Publicity from the Baskets by Carole Web site has generated several requests for examples of Carole's baskets. Carole has asked you to add a page to the site that shows some of her creations and the price of each piece. The new Web page will be named specials and should include a link to the home page. The new page is shown in Figure 3–78.

Software and hardware settings determine how a Web page is displayed in a browser. Your Web page may appear different from the one shown in Figure 3–78. Appendix C contains instructions for uploading your local site to a remote site.

Figure 3–78

Perform the following tasks:

1. Start Dreamweaver, and then copy the two image data files from the Chapter03\baskets\images data files folder into the images folder for your Gift Basket Designs local Web site. (For example, the images folder might be stored on H:\edwardsd\baskets\images.)

2. Open the Gift Basket Designs site.

3. Create a new blank HTML page named specials.htm for this Web site.

4. Use the Page Properties dialog box to apply the baskets_bkg background image to the Web page. Title the page Baskets by Carole.

4. Click the upper-left corner of the page, type `Carole's Basket Specials` as the page heading, and then press the ENTER key to insert a blank line. Format the heading as Heading 1 text, and then center it.

5. Below the heading, insert a table with the following properties:

   Rows: 6

   Columns: 3

   Table width: 80 percent

   Border thickness: 3

   Cell padding: 3

   Cell spacing: 3

   Summary: Basket examples

6. Merge the three cells in row 1 into one cell. Center row 1 horizontally. Type the following heading for the table in row 1: `Baskets by Carole Specialty Pieces`. Apply Heading 2 to the table heading.

7. Center rows 2 through 6 horizontally and apply a Middle vertical alignment. Set the width of each column to 33%.

8. Using the Assets panel, drag images to row 2 as follows:

   Column 1   basket01

   Column 2   basket02

   Column 3   basket03

9. Enter the following information in row 3:

   Column 1 $18.50

   Column 2 $19.50

   Column 3 $20.00

10. Merge the three cells in row 4.

11. Add the following images in row 5:

    Column 1   basket04

    Column 2   basket05

    Column 3   basket06

12. Enter the following information in row 6:

    Column 1 $21.00

    Column 2 $28.00

    Column 3 $29.00

13. Resize each image in the table so the width and height are each 250.

14. Select the table, enter baskets as the ID, and then use the Property inspector to center-align the table.

15. Insert a blank line after the table. On the new line, type **Home** and then use this text to create a link from the specials.htm page to the index.htm page. Save the specials.htm page.

16. Open the index.htm page and click to the right of the Company History link. Press ENTER. Type **Specials** and then use this text to create a link to the specials.htm page. Save the index.htm page.

17. View the pages in your browser. Verify that your links work.

18. Submit your Web pages in the format specified by your instructor.

In the Lab

Lab 3: Adding a Page with a Table to the Credit Web Site

Problem: The Credit Protection Web site has become very popular. Jessica Minnick receives numerous e-mail messages requesting that the Web site be expanded. Several messages have included a request to provide some hints and tips about how to save money. Jessica asks you to create a new page for the Web site so she can share some of this information. Figure 3–79 shows the completed Web page.

Software and hardware settings determine how a Web page is displayed in a browser. Your Web page may appear different from the one shown in Figure 3–79. Appendix C contains instructions for uploading your local site to a remote site.

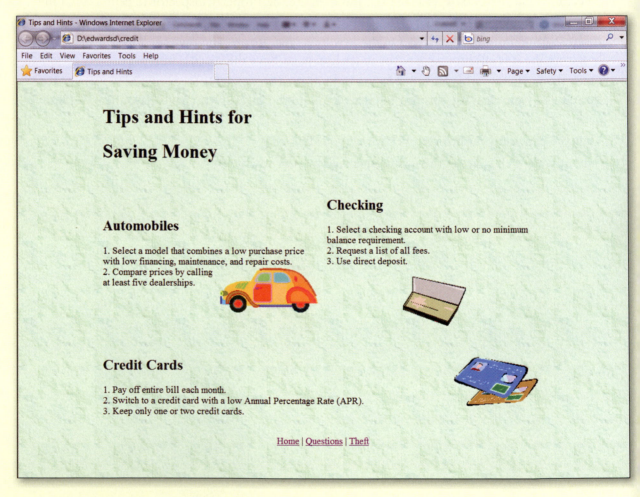

Figure 3–79

Perform the following tasks:

1. Start Dreamweaver, and then copy the three image files from the Chapter03\credit\images data files folder into the images folder for your Credit Protection local Web site.

2. Open the Credit Protection site, and then create a new blank HTML page named saving.htm for this Web site.

3. Apply the credit_bkg background image to the new page. Title the page Tips and Hints.

4. Create a table with four rows, two columns, a width of 75%, border thickness of 0, cell padding of 5, and cell spacing of 5. Add the following summary text: Tips and hints for saving money. Set the width of each column to 50%.

5. Use Figure 3–79 as a guide to add content to the table. Use the information in Table 3–10 for the specific properties and as a reference for the cell contents. Type the specified text into each cell.

Table 3–10 Credit Protection Table Guide						
Cells	**Merge**	**Cell Text**	**Image Name**	**Image Location**	**Image Alignment**	**Alt Text**
Row 1, columns 1 and 2	Cells in columns 1 and 2	Tips and Hints for <ENTER> Saving Money	None	None	None	None
Row 2, column 1	None	Automobiles <ENTER> 1. Select a model that combines a low purchase price with low financing, maintenance, and repair costs. 2. Compare prices by calling at least five dealerships.	car.gif	End of Step 1, after "repair costs."	Right	Car
Row 2, column 2	None	Checking <ENTER> 1. Select a checking account with a low or no minimum balance requirement. 2. Request a list of all fees. 3. Use direct deposit. <ENTER>	check.gif	Below Step 3, "Use direct deposit."	Center	Checking Account
Row 3, columns 1 and 2	Cells in columns 1 and 2	Credit Cards <ENTER> 1. Pay off the entire bill each month. 2. Switch to a credit card with a low Annual Percentage Rate (APR). 3. Keep only one or two credit cards.	credit_card.gif	End of the "Credit Cards" heading	Right	Credit Cards
Row 4, columns 1 and 2	Cells in columns 1 and 2	Home	Questions	Theft	None	None	None	None

6. Apply Heading 1 to the text in the first cell. Apply Heading 2 to the "Automobiles," "Checking," and "Credit Cards" headings.

7. Insert the images into the cells in the locations specified in Table 3–10. Format the images as shown in Table 3–10.

8. Center the last row of the table horizontally. Add the appropriate relative links to this text, using Table 3–11 as a guide.

Table 3–11 Links for Last Row	
Text	**Link**
Home	index.htm
Questions	questions.htm
Theft	theft.htm

9. Select the table, and then center it.

10. Add the following keywords to the Head section: credit, money, tips, checking, saving, your name. Add the following description: Tips and hints on how to save money. Save the Web page.

11. Open the index.htm page and click to the right of the last bulleted item. Press the ENTER key twice. Type **Saving Tips** and create a link from this text to the saving.htm page. Save the index.htm page.

12. View the pages in your browser. Verify that your links work.

13. Submit your Web pages in the format specified by your instructor.

Cases and Places

Apply your creative thinking and problem solving skills to design and implement a solution.

• Easier ••More Difficult

• 1: Add a Web Page to the Favorite Sports Web Site

The Favorite Sports Web site has become very popular. Several of your friends have suggested that you add a statistics page. You agree that this is a good idea. Create the new page. Using the Internet or other resources, find statistics about your selected sport. Add a background image to the page and use Standard mode to insert a table that contains your statistical information. Add an appropriate heading to the table and an appropriate title for the page. Create a link to the home page. Save the page in the sports subfolder of the Favorite Sports Web site. For a selection of images and backgrounds, visit the Dreamweaver CS5 Media Web page (scsite.com/dwcs5/media) and then click Media below Chapter 3.

• 2: Expand the Hobby Web Site

Modify your Hobby Web site. Add a new page that includes a table created in Standard mode. The table should contain a minimum of three rows and three columns, and a border. Include information in the table about your hobby. Include a minimum of two images in the table. Merge one of the rows or one of the columns and change the default border thickness. Add a background image to the page and give your page a title. Create a link to the home page. Save the page in the hobby subfolder of the Hobby Web site. For a selection of images and backgrounds, visit the Dreamweaver CS5 Media Web page (scsite.com/dwcs5/media) and then click Media below Chapter 3.

•• 3: Add a Web Page to the Politics Web Site

Your campaign for office is going well. You want to add a new page to the Politics Web site to include pictures and text listing some of your outstanding achievements. Apply a background image to the page. Insert a table with a minimum of four cells. Include your picture in one of the cells. Add an appropriate title, keywords, and a description to the page. Center the table. Save the page in the subfolder for the Politics site and then view the page in your browser. Appendix C contains instructions for uploading your local site to a remote site. For a selection of images and backgrounds, visit the Dreamweaver CS5 Media Web page (scsite.com/dwcs5/media) and then click Media below Chapter 3.

•• 4: Modify the Favorite Music Web Site

Make It Personal

Modify your Favorite Music Web site by adding a new page. The new page should contain a table with four rows and three columns. Merge one of the rows and add a background color to the row. Add at least two images to your table. Center the images in the cell. View your Web pages in your browser. Give your page a title and save the page in the folder for the Favorite Music site. Appendix C contains instructions for uploading your local site to a remote site. For a selection of images and backgrounds, visit the Dreamweaver CS5 Media Web page (scsite.com/dwcs5/media) and then click Media below Chapter 3.

• • **5: Upgrade the Student Trips Web Site**

Working Together

The students at your school are requesting more information about the student trips. To accommodate the request, the members of your team decide to add another page to the Web site. Each team member is responsible for researching possible destinations and developing content for the selected destination. Add a heading to the new page and format it appropriately. Insert a table with a minimum of six cells. Each member adds at least one image and text content to a cell. One member formats the page — including the text and images. Add a title, keywords, and a description. Save the page and view it in your browser. Appendix C contains instructions for uploading your local site to a remote site. For a selection of images and backgrounds, visit the Dreamweaver CS5 Media Web page (scsite.com/dwcs5/media) and then click Media below Chapter 3.

Appendix A
Adobe Dreamweaver CS5 Help

Getting Help with Dreamweaver CS5

This appendix shows you how to use Dreamweaver Help. The Help system is a complete reference manual at your fingertips. You can access and use the Help system through the Help menu in Dreamweaver CS5, which connects you to up-to-date Help information online at the Adobe Web site. Or, if you prefer, you can download the Help topics to your computer in a single PDF file, which you can open and read with Adobe Reader. The Help system contains comprehensive information about all Dreamweaver features, including the following:

- A table of contents in which the information is organized by subject.
- A link to Popular resources, which includes a variety of examples, instructional tutorials, support articles, videos, and other instructional links.
- A search tool, which is used to locate specific topics.

Additional tutorials and online movies are available on the Adobe Dreamweaver resources Web site at *http://help.adobe.com*.

The Dreamweaver Help Menu

One way to access Dreamweaver's Help features is through the Help menu and function keys. Dreamweaver's Help menu provides an easy system to access the available Help options (see Figure A–1). Most of these commands open a Help window that displays the appropriate up-to-date Help information from the Adobe Web site. Table A–1 on the next page summarizes the commands available through the Help menu.

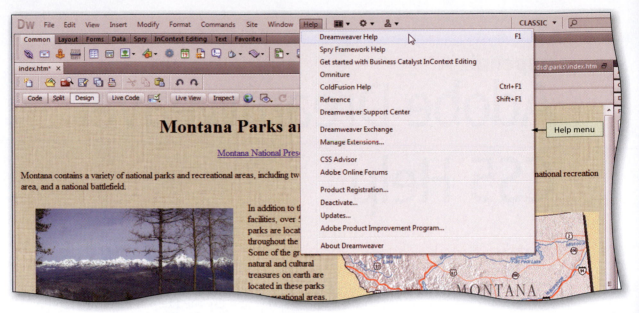

Figure A–1

Table A–1 Summary of Commands on the Help Menu	
Command on Help menu	**Description**
Dreamweaver Help	Starts your default Web browser and displays the Dreamweaver CS5 online help system at the Adobe Web site.
Spry Framework Help	Displays a complete Help document for the Spry framework for Ajax, a JavaScript library that provides the Web site developer with an option to incorporate XML data and other kinds of effects.
Get started with Business Catalyst InContext Editing	Provides information on how to make Web pages editable through any common browser so that content editors can revise Web page text while designers focus on design.
Omniture	Extensions that make it easier to measure the performance of online content.
ColdFusion Help	Displays the complete Help document for ColdFusion, a Web application server that lets you create applications that interact with databases.
Reference	Opens the Reference panel group, which is displayed below the Document window. The Reference panel group contains the complete text from several reference manuals, including references on HTML, Cascading Style Sheets, JavaScript, and other Web-related features.
Dreamweaver Support Center	Provides access to the online Adobe Dreamweaver support center.
Dreamweaver Exchange	Links to the Adobe Exchange Web site, where you can download for free and/or purchase a variety of Dreamweaver add-on features.
Manage Extensions	Displays the Adobe Extension Manager window where you can install, enable, and disable extensions. An extension is an add-on piece of software or a plug-in that enhances Dreamweaver's capabilities. Extensions provide the Dreamweaver developer with the capability to customize how Dreamweaver looks and works.
CSS Advisor	Connects to the online Adobe CSS Advisor Web site, which provides solutions to CSS and browser compatibility issues, and encourages you to share tips, hints, and best practices for working with CSS.

Table A–1 Summary of Commands on the Help Menu (*continued*)	
Command on Help menu	**Description**
Adobe Online Forums	Accesses the Adobe Online Forums Web page. The forums provide a place for developers of all experience levels to share ideas and techniques.
Product Registration	Displays your registration information and provides a print option.
Deactivate	Deactivates the installation of Dreamweaver CS5. If you have a single-user retail license, you can activate two computers. If you want to install Dreamweaver CS5 on a third computer, you need to deactivate it first on another computer.
Updates	Lets you check for updates to Adobe software online and then install the updates as necessary.
Adobe Product Improvement Program	Displays a dialog box that explains the Adobe Product Improvement Program and allows you to participate in the program.
About Dreamweaver	Opens a window that provides copyright information and the product license number.

Exploring the Dreamweaver CS5 Help System

The Dreamweaver Help command accesses Dreamweaver's primary Help system at the Adobe Web site and provides comprehensive information about all Dreamweaver features. Two categories of Help are available, as shown in Figure A–2: Adobe reference and Popular resources. In addition, you can view or download the Dreamweaver CS5 Help in a single PDF file.

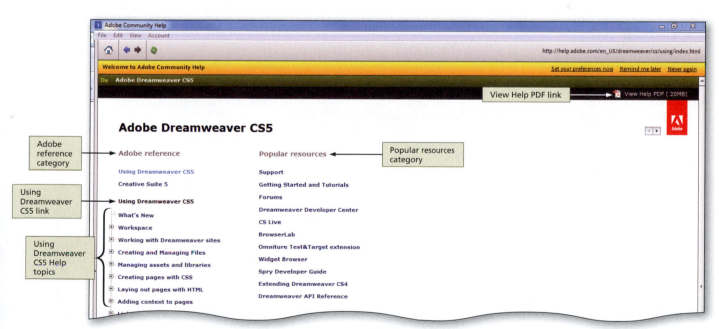

Figure A–2

BTW

Navigating to the Adobe Dreamweaver CS5 Page
If the Dreamweaver Help and Support Web page opens instead of the Adobe Dreamweaver CS5 page shown in Figure A–2 when you click Help on the Application bar and then click Dreamweaver Help (or press F1), click the Dreamweaver CS5 Help link on the Dreamweaver Help and Support page to navigate to the Adobe Dreamweaver CS5 page.

Adobe reference   This section provides extensive Help information, including links to the Using Dreamweaver CS5 Help topics. Using Dreamweaver CS5 is organized into a contents panel on the left and a panel displaying the Help information on the right.

Popular resources   This section provides access to several popular resources, including Support, Getting Started and Tutorials, Forums, Dreamweaver Developer Center, CS Live, BrowserLab, Omniture Test & Target extension, Widget Browser, Spry Developer Guide, Extending Dreamweaver CS4, and Dreamweaver API Reference.

View Help PDF   Click this link to download a Portable Document Format (PDF) file that contains Dreamweaver CS5 Help information. You then can open the PDF file using Adobe Acrobat and use Acrobat features to read, search, and print Help information.

Using the Contents Panel

The **contents** panel is useful for displaying Help when you know the general category of the topic in question, but not the specifics. You use the contents panel to navigate to the main topic, and then to the subtopic. When the information on the subtopic is displayed, you can read the information, click a link contained within the subtopic, or click the Previous or Next button to open the previous or next Help page in sequence. If a Comments link appears on the page, click it to view comments other users or experts have made about this topic.

To Find Help Using the Contents Panel

To find help using the contents panel, you click a plus icon to expand a Help category and display a list of specific topics. Click a link to display a list of specific subtopics. You then can click a link to open a page related to that subtopic. The following steps show how to use the contents panel to find information on displaying toolbars.

- In Dreamweaver, click Help on the Application bar, and then point to Dreamweaver Help (Figure A–3).

Figure A–3

2

- Click Dreamweaver Help to display the Welcome to Adobe Community Help site.

- If necessary, click the Using Dreamweaver CS5 icon to display the Adobe Dreamweaver CS5 page (shown in Figure A–2 on the previous page).

- If necessary, click the plus sign to the left of Workspace to expand that topic, and then click the Workspace link to display the Workspace page, including subtopics about the Dreamweaver workspace (Figure A–4).

Figure A–4

Q&A What is the purpose of the yellow arrow button in the lower-right corner of the window?

Clicking this button displays links to Using Dreamweaver CS4 and Dreamweaver CS3 Help files.

3

- Click 'Using toolbars, inspectors, and context menus' to display that Help page, including links to display toolbars, use the Property inspector, and use context menus.

- Click the Display toolbars link to review the page content, including links to related information (Figure A–5).

Figure A–5

4

- Click the Home link to return to the Adobe Dreamweaver CS5 page.

Using the Search Feature

The Search feature allows you to find any character string, anywhere in the text of the Help system.

To Use the Search Feature

The next steps show how to use the Search feature to obtain help about cropping images.

1

- On the Adobe Dreamweaver CS5 page, click View on the Application bar, and then click Show Search Panel to display the Search panel, including the Search Dreamweaver content text box.

- If necessary, click the Adobe reference only check box to indicate you want to search the Dreamweaver CS5 references only, not all of the Adobe Web site (Figure A–6).

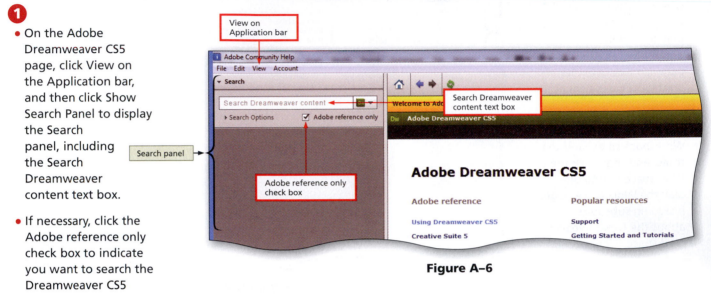

Figure A–6

2

- Click the Search Dreamweaver content text box, type `cropping`, and then press ENTER to display the results.

- Click the Search Options arrow to display additional search options, including Search Location and Filter Results (Figure A–7).

Q&A

Why do the search results include topics related to Creative Suite CS5 products besides Dreamweaver?

Because Dreamweaver CS5 is part of Adobe Creative Suite CS5, help topics related to other Creative Suite CS5 products might provide helpful information.

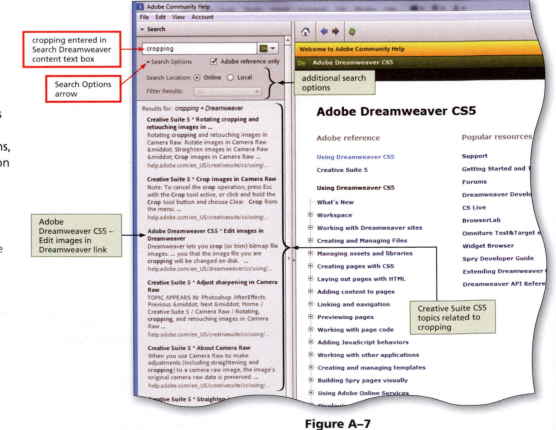

Figure A–7

3

- Click a result of your choice, such as the Adobe Dreamweaver CS5 – Edit images in Dreamweaver link to display the related Help topic (Figure A–8).

4

- If necessary, click a link to a topic.

- Review the instructions and then close the window to return to Dreamweaver.

Edit images in Dreamweaver topic is displayed

Adobe Dreamweaver CS5 – Edit images in Dreamweaver link selected

Edit images in Dreamweaver

links to other image-editing topics

Figure A–8

Context-Sensitive Help

Using **context-sensitive help**, you can open a relevant Help topic in panels, inspectors, and most dialog boxes. To view these Help features, you click a Help button in a dialog box, choose Help on the Options pop-up menu in a panel group, or click the question mark icon in a panel or inspector.

To Display Context-Sensitive Help on Text Using the Question Mark

Many of the panels and inspectors within Dreamweaver contain a question mark icon. Clicking this icon displays context-sensitive help. The following steps show how to use the question mark icon to view context-sensitive help through the Property inspector. In this example, the default Property inspector for text is displayed.

1

- Open a new document in Dreamweaver to prepare for using context-sensitive help.

question mark icon

Property inspector for text

- Right-click the panel groups title bar and then click Close Tab Group to hide the panel groups, if necessary.

- Display the Property inspector, if necessary, to gain access to the question mark icon.

- Point to the question mark icon in the Property inspector (Figure A–9).

Figure A–9

2

- Click the question mark icon to display an online Help page on setting text properties in the Property inspector (Figure A–10).

3

- Close the Adobe Community Help window.

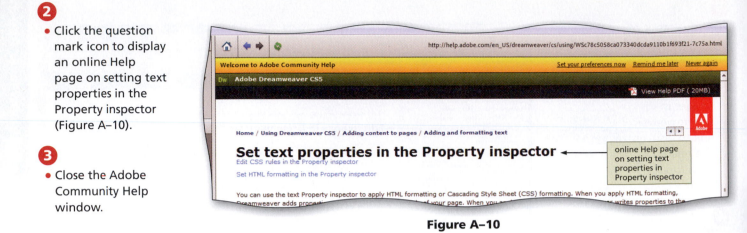

Figure A–10

To Use the Options Menu to Display Context-Sensitive Help for the Files Panel

Panels and dialog boxes also contain context-sensitive help. The following steps show how to display context-sensitive help for the Files panel. In this example, the Files panel is open and displayed within the Dreamweaver window.

1

- Click Window on the Application bar to display the Window menu.

- If the Files command is not displayed with a check mark, click Files to display the Files panel.

Q&A   What should I do if the Files command is displayed with a check mark?

Click outside the Window menu to close the menu.

- Click the Options button on the Files panel, and then point to Help (Figure A–11).

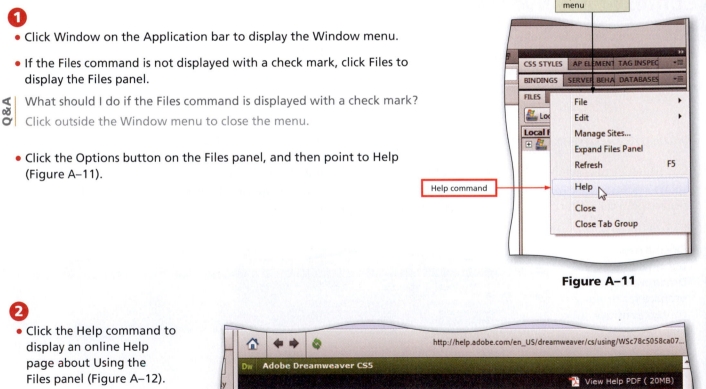

Figure A–11

2

- Click the Help command to display an online Help page about Using the Files panel (Figure A–12).

3

- Close the Adobe Community Help window.

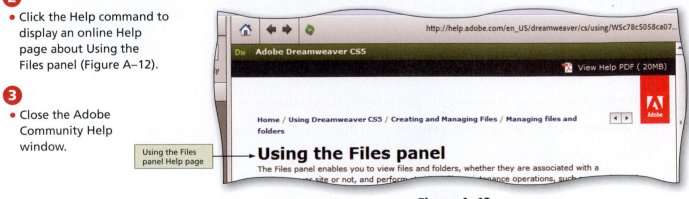

Figure A–12

Using the Reference Panel

The Reference panel is another valuable Dreamweaver resource. This panel provides you with a quick reference tool for HTML tags, JavaScript objects, Cascading Style Sheets, and other Dreamweaver features.

To Use the Reference Panel

The following steps show how to access the Reference panel, review the various options, and select and display information on the <h1> tag.

1

- Click Help on the Application bar, and then point to Reference to highlight that command (Figure A–13).

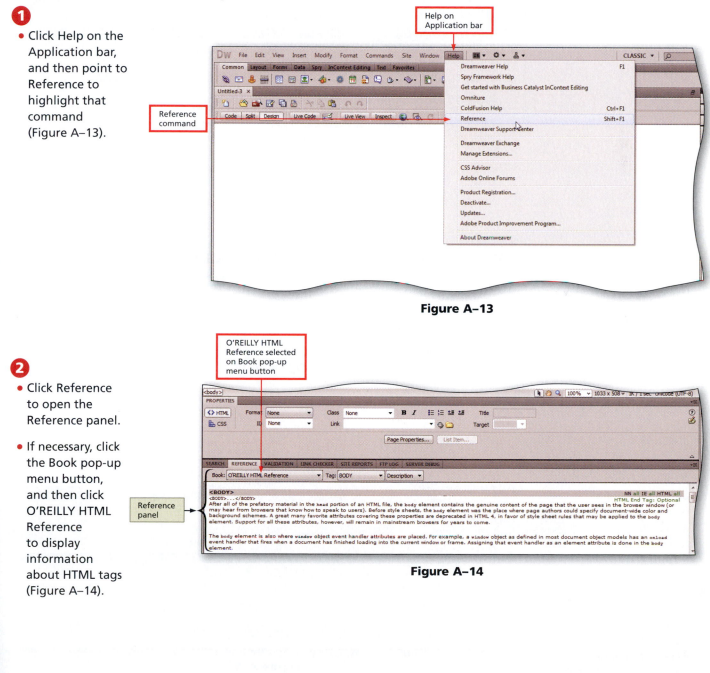

Figure A–13

2

- Click Reference to open the Reference panel.

- If necessary, click the Book pop-up menu button, and then click O'REILLY HTML Reference to display information about HTML tags (Figure A–14).

Figure A–14

3

• Click the Tag button and then point to H1 in the tag list to highlight the H1 tag (Figure A–15).

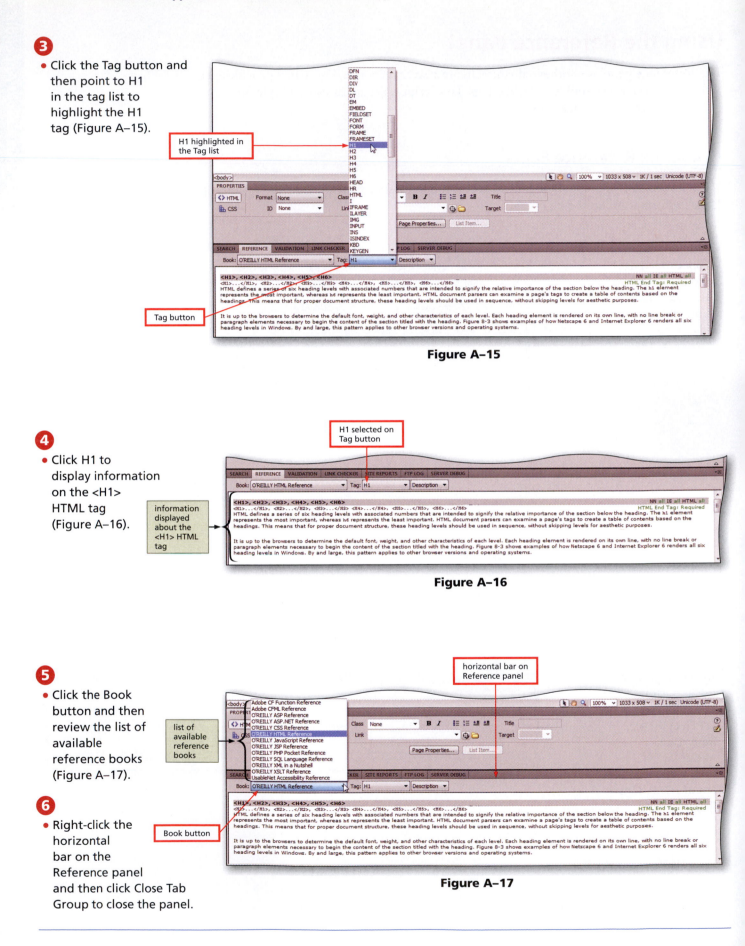

Figure A–15

4

• Click H1 to display information on the <H1> HTML tag (Figure A–16).

Figure A–16

5

• Click the Book button and then review the list of available reference books (Figure A–17).

6

• Right-click the horizontal bar on the Reference panel and then click Close Tab Group to close the panel.

Figure A–17

Apply Your Knowledge

Reinforce the skills and apply the concepts you learned in this appendix.

Viewing the Dreamweaver Help Resources

Instructions: Start Dreamweaver. Perform the following tasks using the Dreamweaver Help command.

1. Click Help on the Application bar and then click Dreamweaver Help.

2. Click the plus sign to the left of Working with Dreamweaver sites, click the plus sign to the left of Setting up a Dreamweaver site, and then click the About Dreamweaver sites link.

3. Read the Help topic, and then use a word processing program to write a short overview of what you learned.

4. Submit your assignment in the format specified by your instructor.

Using the Search Box

Instructions: Start Dreamweaver. Perform the following tasks using the Search box in the Dreamweaver CS5 online Help system.

1. Press the F1 key to display the Using Dreamweaver CS5 Help page.

2. Click the Adobe reference only check box.

3. Click in the Search Dreamweaver content text box, type **adding sound**, and then press ENTER.

4. Click an appropriate link in the search results to open a Help page, click a link on the Help page about embedding a sound file, and then read the Help topic.

5. Use a word-processing program to write a short overview of what you learned.

6. Submit your assignment in the format specified by your instructor.

Using Community Help

Instructions: Start Dreamweaver. Perform the following tasks using the online Community Web page.

1. Click Help on the Application bar, and then click Dreamweaver Support Center.

2. Click the Getting Started and Tutorials link.

3. View the Getting started with Dreamweaver videos and tutorials list and then select the Designing for web publishing link.

4. Review the Designing for web publishing article.

5. Use your word-processing program to prepare a report on three new concepts.

6. Submit your assignment in the format specified by your instructor.

Dreamweaver and Accessibility

Web Accessibility

Tim Berners-Lee, World Wide Web Consortium (W3C) founder and instrumental in the invention of the World Wide Web, indicates that the power of the Web is in its universality. He says that access by everyone, regardless of disability, is an essential aspect of the Web. In 1997, the W3C launched the **Web Accessibility Initiative** and made a commitment to lead the Web to its full potential. The initiative includes promoting a high degree of usability for people with disabilities. The United States government established a second initiative addressing accessibility and the Web through Section 508 of the Federal Rehabilitation Act.

Dreamweaver includes features that assist you in creating accessible content. Designing accessible content requires that you understand accessibility requirements and make subjective decisions as you create a Web site. Dreamweaver supports three accessibility options: screen readers, keyboard navigation, and operating system accessibility features.

Using Screen Readers with Dreamweaver

Screen readers assist the blind and vision-impaired by reciting text that is displayed on the screen through a speaker or headphones. The screen reader starts at the upper-left corner of the page and reads the page content. If the Web site developer uses accessibility tags or attributes during the creation of the Web site, the screen reader also recites this information and reads nontextual information such as button labels and image descriptions. Dreamweaver makes it easy to add text equivalents for graphical elements and to add HTML elements to tables and forms through the accessibility dialog boxes. Dreamweaver supports two screen readers: JAWS and Window-Eyes.

Activating the Accessibility Dialog Boxes

To create accessible pages in Dreamweaver, you associate information, such as labels and descriptions, with your page objects. After you have created this association, the screen reader can recite the label and description information.

You create the association by activating the accessibility dialog boxes that request accessibility information such as labels and descriptions when you insert an object for which you have activated the corresponding Accessibility dialog box. You activate the Accessibility dialog boxes through the Preferences dialog box. You can activate Accessibility dialog boxes for form objects, frames, images, and media. Accessibility for tables is accomplished by adding Summary text to the Table dialog box and adding image IDs and Alt text through the Property inspector.

To Activate the Image Tag Accessibility Attributes Dialog Box

The following steps use the Montana Parks index page as an example to show how to display the Preferences dialog box and activate the Image Tag Accessibility Attributes dialog box.

1

- Start Dreamweaver and, if necessary, open the Montana Parks site.

- Double-click index.htm in the Files panel to open the index.htm page.

- Collapse all the panels, including the Property inspector, to provide additional workspace.

- Click Edit on the Application bar and then point to Preferences (Figure B–1).

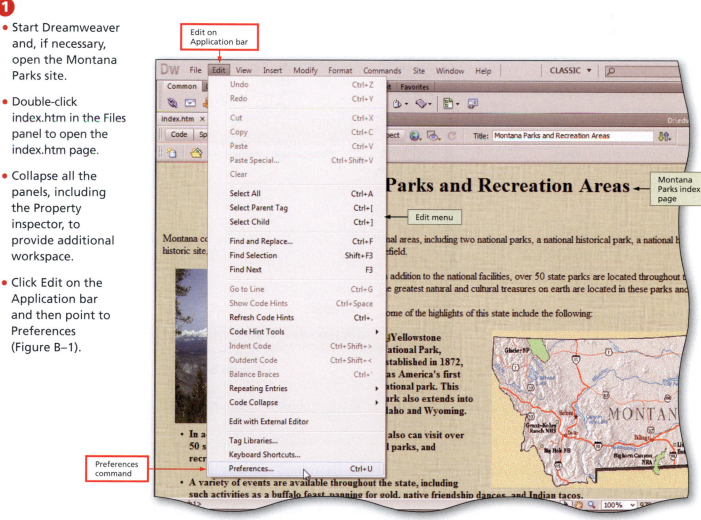

Figure B–1

2

- Click Preferences to display the Preferences dialog box (Figure B–2).

Q&A

When I open the Preferences dialog box, it displays different options. What should I do?

The Preferences dialog box displays the last category of options selected. Continue to Step 3.

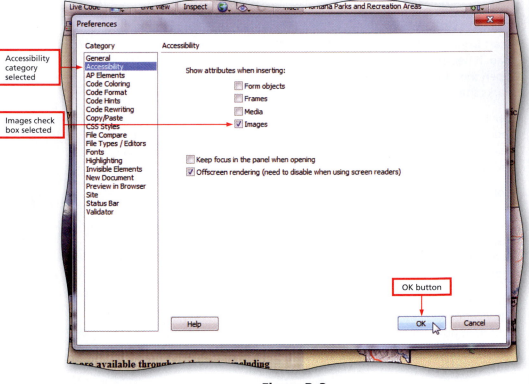

Figure B–2

3

- Click Accessibility in the Category list to display the accessibility options.

- If necessary, click the Images check box in the Accessibility area to select it.

- If necessary, deselect the other check boxes, and then point to the OK button (Figure B–3).

4

- Click the OK button to activate the Image Tag Accessibility Attributes dialog box for images and to close the Preferences dialog box.

Q&A

After clicking the OK button, should I notice a change in the Document window?

No. No change is apparent in the Document window after you click the OK button.

Figure B–3

Inserting Accessible Images

Selecting the Images check box in the Accessibility category of the Preferences dialog box activates the Image Tag Accessibility Attributes dialog box. Thus, any time you insert an image into a Web page, this dialog box will be displayed. This dialog box contains two text boxes: Alternate text and Long description. The screen reader reads the information you enter in both text boxes. You should limit your Alternate text entry to about 50 characters. For longer descriptions, provide a link in the Long description text box to a file that gives more information about the image. It is not required that you enter data into both text boxes.

To Insert Accessible Images

The following steps show how to use the Image Tag Accessibility Attributes dialog box when inserting an image.

1

- Position the insertion point in the Document window where you want to insert the image.

- Click Insert on the Application bar and then point to Image (Figure B–4).

2

- Click Image on the Insert menu to display the Select Image Source dialog box.

- If necessary, open the images folder in the parks folder, and then click an image file name of your choice.

- Point to the OK button (Figure B–5).

3

- Click the OK button to display the Image Tag Accessibility Attributes dialog box (Figure B–6).

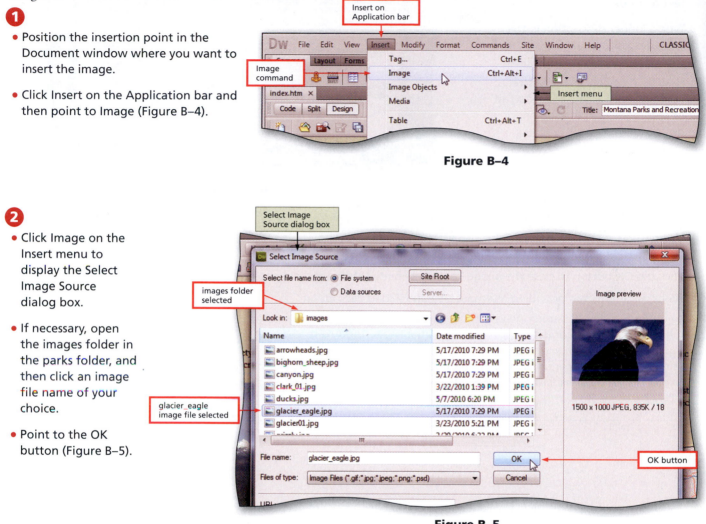

Figure B–4

Figure B–5

Figure B–6

4

- Type a brief description of the image in the Alternate text text box.

- Type a longer description in the Long description text box (Figure B–7).

Q&A

How do I indicate that the screen reader should access a file instead of reading text in the Long description text box?

Click the Browse icon next to the Long description text box, and then use the Select File dialog box to select an .htm file that contains a long description of the image.

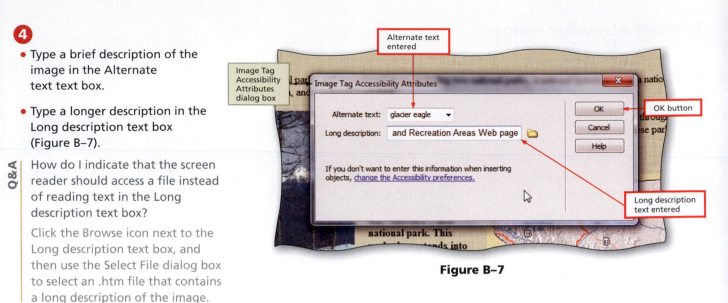

Figure B–7

5

- Click the OK button to close the Image Tag Accessibility Attributes dialog box.

Q&A

What is the effect of providing alternate text and a long description?

Although no changes are displayed in the Document window, when the page is displayed in the browser, the screen reader recites the information you entered in the Image Tag Accessibility Attributes Alternate text text box. If you included a link to a file with additional information in the Long description text box, the screen reader accesses the file and recites the text contained within the file. If you typed additional information in the Long description text box, the screen reader accesses and recites the text.

Navigating Dreamweaver with the Keyboard

Keyboard navigation is a core aspect of accessibility. This feature also is of particular importance to users who have repetitive strain injuries (RSIs) or other disabilities, and to those users who would prefer to use the keyboard instead of a mouse. You can use the keyboard to navigate the following elements in Dreamweaver: panels, inspectors, dialog boxes, frames, and tables.

Using the Keyboard to Navigate Panels

When you are working in Dreamweaver, several panels may be open at one time. A dotted outline around the panel title bar indicates that the panel is selected. Press CTRL+F6 to move from panel to panel. Press the SPACEBAR to select a check box. Placing focus on the panel title bar and then pressing the SPACEBAR collapses and expands the panels. Press the TAB key to move within a panel. Use the arrow keys to scroll the panel.

To Use the Keyboard to Hide and Redisplay the Property Inspector

The following steps use the Montana Parks index page to show how to use the keyboard to hide and display the Property inspector and then change a setting.

1

- With the index.htm page for the Montana Parks Web site open in the Document window, click the first line (the "Montana Parks and Recreation Areas" heading) to place the insertion point in the heading.

- Press CTRL+F3 to redisplay the Property inspector (Figure B–8).

Q&A

How do I hide the Property inspector?

Press the CTRL+F3 keys again to hide the Property inspector.

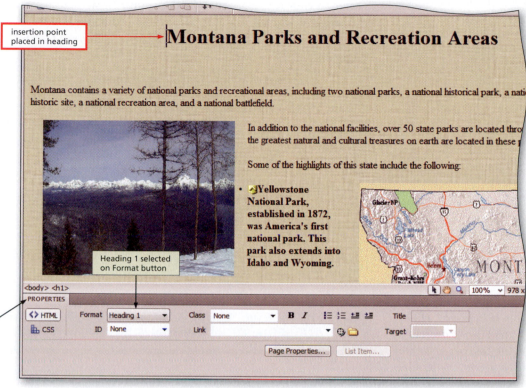

Figure B–8

2

- Press the TAB key three times to move to the Format button and the selected Heading 1 format.

- Press the UP ARROW key to select the Paragraph format (Figure B–9).

3

- Press the DOWN ARROW key to select the Heading 1 format again.

- Close Dreamweaver without saving any of the changes.

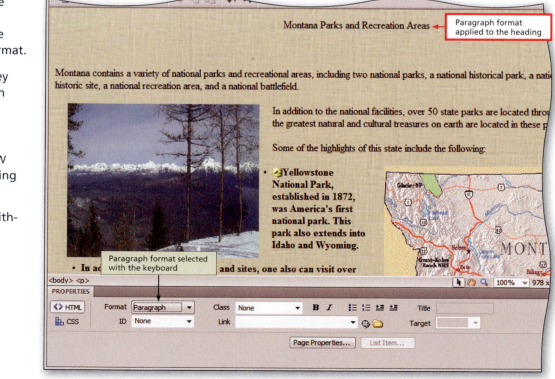

Figure B–9

Operating System Accessibility Features

The third method of accessibility support in Dreamweaver is through the Windows operating system's high contrast settings. **High contrast** changes the desktop color schemes for individuals who have vision impairment. The color schemes make the screen easier to view by heightening screen contrast with alternative color combinations. Some of the high contrast schemes also change font sizes.

You activate this option through the Windows Control Panel. The high contrast setting affects Dreamweaver in two ways:

- The dialog boxes and panels use system color settings.
- Code view syntax color is turned off.

Design view, however, continues to use the background and text colors you set in the Page Properties dialog box. The pages you design, therefore, continue to render colors as they will be displayed in a browser.

To Turn On High Contrast

The following steps show how to turn on high contrast and how to change the current high contrast settings in Windows 7.

1

- In Windows 7, click the Start button on the taskbar and then click Control Panel on the Start menu to open the Control Panel (Figure B–10).

Figure B–10

2

- In the Appearance and Personalization category, click the 'Change the theme' link to display the Personalization window.

- Note your current theme, such as Windows 7.

- Scroll down, if necessary, to display the High Contrast themes (Figure B–11).

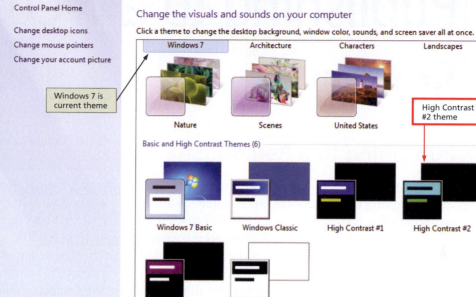

Figure B–11

3

- Click High Contrast #2 to display a preview of the theme on the desktop and in the Personalization window.

4

- Click your original theme to return the settings to their original values.

- Close the Personalization window to redisplay the Windows 7 desktop.

Q&A

What should I do if I want to retain the High Contrast #2 color scheme?

Select the theme, and then close the Personalization window.

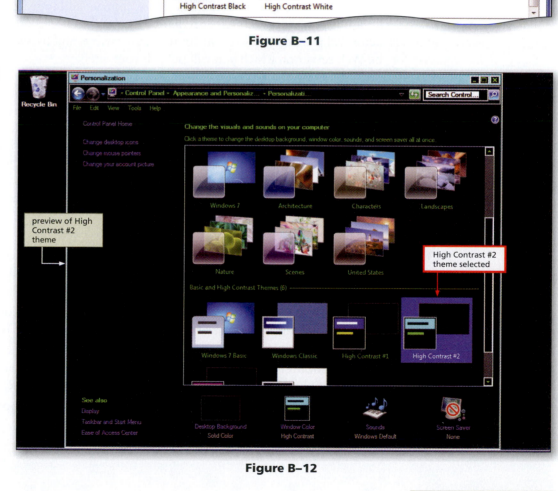

Figure B–12

Other Ways

1. Right-click desktop, click Personalize

Publishing to a Web Server

Publishing to a Remote Site

With Dreamweaver, Web designers usually define a local site and then do the majority of their designing using the local site. You defined a local site in Chapter 1. In creating the projects in this book, you have added Web pages to the local site, which resides on your computer's hard drive, a network drive, a USB drive, or possibly a CD-RW.

To prepare a Web site and make it available for others to view requires that you publish your site by uploading it to a Web server for public access. A Web server is an Internet- or intranet-connected computer that delivers the Web pages to online visitors. Dreamweaver includes built-in support that enables you to connect and transfer your local site to a Web server. Publishing to a Web server requires that you have access to a Web server. Your instructor will provide you with the location, user name, and password information for the Web server on which you will publish your site.

After you establish access to a Web server, you need a remote site folder. The remote folder will reside on the Web server and contain your Web site files. Generally, the remote folder is defined by the Web server administrator or your instructor. The name of the local root folder in this example is the author's first and last name. Most likely, the name of your remote folder also will be your last name and first initial or your first and last name. You upload your local site to the remote folder on the Web server. The remote site connection information must be defined in Dreamweaver through the Site Setup dialog box. You display the Site Setup dialog box, select the Servers category, and then enter the remote site information. Dreamweaver provides five different protocols for connecting to a remote site. These methods are as follows:

- **FTP (File Transfer Protocol)**: This protocol is used on the Internet for sending and receiving files. It is the most widely used method for uploading and downloading pages to and from a Web server.

- **Local/Network**: This option is used when the Web server is located on a local area network (LAN) or a company, school, or other organization intranet. Files on LANs generally are available for internal viewing only.

- **RDS (Remote Development Services) and WebDAV**: These protocols are systems that permit users to edit and manage files collaboratively on remote Web servers.

Most likely you will use the FTP option to upload your Web site to a remote server.

Defining a Remote Site

You define the remote site by changing some of the settings in the Site Setup dialog box. To allow you to create a remote site using FTP, your instructor will supply you with the following information:

- **Server name**: The name of the server where your remote site will be stored
- **FTP address**: The Web address for the remote host of your Web server
- **Username**: Your user name
- **Password**: The FTP password to authenticate and access your account
- **Web URL**: The URL for your remote site

To Define a Remote Site

Assume for the following steps that you are defining a remote site for the Montana Parks Web site.

- If necessary, start Dreamweaver, select the Montana Parks site, and then open the index.htm page.

- Click Site on the Application bar and then click Manage Sites to open the Manage Sites dialog box.

- If necessary, click Montana Parks to select the Montana Parks Web site (Figure C–1).

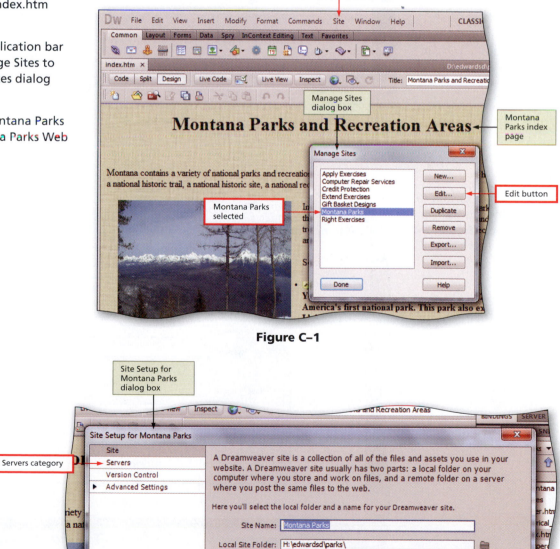

Figure C–1

2

- Click the Edit button to open the Site Setup for Montana Parks dialog box (Figure C–2).

Figure C–2

3

- Click Servers to display an area for entering the server settings in the Site Setup for Montana Parks dialog box (Figure C–3).

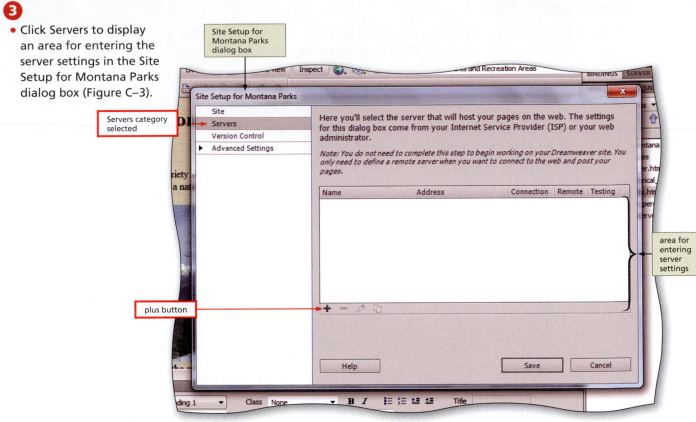

Site Setup for Montana Parks dialog box
Servers category selected
plus button
area for entering server settings
Site Setup for Montana Parks
Site
Servers
Version Control
Advanced Settings
Here you'll select the server that will host your pages on the web. The settings for this dialog box come from your Internet Service Provider (ISP) or your web administrator.
Note: You do not need to complete this step to begin working on your Dreamweaver site. You only need to define a remote server when you want to connect to the web and post your pages.
Name
Address
Connection
Remote
Testing
Help
Save
Cancel

Figure C–3

4

- Click the plus button to display the Basic server information (Figure C–4).

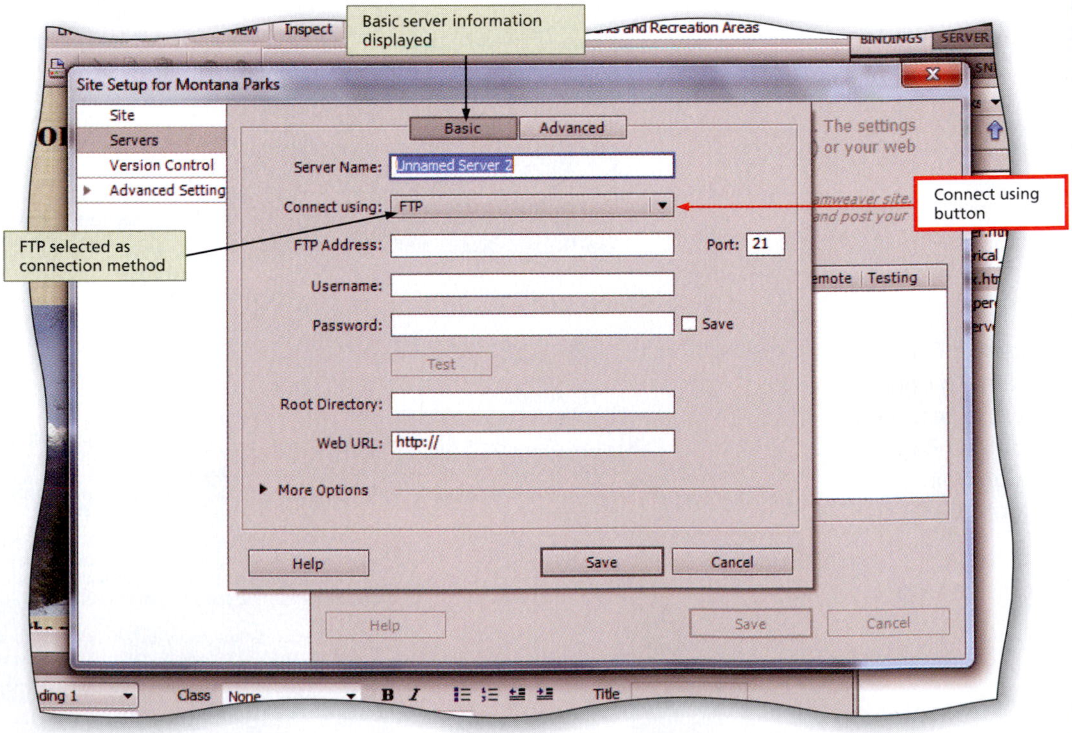

Basic server information displayed
FTP selected as connection method
Connect using button
Site Setup for Montana Parks
Basic
Advanced
Server Name: Unnamed Server 2
Connect using: FTP
FTP Address:
Port: 21
Username:
Password:
Save
Test
Root Directory:
Web URL: http://
More Options
Help
Save
Cancel

Figure C–4

5

- If necessary, click the Connect using button, and then click FTP to select FTP as the protocol for connecting to a remote site.

- In the appropriate text boxes, enter the Server Name, FTP Address, Username, Password, and Web URL information provided by your instructor (Figure C–5).

Q&A

What if I am required to enter different information from that shown in Figure C–5?

Your information will most likely differ from that in Figure C–5.

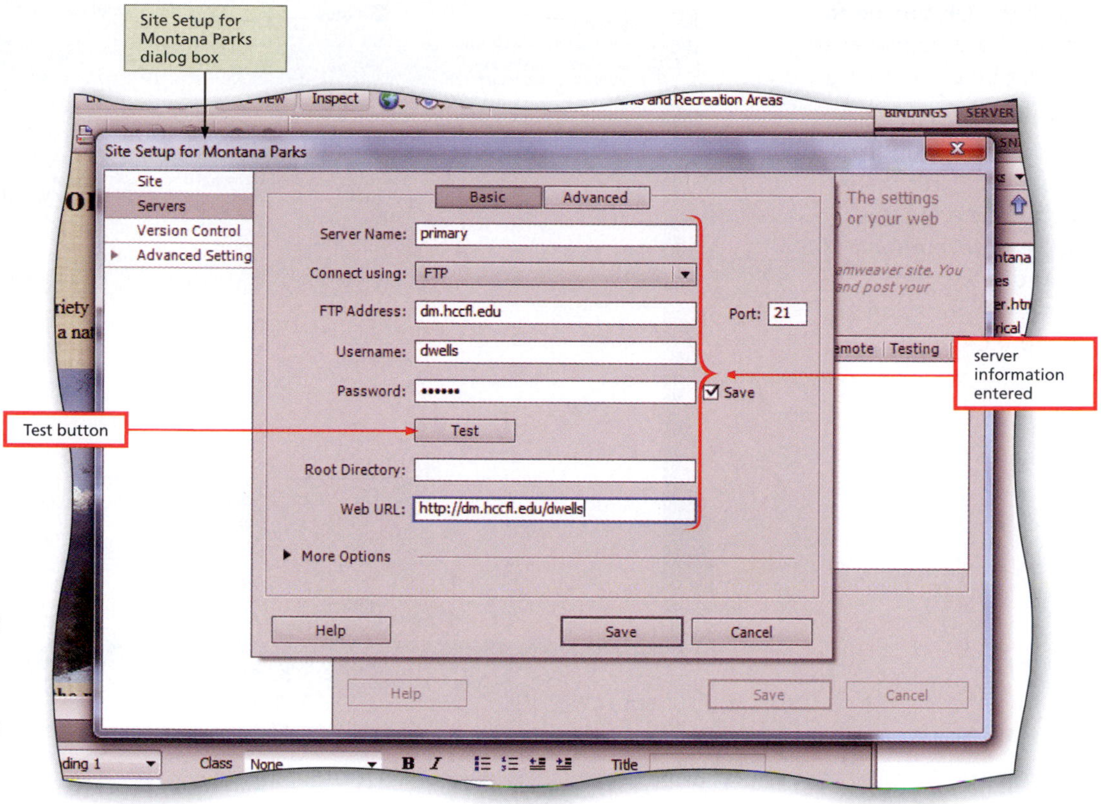

Site Setup for Montana Parks dialog box

Test button

server information entered

Figure C–5

6

- Click the Test button to test the connection and to display the Dreamweaver dialog box (Figure C–6).

Q&A

What should I do if a security dialog box is displayed?

If a Windows Security Alert dialog box is displayed, click the Allow access button.

Q&A

What should I do if my connection is not successful?

If your connection is not successful, review your text box entries and make any necessary corrections. If all entries are correct, check with your instructor. The Site Setup dialog box should look similar to Figure C–5.

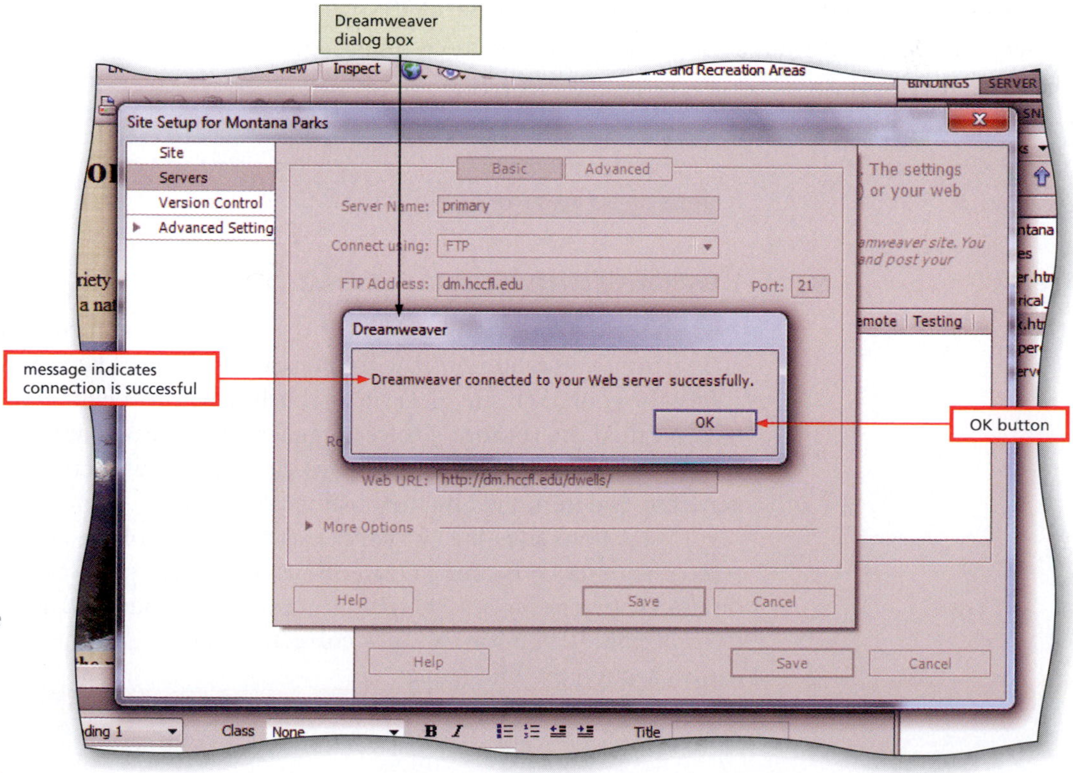

Dreamweaver dialog box

message indicates connection is successful

Dreamweaver connected to your Web server successfully.

OK button

Figure C–6

7

- Click the OK button to close the Dreamweaver dialog box.

- Click the Save button in the Site Setup for Montana Parks dialog box to save the Basic server information and display the server information (Figure C–7).

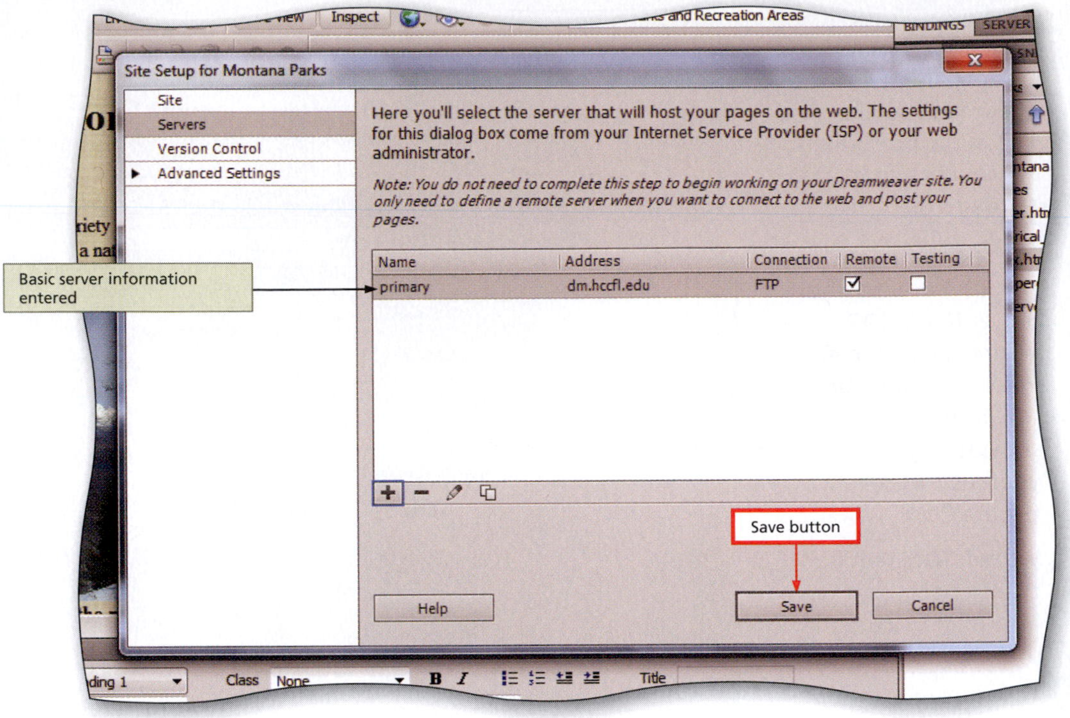

Figure C–7

8

- Click the Save button to save the site information for the Montana Parks Web site.

- Click the Done button to close the Manage Sites dialog box.

Q&A

What should I do if another Dreamweaver dialog box is displayed?

If another Dreamweaver dialog box is displayed, click the OK button.

Connecting to a Remote Site

Now that you have completed the remote site information and tested your connection, you can interact with the remote server. The remote site folder on the Web server for your Web site must be established before a connection can be made. This folder, called the **remote site root**, generally is created automatically by the Web server administrator of the hosting company or by your instructor. The naming convention generally is determined by the hosting company.

This book uses the last name and first initial of the author for the user name of the remote site folder. Naming conventions other than your last and first name may be used on the Web server to which you are connecting. Your instructor will supply you with this information. If all information is correct, connecting to the remote site is accomplished easily through the Files panel.

To Connect to a Remote Site

The following steps illustrate how to connect to the remote server and display your remote site folder.

1
- Click the 'Expand to show local and remote sites' button to expand the Site pane and show both a right (Local Files) and left (Remote Server) pane (Figure C–8).

Q&A What do the right and left expanded panes display?

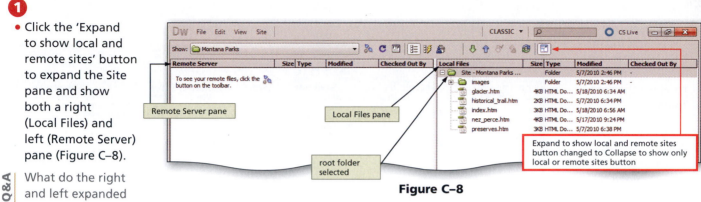

Figure C–8

The right pane contains the local site, and the left pane contains information for viewing your remote files by clicking the Connects to remote host button.

2
- Verify that the root folder for the site is selected in the Local Files pane.

- Click the 'Connects to remote host' button in the Remote Server pane to make the connection (Figure C–9).

Q&A What happens after I click the 'Connects to remote host' button?

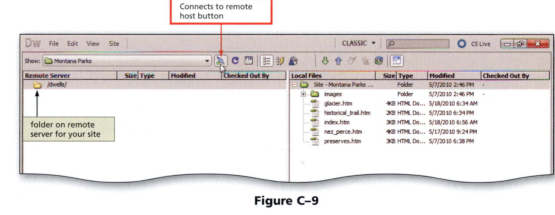

Figure C–9

The 'Connects to remote host/Disconnects from remote host' button changes to indicate that the connection has been made, and a default Home.html folder is created automatically.

Uploading Files to a Remote Server

Uploading is the process of transferring your files from your computer to the remote server. **Downloading** is the process of transferring files from the remote server to your computer. Dreamweaver uses the term **put** for uploading and **get** for downloading.

To Upload Files to a Remote Server

The following steps illustrate how to upload your files to the remote server.

1
• If necessary, click the Montana Parks root folder in the Local Files panel to select the root folder.

• Click the Put File(s) button on the Files panel toolbar to begin uploading the files and display a Dreamweaver dialog box.

• Point to the OK button in the Dreamweaver dialog box (Figure C–10).

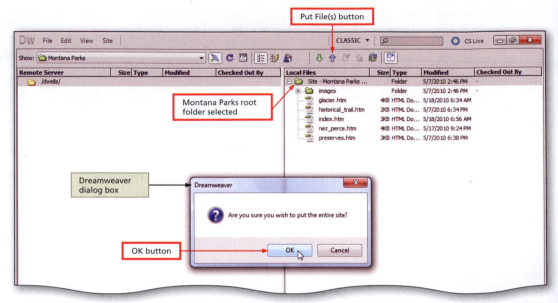

Figure C–10

2
• Click the OK button to begin uploading the files and to display a dialog box that shows progress information (Figure C–11).

Q&A
My files are uploaded, but they appear in a different order. Is that okay?

The files that are uploaded to the server may be displayed in a different order from that on the local site based on the server settings.

3
• Quit Dreamweaver.

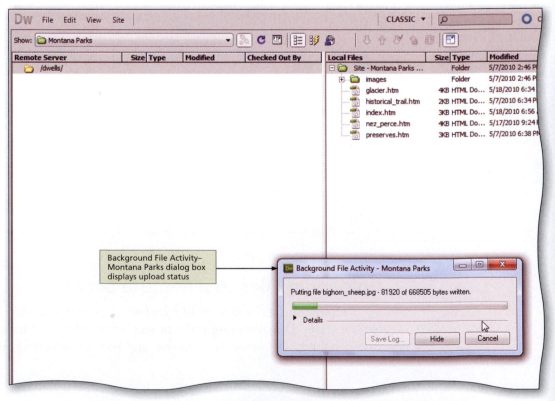

Figure C–11

Remote Site Maintenance and Site Synchronization

Now that your Web site is on a Web server, you will want to continue to maintain the site. When you are connected to the remote site, you can apply many of the same commands to a folder or file on the remote site as you do to a folder or file on the local site. You can create and delete folders; cut, copy, delete, duplicate, paste, and rename files; and so on. These commands are available through the context menu.

To mirror the local site on the remote site, Dreamweaver provides a synchronization feature. Synchronizing is the process of transferring files between the local and remote sites so both sites have an identical set of the most recent files. You can choose to synchronize the entire Web site or select only specific files. You also can specify Direction. Within Direction, you have three options: upload the newer files from the local site to the remote site (put), download newer files from the remote site to the local site (get), or upload and download files to and from the remote and local sites. Once you specify a direction, Dreamweaver automatically synchronizes files. If the files are already in sync, Dreamweaver lets you know that no synchronization is necessary. To access the Synchronize command, you first connect to the remote server and then select Synchronize on the Site menu (Figure C–12).

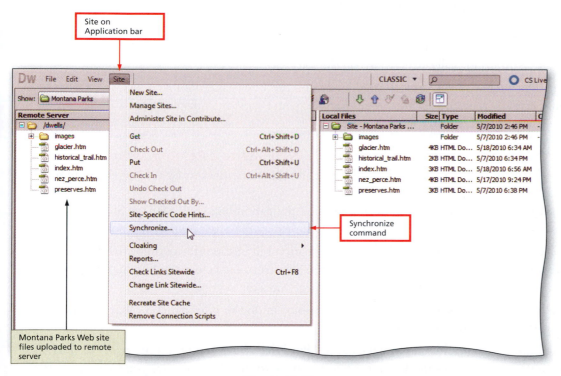

Figure C–12

To save the verification information to a local file, click the Save Log button at the completion of the synchronization process. Another feature within Dreamweaver allows you to verify which files are newer on the local site or the remote site; choose the Remote view by selecting Select Newer Local or Select Newer on Remote Server commands. These options are available through the Files panel Edit menu when the Remote site panel is displayed.

Apply Your Knowledge

Reinforce the skills and apply the concepts you learned in this appendix.

Defining and Uploading the Bryan's Computer Repair Services Web Site to a Remote Server

Instructions: Perform the following tasks to define and upload the Bryan's Computer Repair Services Web site to a remote server.

1. If necessary, start Dreamweaver. Click Site on the Application bar, click Manage Sites, and then click Computer Repair Services. Click the Edit button to display the Site Setup dialog box.

2. In the Site Setup dialog box, click the Servers category, fill in the information provided by your instructor, and then test the connection. Click the Save button to close the Site Setup dialog box, and then click the Done button to close the Manage Sites dialog box.

3. Click the 'Expand to show local and remote sites' button on the Files panel toolbar and then click the 'Connects to remote host button.'

4. Click the local file root folder and then click the Put File(s) button on the Site panel toolbar to upload your Web site. Click the OK button in response to the "Are you sure you wish to put the entire site?" dialog box.

5. Review your files to verify that they were uploaded. The files on the remote server may be displayed in a different order from those on the local site.

6. Click the 'Disconnects from remote host' button on the Files panel toolbar. Click the 'Collapse to show only local or remote site' button on the Files panel toolbar to display the local site and the Document window.

Defining and Uploading the Baskets by Carole Web Site to a Remote Server

Instructions: Perform the following tasks to define and upload the Baskets by Carole Web site to a remote server.

1. If necessary, start Dreamweaver. Click Site on the Application bar, click Manage Sites, and then click Gift Basket Designs. Click the Edit button to display the Site Setup dialog box.

2. In the Site Setup dialog box, click the Servers category. Fill in the information provided by your instructor, and then test the connection. Click the Save button to close the Site Setup dialog box, and then click the Done button to close the Manage Sites dialog box.

3. Click the 'Expand to show local and remote sites' button on the Files panel toolbar and then click the 'Connects to remote host' button.

4. Click the local file root folder and then click the Put File(s) button on the Files panel toolbar to upload your Web site. Click the OK button in response to the "Are you sure you wish to put the entire site?" dialog box.

5. Review your files to verify that they were uploaded. The files on the remote server may be displayed in a different order from those on the local site.

6. Click the 'Disconnects from remote host' button. Click the 'Collapse to show only local or remote site' button on the Files panel toolbar to display the local site and the Document window.

Defining and Uploading the Credit Protection Web Site to a Remote Server

Instructions: Perform the following tasks to define and upload the Credit Protection Web site to a remote server.

1. If necessary, start Dreamweaver. Click Site on the Application bar, click Manage Sites, and then click Credit Protection. Click the Edit button to display the Site Setup dialog box.

2. In the Site Setup dialog box, click the Servers category. Fill in the information provided by your instructor, and then test the connection. Click the Save button to close the Site Setup dialog box, and then click the Done button to close the Manage Sites dialog box.

3. Click the 'Expand to show local and remote sites' button on the Files panel toolbar and then click the 'Connects to remote host' button.

4. Click the local file root folder and then click the Put File(s) button on the Files panel toolbar to upload your Web site. Click the OK button in response to the "Are you sure you wish to put the entire site?" dialog box.

5. Review your files to verify that they were uploaded. The files on the remote server may display in a different order from those on the local site.

6. Click the 'Disconnects from remote host' button. Click the 'Collapse to show only local or remote site' button on the Files panel toolbar to display the local site and the Document window.

Customizing Adobe Dreamweaver CS5

This appendix explains how to change the screen resolution in Windows 7 to the resolution used in this book.

Changing Screen Resolution

Screen resolution indicates the number of pixels (dots) that the computer uses to display the letters, numbers, graphics, and background you see on the screen. When you increase the screen resolution, Windows displays more information on the screen, but the information decreases in size. The reverse also is true: as you decrease the screen resolution, Windows displays less information on the screen, but the information increases in size.

The screen resolution usually is stated as the product of two numbers, such as 1024×768 (pronounced "ten twenty-four by seven sixty-eight"). A 1024×768 screen resolution results in a display of 1,024 distinct pixels on each of 768 lines, or about 786,432 pixels. The figures in this book were created using a screen resolution of 1024×768.

This is the screen resolution most commonly used today, although some Web designers set their computers at a much higher screen resolution, such as 2048×1536.

To Change the Screen Resolution

The following steps change the screen resolution to 1024 × 768 to match the figures in this book.

1

- If necessary, minimize all programs so that the Windows 7 desktop appears.

- Right-click the Windows 7 desktop to display the Windows 7 desktop shortcut menu (Figure D–1).

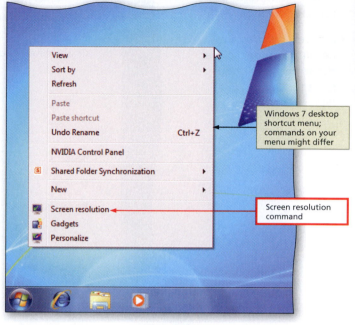

Figure D–1

2

- Click Screen resolution on the shortcut menu to open the Screen Resolution window (Figure D–2).

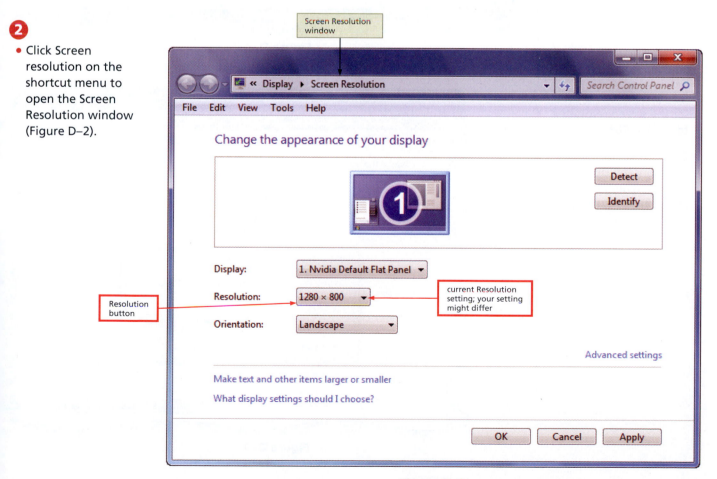

Figure D–2

3

• Click the Resolution button to display a list of resolution settings for your monitor.

• If necessary, drag the Resolution slider so that the screen resolution is set to 1024 × 768 (Figure D–3).

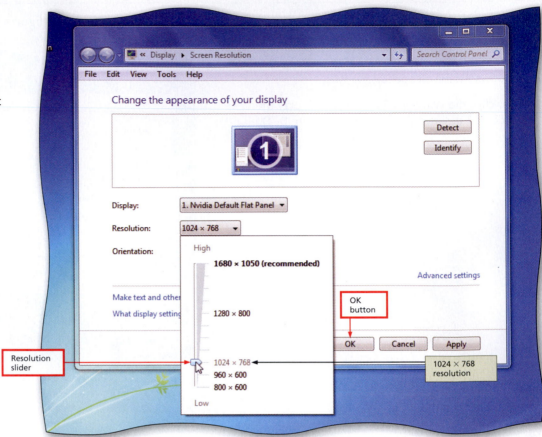

Figure D–3

4

• Click the OK button to set the screen resolution to 1024 × 768.

• Click the Keep changes button in the Display Settings dialog box to accept the new screen resolution (Figure D–4).

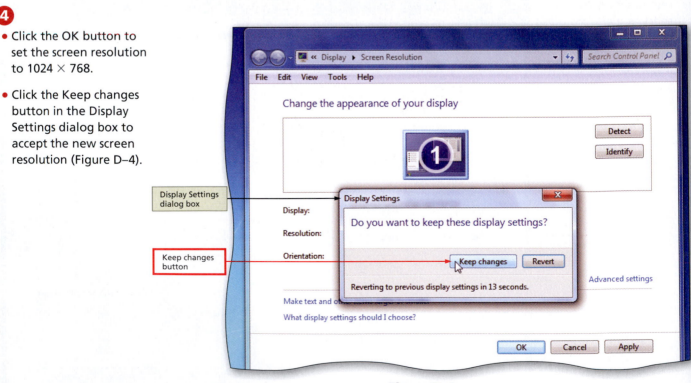

Figure D–4

Quick Reference Summary

In the Adobe Dreamweaver CS5 program, you can accomplish a task in a number of ways. The following table provides a quick reference to each task presented in this textbook. The first column identifies the task. The second column indicates the page number on which the task is discussed in the book. The subsequent four columns list the different ways the task in column one can be carried out.

Adobe Dreamweaver CS5 Quick Reference Summary

Task	Page Number	Mouse	Menu	Context Menu	Keyboard Shortcut
Absolute link, create	DW 155	Link text box in Property inspector	Insert | Hyperlink	Make Link	
Align image	DW 128	Align button in Property inspector		Align	
Align table	DW 195	Align button in Property inspector	Format | Align	Align	
Alt text, specify for image	DW 125	Alt text box in Property inspector *or* drag image to page, enter Alt text (Image Tag Accessibility Attributes dialog box)			
Apply background image to page	DW 60	Page Properties button on Properties	Modify | Page Properties	Page Properties	CTRL+J
Assets panel, display	DW 124	Click Assets panel tab			
Assets panel, open or close	DW 124	Double-click Assets panel tab	Window | Assets		
Background, add to page	DW 60	Page Properties button on Properties	Modify | Page Properties	Page Properties	CTRL+J
Block quote, create	DW 67	Blockquote (Text Indent) button in Property inspector	Format | Indent	List | Indent	CTRL+ALT+]
Block quote, remove	DW 67	Remove Blockquote (Text Outdent) button in Property inspector	Format | Outdent	List | Outdent	CTRL+ALT+[
Bold, apply to text	DW 67, DW 73	Bold button in Property inspector	Format | Style | Bold	Style	CTRL+B
Border, add or change for table	DW 235	Border text box in Property inspector			

Adobe Dreamweaver CS5 Quick Reference Summary *(continued)*

Task	Page Number	Mouse	Menu	Context Menu	Keyboard Shortcut
Border, add to image	DW 235	Border text box in Property inspector			
Brightness and contrast, adjust for image	DW 144	Brightness and Contrast tool in Property inspector	Modify | Image | Brightness/Contrast		
Browsers, select	DW 81		Edit | Preferences | Preview in Browser		
Bulleted list, create	DW 67, DW 72	Unordered List button in Property inspector	Format | List | Unordered List	List | Unordered List	
Cell padding, set for table	DW 194	CellPad text box in Property inspector			
Cell spacing, set for table	DW 194	CellSpace text box in Property inspector			
Cell, change height in table	DW 197	H text box in Property inspector *or* drag cell border			
Cell, change horizontal alignment in table	DW 209	Horz button in Property inspector	Format | Align	Align	
Cell, change vertical alignment in table	DW 203	Vert button in Property inspector	Format | Align	Align	
Cell, change width in table	DW 197	W text box in Property inspector *or* drag cell border			
Center text	DW 70		Format | Align | Center	Align | Center	CTRL+ALT+SHIFT+C
Check spelling	DW 79		Commands | Check Spelling		SHIFT+F7
Classic workspace, switch to	DW 37	Workspace switcher arrow on Application bar	Window | Workspace Layout		
Clear column widths for table	DW 204	Clear Column Widths button in Property inspector	Modify | Table | Clear Cell Widths	Clear All Widths	
Clear row heights for table	DW 204	Clear Row Heights button in Property inspector	Modify | Table | Clear Cell Heights	Clear All Heights	
Collapse Property inspector	DW 66	Double-click title bar	Window | Properties	Minimize	CTRL+F3
Column, change horizontal alignment in table	DW 209	Horz button in Property inspector	Format | Align	Align	
Column, change vertical alignment in table	DW 203	Vert button in Property inspector	Format | Align	Align	
Column, delete in table	DW 215		Modify | Table | Delete Column	Table | Delete Column	DEL
Column, insert in table	DW 215		Modify | Table | Insert Column	Table | Insert Column	TAB
Columns, set for table	DW 194	Table dialog box or Cols text box in Property inspector			
Contrast, adjust for image	DW 144	Brightness and Contrast tool in Property inspector	Modify | Image | Brightness/Contrast		

Adobe Dreamweaver CS5 Quick Reference Summary (continued)

Task	Page Number	Mouse	Menu	Context Menu	Keyboard Shortcut
Convert table width	DW 196	Convert Table Widths to Pixels button *or* Convert Table Widths to Percent button in Property inspector	Modify | Table | Convert Width to Pixels *or* Convert Width to Percent		
Create page	DW 86	Options menu button on Files panel | File | New File	File | New	New File	CTRL+N
Create site	DW 47		Site | New Site		
Crop image	DW 142	Crop tool in Property inspector	Modify | Image | Crop		
Default file name extension, set	DW 57		Edit | Preferences, New Document (Preferences dialog box)		
Definition list, create	DW 67		Format | List | Definition List	List | Definition List	
Delete page	DW 65			Edit | Delete	DEL
Description, add to page	DW 243		Insert | HTML | Head Tags | Keywords		
Design view, display	DW 38	Design button on Document toolbar	View | Design		
Disable Welcome screen	DW 85		Edit | Preferences | General		
Document, save	DW 58	Save button on Standard toolbar	File | Save *or* File | Save As	Save *or* Save As	CTRL+S CTRL+SHIFT+S
Dreamweaver, quit	DW 85	Close button	File | Exit		CTRL+Q
Dreamweaver, start	DW 37	Dreamweaver icon on desktop	Start | All Programs | Adobe Dreamweaver CS5		
Edit site	DW 54	Sites pop-up menu button on Files panel, Manage Sites, site name, Edit button	Site | Manage Sites, *site name*, Edit button		
E-mail link, create	DW 156	Link text box in Property inspector	Insert | Email Link	Make Link	
Expand Property inspector	DW 66	Double-click title bar	Window | Properties	Expand Panel	CTRL+F3
Files panel, collapse	DW	Collapse to Icons		Collapse to Icons	
Files panel, expand	DW 126	Expand Panels		Expand Panels	
Files panel, open or close	DW 147	Double-click Files panel tab	Window | Files	Close	F8
Format, apply to paragraph	DW 66	Format button in Property inspector	Format | Paragraph Format	Paragraph Format	
Heading 1, create	DW 68	Format button in Property inspector	Format | Paragraph Format | Heading 1	Paragraph Format | Heading 1	CTRL+1
Height, change for image	DW 130	H text box in Property inspector *or* drag sizing handle			

Adobe Dreamweaver CS5 Quick Reference Summary *(continued)*

Task	Page Number	Mouse	Menu	Context Menu	Keyboard Shortcut
Help	DW 84		Help | Dreamweaver Help		F1
Horizontal space, increase or decrease around image	DW 130	H Space text box in Property inspector			
Icon color, turn on or off	DW 44		View | Color Icons	Color Icons	
Image brightness or contrast, adjust	DW 142	Brightness and Contrast tool in Property inspector	Modify | Image | Brightness/Contrast		
Image height, change	DW 130	H text box in Property inspector *or* drag sizing handle			
Image width, change	DW 130	W text box in Property inspector *or* drag sizing handle			
Image, align	DW 129	Align button in Property inspector		Align	
Image, crop	DW 142	Crop tool in Property inspector	Modify | Image | Crop		
Image, insert into page	DW 124	Drag image from Assets panel or Files panel	Insert | Image	Insert	CTRL+ALT+I
Image, specify Alt text image	DW 125	Alt text box in Property inspector *or* drag image to page, enter Alt text (Image Tag Accessibility Attributes dialog box)			
Indent text	DW 67	Blockquote (Text Indent) button in Property inspector	Format | Indent	List	CTRL+ALT+]
Insert bar, display	DW 38		Window | Insert		CTRL+F2
Insert bar, display as menu	DW 40			Show as Menu	
Invisible Element preferences, set	DW 119	Visual Aids button on Document toolbar, click Invisible Elements	Edit | Preferences | Invisible Elements		
Italic, apply to text	DW 67	Italic button in Property inspector	Format | Style	Style	CTRL+I
Keywords, add to page	DW 242		Insert | HTML | Head Tags | Keywords		
Layout tab, display in Insert bar	DW 190	Layout tab on Insert bar			
Line break, insert	DW 74		Insert | HTML | Special Characters | Line Break	Insert HTML | br	SHIFT+ENTER
Link, create	DW 67, DW 147	Link text box in Property inspector	Insert | Hyperlink	Make Link	
Link, delete	DW 159	Link text box in Property inspector		Remove Link	
Link, edit	DW 159	Link text box in Property inspector		Change Link	
Links, change color of	DW 159	Page Properties button in Property inspector	Modify | Page Properties	Page Properties	CTRL+J

Adobe Dreamweaver CS5 Quick Reference Summary *(continued)*

Task	Page Number	Mouse	Menu	Context Menu	Keyboard Shortcut
List item, set properties for	DW 67	List Item button in Property inspector	Format | List | Properties	List | Properties	
Live view, display	DW 161	Live View button on Document toolbar	View | Live View		ALT+F11
Merge cells in table	DW 215	Merges selected cells using spans button in Property inspector	Modify | Table | Merge Cells	Table | Merge Cells	CTRL+ALT+M
Numbered list, create	DW 67	Ordered List button in Property inspector	Format | List | Ordered List	List | Ordered List	
Open page	DW 85	Double-click page in Files panel	File | Open *or* File | Open Recent	Open	CTRL+O
Ordered list, create	DW 67	Ordered List button in Property inspector	Format | List | Ordered List	List | Ordered List	
Outdent text	DW 67	Remove Blockquote (Text Outdent) button in Property inspector	Format | Outdent	List	CTRL+ALT+[
Page title, enter	DW 77	Title text box on Document toolbar			
Page, create	DW 86	Options menu button on Files panel | File | New File	File | New	New File	CTRL+SHIFT+N
Page, delete	DW 65			Edit | Delete	DEL
Page, open	DW 85	Double-click page in Files panel	File | Open *or* File | Open Recent	Open	CTRL+O
Panels, open or close	DW 44		Window | Hide Panels	Close Tab Group	F4
Paragraph, center	DW 70		Format | Align | Center	Align | Center	CTRL+ALT+SHIFT+C
Preview Web page	DW 83		File | Preview in Browser	Preview in Browser	F12 CTRL+F12
Primary browser, select	DW 81		Edit | Preferences | Preview in Browser		
Property inspector, collapse or expand	DW 66	Double-click title bar	Window | Properties	Minimize/Expand Panel	CTRL+F3
Property inspector, expand	DW 186	Property inspector expander arrow			
Quick Tag Editor, use	DW 159			Quick Tag Editor	CTRL+T
Quit Dreamweaver	DW 85	Close button	File | Exit		CTRL+Q
Relative link, create	DW 67, DW 147	Link text box in Property inspector *or* Point to File tool in Property inspector *or* Browse icon next to Link text box in Property inspector	Insert | Hyperlink	Make Link	SHIFT+drag to file
Remove site	DW 54	Sites pop-up menu button on Files panel, Manage Sites, *site name*, Remove button	Site | Manage Sites, site name, Remove button		
Row, change horizontal alignment in table	DW 209	Horz button in Property inspector	Format | Align	Align	

Adobe Dreamweaver CS5 Quick Reference Summary *(continued)*

Task	Page Number	Mouse	Menu	Context Menu	Keyboard Shortcut
Row, change vertical alignment in table	DW 203	Vert button in Property inspector	Format | Align	Align	
Row, delete in table	DW 215		Modify | Table | Delete Row	Table | Delete Row	CTRL+SHIFT+M
Row, insert in table	DW 215		Modify | Table | Insert Row	Table | Insert Row	CTRL+M
Rows, set for table	DW 194	Table dialog box *or* Rows text box in Property inspector			
Rulers, show or hide	DW 56		View | Rulers | Show		CTRL+ALT+R
Save document	DW 58	Save button on Standard toolbar	File | Save *or* File | Save As	Save *or* Save As	CTRL+S CTRL+SHIFT+S
Secondary browser, select	DW 81		Edit | Preferences | Preview in Browser		
Site, create	DW 47		Site | New Site		
Site, edit	DW 54	Sites pop-up menu button on Files panel, Manage Sites, site name, Edit button	Site | Manage Sites, site name, Edit button		
Site, remove	DW 54	Sites pop-up menu button on Files panel, Manage Sites, site name, Remove button	Site | Manage Sites, site name, Remove button		
Special character, insert	DW 78		Insert | HTML | Special Characters		
Spelling, check spelling	DW 79		Commands | Check Spelling		SHIFT+F7
Split cells in table	DW 215	Splits cell into rows or columns button in Property inspector	Modify | Table | Split Cell	Table | Split Cells	CTRL+ALT+S
Split view, display	DW 160	Split View button on Document toolbar	View | Code and Design		
Table cell, change height	DW 197	H text box in Property inspector			
Table cell, change width	DW 197	W text box in Property inspector			
Table ID, enter or change	DW 206	ID text box in Property inspector			
Table, delete	DW 216	Click table tag, press DEL			
Table, insert	DW 194	Table button on Layout tab or Common tab of Insert bar	Insert | Table		CTRL+ALT+T
Text, center	DW 70		Format | Align | Center	Align | Center	CTRL+ALT+SHIFT+C
Title, enter for page	DW 77	Title text box on Document toolbar			
Toolbar, add or remove	DW 38		View | Toolbars	Toolbars	

Adobe Dreamweaver CS5 Quick Reference Summary *(continued)*

Task	Page Number	Mouse	Menu	Context Menu	Keyboard Shortcut
Unordered list, create	DW 67, DW 72	Unordered List button in Property inspector	Format | List | Unordered List	List | Unordered List	
Vertical space, increase or decrease around image	DW 135	V Space text box in Property inspector			
Visual Aids, show or hide	DW 119	Visual Aids button on Document toolbar	View | Visual Aids		CTRL+SHIFT+I
Web page, preview in browser	DW 83		File | Preview in Browser	Preview in Browser	F12 CTRL+F12
Welcome screen, disable	DW 85		Edit | Preferences | General		
Width, change for image	DW 130	W text box in Property inspector *or* drag sizing handle			
Width, set for table	DW 212	W text box in Property inspector			

Index

A

absolute links
  described, **DW 145**
  using, creating, DW 155–156
accessibility
  accessibility dialog boxes, APP 13–14
  accessible images, APP 14–16
  Alternate text, DW 131
  Dreamweaver tools for, DW 21
  Image Tag Accessibility Attributes dialog box, DW 34, DW 218
  navigating Dreamweaver with keyboard, APP 16–17
  operating system features, APP 18–19
  screen readers, APP 12
  table defaults and, DW 191–192
accessibility tools, DW 118
accessing the Web, DW 2–5
Accredited Registrar Directory, **DW 15**
actions, undoing, DW 143
Add Browser dialog box, DW 82
adding
  See also inserting
  assets to Favorites list, DW 124
  background images, DW 226
  bullets, DW 74
  e-mail links, DW 156–158
  headings, DW 63–64
  images to tables, DW 219–225, DW 234–239
  images to Web pages, DW 127–141
  keywords, DW 242
  line breaks, DW 74, DW 208
  links to Web pages, DW 213–214, DW 239–240
  name and date, DW 75
  pages to Web sites, DW 106–113, DW 184–187
  rows to tables, DW 195
  tables to Web pages, DW 206–212
  text for relative links, DW 147
  text to tables, DW 230–233
  text to Web pages, DW 62–65, DW 206–209
  Web page backgrounds, DW 59–61
Adobe Browser Lab, DW 18
Adobe Dreamweaver CS5
  See also Dreamweaver CS5
  Help, APP 1–8
  overview of, DW 20–22
Adobe Extension Manager, APP 2

Adobe Photoshop, DW 141
Adobe Roundtrip technology, **DW 20**
Advanced Research Projects Agency (ARPA), DW 2
Advanced Settings category, **DW 46**
advocacy Web sites, **DW 6–7**
Align button, Property inspector, **DW 126**, **DW 195–196**
aligning
  centering text, DW 70–71
  images on Web pages, DW 127–141
alignment, **DW 127**
  Format menu options, DW 222–224
  image options (table), DW 128, DW 234
  table cell options, DW 202–204
Alt box, Property inspector, **DW 126**
Alternate text for accessibility, DW 34, DW 131, DW 192, APP 15–16
America Online, DW 5
American Standard Code for Information Interchange (ASCII), **DW 17**
ampersand (&) and character entities, DW 77–78
anchor points
  and element markers, DW 129
  links, DW 146
angle brackets (<>)
  and Quick Tag Editor, DW 159
  and XHTML, HTML tags, DW 18
animation feature, **DW 114**
Application bar, **DW 41**
ASCII (American Standard Code for Information Interchange), **DW 17**
Assets panel
  resizing, DW 124
  using, **DW 117**
attributes, **DW 18**
audience for Web sites, DW 7

B

background images, **DW 115**
  adding to Web pages, DW 226
  using, DW 115–116
backgrounds, adding Web page, DW 59–61
backslash (\) and folder paths, DW 46
base element (HTML), DW 241
baseband, **DW 7**
Bg (background color) box, Property inspector, **DW 197**

bitmap images, **DW 113**
bitmaps, **DW 113**
bit-resolution, **DW 113**
blogs, **DW 5–6**
bold, **DW 73**
Bold button, Property inspector, **DW 67**
Border box, Property inspector, **DW 126**, **DW 195–196**
Border command, **DW 234**
borders for tables, images, DW 234–239
breaks, commonly used XHTML elements (table), DW 19
Brightness and Contrast tool, DW 142, DW 144–145
broadband, **DW 7**
browse for file method, **DW 146**
Browser Navigation toolbar, **DW 42**
browsers. *See* Web browsers
bullets, adding, removing, editing, DW 71–72, DW 74
business/marketing Web sites, **DW 5–6**
buttons
  See also specific button
  Layout tab, Insert bar, DW 191

C

cable modems, **DW 7**
captions, table, DW 192
Cascading Style Sheets (CSS) styles, **DW 21**
case sensitivity, and Web design, DW 58
cell padding, **DW 189**
cell spacing, **DW 189**
CellPad box, Property inspector, **DW 195–196**
cells, table, **DW 188**
  alignment options (table), DW 202–204
  merging, splitting, deleting, DW 215–218
  selecting, DW 198–200
CellSpace box, Property inspector, **DW 195–196**
centering tables, DW 201–202, DW 227
changing
  font of selected text, DW 68
  link colors, DW 159
  screen resolution, DW 36, DW 104, APP 30–32
  source code, DW 161
  table structure, DW 215–216
  Web page titles, DW 77
character entities

described, **DW 77**

HTML entities supported (table), DW 78

characters

bold, italic, DW 73

commonly used XHTML elements (table), DW 19

Check Spelling command, DW 78–80

checking spelling on Web pages, DW 78–80

Class selector, Property inspector, **DW 66**, **DW 195–196**

Classic workspace, DW 37

Clear Column Widths, Row Heights, Property inspector, **DW 195–196**

clearing table column dimensions, DW 204

client computers, DW 2

closing, **DW 66**

panels, DW 43–44

Property Inspector, DW 66

Web pages, DW 85

code

coding tools and features, DW 20

modifying source, DW 161

viewing elements, DW 119

Code view, **DW 39**, **DW 159–160**

ColdFusion Help, APP 2

collapsing Property inspector, **DW 66**

colors

applying to text, DW 73

background, DW 115–116

changing icon, DW 43–44

changing link, DW 159

inserting in Design view, DW 117

in Web page development, DW 13

on Web pages, DW 8

columns, table, **DW 188**

spanning, DW 228–230

specifying width, DW 204–205

commands

See also specific command

on Application bar, DW 41

default, DW 55

Help menu (table), APP 2–3

on toolbars, DW 42

comparing Web sites, DW 8

CompuServe, DW 5

computers hosts and clients, DW 2

confidentiality of data, DW 76

connecting to remote sites, APP 24–25

content aggregators, **DW 6–7**

contents panel, Help, **APP 4–5**

context menus

creating relative links using, DW 150–151

described, DW 53

context-sensitive help, APP 7–8

contrast, turning on high, APP 18–19

Convert Table Widths to Pixels, Percent, Property inspector, **DW 195–196**

Copy menu, DW 53

copying

data files to local Web site, DW 52–54, DW 102–103, DW 183–184

and pasting text, DW 112

creating

absolute links, DW 155–156

e-mail links, DW 156–158

folders, DW 50

hyperlinks with Property inspector, DW 67

lists, DW 71–72

local Web site, DW 46–54

relative links, DW 146–155

unordered lists, DW 72

cropping, **DW 141**

CSS Advisor Web site, APP 2

CSS options, Property inspector, DW 66, DW 67

CSS styles, **DW 21**

currency, HTML tags and character entities, DW 78

D

data, keeping confidential, DW 76

data files, copying to local Web site, DW 52–54, DW 102–103, DW 183–184

defining

browsers for previewing, DW 80

remote sites, APP 21–24

definition lists, **DW 72**

deleting

See also removing

links, DW 159

table rows, columns, cells, DW 215

tables, DW 216

text, DW 63

Web pages, DW 65

description element (HTML), **DW 241**, DW 244

Design view, **DW 39**, **DW 159–160**

designing Web site navigation, DW 9–11

device icon, **DW 105**

dialog boxes, accessibility, APP 13–14

dictionary, spell-checking, DW 79–80

disabling

Image Tag Accessibility Attributes dialog box, DW 218

Welcome Screen, DW 85

displaying

context-sensitive help, APP 7–8

grid, DW 228

Insert bar, DW 190

invisible element markers, DW 119–121

Property inspector, APP 17

rulers, DW 55–56

toolbars, DW 42

document content, **DW 18**

document tab, **DW 39**

Document toolbar, **DW 42**

Document window

described, **DW 39**

opening new, DW 106, DW 111

document-relative links, **DW 145**

documents

See also Web pages

inserting assets into, DW 117

Domain Name System (DNS), **DW 14**

domain names, **DW 14**

double quotation marks ("), DW 18

Download size and download time, status bar, **DW 40**

downloading, **APP 25**

drag-and-drop method, **DW 146**

Dreamweaver CS5

accessibility. *See* accessibility

customizing, APP 30–32

environment and workspace, DW 38–44

formatting features, DW 65–76

Help system, DW 84

quitting, DW 85, DW 246

starting, DW 85–86

tools and features, DW 34

Dreamweaver site definition, **DW 45**

Dreamweaver Support Center, DW 84

Dreamweaver window, DW 38, DW 104

Dreamweaver workspace

described, **DW 39**

preparing, DW 55–59

DSL (digital subscriber lines), **DW 7**

E

Edit Image Settings, **DW 126**
Edit tools, Property inspector, **DW 126**
editing
  browser preferences, DW 80
  images, tools for, DW 141–145
  links, DW 159
  Web sites, DW 54
educational Web sites, **DW 6–7**
elements, **DW 18**
  commonly used XHTML (table),
    DW 19–20
  invisible, DW 119–121
e-mail links, **DW 146**, **DW 156–158**
encryption, SSL (Secure Sockets Layer),
  DW 16
entertainment Web sites, **DW 6–7**
errors
  correcting with BACKSPACE key,
    DW 63
  undoing actions, DW 143
Expanded Tables mode, DW 190
Extensible Hypertext Markup Language
  (XHTML)
  commonly used elements (table),
    DW 19–20
  described, **DW 17–18**
external links, **DW 145**

F

Favorites list
  adding assets to, DW 124
  described, DW 117
fiber optics, **DW 7**
file formats, image, DW 113–114
file transfer program (FTP), DW 16,
  DW 246
Files panel, **DW 105**
  displaying context-sensitive help, APP 8
  icons in, DW 51
  opening files from, DW 86
Firebox browser. *See* Mozilla Firefox
  browser
Flash plug-in, DW 161
folder icon, **DW 105**
folders
  creating, DW 50
  master, defined, DW 46
  nested, **DW 45**
  publishing, DW 246
fonts

Web page default, DW 68
Web-safe, **DW 12**
Format button, Property inspector,
  DW 66
Format menu, alignment options,
  DW 222
formatting, **DW 65**, DW 68
  Format button, Property Inspector,
    DW 66
  paragraph, **DW 66**
  text, DW 66–76
forward slashes (/) and XHTML,
  HTML tags, DW 18
FTP (file transfer programs), DW 16,
  APP 20, DW 246

G

get (download), **APP 25**
GIF format, DW 113, **DW 114**,
  DW 141
goal of Web sites, DW 7
Google Chrome browser, **DW 3**
graphic image file formats, DW 113–114
Graphics Interchange Format, **DW 114**
grid
  described, **DW 113**
  displaying, DW 228
grid structure, **DW 11**
group tests, **DW 14**

H

H box, Property inspector, **DW 127**,
  DW 141, **DW 195–196**, **DW 197**
H Space box, Property inspector,
  DW 127, DW 129, DW 130
</h1>, DW 18
Hand tool, status bar, **DW 40**
<head> tags, DW 241
Header, Property inspector, **DW 197**
header elements, DW 18
headers, table, DW 192, DW 193
Heading 1 <h1>, **DW 68**
Heading 6 <h6>, **DW 68**
heading styles, **DW 66**
headings
  adding, DW 63–64
  centering, DW 70–71
  commonly used XHTML elements
    (table), DW 19
  text, DW 66–70
  using, DW 62
Help

contents panel, **APP 4–5**
context-sensitive help, APP 7–8
Dreamweaver system, APP 1–4, DW 84
hiding
  invisible elements, DW 119
  panel groups, DW 62
  Property inspector, APP 17
  rulers, DW 55–56
  toolbars, DW 42
hierarchical structure, **DW 10**
high contrast, turning on, APP 18–19
home pages, **DW 4**, **DW 55**, DW 105
Horz box, Property inspector, **DW 197**
host computers, DW 2
Hotspot tools, Property inspector,
  DW 127
HTML
  character entities, DW 77–78
  head content elements, DW 241–245
  structure in tables, DW 198
  tables. *See* tables
  using Quick Tag Editor, DW 159
HTML button, Property inspector,
  DW 66
HTML editors, **DW 17**
HTML Property Inspector, DW 66–67
HTML tags, and Property inspector,
  DW 196–197
hybrid structure, **DW 11**
hyperlinks
  See also links
  described, **DW 4**
Hypertext Transfer Protocol (HTTP),
  DW 14

I

ICANN (Internet Corporation for
  Assigned Names and Numbers),
  DW 15
icons
  changing colors, DW 43–44
  in Files panel, DW 51
ID, Property inspector, **DW 67**
IDs, adding table, DW 205–206,
  DW 212–213
Image Tag Accessibility Attributes dialog
  box, DW 34
  activating, APP 13–14
  disabling, DW 218
images
  adding, sizing, positioning,
    DW 127–141

adding background, DW 226

adding to tables, DW 219–225, DW 234–239

adding Web page backgrounds, DW 59–61

alignment options (table), DW 128

and Assets panel, DW 117

background, DW 115–116

borders, DW 234–239

commonly used XHTML elements (table), DW 20

creating links from, DW 150

editing tools, DW 141–145

file formats, DW 113–114

inserting accessible, APP 14–16

inserting into Web pages, DW 123–125

Property inspector tools for, DW 126–127

resizing, DW 141

in Web page development, DW 12

on Web pages, DW 8

Import command, DW 106

importing documents from other programs, DW 106

index pages, **DW 4**

index.htm, index.html

adding keywords, description to, DW 242–244

described, DW 55, **DW 105**

informational Web sites, **DW 5–6**

Insert bar

described, **DW 40**

using, DW 189–191

inserting

See also adding

accessible images, APP 14–16

assets into documents, DW 117

content with Insert bar, DW 189

images into Web pages, DW 123–125

table rows, columns, DW 215

tables, DW 188–191, DW 193–195, DW 227

Inspect Mode, **DW 39**

interlacing feature, **DW 114**

internal links, **DW 145**

Internet, **DW 2**

Internet Corporation for Assigned Names and Numbers (ICANN), **DW 15**

Internet Explorer, DW 81

Internet service providers. *See* ISPs

invisible element marker, **DW 119**

invisible elements, using, displaying codes, DW 119–121

IP address (Internet Protocol address), **DW 14–15**

ISDN (Integrated Services Digital Network), **DW 7**

ISPs (Internet service providers)

described, DW 4, **DW 5**

and planning Web sites, DW 16

italic, **DW 73**

Italic button, Property inspector, **DW 67**

J

Joint Photographic Experts Group, **DW 114**

JPEG format, DW 113, **DW 114**, DW 141

K

keyboard, navigating Dreamweaver using, APP 16–17

keywords

adding, DW 242

described, **DW 241**

L

layout, **DW 188**

invisible elements and precision, DW 119

table, DW 193–195

templates, **DW 13**

Web page, DW 12–13

Layout tab, Insert bar, DW 190–191

left angle brackets (<) and XHTML, HTML tags, DW 18

line breaks

adding, DW 74, DW 208

described, DW 18, **DW 62**

linear structure, **DW 10**

Link (Hyperlink) box, Property inspector, **DW 67**

Link box, Property inspector, **DW 127**

link element (HTML), DW 241

links, **DW 4**, **DW 146**

absolute, DW 155–156

adding to Web pages, DW 213–214, DW 239–240, DW 244–245

anchors, DW 146

commonly used XHTML elements (table), DW 20

editing, deleting, changing color of, DW 159

relative, DW 146–155

types of, DW 145–146

List Item button, Property inspector, **DW 67**

List Properties dialog box, DW 71–72

lists

creating unordered, DW 72

types of, DW 71

using, DW 62

Live Code, **DW 39**

Live View, **DW 39**

Live view, **DW 159**, **DW 161**

Local Files list, **DW 46**, DW 51

Local folder, DW 47

local root folder

creating, DW 46

described, **DW 45**

local site folder, **DW 45**

local sites, **DW 45**

copying data files to, DW 52–54, DW 102–103, DW 183–184

defining, DW 45–54

opening Web pages in, DW 122–123

Local/Network (protocol), **APP 20**

M

"mailto" protocol, DW 158

maintaining

remote sites, APP 27

Web sites, DW 17

managing Web sites, DW 105

Map box, Property inspector, **DW 127**

mark ups, **DW 18**

master folders, DW 46

menus

See also specific menu

Application bar, DW 41

changing Insert bar to, DW 40

context, DW 53

Dreamweaver Help, APP 1–2

Merges selected cells using spans, Property inspector, **DW 197**

merging table cells, DW 215–218

<meta> tags, **DW 241**

Microsoft Internet Explorer features (table), **DW 3**

mobile Web technologies, **DW 7**

modems, cable, **DW 7**

Montana Parks Web site

additional pages, DW 100–101, DW 178–180

home page, DW 34–36

Mozilla Firefox browser, **DW 3**, DW 81–82
multimedia, **DW 8**

N

name and date, adding, DW 75
named anchors, **DW 146**
names, domain, **DW 14**
naming
  new documents, DW 107–108
  Web page titles, DW 77
  Web pages, DW 55
navigating
  Adobe Dreamweaver CSS page, APP 4
  Web sites, DW 9–11
navigation described, **DW 9**
navigation maps, **DW 9**
nested folders, **DW 45**
nested lists, **DW 67**
Net, **DW 2**
networks
  described, **DW 2**
  online social, DW 5–6
New Document dialog box, DW 86
new Document window, DW 106, DW 111, DW 185
news Web sites, **DW 5–6**
No wrap check box, Property inspector, **DW 197**
No wrap property, **DW 189**
null (link), **DW 146**
number sign (#), HTML tags and character entities, DW 78
numbers, removing from lists, DW 71–72

O

Omniture, APP 2
one-sided elements, **DW 18**
online service providers. *See* OSPs
online social networks, **DW 5–6**
Open Recent command, DW 122
opening
  new Document window, DW 106, DW 111, DW 185
  panels, DW 43–44
  Web pages, DW 85–86, DW 122–123
  Web sites, DW 103–104
Opera browser, **DW 3**
operating system accessibility features, APP 18–19
order or precedence, table formatting, DW 197–198

Ordered List button, Property inspector, **DW 67**
ordered lists, DW 71
organizational charts, DW 12
Original box, Property inspector, **DW 127**
OSPs (online service providers), DW 4, **DW 5**

P

</p>, DW 18
page layout
  described, **DW 188**
  table and, DW 188–189
Page Properties button, Property inspector, **DW 67**
Page Properties dialog box, **DW 59–60**
pages to Web sites, DW 184–187
panel groups
  described, **DW 39–40**
  hiding, DW 62
panels
  See also specific panel
  navigating with keyboard, APP 16–17
  opening and closing, DW 43–44
  resizing, DW 124
paragraph elements, DW 18
Paragraph style, **DW 66**
paragraphs
  commonly used XHTML elements (table), DW 19
  using, DW 62
passwords, FTP, APP 21
pasting text, DW 112
paths, DW 46
percent, **DW 189**
personal Web sites, DW 6–7
picture element, **DW 113**
pixel, **DW 113**, DW 138
pixels, **DW 189**
plug-ins, **DW 8**
PNG format, DW 113, **DW 114**
point to file method, DW 148
Portable Network Graphics, **DW 114**
portals, **DW 5–6**
Preferences dialog box, DW 55, DW 57
Preformatted style, **DW 66**
Preview in Browser command, DW 83
previewing Web pages in browsers, DW 80–83
primary, secondary browsers, DW 81
printing Web pages, DW 83–84
progressive JPEG, **DW 114**

projects
  formatted tables with images, DW 178–180
  Montana Parks Web site home page, DW 34–36
  new pages, links, images, DW 100–102
properties, **DW 18**
Property inspector, **DW 40**
  alignment options, DW 222
  collapsing/hiding, DW 66
  features of, DW 65
  hiding, displaying, APP 17
  HTML-related features of, DW 66–67
  image tools, DW 126–127
  table features, DW 195–198
publishing, **DW 14**
  to Web servers, APP 20–26
  Web sites, DW 14–16, DW 246
purpose of Web sites, DW 7
put (upload), **APP 25**

Q

question mark (?) icons, context-sensitive help, APP 7–8
Quick Tag Editor, DW 159
quitting Dreamweaver, DW 85, DW 246
quotation marks (")
  HTML tags and character entities, DW 78
  and XHTML, HTML tags, DW 18

R

random structure, **DW 10**
RDS (Remote Development Services), **APP 20**
Reference panel, Help system, APP 9–10, DW 84
<refresh> tags, DW 241
relative links
  described, **DW 145**
  using, creating, DW 147–155
Remote folder, DW 47
remote servers, uploading files to, APP 25–26
remote site root, **APP 24**
remote sites, **DW 45**
  connecting to, APP 24–25
  publishing to, APP 20–26
removing
  See also deleting
  browsers, DW 80
  bullets from lists, DW 71
  defining, APP 21–24

Web sites, DW 54
renaming Web page titles, DW 77
resampling, **DW 141**
Reset Size tool, Property inspector, **DW 127**
resizing
  images, DW 141
  panels, DW 124
  tables, columns, rows, DW 216
reviewing Web sites, DW 14–16
right angle brackets (>) and XHTML, HTML tags, DW 18
root, **DW 45**
root directory, **DW 105**, DW 108
root folder, **DW 45**
root-relative links, **DW 146**
rows, table, **DW 188**
  adding, DW 195
  spanning, DW 228–230
Rows and Cols, Property inspector, **DW 195–196**
RSS (Really Simple Syndication), **DW 6–7**
rulers
  described, **DW 55**
  hiding, displaying, DW 55–56

S

Safari browser, **DW 3**
Save as Web Page command, DW 17
saving
  site settings, DW 51
  Web pages, DW 55–59, DW 61
screen resolution, changing, APP 30–32, DW 36, DW 104
ScreenTips, Title, Property inspector, **DW 67**
scripts (link), **DW 146**
Search feature, Help, APP 6–7
secondary, primary browsers, DW 81
Secure Sockets Layer (SSL), **DW 16**
security
  confidentiality of data, DW 76
  Windows Security Alert dialog box, APP 23
Select tool, status bar, **DW 40**
selecting
  table and selected cells, DW 198–200
  tables, DW 201
selection handles, DW 141
self-closing elements, **DW 18**

separators, commonly used XHTML elements (table), DW 19
servers
  ISPs for your Web site, DW 16
  publishing to wEB, APP 20–26, DW 246
Set magnification, status bar, **DW 40**
Sharpening (images), DW 142
Site category, **DW 46**
Site pop-up menu button, **DW 103**
Site Setup dialog box, creating local Web site using, DW 46–54
sites
  See also local sites, remote sites, Web sites
  described, **DW 45**
Sites pop-up menu button, **DW 182**
sizing images on Web pages, DW 127–141
slashes (/) and XHTML, HTML tags, DW 18
Smart Paste, DW 20
source code
  described, **DW 18**
  modifying, DW 161
space
  adjusting around images, DW 129–130
  cell padding, cell spacing, DW 189
special characters
  character entities and, DW 77–78
  described, DW 55
spell-checking text, Web pages, DW 78–80
Split view, **DW 39**, **DW 159**, DW 160
Splits cells into row or columns, Property inspector, **DW 197**
splitting table cells, DW 215–216
Src box, Property inspector, **DW 127**
SSL (Secure Sockets Layer), **DW 16**
Standard mode, DW 190
Standard toolbar
  described, **DW 42**
  displaying, DW 43–44
starting Dreamweaver, DW 36–38, DW 85–86
status bar, **DW 40**
structure of Web sites, DW 10–11
Style Rendering toolbar, **DW 42**
styles
  See also specific style
  Cascading Style Sheets. *See* CSS styles

Class selector, Property Inspector, DW 66
subfolders
  creating for local site, DW 46
  described, **DW 45**
symbols, character entities, **DW 77–78**
synchronization of remote sites, APP 27

T

T1 lines, **DW 7**
Table button, Insert bar, DW 188
Table text box, Property inspector, **DW 195–196**
tables, **DW 188**
  adding images to, DW 219–225, DW 234–239
  adding text to, DW 230–233
  adding to Web pages, DW 206–212
  adjusting width, DW 212–213
  borders, DW 234–239
  cell, row, column properties, DW 196–197
  centering, DW 201–202, DW 227
  column width, DW 204–205
  defaults, accessibility, DW 191–192
  deleting, DW 216
  formatting conflicts, DW 197–198
  inserting, DW 193–195
  layout, DW 193–195
  merging cells, DW 215–218
  modifying structure, DW 215–216
  and page layout, DW 188–189
  Property inspector features, DW 195–198
  selecting cells, DW 198–200
  spanning rows and columns, DW 228–230
  splitting cells, DW 215–216
  using HTML structure in, DW 198
Tag selector, status bar, **DW 40**
tags and styles, formats, DW 66
target audience for Web sites, DW 7
Target box, Property inspector, **DW 127**
Target text box, Property inspector, **DW 67**
templates, **DW 13**
testing
  Web pages, DW 18
  Web sites, DW 14–16
text
  adding for relative links, DW 147

adding to tables, DW 230–233
adding to Web pages, DW 62–65,
  DW 206–209
alignment in table cells, DW 202–204
Alternate, for accessibility, DW 34,
  DW 192
bold, italic, DW 73
centering, DW 70–71
copying and pasting, DW 112
deleting, DW 63
formatting with Property inspector,
  DW 66–70
headings, DW 66–70
line breaks, adding, DW 74
name and date, adding, DW 75
spell-checking, DW 78–80
on Web pages, DW 8
wrapping, DW 64
text editors, **DW 17**
Text Indent button, Property inspector,
  DW 67
Text Outdent button, Property inspector,
  DW 67
Title, Property inspector, **DW 67**
titles
  commonly used XHTML elements
    (table), DW 19
  Web page, DW 76–77
toolbars, overview of, DW 42
tools
  accessibility, DW 118
  coding, DW 20
  Dreamweaver CS5, DW 34
  image editing, DW 141–145
  Property inspector image,
    DW 126–127
top-level directory, **DW 105**
transparency feature, **DW 114**
tutorials on Dreamweaver, APP 1
two-sided elements, **DW 18**
typefaces, **DW 12**
typography in Web page development,
  DW 12

U

underlining text, DW 73
undoing
  actions, DW 143
  input with Backspace key, DW 63
Unicode (UTF-8), status bar, **DW 40**
Uniform Resource Locators. *See* URLs

Unordered List button, Property
  inspector, **DW 67**
unordered lists, creating, DW 72
updating Web sites, DW 17
uploading, **APP 25**
  files to remote servers, APP 25–26
  for Web site publication, DW 16
URLs (Uniform Resource Locators),
  DW 2, **DW 14**
USB flash drives
  on Files panel, DW 184
  storing files on, DW 48

V

V Space box, Property inspector,
  DW 127, DW 129, DW 130
value modifiers, **DW 18**
vector images, **DW 113**
Vert box, Property inspector, **DW 197**
vertical/horizontal bars, DW 41
viewing, previewing Web pages in
  browsers, DW 161
views
  Code and Design, DW 159–160
  Dreamweaver, DW 159
Visual Aids command, DW 119,
  DW 121

W

W box, Property inspector, **DW 127**,
  DW 141, **DW 195–196, DW 197**
Web, accessing the, DW 2–5
Web Accessibility Initiative, APP 12
Web applications, **DW 6–7**
Web browsers
  opening linked Web pages in new
    window, DW 153
  popular programs, features, DW 3
  previewing Web pages in, DW 80–83
  selecting your, DW 80
  and World Wide Web, DW 2
Web hosting, DW 246
Web page titles, **DW 76–77**
Web pages
  adding backgrounds, DW 59–61
  adding links to, DW 213–214,
    DW 239–240, DW 244–245
  adding tables to, DW 206–212
  adding text to, DW 62–65,
    DW 206–209
  adding to Web sites, DW 106–113,

    DW 184–187
  and ASCII format, DW 17
  background images, colors,
    DW 115–116
  closing, DW 85
  components of, DW 4
  components of, testing, DW 18
  deleting, DW 65
  inserting images into, DW 123–125
  layout, DW 12
  linked, opening in new browser
    window, DW 153
  name and date, adding, DW 75
  naming, DW 55
  opening, DW 85–86, DW 122–123
  previewing in browsers, DW 80–83
  printing, DW 83–84
  saving, DW 55–59
  spell-checking, DW 78–80
  table layouts, DW 193–195
Web servers
  described, DW 2
  publishing to, APP 20–26, DW 246
Web site development
  basics of, DW 12–13
  methods, tools, languages, DW 17–20
  overview of, DW 2–11, DW 22
  See also Web sites
Web site hosting services (table),
  DW 246
Web sites, **DW 4**, DW 18, **DW 45**
  adding pages to, DW 106–113,
    DW 184–187
  developing, DW 12–13
  managing, DW 105
  navigation for, DW 9–11
  opening, DW 103–104
  planning, DW 7–8
  publishing, DW 14–16, DW 246
  remote site maintenance,
    synchronization, APP 27
  removing, editing, DW 54
  reviewing, testing, DW 14–16
  types of, DW 5–7
Web structure
  described, **DW 10**
  stypes of, DW 104
Web technologies, DW 7
WebDAV, **APP 20**
Web-safe fonts, **DW 12**

Welcome Screen, disabling, DW 85
wikis, **DW 5–6**
Window size, status bar, **DW 40**
windows
  Document, **DW 39**
  Dreamweaver, DW 38
Windows Security Alert dialog box,
  APP 23
Windows Web Publishing Wizard,
  DW 16
wireless service providers (WSPs),
  DW 5
World Wide Web Consortium (W3C),
  DW 17
World Wide Web (WWW), Web
  browsers and, DW 2
wrapping text, DW 64
WSPs (wireless service providers),
  DW 5
WYSIWYG text editors, DW 17,
  DW 20

X

XHTML compliant code, DW 160
XHTML described, DW 107
XHTML editors, **DW 17**

Z

Zoom tool, status bar, **DW 40**